Newnes Television and Video Engineer's Pocket Book

Eugene Trundle, TMIEEIE, MRTS, MISTC

Newnes
An imprint of Butterworth-Heinemann Ltd
Linacre House, Jordan Hill, Oxford OX2 8DP

PART OF REED INTERNATIONAL BOOKS

OXFORD LONDON BOSTON
MUNICH NEW DELHI SINGAPORE SYDNEY
TOKYO TORONTO WELLINGTON

First published 1987
Reprinted 1987
Second edition 1992

British Library Cataloguing in Publication Data
Trundle, Eugene
Newnes Television and Video Engineer's
Pocket Book.–2Rev.ed
I. Title
621.388

ISBN 0 7506 0677 0

Library of Congress Cataloguing in Publication Data
Trundle, Eugene.
Newnes television and video engineer's pocket book/Eugene
Trundle/ – 2nd ed.
p. cm.
Includes bibliographical references and index.
ISBN 0 7506 0677 0
1. Television – Handbooks, manuals, etc. 2. Video tape recorders and recording – Handbooks, manuals, etc. I. Title.
TK6642.T74 1992
621.388–dc20 92–10300
CIP

Typeset by TecSet Ltd, Wallington, Surrey
Printed and bound in Great Britain

Contents

Preface

The purpose of this book is to present a reasonably full picture of the systems, formats and technology of contemporary TV and video equipment, primarily for the practising service engineer. Recent years have seen tremendous diversification of home entertainment and educational products; embodied in them are techniques and artifices drawn from all branches of electronics, as well as high-precision mechanics. The engineer is expected to take all of them in his stride.

Like the equipment it describes, the book contains a unique mixture of analogue and digital systems. Few chapters are completely devoid of references to digital techniques, and Chapter 19 is wholly devoted to them – such are the trends in consumer equipment. When the picture-display tube finally appears in 'flat' form (and tube-type camera image sensors are rapidly being ousted by flat MOS/CCD devices) the TV receiver and the monitor will become almost wholly digital in their operation, and at that point all the textbooks will have to be rewritten. . . .

My thanks are due, as on many past occasions, to the UK and Irish broadcasting authorities; to Mullard and the equipment manufacturers; and others, all of whom supplied data and diagrams to assist in the preparation of the book. Again my wife Anne provided invaluable moral support and expertly typed the manuscript.

As a full-time service engineer, I can strongly identify with the readers of this book. Few people appreciate what is involved in fault-diagnosis and servicing of modern equipment, or the struggles and problems it brings – not all of which arise from the equipment itself! The book, then, is dedicated to service engineers everywhere, who are daily expected to competently deal with lasers and LOPTs, microvolts and kilovolts, data buses and dirty switch contacts, camcorders and convergence.

Eugene Trundle,
Hastings, East Sussex

1

Components and assemblies

All electronic equipment uses components, passive (R, C, L and some diodes) and active (transistors, ICs etc.), built up into assemblies to make complete operational units; some units, like the videorecorders and disc players examined later in this book, have mechanical assemblies as well. This section surveys the most common building blocks in electronic systems. Type-coding and formulae are given in Chapter 21.

RESISTORS

The basic function of a resistor is to impede the passage of an electrical current, absorbing energy and dissipating it as heat. The vast majority of resistors in use dissipate less than 500 mW, and the most common are metal-oxide and metal-film types, which (due to their superior accuracy and stability) have superseded carbon composition types. Metal-film resistors have low inherent noise and high stability, and are available in a wide range of values and sizes. Metal-oxide types have better power-dissipation capabilities, and are generally based on the resistive properties of stannic oxide, SnO_2.

Wire-wound resistors are used for higher-dissipation applications, from about 2 W upwards – as equipment becomes more efficient, high-power resistors are being ousted, along with the unwelcome heat they generate. Wire-wound resistors can be made to close tolerances and high accuracy, and thus find 'precision' applications – in test equipment, for instance.

Other types of resistor are: *metal glaze*, whose characteristics are high resistance in small sizes, and resistance to external heating; *Cermet*, with similar virtues; and *thick-film*, made by screen-printing a carbon-loaded ink onto a substrate, and, typically in the form of 'packages', incorporating several resistors for non-critical applications.

There is a wide range of *non-linear* resistors for special applications. Amongst the most common types are VDR (Voltage Dependent Resistors), whose value depends on applied voltage, and *thermistors*, whose resistance varies with temperature. They are usually made of manganese oxide or nickel oxide, giving the thermistor a negative (falling resistance) reaction to heat, either externally supplied or generated internally by the passage of current.

Variable resistors have some form of conductive wiper which can be set to any point on the resistive track, and in domestic equipment these range from large double-gang volume controls to tiny PCB-mounted presets. Their tracks are carbon-coated or carbon-suffused, and may have a linear, logarithmic (volume controls) or other relationship to the physical position of the slider. In many cases variable resistors are being superseded by 'software-control' from microprocessor ICs.

Fixed resistors are available in various logarithmic series of standardised values, designated E12, E24, E96 etc., the number indicating how many different values are available in each decade. The standard range is E24: 1.0, 1.1, 1.2, 1.3, 1.5, 1.6, 1.8, 2.0, 2.2, 2.4, 2.7, 3.0, 3.3, 3.6, 3.9, 4.3, 4.7, 5.1, 5.6, 6.2, 6.8, 7.5, 8.2, 9.1 and their decades.

CAPACITORS

A capacitor consists basically of two conductive plates separated by an insulator (*dielectric*). It has the ability to store a charge of electricity, proportional to its capacitance, which for general use may range from 1 pF to 10 000 μF, and may be more for special applications like clock back-up stores in videorecorders. Capacitors are broadly divided into two classes, non-polarised and electrolytic.

The first category has a dielectric typically of ceramic or plastic-film material. Ceramic capacitors are formed by evaporating metal electrodes onto a ceramic insulator, and can take many physical forms: tube, disc, plate and multilayer. With different ceramic types, characteristics like temperature coefficient, physical volume and capacitance can be traded off. Plastic-film capacitors are generally larger than ceramic types for the same electrical ratings; they have metal-foil or metal-film electrodes and dielectrics of polyester, polystyrene, polypropylene or polycarbonate. With their relatively large physical volume and dislike of high body temperatures during soldering, film capacitors do not lend themselves to modern PCB techniques as well as ceramic types.

Electrolytic capacitors have the highest capacitance per unit size, and are generally used in values above 0.1 μF. They depend for their operation on a very thin oxide film formed on the surface of the positive plate by electrolysis when a d.c. polarising voltage is applied. There are two basic types of electrolytic capacitor: aluminium and tantalum. Aluminium types are available in higher capacitance ranges than tantalum, and are commonly used as PSU reservoirs and for smoothing and decoupling on supply lines. Tantalum capacitors are marginally less reliable, but have a size advantage (smaller) and higher permissible operating temperature.

Variable capacitors are now rare, except in *varicap diode* form, described below.

INDUCTORS

Inductance concerns the magnetic properties of a current-carrying conductor; all conductors are surrounded by magnetic fields. Practical inductors concentrate the magnetic field by winding the conductor into a coil with (usually) a magnetic core of ferrite or laminated iron. A basic property of an inductor is its ability to turn electrical energy into magnetic energy and vice versa. Examples are solenoids, relays, recording heads and loudspeakers in the one case, and replay heads, ferrite-rod aerials, phono pick-ups and VCR-motor PG/FG generators in the other. *Transformers* convert an alternating current into a strong, 'tight' magnetic field which induces a current in the secondary winding, usually at a different voltage: transformation ratio is proportional to wire-turns ratio.

The size of an inductor, for practical purposes, is generally proportional to the current it carries, and inversely proportional to the frequency at which it works. In conjunction with capacitors, inductors can form resonant circuits, the formulae for which are given in Chapter 21. The unit of inductance is the *henry*, which is too large for most purposes: millihenries (mH) and microhenries (μH) are more common terms. Because of the relative cost, size and complexity of inductors they are avoided where possible in modern design; in low-power applications they have been largely superseded by, for example, ceramic filters and 'electronic' substitutes.

DIODES

The diode is the simplest form of semiconductor, and consists of a single PN junction with the basic characteristic of conducting in one direction only. Most general-purpose diodes are based on silicon, with a forward voltage drop of about 700 mV and a very high reverse resistance.

In TV and video applications there are many significant variants of the diode. Some of the most important are: the *zener diode*, which has a specific and (with limited current) non-destructive reverse breakdown voltage, used as a reference; the *varicap diode*, always operated in reverse-bias, with an effective capacitance dependent on applied voltage; the light-emitting diode, *LED*, which emits infra-red or coloured light proportional to its forward current; the *PIN diode*, used as a modulator, switch or attenuator in UHF and SHF applications; laser diodes, allied to LEDs, but capable of producing high-intensity, spectrally-pure beams of light; and *photodiodes*, whose conduction depends on the intensity of light falling on the junction.

TRANSISTORS

A transistor is a semiconductor device whose output can be controlled by the signal applied to one or more input electrodes, in the form of current in the base-emitter junction (bipolar type) or voltage at the gate (field-effect type). Most transistors are based on silicon, and have three terminals, base/emitter/collector or gate/drain/source. Basically transistors are classified by their semiconductor material (germanium, Ge; or silicon, Si) and their polarity (PNP or NPN). Within these categories there is a very wide range of types: *general purpose*, for linear or switching applications up to about 3 MHz at about 500 mW dissipation; *power devices*, typically used in audio amplifier output stages, whose main characteristic is an ability to dissipate heat; *high-voltage* types, for, for example, RGB output stages driving picture-tube cathodes, and (combined with high power capability) for PSU switching and line deflection; *high-frequency* devices with short transit times and often low-noise characteristics for use in VHF, UHF, and SHF front-ends; *low-noise* types for amplification of very small baseband signals; *Darlington pairs* which give very high power gain; *switching* transistors for fast pulse or logic signal handling; and *complementary pairs*, matched NPN/PNP devices generally used for audio class B power amplification. These categories are the main ones encountered in TVs and VCRs.

INTEGRATED CIRCUITS

Most of the components described so far (but primarily semiconductor devices) can be formed on a silicon wafer substrate in subminiature form with very high density to form integrated circuits (ICs), whose advent and development is alone responsible for the very advanced state of consumer electronics, and the low – in real terms – cost of equipment.

ICs fall into two main groups, analogue and digital, with many subdivisions in each. Analogue ICs used in TV and video sets are almost invariably purpose-designed for the role they play: field timebases, PAL decoders, audio power amplifiers and scan-timing generators in TV sets; f.m. modulators/demodulators, colour-under processors, motor drivers and audio record/playback amplifiers in VCRs; and power-supply regulators, i.f. amplifiers and video demodulators/amplifiers in both. High-power IC amplifiers, usually driving 'magnetic' loads, have heat sinks and can provide powers up to many tens of watts.

Digital ICs have a huge variety, and most of those used in home-entertainment equipment fall into these four classes: *general-purpose* chips, containing relatively simple counting, logic and switching functions, used as 'building blocks' of a system; *microprocessors*, generally used for overall control and co-ordination of the functions of a complete unit, many of which are mask-programmable to suit specific products, with the 'software' denoted by a suffix to the type number; *peripherals*, which typically interface microprocessors to other devices like display panels, memory chips and data buses; and *memories*, which can be as simple as a 1K bit RAM for tuning data storage or as complex as a 2M bit DRAM capable of holding a complete TV field in digital form. Many ICs are static-sensitive: see *static precautions* in Chapter 20.

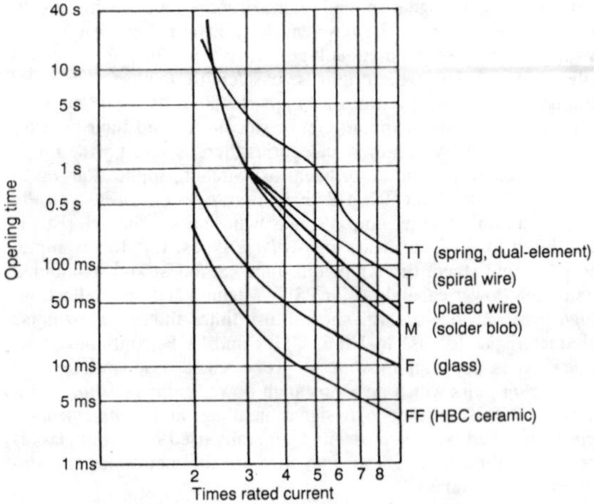

Fig. 1.1 *Time-delay curves for six types of tubular fuses*

FUSES

Fuses and fusible devices are essential for protection against overheating, damage, fire and shock. The most common type of fuse is the 20 × 5 mm glass type, which comes in five classes, TT, T. M. F. and FF, in ascending order of operating speed (see Fig. 1.1). Glass fuses are available in current ratings from 32 mA upwards, the rated current being the one which the fuse can carry continuously without degradation. To blow the fuse a much higher current must be passed for a period depending on the 'time' rating of the fuse. This *minimum fusing current* is typically 50–100% more than the rated current. All fuses have internal resistance and hence a voltage drop while in operation; fast fuses have higher resistance than delay types, and a drop of 1 V across an HBC fuse rated at (and carrying) 500 mA is normal. Delay fuses are used where inrush or transient currents are expected to significantly exceed the normal steady-state current.

ICP (Integrated Circuit Protector) fuses are commonly used in consumer equipment. They are plastic-encapsulated in the shapes shown in Fig. 1.2. They are fast-acting (200 ms at 300% current) and non-polarised, with low voltage drop and low (50–150 V) voltage ratings. The figure following the type letters must be multiplied by 40 to give the rated current in milliamps: thus an ICP-N15 is a 600 mA and an ICP-F10 is a 400 mA type.

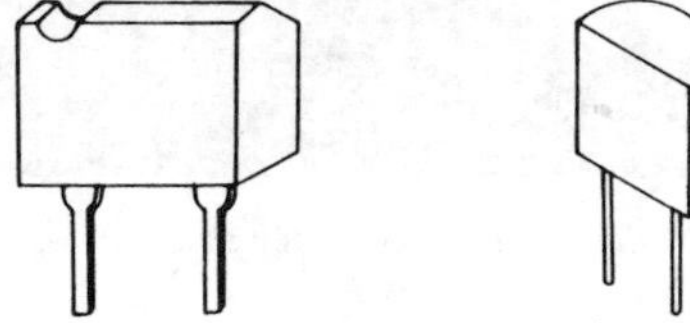

Fig. 1.2 *ICP fuse encapsulation: F-type at left, N-type at right*

PRINTED CIRCUIT BOARDS

PCBs are the basis of virtually all electronic assemblies. A PCB consists of a substrate of SRBP (Synthetic Resin-Bonded Paper) or epoxy-bonded glass fibre, 1–2 mm thick, with a network of copper conductors, about 35 microns thick, 'printed' on its surface. The copper pattern has *lands* or *pads* aligned with the legs and leadouts of the components, which both secure them and connect them to the board. Conventional PCBs have all the components on one side, and the printed pattern on the other, with all the legs and leadouts passing through holes in the board. A later development uses a print-through-holes technique, which permits higher-density packing by virtue of having conductors on both sides of the board. In domestic products SRBP boards are conventionally used for economy. They have a lower operating temperature (85°C) than fibre boards (120°C) and a risk of carbonisation under fault conditions, which can render the board conductive.

A variant of PCB technology is the *surface-mounting* (SM) assembly, in which subminiature components and printed conductors share the same surface, permitting both sides of the board to be densely covered. Through-board links provide interconnections as necessary. SM assemblies have many advantages for the manufacturer and user: their high-frequency performance (e.g. in tuners) is good; and they offer very high packing density (tiny but complex products) and consistent and reliable performance. The components have to be able to withstand immersion in molten solder, and must be very accurately placed on the board during manufacture. All components, active and passive, are available in SM versions, and resistors and capacitors are typically 2 × 1.25 mm outline. Value-coding for these devices is listed in Chapter 21, and Fig. 1.3 gives an example of the use of SM PCBs in a consumer-market camcorder. Practical advice on servicing PCBs and SM devices is given in Chapter 20.

Fig. 1.3 *Surface-mount technology saves space, weight and energy*

SOLDER

Most electrical joints, on PCBs and elsewhere, are made with solder, which for general purposes is a 60/40 alloy of tin and lead with a melting point around 183°C. For applications where operating temperatures may approach this, high melting point (HMP) solders are available. Solders are generally prepared in wire form with one or more internal cores of non-corrosive flux. For general servicing purposes 18 or 22 s.w.g. is suitable, though finer grade (26 s.w.g.) is useful for fine work and for rework of SM PCBs. Special-purpose solders also relevant to these are various preforms, and *solder-paste*, in which tiny globules of solder are suspended in a semi-liquid flux and dispensed onto the board as required during manufacture or repair, in the latter case from a syringe. All soldering is accompanied by fluxing, the application of an agent (e.g. resin) to remove oxides from the surfaces of both metals to be bonded.

2

TV and video waveforms and standards

'Television' and 'video' are wide-ranging words. For our purposes, television means seeing over long distances by means of an electrical link, and video (in the everyday usage of the word) means a recording and playback system with which TV programmes can be stored on disc or magnetic tape for subsequent replay via a TV set or monitor. In all cases the picture information is conveyed as an electrical waveform. Since a single link between TV sender and receiver can only handle one signal at a time, and because a TV picture consists of many hundreds of thousands of individual picture elements, a scanning system is required at each end. At the sending end it breaks down the composite picture into separate picture elements which are then sequentially transmitted. At the receiving end this 'serial' video signal is used to modulate the light output of the display in order to recreate the original scene. Provided that the scanning system at the receiver runs in perfect synchronism with that at the transmitter the positioning of each picture element in the display will be correct, and a complete two-dimensional picture is built-up.

The fidelity of the reproduced picture depends on many things. The scanning process consists of analysing the picture in terms of horizontal lines: the duration and number of these lines is the basic arbiter of picture definition and quality. Many other factors are present, such as the bandwidth of the entire video path from camera to picture tube; the screen structure of a colour display tube; the method of encoding the colour signal, and so on.

SCANNING STANDARDS

The number of horizontal scanning lines used in TV picture analysis is a fundamental characteristic of a TV *standard*. So far as line standards are concerned there are now only two in general broadcast use – 525 lines in the Americas, Greenland and Japan, and 625 lines elsewhere, including Eastern and Western Europe, Africa and Australia. More specific details appear later in this chapter. Of course the number of lines only describes how each *stationary* picture is analysed. For moving pictures it is necessary to present a series of frames at a rate which will fool the human eye into believing that it perceives continuous movement; and which avoids noticeable flicker. This depends for its success on 'persistence of vision', that characteristic of the eye which retains an impression of an image for a fraction of a second after the object itself has disappeared. A series of still images presented at a rate of about 14 per second would provide an illusion of continuous movement, but would give rise to a very distracting flicker. Increasing the rate to 25 per second would reduce the effect but not eliminate it. A repetition rate of 50 per second is satisfactory for most purposes, though 60 is better, especially where the picture is bright. For historical reasons having to do with the frequency of the public electricity supply, 625 line systems generally have a 50 Hz field rate, while 525 line systems have a 60 Hz field rate.

Taking the European 625/50 standard as an example, then, the requirement is for the picture to 'light-up' 50 times per second to avoid a bad flicker effect. Since 25 pictures per second are adequate to fulfil the continuous movement requirement, however, it would be wasteful of bandwidth and broadcast spectrum space to transmit 50 complete pictures per second. The problem is neatly solved by the adoption (universal for broadcast TV) of *interlaced* scanning. In this system, instead of transmitting each line of the picture in sequence (Fig. 2.1(a)) the first vertical scanning sweep is done at twice-speed, as it were. The left-to-right scan-line paths are double spaced as a result, and so only 312½ lines (half the total of 625) are traced out, corresponding to lines 1, 2, 3, 4 etc. in Fig. 2.1(b). The second vertical sweep, by virtue of a very precisely-timed start point, scans the gaps left between the lines of the first field – lines A, B, C and D in Fig. 1.1(b). By this means, although only 25 complete pictures (*frames*) are presented per second, the entire screen is scanned 50 times (50 *fields*) per second. Since at normal viewing distances individual scanning lines are not perceptible, the effect is to secure a 50 Hz flicker rate while using no more video or spectrum bandwidth than required for a 25 fields/second sequentially-scanned system.

Fig. 2.1 *TV scanning: (a) sequential; (b) interlaced*

THE VIDEO SIGNAL

A standard video signal is an electrical analogy of the brightness of the TV picture at the point on the screen being described at that instant. The brighter the picture-point the higher the voltage, with 'peak-white' – corresponding to maximum drive – being standardised at the level of +1 V. Black is standardised at 0.3 V (300 mV). All the levels of grey therefore fall between these two voltages, and where a lot of detail is present in the scene the video voltage will very quickly alternate between different levels, giving rise to high frequencies in the video waveform. The range of possible frequencies goes from zero (d.c.) when an even tone (i.e. all black, all grey, all white, etc.) is being transmitted, up to about 5.5 MHz for a fine network of vertical black and white bars. Three lines of a TV waveform are shown in Fig. 2.2.

Along with the video signal itself synchronising pulses must be sent to keep the scanning at the receiver in step with that in the camera. The 'blacker than black' area between 0 V and 0.3 V is reserved for sync pulses – two types are sent, one at 64 μs intervals

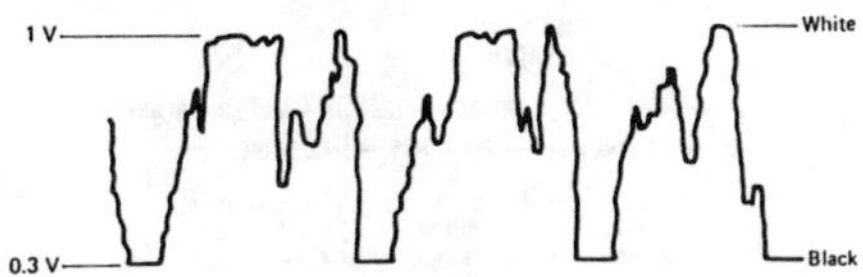

Fig. 2.2 *Basic video waveform. The voltage is analogous to the strength of light*

to trigger the line scan generator, and one at 20 ms intervals to synchronise field scanning sweeps. In the receiver these pulses are stripped off the video signal by an amplitude limiter (sync separator) and then split into line- and field-rate pulses by frequency (time)-conscious circuits.

A section of this basic waveform, showing one complete line period of 64 μs is shown in Fig. 2.3. It is made up of 52 μs of picture information and a 12 μs line blanking period. The time-reference point for the whole waveform is the beginning of the 4.7 μs line sync pulse. Following the pulse is a 'back porch' period of 5.8 μs during which the waveform remains at black level. At the finish of picture information comes a 'front porch' of 1.55 μs. This short blanking interval is introduced to ensure that (regardless of the voltage level on which the line ends) the signal level has dropped fully to black level at the instant of the crucial leading edge of the line sync pulse. Because the path of the video signal does not offer infinite bandwidth it takes a finite time for the signal voltage to change state, hence the need for the front porch. For precise triggering of line and field scan generators in the receiver it is important that the steep leading edges of synchronising pulses are maintained.

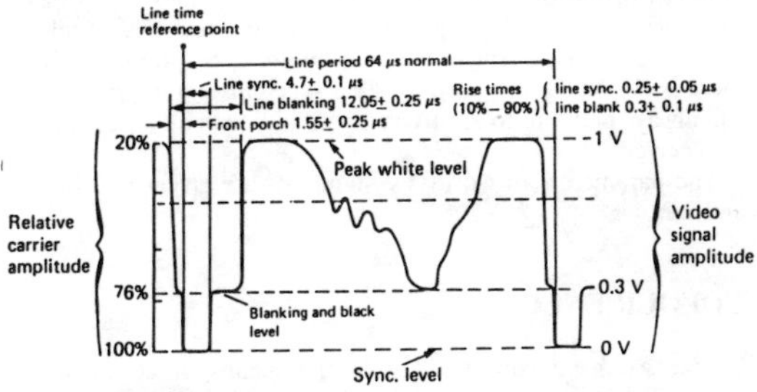

Fig. 2.3 *Composite video signal, with important parameters*

At intervals of 20 ms it is necessary to insert a triggering pulse for the field timebase. This will initiate flyback at the end of line 625 and halfway through line 313. The field triggering signal is in fact a series of five *broad* pulses as shown in Fig. 2.4. To give sufficient time for retrace or flyback of the scanning spot to take place in the picture tube (and to give some useful 'spare' lines for various forms of data transmission) picture information is suppressed for some 20 lines after the field sync pulse train. Since the broad field sync pulses occupy 2½ lines and the preceding equalising pulses a further 2½ lines, the picture is suppressed for a total of 25

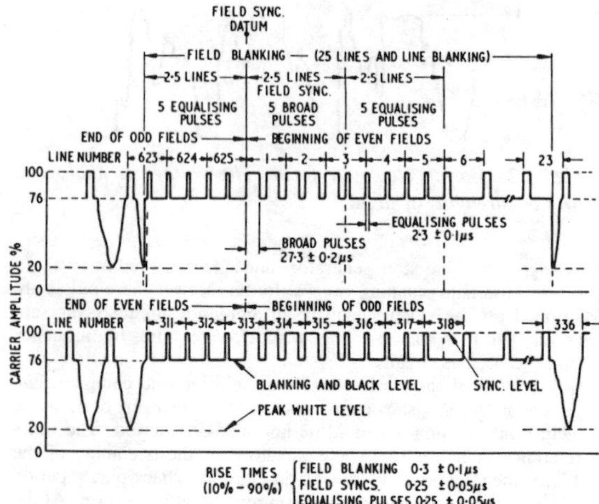

Fig. 2.4 *UK 625-line transmission: the field sync period in detail*

(20 + 2½ + 2½) lines in each field period. So our total of 625 lines is thus reduced by 50, and close examination of an actual TV picture would reveal it to be composed of 574 complete lines and two half-lines.

The fact that the broad field sync pulses have a component at line rate ensures that synchronisation of the line oscillator is maintained throughout the field sync period. This is less relevant in modern TV design where flywheel line synchronisation (fully covered later) is used, as opposed to the *direct sync* of the earliest TV designs. Current receiver technology also permits the use of a counter to directly derive field trigger pulses from line sync, so that in theory there is no longer any need for field sync pulses – in practice they will always be there to ensure compatibility with all types and ages of receiver.

The parameters of world TV standards are given in Tables 2.1 and 2.2.

COLOUR ENCODING

So far we have considered only the means of conveying the *brightness* information of a TV picture, and virtually all modern television, be it sourced from a home camera, a videorecorder, disc player or broadcast transmission is in colour. It is necessary, then, to add further information to this basic *luminance* waveform to describe the colours in the picture. The colouring (*chrominance*) signal is kept separate from the luminance information throughout much of the circuitry of TV equipment: the two are separated early in the camera's electronics and recombined at a late stage in the TV set or monitor. The derivation and processing of chrominance signals will be fully discussed in Chapters 6 and 7, and our concern here is with the chroma (for short) component of the composite video waveform.

Chroma signals are not carried in basic form over any but the shortest links. They are encoded and modulated onto a *subcarrier* which by its phase and amplitude conveys all the necessary information to describe the colour in the picture. Because this subcarrier is carried on the video waveform the two signals are time-synchronised, and at any given moment the luminance signal and accompanying chroma signal together carry all the information required to precisely define the brightness and colour of a single picture element. By virtue of the elapsed time since the last sync pulse occurred the position of the picture element on the screen is also defined – its 'longitude' by the period since the last line pulse, and its 'latitude' by the period since the last field pulse.

For the PAL system used in the UK and much of Western Europe the colour subcarrier frequency is at 4.43361875 MHz: we shall shorten it here to 4.43 MHz for convenience. It is added to the luminance waveform as a sinusoidal wave whose amplitude is proportional to the degree of saturation of the colour being described, and whose phase, or timing, describes the hue of the colour. Since phase and timing are relative terms a reference must be provided against which to measure them. It takes the form of a 'colour burst' consisting of a ten-cycle sample of subcarrier frequency sitting on the back-porch of the video waveform – Fig. 2.5. This waveform, drawn here as representing a colour-bar signal, is often known as a CVBS (Chroma, Video, Blanking and Syncs) signal, and is the standard form which will be found at the video input and output sockets of cameras, videorecorders, monitors and so on. Its level is invariably 1 V peak to peak, though as Fig. 2.5 shows, this refers to the luminance and sync components; a heavily-saturated and bright picture section can take the waveform amplitude up to 1.234 V as is happening here on the first (yellow) bar. In conventional practice the signal is produced across an impedance of 75 Ω. The colour burst signal is also used as an amplitude reference for the chroma signals; its peak-to-peak amplitude is fixed at 0.3 V – the same as the sync pulses. Other characteristics of the chroma signal are given in Table 2.1.

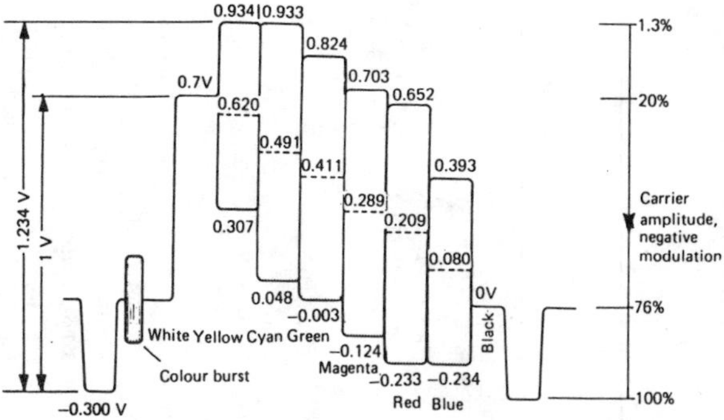

Fig. 2.5 *The waveform of a single line of a colour-bar pattern*

Table 2.1

System / Standard	NTSC M	PAL B, G, H	PAL I	PAL M	PAL N	SECAM B, G, H	SECAM D, K, K1	SECAM L
Luminance signal	$E'_Y = 0.3\,E'_R + 0.59\,E'_G + 0.114\,E'_B$							
Colour difference signals (chrominance signals)	$E'_I = -0.27(E'_B - E'_Y + 0.74(E'_R - E'_Y$ $E'_Q = -0.41(E'_B - E'_Y + 0.48(E'_R - E'_Y$	$E'_U = 0.493(E'_B - E'_Y)$ $E'_V = 0.877(E'_R - E'_Y)$				$D'_R = -1.9(E'_R - E'_Y$ $D'_B = 1.5(E'_B - E'_Y$		
Correction of colour difference signals	—					$D'^*_R = A \cdot D'_R$ $D'^*_B = A \cdot D'_B$ $A = \frac{1 + j \cdot \frac{f_R}{85}}{1 + j \cdot \frac{f_B}{255}}$ (f in kHz)		
Composite colour video signal	$E_M = E'_Y + E'_I(\cos\omega_{SC}t + 33°) + E'_Q(\sin\omega_{SC}t + 33°)$	$E_M = E'_Y + E'_U \sin\omega_{SC}t \pm E'_V \cos\omega_{SC}t$				$E_M = W'_Y + B \cdot \cos 2\pi(f_{oR} + D'^*\Delta f_{oR}) \cdot t + B \cdot \cos 2\pi(f_{oB} + D'^*_B \Delta f_{oB}) \cdot t$ B=function of f_o and f_{RB}; see f_{SC}		
Type of modulation	Suppressed-carrier amplitude modulation of two subcarriers in quadrature					FM		
Line frequency f_H	15734.264±0.05Hz	15625±0.016Hz		15734.264±0.05Hz	15625±0.016Hz	15625±0.016Hz		
Field frequency	59.95Hz	50Hz		59.94Hz	50Hz	50Hz		
Chrominance subcarrier freq. f_{SC}	3579545±10Hz	4433618.75±5Hz	4433618.75±1Hz	3582056.25÷5Hz		$f_{oR} = 4406250 \pm 2000Hz$ $f_{oB} = 4250000 \pm 2000Hz$ ($f_o = 4286 \pm 20kHz$)		
Relationship between f_{SC} and f_H	$f_{SC} = \frac{455}{2} \cdot f_H$	$f_{SC} = \left(\frac{1135}{4} + \frac{1}{625}\right) \cdot f_H$		$f_{SC} = \frac{909}{4} \cdot f_H$	$f_{SC} = \left(\frac{917}{4} + \frac{1}{625}\right) \cdot f_H$	$f_{oR} = 282 \cdot f_H$, $f_{oB} = 272 \cdot f_H$		

Bandwidth/ deviation of colour difference signal	$f_{SC}+620/$ $-1300kHz$	$f_{SC}+570/$ $-1300kHz$	$f_{SC}+1070/$ $-1300kHz$	$f_{SC}+600/$ $-1300kHz$	$f_{SC}+600/$ $-1300kHz$	$\Delta f_{oR}=280+70/-226kHz$, $\Delta f_{oB}=230+276/-120kHz$
Amplitude of chrominance subcarrier	$\sqrt{(E'_I)^2+(E'_Q)^2}$		$\sqrt{(E'_U)^2+(E'_V)^2}$			$M_o \left\lvert \frac{1+j\cdot 16F}{1+j\cdot 1.26F} \right\rvert$; M_o = 11.5% of luminance amplitude; $F = \frac{f_{RB}}{f_o} - \frac{f_o}{f_{RB}}$
Duration of burst	min. 8 cycles	10±1 cycles		9±1 cycles		—
Phase of burst	180°, relative to $(E'_B-E'_Y)$axis	+135° for odd lines in 1st and 2nd fields −135° for even lines in 1st and 2nd fields +135° for even lines in 3rd and 4th fields −135° for odd lines in 3rd and 4th fields		relative to E'_U axis		—
Identification	—		by E'_V component of burst			for lines D'_R: + 350kHz deviation at max. 540mV for lines D'_B: −350kHz deviation at max. 500mV

E′ and D′ are gamma-precorrected values of chrominance components E and colour difference signals D

Table 2.2

Standard	*FCC*	*CCIR*	*British*	*OIRT**
Number of lines	*525*	*625*	*625*	*625*
Field frequency	*60 Hz*	*50 Hz*	*50 Hz*	*50 Hz*
Standard code	M	B/G	I	D/K
Channel width	6 MHz	7/8 MHz	8 MHz	8 MHz
Vision/sound carrier spacing	4.5 MHz	5.5 MHz 5.74 MHz	6 MHz	6.5 MHz
Vestigal sideband	0.75 MHz	0.75 MHz	1.25 MHz	0.75 MHz (1.25 MHz)
Vision IF	45.75 MHz	38.9 MHz	39.5 MHz	38.9 MHz (38 MHz)
Vision/sound ratio	5:1	10:1 20:1	10:1	10:1

* Organisation Internationale de Radiodiffusion-Télévision

VISION MODULATION

To carry a vision signal through a transmission channel, whatever the media may be, some form of modulation system is generally necessary. The carrier itself is usually a high-frequency r.f. wave, though light (visible or more usually infra-red) is increasingly being used: the medium here is generally fibre-optic cable. The carrier may be regarded as a 'vehicle' which is generated at the sending end and discarded at the receiver. There are various ways in which the basic video signal (complete with colour subcarrier) can be impressed or modulated onto a carrier. For satellite transmissions, for twisted-pair cable distribution and for passage through the tape/head interface of a videorecorder, f.m. (frequency modulation) is used; for terrestrial broadcasting in the VHF and UHF bands a.m. (amplitude modulation) is used. Although r.f. modulators form no part of a TV receiver they are increasingly being used in the home – modulators operating in the region of UHF channel 36 are fitted to videorecorders, satellite boxes, disc players and home computers for easy interfacing with conventional TV sets; and more specialised modulators are used in the sound and vision circuits of videorecorders.

AM MODULATION

In terrestrial TV broadcasting an a.m. modulation system is used for the video signal. Here the carrier is a VHF or (especially in the UK) a UHF wave whose amplitude is varied in sympathy with the excursions of the composite video signal. Unlike an audio waveform the picture signal is asymmetrical, so either positive modulation or negative modulation can be adopted. Very early TV transmissions used positive modulation, but all current broadcasts, with the exception of French system L transmissions, are negatively modulated, so that sync pulses give rise to maximum carrier power, and peak white (plus chroma) corresponds to minimum carrier power. This has several advantages, a major one of which is the reduced effect of impulse interference on the reproduced picture: the sharp spikes characteristic of ignition and similar spurious pulses give rise, after demodulation, to negative-going pulses on the recovered video signal. The resulting small black spots on the picture are less intrusive than the large defocused white spots which would result from an interference-laden positive-modulation signal.

The standard for an a.m. transmission is given in Fig. 2.5. Carrier power is 100% on sync pulse tips, falling to 76% on blanking and black level, 20% on peak white and 1.3% as an absolute minimum on fully colour-saturated bright scenes, again here represented by the yellow colour bar.

SIDEBANDS

In an a.m. transmission system sidebands are generated, taking the form of a 'spreading' of the carrier wave on each side of its nominal frequency. The extent of these sidebands depends on the frequency of the modulating signal. In an a.m. radio transmission sidebands are present on both sides of the carrier so that the total bandwidth of the transmission (and the spectrum space taken up) equals twice the highest audio frequency used. A simple r.f. modulator as fitted to home videorecorders operates in the same way, producing a double-sideband negatively-modulated UHF carrier signal, which for a full-bandwidth (5.5 MHz) vision signal will spread itself over more than 12 MHz of the UHF band.

The requirements of a national television service make it necessary to use the available frequency band as effectively as possible, and this has led to the use of *vestigial* sideband working. Since the information in the upper and lower sidebands is the same, it is theoretically necessary to transmit only one set of sidebands. Single sideband television transmission would, however, lead to great difficulties in the design of transmitter and receiver. An acceptable compromise is found in the vestigial sideband system, where one set of sidebands is partially suppressed. As an example, Fig. 2.6(a) shows the channel 23 sound and vision bandwidths, with a vision carrier frequency of 487.25 mHz. As can be seen, double sideband transmission of the video signal is retained up to 1.25 mHz on each side of the carrier frequency, but vision frequencies above 1.25 MHz are transmitted on the upper sideband only. In this way the total bandwidth required for the vision and sound signals and guard bands is reduced to 8 MHz.

Vestigial sideband transmission means that the energy in the vision signals received is doubled for frequencies up to 1.25 MHz. To re-balance the energy distribution in the demodulated video signal the pre-detector response curve of the receiver's signal amplifier is arranged to follow the shape of Fig. 2.6(b). Here the response at the vision carrier frequency is one-half (i.e. 6 dB down) that at higher frequencies. This will be examined more closely in the next chapter.

TV SOUND TRANSMISSION

The sound that accompanies TV transmissions is better than the audio system and loudspeakers of many TV sets (and VCRs using longitudinal sound recording systems) can do justice to, though contemporary high-quality TV sets and videorecorders are much better, thanks to the use of large loudspeakers and Hi-Fi sound

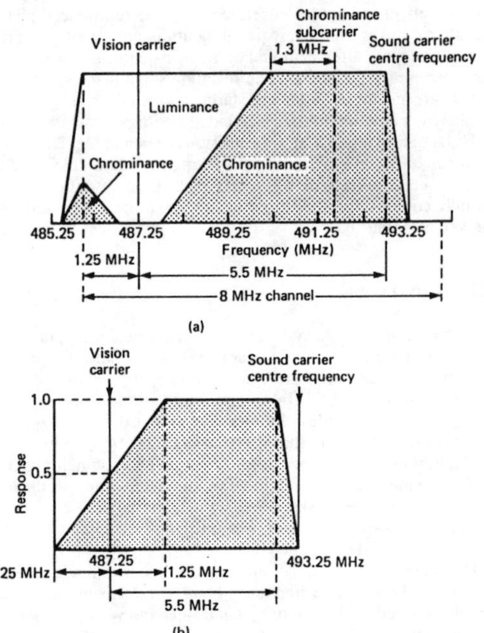

Fig. 2.6 *(a) RF spectrum of a 625 line colour transmission, showing vestigial sideband shaping for bandwidth conservation. (b) Response shaping in the receiver*

recording techniques respectively. In many countries broadcast TV sound is still monaural. It is (except for French System L) transmitted by frequency-modulation (f.m.) of its own carrier wave, whose spacing above the vision carrier frequency varies with the transmission system in use. These systems are summarised in Table 2.7 where it can be seen that for the UK System I the sound-to-vision carrier spacing is 6 MHz. Frequencies up to 15 kHz are transmitted on a carrier whose power is 10% of that of peak vision power. Peak sound carrier deviation is ± 50 kHz, and to reduce the effect of noise a pre-emphasis characteristic corresponding to a time constant of 50 μs is introduced at the transmitter.

STEREO-SOUND TV TRANSMISSIONS

Although stereo sound transmissions have long been established on the Band II VHF radio network, they are only now becoming common as an accompaniment to TV broadcasts. Satellite TV transmission systems (see later) have designed-in provision for stereo sound, especially MAC, to be described in Chapter 4.

So far as terrestrial TV transmitters are concerned, the pilot-tone systems used for stereo radio are impractical due to their vulnerability to interference from the vision signal. Alternative systems are in use in Japan (FM-FM system, with subcarrier based on 2 fh carrying a frequency-modulated L-R signal); and West Germany, where a second sound carrier, spaced 240 kHz from the main (L + R) sound carrier, conveys a 2 R signal.

The advance of digital IC technology and the low cost (in mass-production) of sophisticated processing chips has made practical the use of digital sound systems in domestic equipment. Examples of this will be found in the later sections of this book dealing with MAC, Nicam, Compact Disc and Hi-Fi videorecorder sound systems.

THE TELEVISION NETWORK

Broadcast TV takes place in the VHF (Bands I and III) and UHF (Bands IV and V) spectra for terrestrial transmitters. In the UK it is currently confined to UHF, with a network of 51 main stations (Fig. 2.7) and 900-odd relay stations, the latter acting as transponders in that they receive signals from the nearest main transmitter and rebroadcast them locally on different channels. The signals from main transmitters are horizontally polarised while those from relays are with a few exceptions vertically polarised, requiring corresponding orientation of the rods of receiving aerials. Each transmitting site is shared by the two broadcasting authorities BBC and ITC so that a signal receiving aerial will receive all four transmissions BBC 1, BBC 2, ITV and Channel 4 from the single transmitting array. The details of main transmitters for the UK are given in Table 2.3, and those for Eire in Table 2.4. The Irish broadcasting authority Radio Telefis Eireann (RTE) provides two channels RTE1 and RTE2, some of which are radiated at VHF as Table 2.4 shows. Irish receivers, then, need to be equipped with both VHF and UHF tuners though at any given receiving site only one band will be in use with an appropriate aerial.

The TV broadcast bands are divided into channels, which for System I countries are 8 MHz wide to provide a small guard band between channels. The channel frequencies for sound and vision for the UK and Eire are given in Table 2.5, though the VHF channels are currently unallocated in the UK. The transmission channels and polarisation of each transmitter in the network is very carefully worked out to provide minimum mutual interference to receivers, and except in unusual barometric conditions the plan works very well. UHF receiving aerial groups and their colour coding is given in Table 2.6.

WORLDWIDE TV STANDARDS

While System I (625/50/PAL) with 6 MHz sound spacing is used in the UK and Eire there are many other permutations of scanning rates, encoding systems and transmission parameters in use around the world for terrestrial transmissions. The three main colour encoding systems are NTSC, generally used with the 525/60 standard; SECAM, used with 625/50 scanning in France and Eastern Europe; and PAL in the rest of Europe, Australia and some South American countries. Characteristics of the main systems in current use are given in Table 2.7, and a comprehensive worldwide listing of countries with their systems in Table 2.8. European VHF channel allocations are shown in Figs 2.8 and 2.9. Vision carrier frequencies per channel are listed in Table 2.9. Some guidance on converting between standards is given in the next chapter.

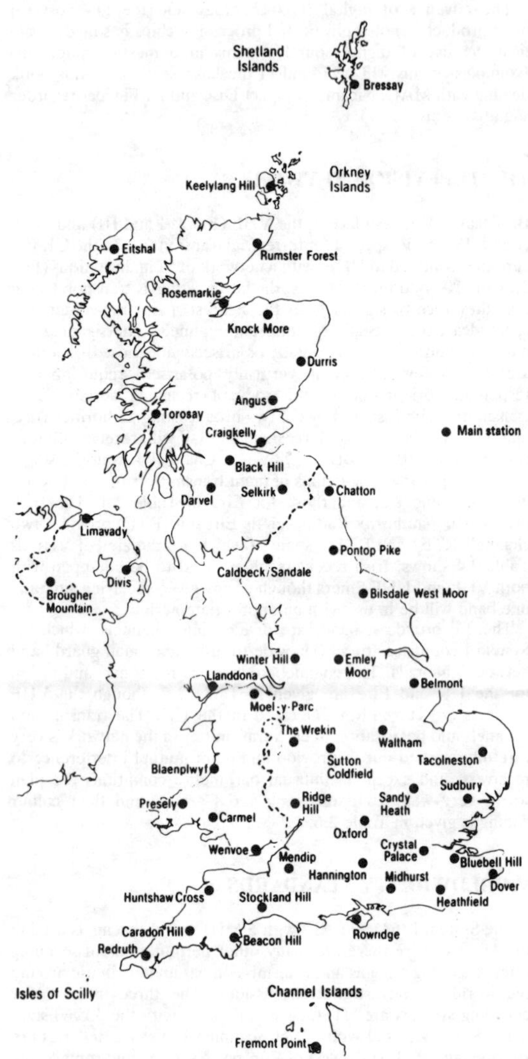

Fig. 2.7 *Main transmitter positions in the UK*

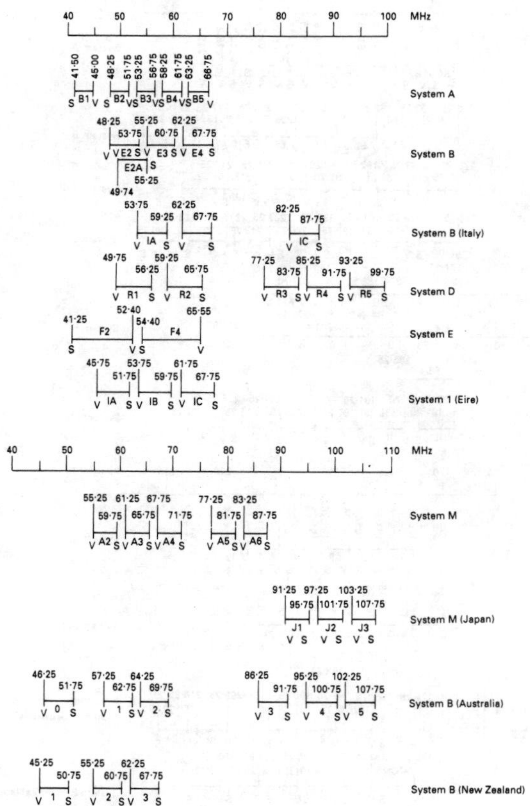

Fig. 2.8 *Channel allocations, band I/II*

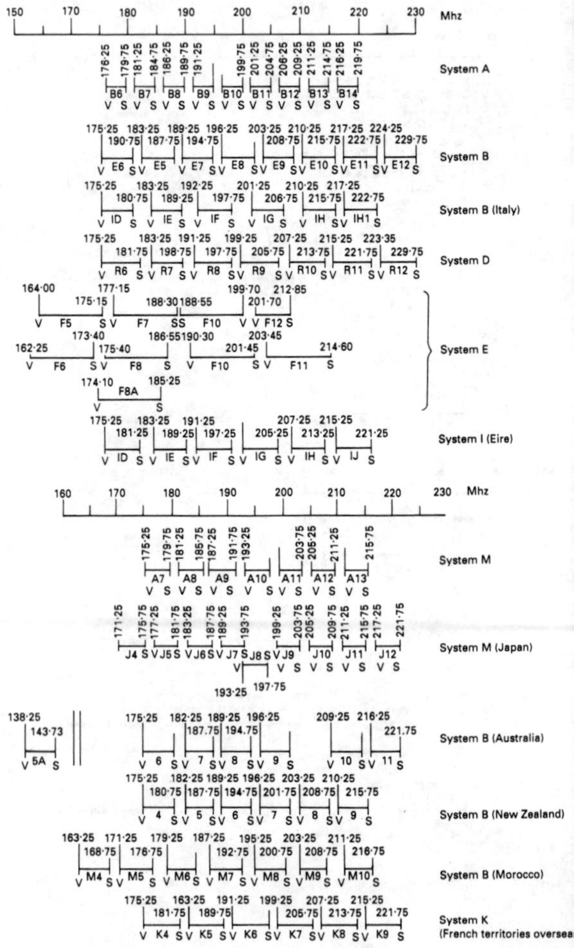

Fig. 2.9 *Channel allocations, band III*

Table 2.3 *UK main transmitter sites and channel allocations*

	ITV1	*CH4*	*BBC1*	*BBC2*
East of England				
Tacolneston	59	65	62	55
Sudbury	41	47	51	54
Sandy Heath	24	21	31	27
Midlands East				
Waltham	61	54	58	64
Midlands West				
Sutton Coldfield	43	50	46	40
Oxford	60	53	57	63
The Wrekin	23	29	26	33
Ridge Hill	25	32	22	28
The Borders and Isle of Man				
Caldbeck	28	32	30	34
Selkirk	59	65	55	62
Channel Islands				
Fremont Point	41	47	51	44
North East Scotland				
Durris	25	32	22	28
Angus	60	53	57	63
Keelylang Hill (Orkney)	43	50	40	46
Bressay	25	32	22	28
Rumster Forest	24	21	31	27
Knock More	23	29	33	26
Eitshal (Lewis)	23	29	33	26
Rosemarkie	49	42	39	45
Lancashire				
Winter Hill	59	65	55	62
Wales				
Wenvoe	41	47	44	51
Llanddona	60	53	57	63
Carmel	60	53	57	63
Presely	43	50	46	40
Blaen-Plwyf	24	21	31	27
Moel-y-Parc	49	42	52	45
West of England				
Mendip	61	54	58	64
London				
Crystal Palace	23	30	26	33
Central Scotland				
Black Hill	43	50	40	46
Torosay	25	32	22	28
Craigkelly	24	21	31	27
Darvel	23	29	33	26
South of England (south)				
Rowridge	27	21	31	24
Midhurst	58	68	61	55
Hannington	42	66	39	45
South of England (east)				
Bluebell Hill	43	65	40	46
Dover	66	53	50	56
Heathfield	64	67	49	52

Table 2.3 *Contd*

	ITV1	*CH4*	*BBC1*	*BBC2*
North-east England				
Pontop Pike	61	54	58	64
Bilsdale	29	23	33	26
Chatton	49	42	39	45
Northern Ireland				
Divis	24	21	31	27
Limavady	59	65	55	62
Brougher Mountain	25	32	22	23
South-west England				
Caradon Hill	25	32	22	28
Stockland Hill	23	29	33	26
Beacon Hill	60	53	57	63
Huntshaw Cross	59	65	55	62
Redruth	41	47	51	44
Yorkshire				
Emley Moor	47	41	44	51
Belmont	25	32	22	28

This list includes all main transmitting stations used for both ITC and BBC transmitters. Aerial polarisation in all cases is horizontal. Since about 900 transmitters are now in use, mainly relay stations, further details can be obtained from the broadcasting authorities since there is insufficient space here for a complete list. With a few exceptions, all relay transmitters use vertically polarised aerials.

The use of videorecorders and cassettes in various countries gives rise to many questions. Provided the scanning standards for line and field, and the encoding system is the same, a cassette recorded on a machine of a given format (i.e. VHS, Beta, etc.) will replay satisfactorily elsewhere in the world on a machine of the same format. Thus a UK-made tape will replay in Jordan, for example, where PAL system B is in use. Video machines themselves, however, are less versatile since they incorporate, in effect, a TV transmitter and receiver/demodulator, and require a specific mains voltage to power them. Some are internally switchable between 240, 220, 117 and 110 V, which embraces all the world's domestic electricity supply systems. There are multi-standard videorecorders manufactured, mainly intended for the Middle Eastern market, which can deal with video signals in both VHF and UHF bands, and encoded to PAL, SECAM or NTSC standards. Not all of them have facilities for the 6 MHz sound spacing of the I system, however, and in NTSC mode many utilise a 'hybrid' system called 'NTSC 4.43' for use with which the TV's colour decoder must be specially adapted or designed. A conventional multi-standard VCR can only replay a tape in the form in which it was recorded unless it incorporates a digital field store. It is important to understand the capabilities of the machine at the time of purchase if multi-standard use is envisaged.

Table 2.4 *RTE television transmitters*

	Channel and RTE 1	*Polarisation RTE 2*	*Frequency band/ UHF group*	*Max ERP (kW vision)*
Main transmitters (625)				
Three Rock (Dublin)	29 Horiz	33 Horiz	UHF Group A	25
Cairn Hill (Longford)	40 Horiz	43 Horiz	UHF Group B	800
Kippure	H Horiz	J Horiz	VHF Band 111	100
Maghera	B Horiz	H Vert	VHF Band 1 & 111	100
Mt Leinster	F Vert	I Vert	VHF Band 111	100
Mullaghanish	D Vert	G Vert	VHF Band 111	100
Truskmore	I Horiz	G Horiz	VHF Band 111	100
Clermont Carn (Co. Louth)	52 Vert	56 Vert	UHF Band C/D	250
Holywell Hill (North-East Donegal)	23 Horiz	26 Horiz	UHF Band A	20
Transposers (625)				
Abbeyfeale	F Horiz	I Horiz	VHF Band 111	0.012
Achill	E Horiz	H Horiz	VHF Band 111	1.00
Ballydavid	22 Vert	25 Vert	UHF Group A	0.020
Cahir	21 Vert	24 Vert	UHF Group A	0.030
Cahirciveen	F Horiz	I Horiz	VHF Band 111	1.00
Cappoquin/Dungarvan	H Horiz	E Horiz	VHF Band 111	0.250
Carlingford	61 Vert	67 Vert	UHF Group C/D	0.60
Castlebar	D Vert	F Vert	VHF Band 111	1.00
Castletownbere	E Vert	H Vert	VHF Band 111	0.250
Clifden	D Horiz	F Horiz	VHF Band 111	1.00
Clonakilty	F Horiz	I Horiz	VHF Band 111	0.030
Cork (Spur Hill)	H Vert	E Vert	VHF Band 111	0.250
Cork (Spur Hill)	29 Horiz	33 Horiz	UHF Group A	0.500
Cork City (Collins	39 Vert	49 Vert	UHF Group B	0.165
Barracks)	F Horiz		VHF Band 111	0.130
Crosshaven	55 Vert	59 Vert	UHF Group C/D	0.250
Dingle	23 Vert	26 Vert	UHF Group A	0.100
Ennistymon	I Horiz	F Horiz	VHF Band 111	0.012
Fanad	F Horiz	D Horiz	VHF Band 111	2.00
Fermoy	F Horiz	I Horiz	VHF Band 111	0.006
Glanmire	C Horiz	E Horiz	VHF Band 1 & 111	0.050
Glencolumcille	E Vert	H Vert	VHF Band 111	0.006
Glengarriff/Bantry	F Horiz		VHF Band 111	0.060
	39 Horiz	49 Horiz	UHF Group B	0.250
Kilmacthomas	E Horiz	H Horiz	VHF Band 111	0.006
Laragh/Glendalough	D Horiz	G Horiz	VHF Band 111	0.012
Letterkenny	H Vert	J Vert	VHF Band 111	0.500
Listowel	F Horiz	I Horiz	VHF Band 111	0.012
Monaghan	D Horiz		VHF Band 111	1.00
Mt Eagle	40 Vert	43 Vert	UHF Group B	0.020
Moville	H Horiz	J Horiz	VHF Band 111	0.200
Roscarbery	F Horiz	I Horiz	VHF Band 111	0.012
Suir Valley	H Vert	E Vert	VHF Band 111	0.400

Table 2.5 *VHF/UHF channels and frequencies in UK and Ireland*

	Vision	*Sound*			*Vision*	*Sound*	
Band I				*Band V*			
A	45.75	51.75	A	39	615.25	621.25	39
B	53.75	59.75	B	40	623.25	629.25	40
C	61.75	67.75	C	41	631.25	637.25	41
Band III				42	639.25	645.25	42
D	175.25	181.25	D	43	647.25	653.25	43
E	183.25	189.25	E	44	655.25	661.25	44
F	191.25	197.25	F	45	663.25	669.25	45
G	199.25	205.25	G	46	671.25	677.25	46
H	207.25	213.25	H	47	679.25	685.25	47
I	215.25	221.25	I	48	687.25	693.25	48
J	223.25	229.25	J	49	695.25	701.25	49
Band IV				50	703.25	709.25	50
21	471.25	477.25	21	51	711.25	717.25	51
22	479.25	485.25	22	52	719.25	725.25	52
23	487.25	493.25	23	53	727.25	733.25	53
24	495.25	501.25	24	54	735.25	741.25	54
25	503.25	509.25	25	55	743.25	749.25	55
26	511.25	517.25	26	56	751.25	757.25	56
27	519.25	525.25	27	57	759.25	765.25	57
28	527.25	533.25	28	58	767.25	773.25	58
29	535.25	541.25	29	59	775.25	781.25	59
30	543.25	549.25	30	60	783.25	789.25	60
31	551.25	557.25	31	61	791.25	797.25	61
32	559.25	565.25	32	62	799.25	805.25	62
33	567.25	573.25	33	63	807.25	813.25	63
34	575.25	581.25	34	64	815.25	821.25	64
				65	823.25	829.25	65
				66	831.25	837.25	66
				67	839.25	845.25	67
				68	847.25	853.25	68

Table 2.6 *Colour coding for UHF receiving aerial groups*

Group	A	B	C/D	E	W
Channels	21–34	39–53	48–68	39–68	21–68
Colour code	Red	Yellow	Green	Brown	Black

Table 2.7 *TV standards of the world*

System	*Line no.*	*Overall channel band-width (MHz)*	*Vision band-width (MHz)*	*Sound/ vision spacing (MHz)*	*Vision modula-tion*	*Sound modula-tion*	*Areas in use*
B	625	7	5	+5.5	–	FM	Western Europe, Parts of Africa, Middle East, Australasia (VHF)
D	625	8	6	+6.5	–	FM	Eastern Europe, USSR, China (VHF)
G/H*	625	8	5	+5.5	–	FM	Western Europe (UHF)
I	625	8	5.5	+6	–	FM	UK (UHF) Eire
K	625	8	6	+6.5	–	FM	French Territories Overseas
L	625	8	6	+6.5	+	AM	France (UHF), Luxembourg (VHF/UHF)
M	525	6	4.2	+4.5	–	FM	North and South America, Caribbean, Parts of Pacific, Far East, US Forces Broadcasting (AFRTS) Japan
N	625	6	4.2	+4.5	–	FM	Argentina, Uruguay, Bolivia

*System H has 1.25 MHz vestigial sideband

Table 2.8 *World television and colour systems*

	System	*Colour*	*Sound carrier MHz*	*Channels*	*Mains*
Abu Dhabi	B	PAL	+5.5		240/50
Afghanistan	D	PAL	+6.5		220/50
Alaska (USA)	M	NTSC	+4.5	A2–13	120/60
Albania	B, G	PAL	+6.5	E6–12	220/50
Algeria	B	PAL	+5.5	E5–11	220/50
Andorra	B	PAL	+5.5		220/50
Angola	I	PAL	+6.0	E9	220/50
Antigua and Barbuda	M	NTSC	+4.5	A7–10	230/60
Antilles	M	NTSC	+4.5	A3–13	120/60
Argentina	N	PAL	+4.5	A2–13	220/50
Ascension Is.	I		+6.0		
Australia	B	PAL	+5.5	0–11	240/50
Austria	B, G	PAL	+5.5	1–12, 21–68	220/50
Azores	B	PAL	+5.5	E7–9	220/50
(US Forces)	M	NTSC	+4.5	A5	
Bahamas	M	NTSC	+4.5		120/60
Bahrain	B	PAL	+5.5	E4	230/50
Bangladesh	B	PAL	+5.5	E5–11	230/50
Barbados	N	NTSC	+4.5	A3	110/50
Belgium	B, H	PAL	+5.5	1–12, 21–68	220/50
Bermuda	M	NTSC	+4.5	A8–10	120/60
Bolivia	N	NTSC	+4.5	A7, 10	120/50
Botswana	I	PAL	+6.0		220/50
Brazil	M	PAL	+4.5	A2–13	110/50
Brunei	B	PAL	+5.5	E5–8	230/50
Bulgaria	D	SECAM(V)	+6.5	R7–12	220/50
Burma	M	NTSC	+4.5		220/50
Burundi	K		+6.5		220/50
Cambodia	M		+4.5		120/50
Cameroon	B	PAL	+6.5		127/50
Canada	M	NTSC	+4.5	A2–13, A15–30	120/60
Canary Is.	B	PAL	+5.5	E3–10	220/50
Cape Verde Is.	I		+6.0		
Central African Republic	K		+6.5		220/50
Chad	K		+6.5		220/50
Chile	M	NTSC	+4.5	A2–13	220/50
China	D	PAL	+6.5	R1–5	220/50
Colombia	M	NTSC	+4.5	A2–13	110/60

Table 2.8 Contd

	System	Colour	Sound carrier MHz	Channels	Mains
Congo	D	SECAM(V)	+6.5	R7	220/50
Costa Rica	M	NTSC	+4.5	A2–12	120/60
Cuba	M	NTSC	+4.5	A2–13	120/60
Cyprus	B, G	SECAM	+5.5	E6–11, 35–38	240/50
Czechoslavakia	D, K	SECAM(V)	+6.5	R1–12, 21–39	220/50
Denmark	B, G	PAL	+5.5	E3–11	220/50
Diego Garcia	M	NTSC	+4.5	A8	
Djibouti	K	SECAM	+6.5	K5	
Dominican Republic	M	NTSC	+4.5	A2–13	110/60
Dubai	B, G	PAL	+5.5		220/50
Ecuador	M	NTSC	+4.5	A2–10	110/60
Egypt	B	SECAM(V)		E3–11	220/50
El Salvador	M	NTSC	+4.5	A2–20	115/60
Ethiopia	B	PAL	+5.5	E7	220/50
Fernando Po	B		+5.5		220
Fiji	B	PAL	+5.5		240/50
Finland	B	PAL	+5.5	E1–12	220/50
France	L	SECAM(V)	+6.5	F1–12, 21–68	220/50
Gabon	K	SECAM(V)	+6.5	K3, 10	220/50
Gambia	I		+6.0		
Germany, East	B, G	SECAM(V)	+5.5		220/50
Germany, West	B, G	PAL	+5.5	E2–11, 21–60	220/50
(US Forces)	G	NTSC	+4.5		220/50
Ghana	B	PAL	+5.5	E2–5	220/50
Gibraltar	B	PAL	+5.5	E6, 11	240/50
Greece	B,G	SECAM	+5.5	E5–11, 23–49	220/50
Greenland	B	PAL	+5.5		220/50
Greenland (US Forces)	M	NTSC	+4.5	A8	220/50
Guadeloupe	K	SECAM(V)	+6.5	K5–8	220/60
Guam	M	NTSC	+4.5	A8, 12	110/60
Guatemala	M	NTSC	+4.5	A3–13	120/60
Guinea (Bissau)	I		+6.0		
Guinea (Rep.)	K		+6.5		220/50
Guyana (French)	K	SECAM(V)	+6.5	K4–6	220/50
Guyana (Rep.)	B, G		+5.5		
Haiti	M	NTSC	+4.5	A2–5	115/60
Hawaii	M	NTSC	+4.5	A2–13	115/60
Honduras	M	NTSC	+4.5	A3–13	110/60
Hong Kong	I	PAL	+6.0	E1–12, 21–68	200/50
Hungary	D, K	SECAM(V)	+6.5	R1–12, 24–32	220/50
Iceland	B, G	PAL	+5.5	E3–10	220/50
India	B	PAL	+5.5	E4–7	230/50
Indonesia	B	PAL	+5.5	E1–3, 4–11	220/50
Iran	B, G	SECAM(H)	+5.5	E3–11	220/50
Iraq	B	SECAM(H)	+5.5	E5–11	220/50
Ireland	I	PAL	+6.0	A–J, 21–68	220/50
Israel	B, G	PAL	+5.5	E5–11, 24–56	230/50
Italy	B, G	PAL	+5.5	A–H, 21–34	220/50
Ivory Coast	K	SECAM(V)	+6.5	K4–10	220/50
Jamaica	M	NTSC	+4.5	A7–13	110/50
Japan	M	NTSC	+4.5	J1–12, 28–62	100/60
Johnston Is.	M	NTSC	+4.5	A10	
Jordan	B, G	PAL	+5.5	E3–9	220/50
Kenya	B, G	PAL	+5.5	E2–10	240/50
Korea, North	D	SECAM	+6.5	R5–12	110/60
Korea, South	M	NTSC	+4.5	A4–13	110/60
Kuwait	B, G	PAL	+5.5	E5–10	240/50
Lebanon	B	SECAM(V)	+5.5	E2–11	220/50
Leeward Is.	M		+4.5	A7–8	230/60
Lesotho	I		+6.0		220/50
Liberia	B, H	PAL	+5.5	E6–10	120/60
Libya	B, G	SECAM	+5.5	E5–11	230/50
Luxembourg	C, L	PAL/SECAM	+6.5	E7, 21	220/50
Macao	I		+6.0		110/50
Madagascar	K	SECAM	+6.5	K5	220/50
Madeira	B	PAL	+5.5		220/50
Malawi	B, G		+5.5		230/50
Malaysia	B, G	PAL	+5.5	E2–10	230/50
Mali	K		+6.5		220/50
Malta	B, G	PAL	+5.5	E10	240/50
Martinique	K	SECAM(V)	+6.5	K4–8	220/50
Mauretania	K		+6.5		220/50
Mauritius	B	SECAM(V)	+5.5	E4–11	230/50
Mexico	M	NTSC	+4.5	A2–13, 14–45	120/60
Midway Is.	M	NTSC	+4.5	A4	
Monaco	G, L	SECAM(V)	+6.5	E10, 30, 35	220/50
Mongolia	D		+6.5		
Morocco	B, H	SECAM(V)	+5.5	M4–10	220/50
Mozambique	I		+6.0		220/50
Netherlands	B, G	PAL	+5.5	E1–12	220/50

Table 2.8 Contd

	System	Colour	Sound carrier MHz	Channels	Mains
New Caledonia	K	SECAM(V)	+6.5		220/50
New Zealand	B	PAL	+5.5	NZ1–9	230/50
Nicaragua	M	NTSC	+4.5	A2–13	120/60
Niger	K		+6.5		220/50
Nigeria	B	PAL	+5.5	E2–10	230/50
Norway	B, G	PAL	+5.5	E2–10, 44	230/50
Okinawa	M	NTSC	+4.5		
Oman	B, G	PAL	+5.5	E5–12	220/50
Pakistan	B	PAL	+5.5	E4–10	230/50
Panama	M	NTSC	+4.5	A2–12	120/60
Paraguay	N	PAL	+4.5	A9	220/50
Peru	M	NTSC	+4.5	A2–13	220/60
Philippines	M	NTSC	+4.5	A2–14	110/60
Poland	D, K	SECAM(V)	+6.5	R1–12, 21–37	220/50
Portugal	B, G	PAL	+5.5	E2–11, 25–46	220/50
Puerto Rico	M	NTSC	+4.5	A2–12	120/60
Qatar	B	PAL	+5.5	E9, 11	240/50
Reunion	K	SECAM(V)	+6.5	K4–9	220/50
Rumania	D, K	PAL	+6.5	R2–12	220/50
Rwanda	K		+6.5		220/50
Sabah and Sarawak	B	PAL	+5.5	E2–10	240/50
Samoa	M	NTSC	+4.5	A2–12	230/50
Saudi Arabia	B, G	SECAM(H)	+5.5	E5–10	220/50
Senegal	K	SECAM(V)	+6.5	K7	220/50
Seychelles	I				
Sierra Leone	B, G	PAL	+5.5	E2	230/50
Singapore	B, G	PAL	+5.5	E5, 8	230/50
Somalia	B, G		+5.5		230/50
South Africa	I	PAL	+6.0	I4–13, 21–68	220/50
Soviet Union	D, K	SECAM(V)	+6.5	R1–12, 21–68	220/50
Spain	B, G	PAL	+5.5	E2–11, 21–65	220/50
Sri Lanka	B, G	PAL	+5.5		230/50
St Helena	I				
St Kitts	M	NTSC	+4.5	A2–13	220/60
St Pierre and Miquelon	K	SECAM	+6.5	K4–8	115/50
Sudan	B	PAL	+5.5	E5–7	240/50
Surinam	M	NTSC	+4.5	A7–12	115/60
Swaziland	B, G	PAL	+5.5		230/50
Sweden	B, G	PAL	+5.5	E2–11, 21–68	220/50
Switzerland	B, G	PAL	+5.5	E2–12, 21–63	220/50
Syria	B, H	SECAM	+5.5	E4–9	220/50
Tahiti	K	SECAM(V)	+6.5	K4–8	240/60
Taiwan	M	NTSC	+4.5	A7–12	110/60
Tanzania	B, I	PAL	+5.5	E21	230/50
Thailand	B, G	PAL	+5.5	A2–13	220/50
Tibet	D	PAL	+6.5		220/50
Togo	K	SECAM	+6.5	K6–8	220/50
Trinidad and Tobago	M	NTSC	+4.5	A2–13	115/60
Trust Islands (Micronesia)	M	NTSC	+4.5	A8–10	
Tunisia	B	SECAM(V)	+5.5	E5–12	220/50
Turkey	B, G	PAL	+5.5	E5–10	220/50
United Arab Emirates	B, G	PAL	+5.5	E2–11	220/50
Uganda	B, G	PAL	+5.5	E5–10	240/50
United Kingdom	I	PAL	+6.0	21–68	240/50
Upper Volta	K		+6.5	K6	220/50
Uruguay	N	PAL	+4.5	A3–13	220/50
USA	M	NTSC	+4.5	A2–13, A14–83	120/60
USSR	D, K	SECAM(V)	+6.5	R1–12, 21–68	220/50
Venezuela	M	NTSC	+4.5	A2–13	120/60
Vietnam	D, M	NTSC	+4.5	R6, A7–13	230/50
Virgin Is.	M	NTSC	+4.5	A5–12	110/60
Yemen Rep.	B		+5.5	E4–10	220/50
Yugoslavia	B, H	PAL	+5.5	E2–12, 21–68	220/50
Zaire	B, K	SECAM(V)	+5.5	K5–9	220/50
Zambia	B, G	PAL	+5.5	E2–4	230/50
Zanzibar	I	PAL	+6.0		220/50
Zimbabwe	B, G	PAL	+5.5	E2–4	230/50

Table 2.9 *UHF television vision carrier frequencies*

21 471.25	36 591.25	51 711.25	66 831.25
22 499.25	37 599.25	52 719.25	67 839.25
23 487.25	38 607.25	53 727.25	68 847.25
24 495.25	39 615.25	54 735.25	
25 503.25	40 623.25	55 743.25	
26 511.25	41 631.25	56 751.25	
27 519.25	42 639.25	57 759.25	
28 527.25	43 647.25	58 767.25	
29 535.25	44 655.25	59 775.25	
30 543.25	45 663.25	60 783.25	
31 551.25	46 671.25	61 791.25	
32 559.25	47 679.25	62 799.25	
33 567.25	48 687.25	63 897.25	
34 575.25	49 695.25	64 815.25	
35 583.25	50 703.25	65 823.25	

3

Aerials and receivers

For the purpose of this chapter we shall regard a receiver as that section of a TV or videorecorder installation concerned with the selection, tuning, filtering, amplification and demodulation of transmitted TV signals, culminating in the deliverance of the standard 1 V video waveform, and a 0 dB (0.775 V r.m.s.) base-band audio signal.

AERIALS

The first, and one of the most critical links in the receiving chain is the aerial. In effect it forms the first tuned circuit of many, and its performance is crucial to the recording and display of good pictures. The basic pick-up element is the dipole, consisting in practice of a metal rod, divided at its centre by an air gap of about 20 mm for connection to the transmission line. Its overall length is approximately half that of the wavelength on which optimum reception is required. The impedance at the centre is approximately 72 Ω, a reasonable match to the 75 Ω co-axial cable used to link the dipole to the r.f. input of the tuner, whose characteristic input impedance is likewise 75 Ω. Normally the centre conductor of the co-axial cable is connected to the upper half of the dipole and the outer (screening) braid to the lower half.

Parasitic elements

The basic half-wave dipole is omnidirectional, and this can be a disadvantage in terms of susceptibility to interference and the pick-up of unwanted signals. To overcome this, and to add some useful gain, further elements are usually fitted. The H-type aerial, much used on VHF band I, consists of a half-wave dipole and a reflector: a second and slightly longer metal rod. The reflector is mounted one-quarter or one-eighth of a wavelength behind the dipole. It has no electrical connection with the dipole, but influences the dipole impedance and its directivity. By reflecting an in-phase signal back to the dipole an improvement in gain of some 3 dB is made by the reflector for signals in the 'forward' direction, while signals arriving from the rear are attenuated; a front-to-back ratio of 9 dB is typical of an H-type aerial. See Fig. 3.1 for an explanation of dB ratios, and Table 21.6 for conversions.

Further gain and directivity can be gained by adding directors in front of the dipole. They have the effect of concentrating the signal on the dipole element, and up to sixteen may be fitted to high-gain aerials in a Yagi configuration, Fig. 3.2. Here the reflector takes the form of a mesh or grid for high gain and good back-to-front ratio. The dipole is a folded type for greater bandwidth and better

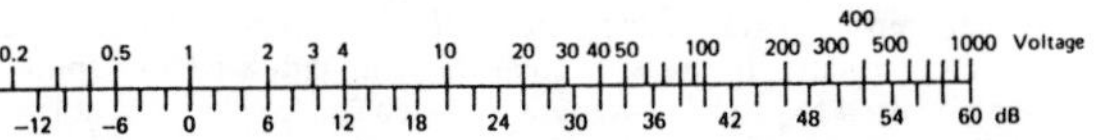

Fig. 3.1 *Voltage-dB conversion chart*

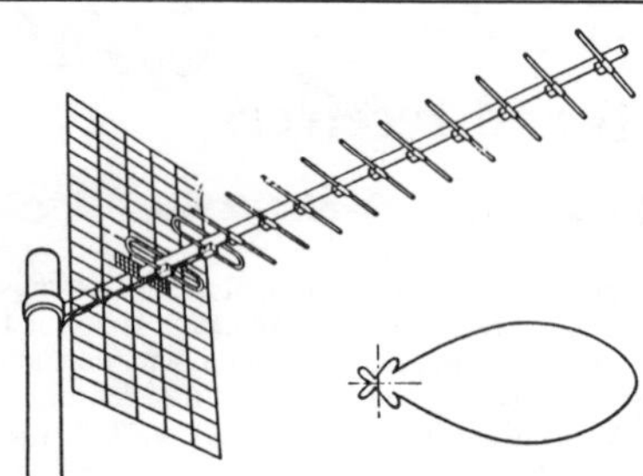

Fig. 3.2 *UHF aerial with mesh reflector element. Inset: polar response*

impedance matching to the co-axial feeder; the presence of parasitic elements tends to reduce dipole impedance. The polar diagram in Fig. 3.2 gives an idea of the directive properties of the multi-element Yagi aerial.

Bandwidth

As a 'tuned circuit' a receiving aerial has a certain bandwidth, determined by its physical characteristics. For reception from UHF transmitting sites in the UK an aerial bandwidth sufficient to cover all four local channels is required; with few exceptions the signals from each BBC/IBA site fall within one of the aerial groupings given in Table 2.6.

FEEDERS

The transmission line between aerial and tuner is an important component. For minimum loss, thick coaxial cable should be used: semi-air-spaced coaxial cable is best, though cellular-polythene spaced types are a good compromise between performance and cost in areas of good signals and where the cable run is not too long. The performance of the feeder (and other distribution components like amplifiers) is particularly critical where teletext receivers are in use. Short-term reflections due to poor cable routing and mismatch at terminations and connections will upset text reception and lead to the display of blanks and errors in the characters and graphics.

DISTRIBUTION AMPLIFIERS FOR UHF

Apart from MATV installations in blocks of flats, hotels and shops, there is an increasing demand for multiple aerial outlet points in ordinary dwellings, where several TV sets may be found in different rooms, and videorecorders are burgeoning. For this purpose a simple mains-powered distribution amplifier is used, mounted at the rear of the main TV, or (to save difficult cable-routing and redecoration problems) in the loft or even on the aerial pole itself. From here separate cables are routed to up to six outlets in different rooms. In areas of good field strength a passive splitter may be used to provide two outlets from a single cable, but at least 6 dB attenuation is introduced in each path.

SATELLITE AERIALS

At microwave frequencies a form of dipole (in fact a *probe*) is still used for signal pick-up, but unaided it would intercept virtually none of the very low-level signals from space. Even the addition of parasitic elements in Yagi form would not be effective – the signal capture area would not be great enough. Instead a parabolic dish is used to intercept r.f. energy over a larger area. The surface of the dish is carefully formed into a true uniform parabola so that the centimetric waves are all reflected, uniformly and *in phase*, to the focal point. Here may be mounted the pick-up probe, though sometimes a subreflector is fitted to redirect the energy to the centre-point of the dish, where sits a waveguide in which the pick-up probe is mounted. The difficulties of conveying SHF signals is such that a low-noise amplifier or mixer stage is connected direct to the pick-up probe itself – more on this in Chapter 4.

TUNERS

The UHF tuner has several functions. It has to reject out-of-band transmissions, amplify the incoming signal and then mix it with an internally generated c.w. (continuous-wave) signal to give an output on the *difference* frequency between the two UHF signals – the incoming a.m. modulated one and the local oscillator output. The tuner's local oscillator runs (for UK receivers) at a frequency 39.5 MHz above the required vision carrier frequency, so that for instance in the case of channel 23 (Fig. 2.6(a)) whose vision carrier has a frequency of 487.25 MHz the local oscillator would need to run at precisely 526.75 MHz. The two signals come together in a *mixer*, a non-linear device which produces outputs at the sum and difference frequencies of its two inputs. In this case the difference frequency of 39.5 MHz (i.f., intermediate frequency) is selected by a tuned-circuit filter which rejects other frequencies. This filter and subsequent circuits have a bandwidth sufficient to embrace not only the sideband signals corresponding to high frequencies in the vision signal, but also the sound i.f. which will appear at 33.5 MHz. This arises from the difference between the channel 23 sound carrier at 493.25 MHz and the same local oscillator frequency of 526.75 MHz. What has been described is in fact the superheterodyne principle, which is used in virtually all r.f. receiving equipment from pocket radios up to satellite installations.

The great virtue of superhet operation is that by altering the local oscillator frequency any required incoming signal can be translated to a single, common frequency carrier – the i.f. Provided the local oscillator is made to run at a frequency (in this case) 39.5 MHz higher than the wanted one, the signal (complete with sidebands) is translated to a single low frequency where it can be dealt with by a fix-tuned amplifier with fix-tuned filters to shape the required passband. Thus the need for 'movable' tuned circuits is confined to three or four within the tuner itself.

Apart from offering gain to overcome the inherently noisy mixing process, and isolating the local oscillator signal from the aerial, the r.f. amplifier is required to reject the image frequency. At a given local oscillator rate ($f$osc) there are two input frequencies which can give rise to a 39.5 KHz. i.f. signal – the wanted frequency at $f$osc – 39.5 MHz; and an unwanted (image) frequency at $f$osc + 39.5 MHz. The bandwidth of the tuned r.f.

amplifier (generally a two-stage section) is tailored to offer approaching 60 dB of image frequency reception at a frequency 79 MHz above the wanted carrier. Calculation shows that the sound carrier of channel n + 4 (where *n* is the required channel) will give rise to a spurious i.f. signal 1.5 MHz away from the required vision i.f. carrier. To avoid beat pattern effects on the picture the r.f. amplifier's response to the n + 4 channel must be at least 55 dB down.

On VHF bands I and III, conventional inductors and capacitors can be used in the tuned circuits required for oscillator and r.f. amplifier tuning. On UHF bands IV and V such inductors would consist of less than one turn, and designing a tuner along such lines would be difficult. An alternative technique is the use of distributed constants in tuned circuits making use of *lecher lines* printed on the surface of a low-loss insulating board. Each line is equivalent in length to an electrical half-wavelength, having one end grounded and the other end (nodal point) tuned by a variable capacitor with which its resonant frequency can be swung over the required range.

Fig. 3.3 shows a typical varicap tuner's circuit diagram. For optimum noise performance and matching over the entire UHF band 470 to 860 MHz the input circuit is untuned. TR701 forms the first r.f. amplifier and operates in grounded-base mode, with the input signal applied to the emitter via the diode attenuator D600/D601. TR701 collector circuit incorporates a tuned load L510 whence the signal is transferred via C213 to bandpass tuned circuit L511/L512. The local oscillator is TR702, whose frequency is governed by the capacitive loading at the top end of lecher line L518. Local and broadcast signals are applied via C220 and L513 respectively to Schottky mixer diode D603. At its anode appears the wanted *beat* signal, selected and filtered by the LC network en route to i.f. amplifier TR703, again a common-base stage. TR703 collector circuit is returned to ground externally of the tuner, and further selection and filtering takes places in L523 and associated components.

AGC is applied in two ways in this tuner. The attenuation offered by the PIN diode pair D600/601 depends on the amount of current 'sinked' from the gain control pin 3 by the external a.g.c. control circuit; at high current levels (9 mA) D601 is fully on and D600 off so that the full signal level is applied to TR701 emitter. As the a.g.c. current decreases D601 turns off and D600 becomes progressively more conductive, attenuating the UHF input signal. The very linear attenuator so formed offers excellent performance in the face of high levels of unwanted signal, thus very good *cross-modulation* performance.

VARICAP TUNING

Traditionally a variable capacitor is a mechanical device in which interleaving vanes are rotated by a shaft, their degree of mesh determining the total capacitance. The same effect can be achieved by the use of a varicap diode, the junction capacitance of which can be varied between typically 20 pf and 2 pf for applied reverse-bias voltages between 1 V and 28 V. The three varicap diodes in the tuner of Fig. 3.3 D605, D606 and D607 are carefully matched and selected in manufacture to have identical voltage/capacitance curves. The two bandpass tuned circuits L510/L511-12 in the r.f. stage are thus tuned exactly in step, and the oscillator frequency maintained exactly 39.5 MHz higher in frequency – a process

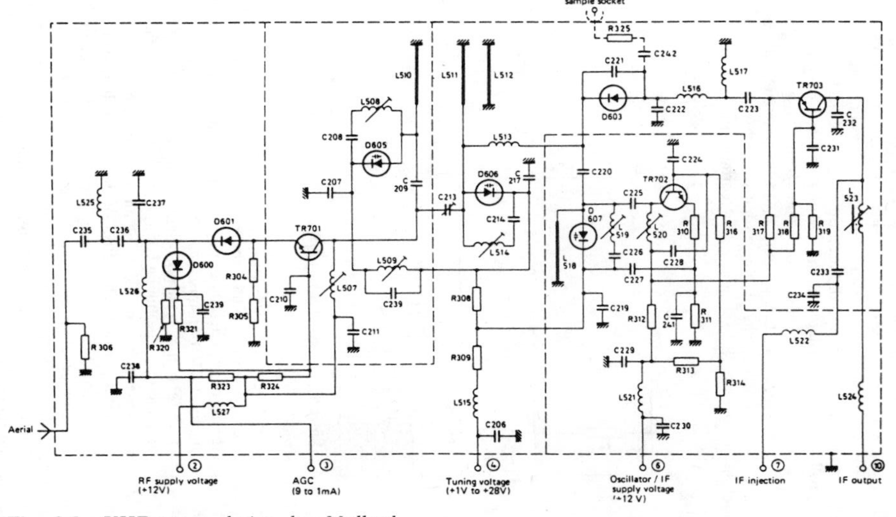

Fig. 3.3 *UHF tuner design by Mullard*

known as *tracking*. Correct tracking ensures optimum gain and performance throughout UHF bands IV and V. The channel selected, then, depends on the d.c. voltage applied to tuner pin 4.

Deriving the tuner control voltage

With received channel number depending purely on the d.c. voltage applied to the varicap tuner, a wide range of options is open to the TV set designer, including self-seeking systems, remote control and station memory, all based on modern IC technology. They will be examined later in this chapter and in Chapter 19. While the simplest types of monochrome receiver use a single rotary potentiometer as tuning control, in conjunction with a stabilised 30 V source, a slightly more sophisticated tuning system is used in inexpensive TV sets and videorecorders: Fig. 3.4 shows its basis.

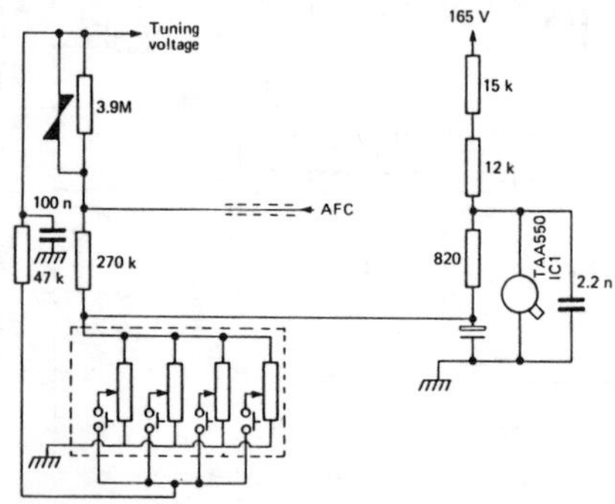

Fig. 3.4 *Simple press-button circuit for varicap tuning control*

A specially-developed two-terminal chip, IC1, acts as a temperature-compensated voltage source for a series of potentiometers in a tuning bank. Each slider taps off a potential appropriate to one of the local TV transmissions, and is selected by a push-button, of which there may typically be eight, marked BBC 1, BBC 2, ITV, Channel 4, etc. The tuning voltage thus set passes into the varicap tuner, having had added to it an a.f.c. control voltage derived from the i.f. carrier. The effect of the a.f.c. voltage is to correct for slight tuning errors by 'pulling' the local oscillator up or down to achieve an exact vision i.f. frequency of 39.5 MHz, when tuning is spot-on. Because the influence of a.f.c. control can mask the correct tuning point, provision is often made to switch it off when manual tuning is carried out: the most common artifice is a switch operated by the flap or door which conceals the tuning potentiometers.

Touch-tuning

One disadvantage of the simple tuning system outlined above is its use of switches with moving contacts which can deteriorate with wear and oxidation. To counter this, various *touch-tuning* systems were evolved whereby the tuning potentiometers are selected by finger contact with sensitive 'touch pads' which depend for their operation on either the 50 Hz mains-induced hum present in the human body, or more commonly the leakage resistance introduced by the presence of a finger across two adjacent conductive pads. For safety reasons these are very high impedance circuits, and an early example of the latter type is shown in Fig. 3.5.

In this system there are six touch buttons. IC1 controls the switching for the first three, and IC2 that for the remainder. Both ICs are similar except for the provision in IC1 of an extra stage to ensure that the number 1 position is always selected at switch-on of the set. All switching operations are identical, so only that for the second position will be described.

Initially the number one lamp will be lit and number 1 potentiometer in use due to the closing of two separate switches within IC1 – one between its pins 8 and 9, one between its pins 7 and 6, passing 12 V to the bulb and 33 V to the potentiometer respectively. Touching the channel 2 button effectively earths IC pin 14 via R29 whereupon an internal switch changes state to turn on two separate transistors: one linking pins 8 and 13 to light up the no. 2 lamp and one linking pins 7 and 4 to bring in the appropriate potentiometer. As the electronic switch latches, its emitter current passes through R15, which is the common emitter return for all six stages. R15 voltage rises as a result, unlatching channel 1 (or whichever was on) and switching the selected amplifier hard on. This simple circuit is representative of many, including those incorporating bandswitching for VHF/UHF reception. Early sets with touch tuning employed somewhat troublesome neons as indicators; later types use LEDs or a numicator (digital display) in neon, LED or even on-screen form, the latter employing a simple character-generator chip with access to a video channel, typically the G-amplifier.

IF AMPLIFIERS

As with the tuner, the i.f. amplifier has several functions, not all of them immediately obvious. Its primary task is to amplify the tuner's output signal to a level where it can be practically demodulated. It is also required to maintain a constant output signal level in the face of very wide variations in signal input level; to provide a closely

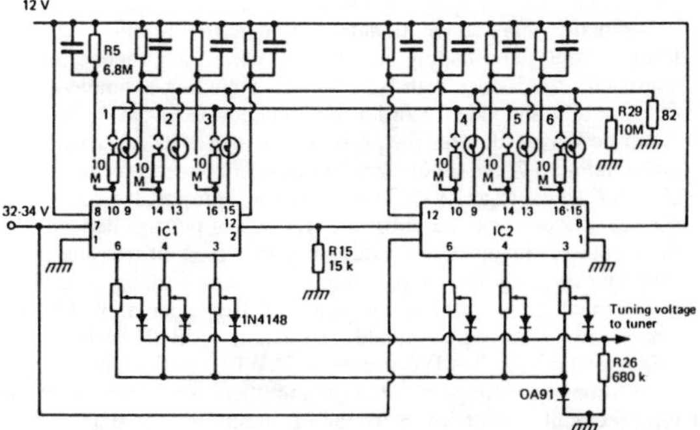

Fig. 3.5 *Touch tuning circuit using purpose-designed ICs*

defined passband, selectively amplifying wanted signals and rejecting adjacent ones; to furnish a.g.c. and a.f.c. control lines for the tuner; and to offer a reasonably linear phase response or group-delay characteristic, important for colour reproduction and crucial to good teletext reception.

Bandpass shaping

The tuner's r.f. stage offers rejection of unwanted signals which are widely spaced from the carrier in use, but is not sufficiently selective to reject frequencies within a few MHz of it. Thus adjacent channel and other spurious signals emerge unscathed from the tuner and must be rejected in the i.f. stage. For use with a synchronous demodulator (see later) the required response curve is as shown in Fig. 3.6. Deep rejection notches are provided at 41.5 MHz (adjacent sound carrier) and 31.5 MHz (adjacent vision carrier), and a shallower one at 33.5 MHz, corresponding to the co-sound i.f. frequency. The need for the 33.5 MHz notch is twofold: to prevent a high level of sound carrier beating with the colour subcarrier at 35.07 MHz to produce a 1.57 MHz pattern on highly coloured areas of the picture; and to depress the sound carrier to a level where it remains below the minimum excursion of the vision signal (i.e. peak white) so that it will not become a.m. modulated by picture frequencies to cause difficulties with buzz on sound.

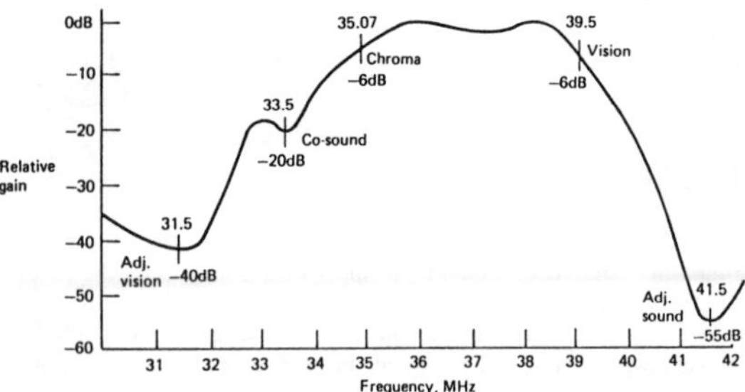

Fig. 3.6 *Typical response curve for a TV i.f. amplifier*

For many years conventional LC tuned circuits were used for filtering and bandshaping in i.f. circuits, which then typically consisted of a 3-stage transistor amplifier feeding a simple diode detector. TV and videorecorder receivers now use a SAW (Surface Acoustic Wave) filter for the purpose. An idea of its construction is given in Fig. 3.7. An input signal transducer converts the incoming electrical signal to an acoustic wave which is propagated across the surface of a piezoelectric substrate. Its ease of passage depends on the frequency involved – the design of the resonant transducers is such that the response curve of Fig. 3.6 is closely maintained. The most critical area is around the vision i.f. frequency of 39.5 MHz, where the output signal should be excactly 6 dB down from full gain, see Fig. 2.6(b). The use of a SAWF greatly simplifies the fabrication and setting-up of the i.f. amplifier, as can be seen in the typical circuit of Fig. 3.8. Here the i.f. input signal is amplified by about 26 dB within IC50 before application to the SAWF, whose output passes direct to the balanced inputs of IC51.

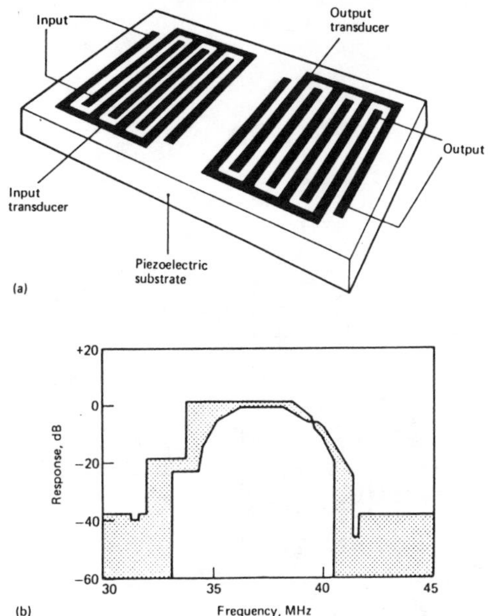

Fig. 3.7 *SAW filter: (a) basic construction; (b) tolerance — response curve must lie within the shaded area*

Amplification and detection

The TDA2540 chip IC51 contains amplifier, demodulator, a.g.c. and a.f.c. stages, together with some noise-reducing circuitry. The level of the recovered video signal is sampled in the a.g.c. detector, which regulates the amplifier gain to maintain constant output level. Normally the UHF tuner is kept at full gain to minimise noise, but when the TDA2540 chip is turned fully down (at an r.f. input level of around 5 mV) control over the tuner gain takes place via IC pin 4. The onset of r.f. a.g.c. is governed by the crossover control VR36. L36 is associated with the vision demodulator and is tuned with C45 to the vision i.f. of 39.5 MHz. If the i.f. frequency increases, the potential at IC pin 5 reduces and vice-versa, and this is fed back to the tuner's tuning voltage input to form an a.f.c. loop; a *defeat* line is provided at IC pin 6 whereby the a.f.c. action can be cancelled when fine-tuning or changing channels. With the a.f.c. on, L36 is adjusted for correct tuning, thereafter compensating for ageing and thermal drift in the tuner's local oscillator, or for carrier drift in any local r.f. signal source.

The demodulator works on the synchronous principle. A sample of carrier signal is amplified, clipped and applied to the 'tank' tuned circuit L34/C43. The result is a train of sampling pulses at 39.5 MHz, and these are used to gate the amplitude-modulated vision i.f. signal, taking a sample of its level on each carrier cycle. The succession of these samples forms the demodulated vision

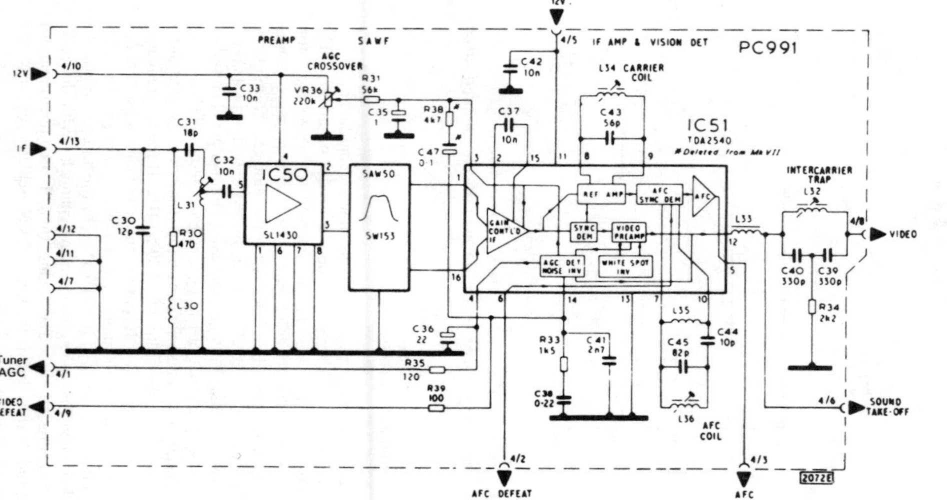

Fig. 3.8 *IF system using SAW filter — Ferguson*

signal. The synchronous demodulator is capable of linear operation and has good intermodulation performance.

The video signal is pre-amplified within the chip, whence it emerges on pin 12. At this point it carries a 6 MHz intercarrier sound signal – the product of the 33.5 MHz sound i.f. signal – which is removed from the video signal by bridged-T notch filter L32/C39/C40/R34. At point 4/8 in the diagram, then, appears the 1 V pk-pk CVBS signal in the form shown in Fig. 2.5.

SOUND DEMODULATION

Since the deviation of the sound carrier (now in 6 MHz form) is ±50 KHz, a sharply tuned circuit with at least 100 KHz bandwidth, and centred on 6 MHz, is required to filter out the sound carrier from the video waveform. It takes the form of a ceramic filter, a very small mechanical resonator with sharp cut-off characteristics. After passing through one or two of these the sound carrier is 'clean' and ready for delivery to its demodulator. First (Fig. 3.9) it passes through several *limiter* stages, in which it is repeatedly amplified and clipped to remove all traces of amplitude modulation, and with them the influence of interference spikes and noise. The sound detector is also a synchronous type, but here working in *quadrature* mode, with the 6 MHz tank coil L1 adjusted so that the carrier-sampling pulses are 90° out of phase with the cycles of the unmodulated carrier. The output from this arrangement is proportional to phase angle of the sound carrier, which is what is required for f.m. demodulation. A preamplifier within the IC brings the level up to the 0 dB (0.775V r.m.s.) point, or indeed any other required level; its gain is adjustable in many chip designs by virtue of an internal voltage-controlled attenuator (VCA). By this means sound level can be controlled by application of a variable d.c. voltage, useful for local control and muting purposes and essential

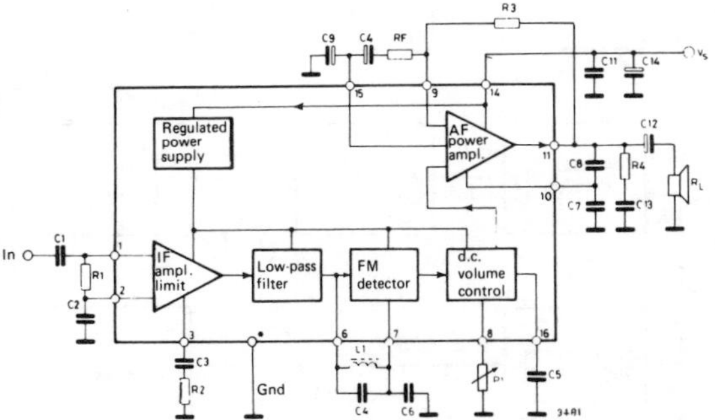

Fig. 3.9 *Sound IF and detector circuit by SGS-Ates. This one also incorporates a power output stage with feedback, forming the entire sound section of a TV receiver in one IC package*

for remote control applications. In Fig. 3.9 the VCA is controlled via pin 8 of the chip.

FREQUENCY-SYNTHESIS TUNING

Since the received channel depends purely on the frequency of the local oscillator within the tuner, and since broadcast transmissions – be they from terrestrial or space-based transmitters – are held very accurately to their nominal frequencies, there is no theoretical need for any trial-and-error tuning systems. Very accurate and stable crystal control of the receiver's local oscillator would suffice for a fixed-tuning system. In practical frequency-synthesis tuning systems the 'analogue' oscillator is still present within the tuner, and still controlled by a d.c. potential acting on an array of varicap diodes. Here, however, the oscillator is made part of a phase-lock-loop (PLL) in which it comes under the influence of a stable local frequency reference in the form of a quartz crystal.

A basic block diagram is given in Fig. 3.10. Inside or adjacent to the tuner is a prescaler which divides the local oscillator frequency *f*osc by 64, and is capable of working with input frequencies up to 1 GHz (1000 MHz). The counted-down frequency is *f*osc/64, and this is applied to an LSI (Large Scale Integration) digital IC called a programmable divider which further divides *f*osc/64 by a factor determined by its programming instructions. Their derivation will be described shortly. Thus at the phase detector's 'A' input appears a signal frequency which depends on (a) the tuner's local oscillator frequency, and (b) the division ratio of the programmable divider. At the top of the diagram appears a reference crystal oscillator running at 3 MHz and feeding a fixed divider (counter) whose division ratio is fixed at 1536. 3 MHz divided by 1536 is 1.953 kHz and this is the frequency applied to the 'B' input of the phase detector. Whenever the frequency or phase of the A and B inputs

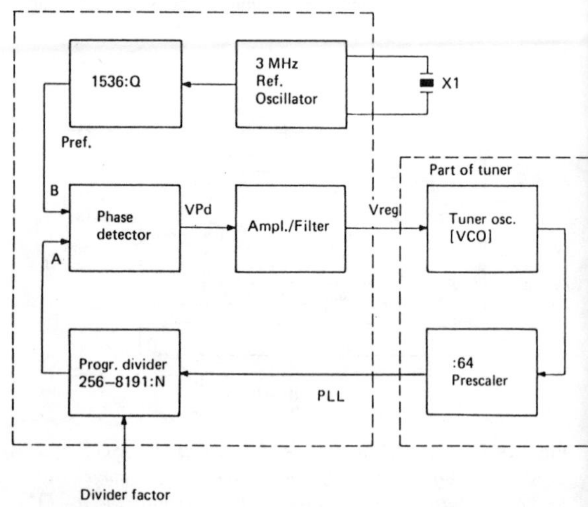

Fig. 3.10 *Skeleton block diagram of an FS TV tuning system*

differ the phase detector produces a d.c. *error* output whose polarity is dependent on the direction of the error (i.e. whether B input is faster or slower than A input); and whose magnitude is proportional to the difference in speeds between the two inputs. The error voltage is amplified and filtered and appears as a control potential on the tuner's varicap control line. Since the local oscillator is in effect a VCO (Voltage Controlled Oscillator) its frequency changes until the two inputs of the phase detector come into frequency and phase coincidence, when the varicap control potential stabilises. What we have set up is a phase-lock-loop (PLL) in which *fosc* is locked to a multiple of the 3 MHz crystal reference, the exact multiple being set by the division ratio of the programmable divider (PD) block. In fact the PD can divide by numbers between 256 and 8191.

To set a required channel, then, we merely give the divider a coded instruction to correspond with the known and pre-programmed channel frequency. We know that the local oscillator must run 39.5 MHz above incoming r.f. and we know the CCIR standard vision carrier frequencies for each TV channel. Taking a numerical example, suppose it is required to tune channel 41 whose vision carrier is 631.25 MHz. Required tuner *fosc* is 631.25 + 39.5 = 670.75 MHz, giving rise to 10.48 MHz from the prescaler. To satisfy the 1.953 kHz input requirement of the phase detector we need to set a division ratio in the PD of the 10480/1.953 = 5366. This ratio is one of say 100 available to cover all CCIR-approved TV channels on the four bands available to terrestrial transmissions. Each channel instruction is held in a ROM (read-only memory) as a group of thirteen binary digits (bits), and for the channel 41 division ratio of 5366 the binary code happens to be 1010011110001. For UHF channel 64 the division ratio is 6838 and the corresponding binary code 1101010110001.

The ROM needs in this case to have 100 memory addresses with the appropriate code for the division ratio for each possible channel permanently stored there. Thus (in simple terms) if channel 41 is requested on the user's keypad, address no. 41 will be accessed and its contents 1010011110001 read out into the instruction register of the programmable divider. Some of the digits contain bandswitching instructions (not currently needed in the UK except for a satellite receiver option) which are decoded and passed to the tuner(s) to enable the appropriate section to operate.

Most frequency-synthesis tuning systems have facilities for sweep-search. An alternative name for it is self-seek, and when this function is invoked the control system steps through the 100 addresses in the programme ROM sequentially, presenting their contents in turn to the programmable divider. The tuner is thus stepped through all available transmission channels in its search for a broadcast transmission. When one is found the TV's line oscillator quickly synchronises to it: an output pin on the line generator chip signals 'locked' to the tuning control microcomputer, instructing it to stop seeking. What happens next depends on the user's requirements. If he wishes the set to memorise that channel, a touch of the 'memory' button will write the PD instructions into a RAM (Random Access Memory) for instant call-up when that channel is next required. These binary-coded instructions may typically be held at 'Address 1' in the RAM and contain data corresponding to the local BBC 1 transmission channel. Further seeking will find the other three local channels and the output channels of other equipment like videorecorders, TV games and home computers, and each can be assigned to memory in turn. This

RAM (*programmable memory*) is built in 'floating gate technology' which means that the data is held in the form of electrostatic charges in the isolated gate regions of an array of FETs (Field Effect Transistors). Such a memory is called *non-volatile* because the data can be held for several *years* without any need for external power. This type of memory is ideal for TV channel data storage in a set which may not be continuously powered. In fact the contents can be erased and overwritten by means of applying a high 'erase voltage' of +33 V, and this is carried out whenever the user or installer re-programmes the memory.

A basic block diagram of the synthesis control system is given in Fig. 3.11. The need for a.f.c. control may well be questioned in view of the accuracy and stability of the crystal reference. In fact none is needed for broadcast transmissions, but the r.f. modulators fitted to home computers and videorecorders can drift in frequency, and will probably nor produce a vision carrier exactly on the frequency specified for a CCIR channel. Hence the 'fine tune minus' and 'fine tune plus' buttons, Plainly, continuous tuning is not possible with a frequency synthesis system, but very small discrete steps can be made. In the present case the (divided) reference frequency of 1.953 kHz and prescaler division factor of 64 gives a minimum step of 1.953 × 64 = 125 kHz, sufficient for 64 separate tuning points across one 8 MHz wide television channel; to all intents and purposes this approximates to continuous tuning.

SYSTEMS CONVERSION

On occasion it is required of a service engineer to convert receivers, be they part of TV or videorecorder or separate, to different reception standards. Where different mains supply voltages, encoding systems and r.f. bands are encountered, economic and practical limitations seldom render the project worthwhile unless the power supply system is switchable, the decoder has provision for alternate modes (see Chapter 7) and the r.f. tuner is easily replaced by a suitable type.

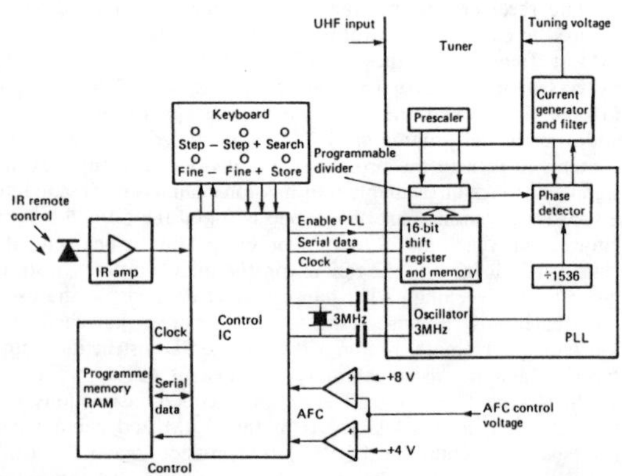

Fig. 3.11 *Practical implementation of FS tuning. Three main ICs are involved*

The easiest conversion project is that involving a receiver with different sound carrier characteristic but otherwise similar parameters, and typical of these are receivers designed for CCIR system PAL G imported to the UK from continental Europe. This category of receiver can be made to work with UK system I transmissions merely by retuning the intercarrier sound channel from 5.5 to 6 MHz; this may involve adjustment of filter coils and quad-f.m. detector coil, or replacement of fix-tuned ceramic filters. In the latter case it is important to order the correct filter type – those used for bandpass tuning have different characteristics to those used as resonators in quadrature demodulators. In videorecorders it is also necessary to retuned to 6 MHz the sound generator coil in the r.f. output modulator (sometimes called *convertor*) module.

Merely retuning the sound circuits is not sufficient for correct performance, however. To avoid buzz on sound, vision beat patterns and vulnerability to adjacent-channel interference, the i.f. response curve must also be changed to conform to the 6 MHz sound-vision carrier spacing, with regard to co-sound and adjacent-sound traps, see Fig. 3.6. In old sets using discrete bandpass-shaping circuits, retuning of these traps (to 33.5 and 41.5 MHz respectively where the vision i.f. is 39.5 MHz) is required; in more modern equipment the SAW filter must be replaced with a system I type. This can often be ordered from importer or manufacturer as a standard spare part for the UK (etc.) version of the equipment. A final point concerns the sound trap in series with the vision/luminance channel, which may be in ceramic or LC form. Unless it is replaced or retuned, a fine dot pattern and tonal distortion of the picture highlights will result.

TV and videorecorder equipment marketed in the Middle East is very often triple-standard (PAL, SECAM, NTSC) and in spite of the basic PAL-B (VHF) specification for local broadcasts, is invariably capable of both VHF and UHF reception. Such machines can easily be converted for system I as described above, but will then be incompatible with broadcasts and interfacing equipment if returned to their country of origin.

CCIR system PAL-B receivers (Australia, New Zealand, etc.) also require sole-VHF tuners (and/or r.f. modulators for videocassette recorders) to be replaced by their UHF equivalents – viable where pin-compatible units are available as spares, time-consuming otherwise.

In situations other than commercial domestic service departments, i.e. where time and money factors are less pressing, conversion and multi-standard switching can be interesting and rewarding projects. Diode switching of filters can be arranged if required, and different decoding arrangements made by means of the ICs to be described at the end of Chapter 7.

4

Satellite television

During the 1980s satellite television was primarily a means of conveying broadcasts to cable distribution networks and relaying live news feeds over long distances point-to-point. A handful of enthusiasts set up receiving equipment and 'pirated' these transmissions, but the low-power telecommunications satellites of those days demanded large dishes and specialised equipment, and this had little appeal for ordinary TV viewers.

With the advent of the Astra 1A direct-to-home satellite in early 1989, relatively inexpensive tuner/dish outfits became available to the general public, and the establishment of true DBS (Direct Broadcast by Satellite) by BSB's Marcopolo satellite a year later further increased interest in the new broadcast medium. Satellite TV has now become well established, with small dishes and plates sprouting from millions of homes across Europe.

TV FROM SPACE

The concept of modern communications satellites was first put forward by Arthur C. Clarke in 1945, and first implemented in 1965 by *Early Bird*, built and launched in the USA. It is based on the use of a geosynchronous orbit in the plane of the equator, wherein the satellite orbits at an altitude of 36 000 km at a speed of 11 000 km/h. Under these circumstances it appears stationary to an observer on earth, and can act as a 'mirror in the sky' to radio waves. The sky-path 36 000 km above the equator is called the *Clarke belt* and individual spots on it are known as orbital slots. These slots are defined and allocated by international agreement. The governing body for satellite slot allocation is the World Administrative Radio Conference (WARC), whose allocations are given in Table 4.1 and channel frequencies in Table 4.2.

The satellites are powered, for both transmission and internal 'housekeeping' services, by solar energy, intercepted by banks of solar cells on dragonfly-type wings which are kept facing the sun. Transmissions to and from the satellite are in the Ku band, 10.95–14.5 GHz, concentrated into very narrow (and thus intense) beams by parabolic reflectors – dishes – at each end. Medium-power satellites like Astra 1A and 1B typically have transponder powers of 45 W, receivable with a dish of about 60 cm diameter in the primary service area. The DBS transmissions have higher power (say 100 W per transponder) and call for an antenna of about 35 cm diameter in the primary service area, centred on the receiving *footprint*. Typical footprint diagrams are given in Fig. 4.1.

A medium-power satellite typically has 16 transponders, whose footprints are not necessarily the same: by special antenna arrangements *spot beams* can be designed to cover different areas on the earth. The higher-power DBS satellites have five or ten transponders. All TV transmissions from satellites are frequency-modulated to take advantage of the f.m. system's greater immunity from noise interference. The carrier wave from a satellite can be polarised in either linear or circular fashion. The polarisation characteristic is used to discriminate between co-channels or

Table 4.1 *DBS allocations – positions, channels and polarisation*

Band	*Orbital position*			
	5°E	*19°W*	*31°W*	*37°W*
11.7–12.1 GHz RH polarised	*Turkey:* CH. 1, 5, 9, 13, 17 *Greece:* CH. 3, 7, 11, 15, 19	*France:* CH. 1, 5, 9, 13, 17 *Luxembourg:* CH. 3, 7, 11, 15, 19	*Eire:* CH. 2, 6, 10, 14, 18 *UK:* CH. 4, 8, 12, 16, 20	*San Marino:* CH. 1, 5, 9, 13, 17 *Liechtenstein:* CH. 3, 7, 11, 15, 19
11.7–12.1 GHz LH polarised	*Finland:* CH. 2, 6, 10 *Norway:* CH. 14, 18 *Sweden:* CH. 4, 8 *Denmark:* CH. 12, 16, 20	*W. Germany:* CH. 2, 6, 10, 14, 18 *Austria:* CH. 4, 8, 12, 16, 20	*Portugal:* CH. 3, 7, 11, 15, 19	*Andorra:* CH. 4, 8, 12, 16, 20
12.1–12.5 GHz RH polarised	*Cyprus:* CH. 21, 25, 29, 33, 37 *Iceland, etc.* *CH. 23, 27, 31, 35, 39*	*Belgium:* CH. 21, 25, 29, 33, 37 *Netherlands:* CH. 23, 27, 31, 35, 39		*Monaco:* CH. 21, 25, 29, 33, 37 *Vatican:* CH. 23, 27, 31, 35, 39
12.1–12.5 GHz LH polarised	*Nordic group** CH. 22, 24, 26, 28, 30, 32, 36, 40 *Sweden:* CH. 34 *Norway:* CH. 38	*Switzerland:* CH. 22, 26, 30, 34, 38 *Italy:* CH. 24, 28, 32, 36, 40	*Iceland:* CH. 21, 25, 29, 33, 37 *Spain:* CH. 23, 27, 31, 35, 39	

* Wide beam channels: Denmark, Finland, Norway, Sweden.

Table 4.2 *SHF Band VI DBS channel frequencies*

	Lower half		*Upper half*
1	11.727 48	21	12.111 08
2	11.746 66	22	12.130 26
3	11.765 84	23	12.149 44
4	11.785 02	24	12.168 62
5	11.804 20	25	12.187 80
6	11.823 38	26	12.206 98
7	11.842 56	27	12.226 16
8	11.861 74	28	12.245 34
9	11.880 92	29	12.264 52
10	11.900 10	30	12.283 70
11	11.919 28	31	12.302 88
12	11.938 46	32	12.322 06
13	11.957 64	33	12.341 24
14	11.976 82	34	12.360 42
15	11.996 00	35	12.379 60
16	12.015 18	36	12.398 78
17	12.034 36	37	12.417 96
18	12.053 54	38	12.437 14
19	12.072 72	39	12.456 32
20	12.091 90	40	12.475 50

adjacent channels: interfering carriers in the wrong polar field are rejected by up to 22 dB, enabling the carriers from individual transponders on a single satellite to overlap without mutual interference. Fig. 4.2 shows the 'staggered' arrangement of carriers on the Astra 1A transmissions, and Table 4.3 the transponder occupancies of Astra 1A and 1B.

Most satellite channels are 27 MHz wide; the Eutelsat II transponders are an exception at 36 MHz. The f.m. transmissions carry an energy-dispersal waveform which prevents the carrier frequency dwelling at one spot during such repetitive picture features as black-level, syncs and peak white: this avoidance of spot-frequencies lessens the risk of interference to other services.

The orbital slots in the Clarke belt of interest to European viewers are shown in Fig. 4.3. At present the most popular of these for direct-to-home services is the Astra group at 19.2°E. The UK DBS allocation is 31°W, from which the Marcopolo bird, operated by British Sky Broadcasting, delivers five high-power channels using the MAC transmission system. A single receiving antenna/dish can be fixed to a *polar mount* and made to scan the entire Clarke belt by manual or automatic (governed by the receiver's microprocessor control system) means, but polar installations are not nearly so popular as simple, inexpensive fixed-dish outfits. World allocations for DBS satellite positions are the subject of Fig. 4.4.

Many satellite picture transmissions are scrambled or encrypted to prevent unauthorised viewing, generally by those who have paid no subscription, or by those who live in areas for which copyright release has not been obtained for the broadcast material. Many different scrambling systems are in use, some of which have to be frequently updated to keep ahead of the designers of 'pirate' decoders. Authorised decoders typically use a 'smart-card' containing data which, with the descrambling information carried in the broadcast itself, provides clear reception for a month, after which

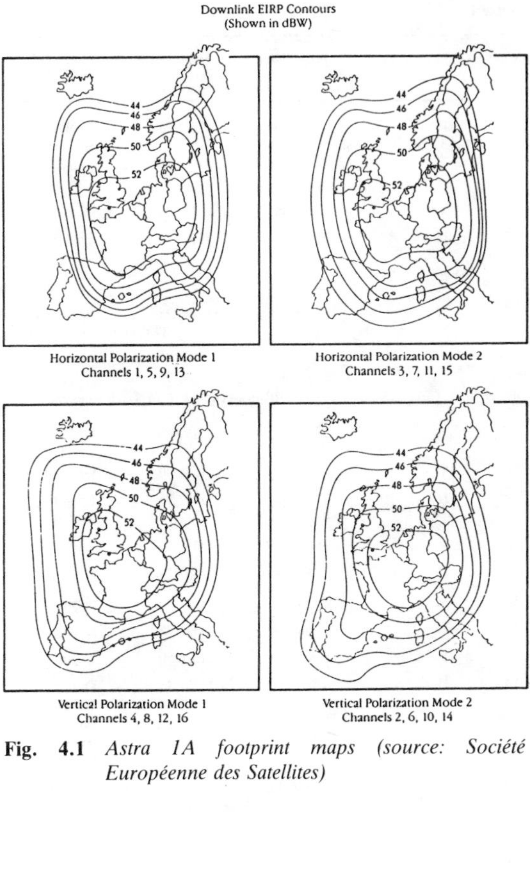

Downlink EIRP Contours
(Shown in dBW)
44
46
48
50
52
Horizontal Polarization Mode 1
Channels 1, 5, 9, 13
Horizontal Polarization Mode 2
Channels 3, 7, 11, 15
Vertical Polarization Mode 1
Channels 4, 8, 12, 16
Vertical Polarization Mode 2
Channels 2, 6, 10, 14

Fig. 4.1 *Astra 1A footprint maps (source: Société Européenne des Satellites)*

Horizontal polarized channels (MHz)
11214.25
11243.75
11273.25
11302.75
11332.25
11361.75
11391.25
11420.75
1
3
5
7
9
11
13
15
11.20 GHz
11.45 GHz
2
4
6
8
10
12
14
16
11229.0
11258.5
11288.0
11317.5
11347.0
11376.5
11406.0
11435.5
Vertical polarized channels (MHz)

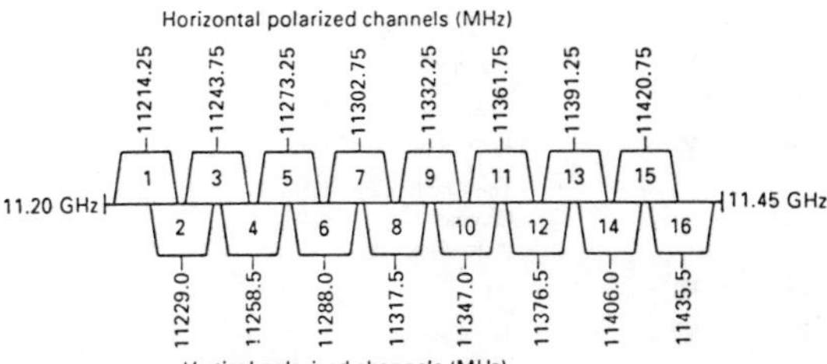

Fig. 4.2 *Transponder frequencies for Astra 1A*

Table 4.3

Channel	*Polarisation*	*Programme*	*Frequency (MHz)*	*Language*
1	H	Screensport Sportkanal TV Sport Sportnet	11214.25	English German French Dutch
2	V	RTL Plus	11229.00	German
3*	H	TV 3	11243.75	English Swedish
4	V	Eurosport	11258.50	Eng/Ger/Dutch
5	H	Lifestyle (10 am–6pm weekdays, 12am–6pm weekends)	11273.25	English
		The Children's Channel (6am–10am weekdays, 6am–12am weekends)		English
		JSTV (8pm–10pm)		Japanese
6	V	SAT 1	11288.00	German
7*	H	TV 1000	11302.75	English Swedish
8	V	Sky One	11317.50	English
9*	H	Teleclub	11332.25	German
10	V	3 SAT	11347.00	German
11*	H	Filmnet	11361.75	English
12	V	Sky News	11376.50	English
13*	H	RTL 4	11391.25	Dutch German French English Italian
		Channel e (8.50am–9.20am, Mon–Fri)	11381.25	English
14	V	Pro 7	11406.00	German
15	H	MTV Europe	11420.75	English
16+	V	Sky Movies	11435.50	English
17*	H	Premiere	11464.25	German
18+	V	Movie Channel	11479.00	English
19	H	ARD/1 Plus	11493.75	German
20	V	Sky Sports	11508.50	English
21	H	Tele 5	11523.25	German
24	V	JSTV(8–10pm)	11567.50	Japanese
		The Children's Channel (6am–7pm)	11567.50	English
25	H	N3	11582.25	German
26+	V	The Comedy Channel	11597.00	English

27	H	SES Video	11611.75	Eng/Ger/Fre
29*	H	TV 3 Denmark	11641.25	Danish/English
30	V	SES Info	11656.00	Eng/Ger/Fre
31*	H	TV 3 Norway	11670.75	Norwegian/Eng

+ Subscription channel. Decoder required.
* Scrambled or partially scrambled channel – not available in the UK
Note: All non-digital channels carry main sound additionally at 6.5 MHz and 7.02 MHz

another card must be purchased. With MAC transmissions each individual receiver is separately addressed and enabled by the satellite, so that subscription can be made directly to the broadcaster.

The MAC system is the only one in current use which was designed specifically for use with satellites, and gives far superior results to other systems. Non-MAC satellite transmissions, scrambled or not, use the same basic TV system as the terrestrial transmissions in the country for which they are intended, which generally means PAL/625 for Western Europe, Secam/625 for Eastern Europe and parts of the Middle East, and NTSC/525 for North America and Japan. Other, higher-definition systems are being used on a limited basis, notably by NHK of Japan. The use of established colour-encoding systems is far from ideal for satellite use with frequency modulation, but confers compatibility with existing TV equipment in the home, a compromise which most viewers seem very ready to accept.

Again excepting the MAC transmissions, sound is broadcast on f.m. carriers typically spaced 6.5 MHz above the vision carrier. Stereo sound, using an analogue modulation format and a noise-reduction artifice such as the Wegener-Panda system, is often used, and certain programmes offer bi-lingual sound channels. For these 'audio extras', narrowband sound carriers are used: in Astra transmissions they sit 7.02, 7.20, 7.38 and 7.56 MHz above the demodulated vision carrier. The audio signals on these carriers are not necessarily related to the video images on whose backs they ride; specialised and general 'radio' stations occupy them in some transponders, see Table 4.4.

This plethora of transmissions, sound and vision, from the sky is uplinked from control/relay stations on Earth, using frequencies in the region of 14 GHz to convey not only programme signals, but also control, monitoring and telemetry commands and feedback. Thus is the satellite kept in position and on target.

SATELLITE RECEIVING ANTENNAS

Even though the broadcast signal from a satellite is concentrated into a narrow and relatively powerful beam, it cannot be usefully intercepted by a dipole in the same way as longer-wavelength signals. It is necessary, then, to use a large-area collector of SHF signals in the form of a dish or plate to increase the capture area. Most common is the dish aerial in which a parabolic reflector

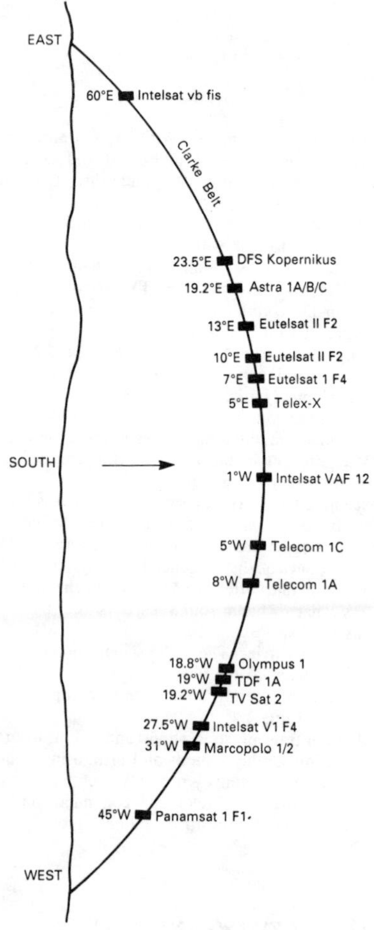

Fig. 4.3 *The main broadcast satellites seen from Europe*

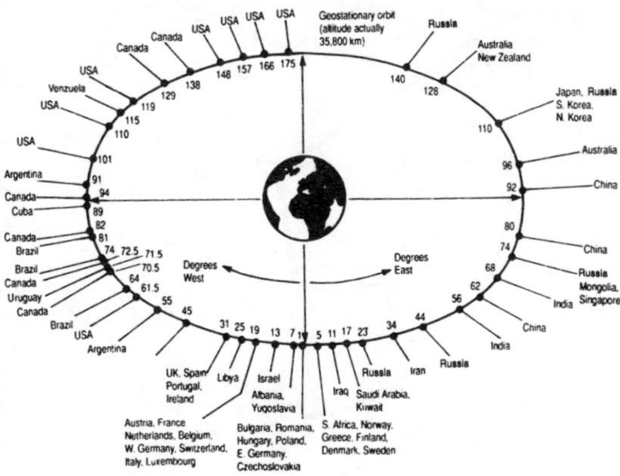

Fig. 4.4 *DBS satellites: world allocations*

Table 4.4 *Radio programmes from the Astra satellites*

Name	*Ch*	*Frequency (MHz)*
Deutsche Welle (14 languages including English)	2	7.56 mono
Deutschland-funk II (various languages)	6	7.92 mono
Hit Radio	8	7.74/7.92
Sky Radio	8	7.38/7.56
Chiltern Radio	12	7.92
Radio Luxembourg	13	7.38/7.56
Power FM	15	7.38/7.56
Quality Europe FM	16	7.38/7.56
Sunrise Radio (Pan-European) channel for Asian listeners)	18	7.38 mono
Eclipse FM	20	7.56

All are stereo unless marked 'mono'

concentrates the signal beam onto a tiny metal patch or probe inside the *low-noise-block* (LNB) at the focal point of the dish. Manufacture and handling of the dish is crucial because its surface must be true enough to ensure *in-phase* arrival of all the SHF carrier cycles at the pick-up point.

Practical satellite dishes do not have to be completely parabolic in shape: it is sufficient for them to take the form of a section of a

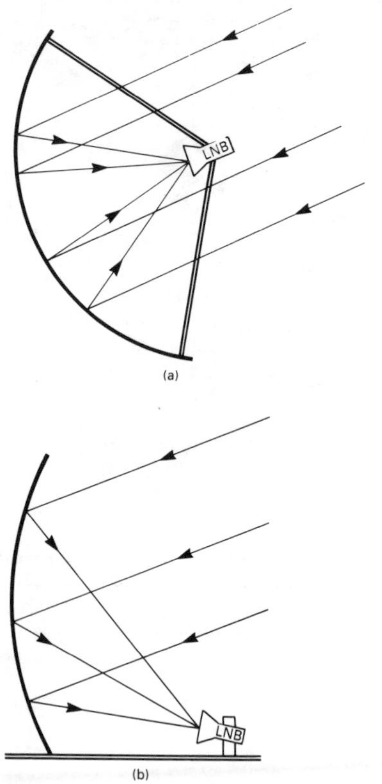

Fig. 4.5 *Dish configurations: (a) prime-focus, (b) offset*

parabola so long as the LNB is at the effective focal point. Thus the two main variations for home use are the prime-focus and the offset dish, shown respectively in Fig. 4.5(a) and (b), with the latter type most common: it has the two advantages of keeping the LNB's 'shadow' out of the path of incoming signals, and presenting a more nearly vertical face from which water and snow easily fall away. There are other dish configurations, one of which has the LNB at the rear of the dish, looking at a sub-reflector at the main focal point.

Dish gain and efficiency

A typical efficiency figure for a receiving dish is 60%. The gain increases with dish size, of course, and the larger the dish the better the received signal. Dish size is a compromise between many factors; for aesthetic, economic and physical reasons home-mounted dish antennas need to be as small and unobtrusive as possible. A large dish has the advantages of providing a greater margin to accommodate losses due to rain, snow and gradual deterioration of efficiency in the system; and a narrower beam-width, giving greater immunity from interference by other satellites in the burgeoning Clarke belt. It is, however, marginally more difficult to install, more obtrusive, and imposes more strain on its mountings in high winds.

The continuing improvement in LNB noise figures has made it possible to use smaller dishes to achieve the required carrier/noise (C/N) ratio, and the greater the EIRP (Effective Isotropic Radiated Power) of the satellite on which it is targeted, the smaller the dish needs to be. In general, dishes of less than 40 cm effective diameter run the risk of picking up interference from other satellites. Thus it is unlikely with current technology that the norm will be less than 35 cm for DBS broadcasts, and 60 cm for medium-power DTH birds like the Astra group.

Rain or snow in the air tends to absorb microwave radiation, and short-term signal losses of 3–10 dB can be experienced in heavy weather. In an average installation very heavy rain will reduce the C/N ratio below the system's noise threshold, the effect of which is *sparklies* (black and white horizontal dashes) superimposed on the picture. Seldom in Europe or North America does it rain hard enough or long enough for this to be a significant problem, however.

For fixed-dish installations, manufacturers generally provide a complete kit consisting of antenna, LNB, mountings and receiver, all matched to a specific satellite whose EIRP is well established and defined. Used together, the components of such a kit work well so long as the installation is correctly done and the maker's recommendations of dish-size/LNB specification for different geographical areas is followed. If, however, it is required to mix head-end components of different makes; to match two LNBs to a single dish; to receive low-power or footprint-margin transmissions; or to install a polar-mounted dish other than a custom-made outfit, it is necessary to take into account many factors when specifying the dish, LNB and receiver. This is called a *linked budget calculation*, covered (with computer program details) in *Newnes Guide to Satellite TV*.

Beamwidth

The beamwidth of a dish is inversely proportional to its size, whether it is transmitting or receiving. Footprint shapes and sizes are wholly determined by the design of the satellite-mounted dish, which is 'fine-tuned' to give the coverage required by the broadcaster in terms of countries and areas – see Fig. 4.1. Regardless of which end of the chain a dish may be, the beamwidths are represented by cones of 2° angle for 1 m types, 3° angle for 50 cm, and 4.5° angle for 35 cm. The angles are based on half-power (−3 dB) points as shown in Fig. 4.6. There are also side-lobes (not shown in the diagram) on each side of the main aiming path, but their response is typically 20 dB down on the main beam, so they are less likely to contribute interference than to increase the noise component of the received signal. The nature of the spurious lobes depends greatly on the type and design of the dish and LNB unit.

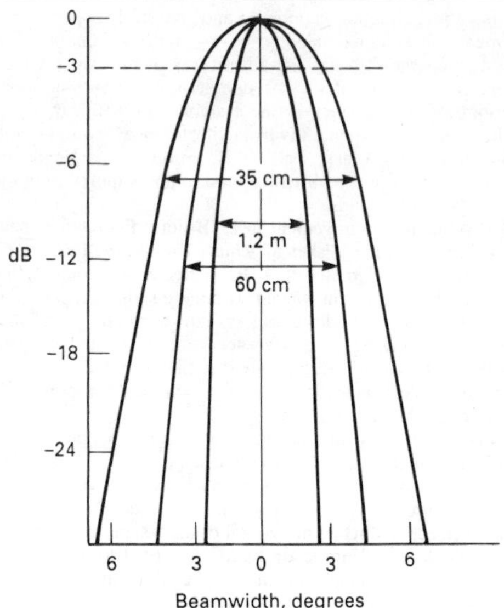

Fig. 4.6 *Beamwidths for three typical dish sizes. The figures given are effective diameters*

C/N ratio

The arbiter of reception quality is the carrier-to-noise ratio. A C/N ratio of 10 dB gives satisfactory results, but leaves little safety margin. We may regard 11 dB as a norm for currently-available equipment, and 13.5 dB or more is excellent. As the C/N ratio decreases, there is little effect on the picture until the threshold level of the receiver's f.m. vision demodulator is reached, when sparklies begin to intrude on the picture. With terrestrial-type (e.g. PAL, NTSC) colour-encoding systems the interference is most obtrusive on highly-coloured areas of the picture. As LNB noise figures and carrier detector designs improve, the required C/N ratio becomes less. An off-screen picture of sparklie interference is shown in Fig. 4.7.

Environment-friendly dishes

The fact that (in the northern hemisphere) satellite receiving antennas have to point south means that the physical positioning of a home dish is seldom a matter of free choice, though a great deal can be done to hide or disguise the antenna with careful thought and choice of type. Where the dish has to be visible, there are three ways in which its obtrusiveness can be reduced: by painting, by making the dish transparent, and by using an open-mesh construction.

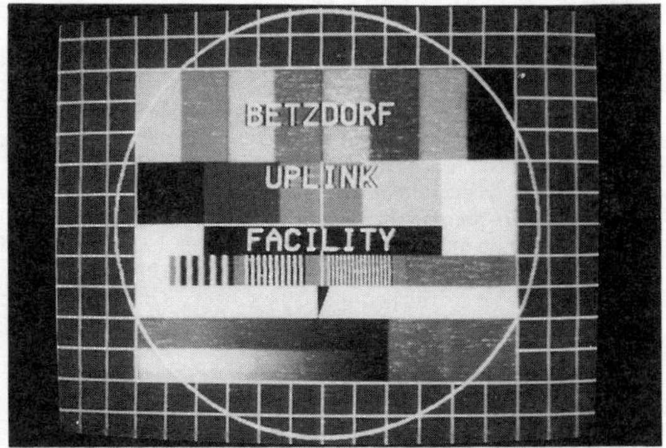

Fig. 4.7 *Sparklies: the effect of noise in an f.m. picture transmission*

Any conventional dish type can be painted – ideally with spray application – to make it merge into the background against which it is seen. Some dishes come in a choice of colours, but it is generally necessary to spray the dish after installation, giving a thin and even coat of matt or eggshell-finish paint.

Glass dishes use metallised armoured glass with 99% reflectivity to microwave radiation. They are more expensive than the simplest (pressed sheet metal) types, but are more rigid, reflect less heat onto the LNB assembly, and of course are less obtrusive.

The reduction of visual impact represented by a mesh dish (they are usually black) is somewhat questionable, but they are established in production. Their weight and wind-resistance is less than that of conventional types for a given size, and the perforations have little or no effect on their efficiency. They tend to be more flexible, however, which can be detrimental in high winds.

Flat-plate antennas

An alternative to the parabolic dish is a flat-plate antenna, sometimes called a squarial. A flat board is fitted with an array of many hundreds of small 'dipoles' in the form of patches, lines or slots. The tiny signal currents induced into them by the r.f. radiation are combined in phase and conveyed by a waveguide of some type to a common point where they enter an LNB. For the same surface area a flat-plate antenna has less gain than a parabolic dish arrangement, and above a certain size (about 50 cm square) the efficiency of a plate array falls rapidly. As technology improves, however, flat antennas may become more popular, especially as they have the potential to be cheaper, easier to install and less obtrusive than dishes. It may also be possible to incorporate 'electronic aiming' of flat plates by internal phase-switching, an attractive possibility for multi-satellite reception. Domestic satellite antennas are the subject of intense research and development.

RECEIVER INSTALLATION

The first step in the installation of a satellite antenna is a *site survey*, consisting basically of a careful assessment of where and how the antenna should be mounted. It must have a clear view of the southern sky in the direction of the satellite of interest. It needs a strong mounting surface, ideally a brick or masonry wall, or for 'patio mounts' a concrete base. It should be as near as possible to the cable's entry point to the viewing room to save the expense and signal attenuation of long cables. It should ideally be out of sight of the street and as unobtrusive as possible anyway. Planning regulations demand that special permission be sought for mounting above the line of the roof apex.

Safety

Strict regulations cover the safety (of the installer, the customer and the general public) of antenna installations. In general, safety has two aspects: that of the installer, customer and bystander while the work is carried out; and that of the dish and fittings themselves throughout their working life.

During installation the main precautions concern ladders, which should be firmly based, perfectly upright and at a slope near 4 : 1; electrical tools, which should be regularly safety-tested; and eye-protection, which should be worn throughout hammering and drilling operations.

Regarding the subsequent safety of the installation, the key points are that the dish-mounts are strong, reliable and fixed to a strong and stable base, and that the equipment presents no shock- or fire-hazard due to bad handling or practice.

Dish mounting

Once the mounting point for the antenna has been decided upon, the first essential is to get as strong and reliable a fix as possible. The most common – and best – fixing is into a brick or concrete wall, avoiding the chimney wherever possible. Whatever type of anchor is used on a brick wall it is important to fix it into brick rather than mortar, and to keep the holes near the centre of the brick where possible. If the brick wall has been rendered, 'test-borings' establish the positions of mortar courses.

Mounting holes are easiest drilled with a powerful electric hammer drill and a tough masonry bit. Hole sizes and anchor types are usually recommended by the dish manufacturer, based on the size and weight of the antenna assembly and particularly its likely *wind loading*, which can increase the effective weight/pull by a factor of 10.

For small light antennas, high-quality plastic wall plugs are perfectly adequate so long as they are matched in size to the fixing screws, which must themselves be of the correct diameter for the fixing holes, and of non-corroding type – plain steel screws rapidly rust out of doors. Larger and heavier antennas require expansion anchors or special purpose-designed variants. They provide the strongest and most rigid fixings, but should be avoided in low-density materials like breeze-blocks, which have low compressive strength. For situations where wall mounting is not possible, pole fixing is an alternative for which special kits are available; the pole must be stout and very rigidly mounted and braced.

Alignment

Once the dish is fixed, alignment can begin. The relatively small antennas used for domestic reception are not difficult to align, given the three essential aids: a compass, an inclinometer (basically an enlarged protractor) and a signal-strength meter, which is incorporated in some receiver designs.

Tighten the securing screws a little so that the dish can be moved, but is not floppy, and then set the azimuth (panning action) according to the published orbital position of the satellite and with reference to the compass. Next, using the inclinometer or the printed/stamped graduations on the mount, set the elevation (tilting action) to the required point. Bear in mind that the elevation setting for an offset dish must take into account the offset angle.

When the aiming is approximately correct some vestige of picture and sound will be present on a pre-tuned receiver or on a simple field-strength meter. The dish can now be trimmed in respect of both azimuth and elevation to peak the signal strength, ensuring

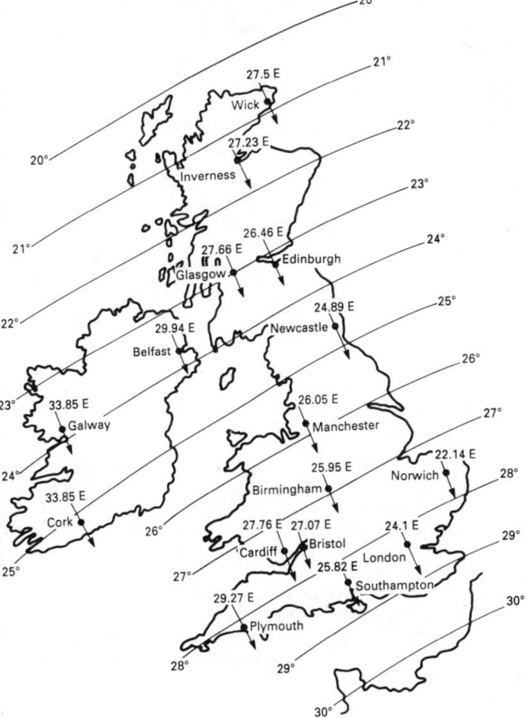

Fig. 4.8 *Dish-setting parameters for Astra group, 19.2°E. The continuous lines indicate elevation angle*

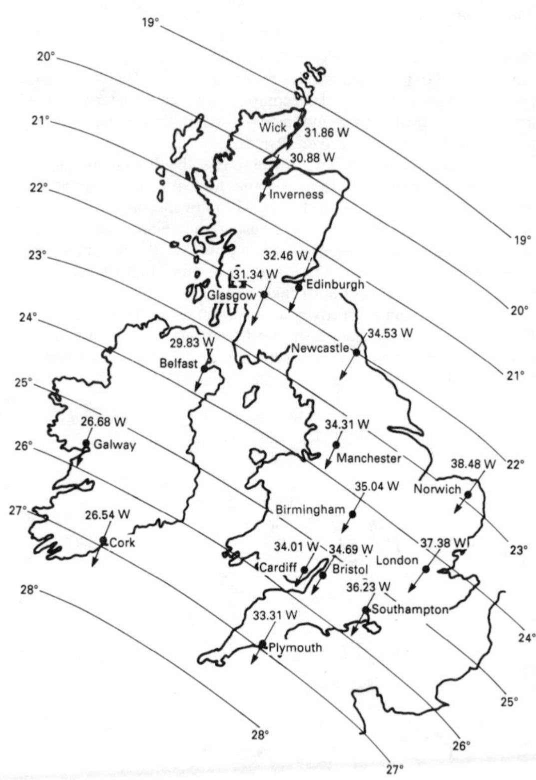

Fig. 4.9 *Dish-setting parameters for BSB Marcopolo, 31°W*

that the installer is not casting a 'shadow' on the front of the dish. When the maximum possible signal strength has been achieved the dish-mounting bolts can be fully tightened, and then greased as a precaution against corrosion. Figures 4.8 and 4.9 show elevation and azimuth settings throughout the UK for the Astra and Marcopolo satellites respectively.

Some dish assemblies require adjustment of the LNB position to optimise focus and polarisation settings. Focus is simply achieved by moving the LNB to or from the dish to achieve best signal strength. Polarisation is set by rotating the entire LNB to the point specified by the manufacturers, or (more accurately) for minimum field strength on the 'wrong' polarisation setting: this gives a sharper null, more accurate alignment and greater immunity from interference/crosstalk than setting for maximum signal with correct polarisation for the transponder to which the receiver or field-strength meter is tuned.

Alignment of a polar-mount antenna is much more demanding. The basic requirements are a very accurate setting of the dish to true south at the *apex*, the centre of its travel, and a true-vertical setting of the mount's position. Polar-mount outfits come with very detailed and specific setting-up instructions, which should be closely followed.

Where the receiver does not incorporate an inbuilt field-strength meter, or where it is physically impractical to use it, a hand-held type can be taken to the dish to aid alignment. The simplest and cheapest type (*dish-peaker*) gives no absolute indication of signal strength and has a broad frequency response: its indication is the sum-total of all the signals picked up by the dish. It is perfectly adequate for the pointing adjustment, however. More expensive meters are tunable to individual transponders and usually give a true strength reading in millivolts or dBu. The most comprehensive (and expensive) meters give a spectrum display of the satellite band on a CRT or LCD indicator to show relative and absolute strength of all the carriers received. Either of the latter types can be used for polarisation setting as well as dish-pointing.

Fig. 4.10 shows a simple and inexpensive dish-peaking meter.

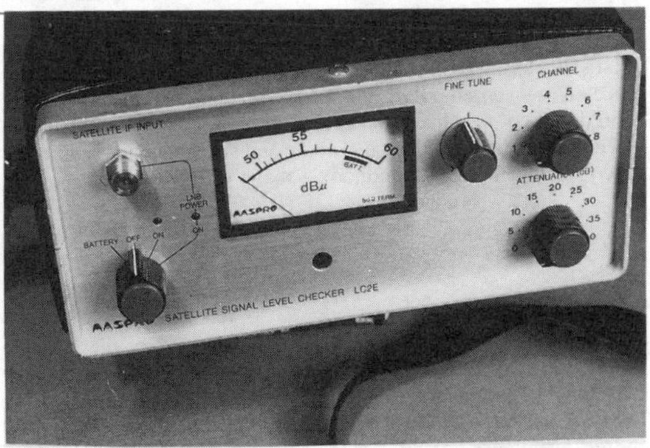

Fig. 4.10 *A portable aid to dish-pointing, the signal-strength meter*

Cables and routing

The link from the dish to the receiver carries frequencies in the range of 950 MHz to 1.7 GHz, too high for use with ordinary UHF TV aerial cables. A special low-loss cable type such as CT100 or H109F must be used: its attenuation at mid-band (1.3 GHz) is about 23 dB per 100 m, and a maximum run of about 40 m is possible without the use of in-line amplifiers.

In most systems the co-ax cable itself carries the operating voltage (typically 15 V) to the LNB, and in some cases it carries a d.c. polarisation switching signal as well. Other designs call for a separate pair of conductors for polarity switching. Special cables containing low-loss co-ax plus separate conductors are available, but it is generally cheaper and more convenient to run a separate (mains-type) twin-core lead alongside the signal cable for this purpose.

The downlead should be provided with a drip loop at each end, and very thoroughly sealed at the points where it enters the LNB and the dwelling: with self-amalgamating tape or a rubber boot at the top, and a mastic sealer at the bottom. Tack up the cable at 50 cm intervals on vertical runs and 20 cm on horizontal runs, following the most unobtrusive route, e.g. under the eaves. Avoid tight bends, which stress the cable physically and cause excessive signal attenuation; a bend radius of 10 times the cable diameter is the minimum acceptable. As a precaution against lightning and static damage it is good practice to ground (earth) the dish metalwork and the braid of the downlead.

Indoor installation

Ensure that the receiver is unplugged (not just switched off) until all wiring and connections are complete. The satellite tuner (some of them run very hot) should be sited on a hard surface with plenty of room for air circulation around it. Most receivers and IRDs (Integrated Receiver/Decoders) come ready-tuned, though some require the presetting of polarisation, either by memorising the setting for each preset channel, or by adjustment of internal presets for each mode, vertical and horizontal. In the latter case, as with LNB positioning, it is more accurate to tune for a null on a *wrongly* polarised transmission than to adjust for minimum sparklie interference on the wanted polarisation. Incorrect polarisation setting and consequent co- or adjacent-channel interference is most noticeable when descramblers are in use. Tuning and station memorisation are described in the user's handbook – many different systems are in use.

Hook-up

The audio and video outputs are available from the satellite receiver in two forms: baseband, from a SCART socket; and r.f. from a UHF modulator tuned to channel 38 or 39, but adjustable over a range of about 10 channels. It is best to use the baseband outputs whenever possible for the better picture and sound quality they offer, their immunity from r.f. interference, and their ability to handle stereo sound signals. Where the TV set or VCR in use does not have SCART sockets, or where they are already fully occupied, the r.f. connection can be used, though careful adjustment of the output channel trimmers of both sat-box and VCR will probably be necessary to avoid mutual interference and the resultant patterning effects.

Even when a baseband connection is present it is still necessary to maintain the r.f. link through the VCR to the TV so that all viewing and recording options are maintained. A typical hook-up is shown in Fig. 4.11. Where the satellite tuner and the VCR are both equipped for stereo sound, their full potential can only be realised with a baseband link: some VCRs and TVs are fitted with two SCART sockets, greatly simplifying hook-up in circumstances like these. SCART pin layout and functions are given in Fig. 21.2.

MAC satellite receivers have RGB outputs as well as those mentioned above, and unless they are connected to the TV set via a SCART lead, wired for RGB, much of the advantage of the MAC TV system is thrown away. VCRs have no means of dealing with RGB signals, but high-band types, e.g. S-VHS format, benefit in terms of picture and sound quality from SCART connections. To help with the sometimes difficult taks of interconnection and

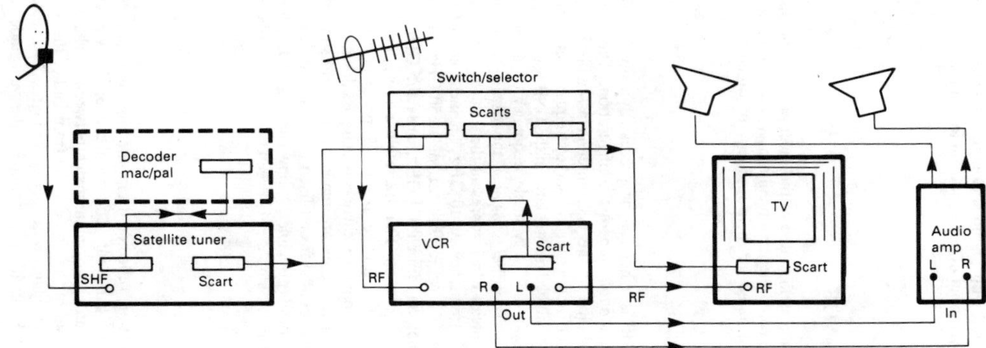

Fig. 4.11 *Representative indoor wiring diagram using AV cables*

interfacing, various switchboxes are available, some with simple mechanical switches and others with sophisticated auto-switching and routing based on the 'status' flags carried on pins 8 and 16 of the SCART connector system.

The high-quality audio transmissions from satellite services, Hi-Fi VCRs and the Nicam broadcasts described in Chapter 9 have led to a tendency to interconnect audio and video equipment; most video gear is fitted with phono sockets from which leads can be taken to the AUX input of a separate audio amplifier as shown on the right of Fig. 4.11.

HEAD-END UNITS

The head-end unit is mounted at the focal point of the dish, and consists of three components: a feedhorn, a polariser and an LNB. All are weatherproofed for their outdoor environment.

Principle

Reception at SHF is a heterodyne process, but involves two i.f. frequencies in a *double superhet* configuration. The first 'local oscillator' is installed at the dish antenna assembly in order to convert to a lower (and easier to handle) frequency as early in the signal chain as possible. The oscillator in the LNB is not adjustable: it runs at a constant and very stable frequency of about 10 GHz. Each incoming carrier beats against the oscillator to produce difference frequencies which represent the first i.f. so that, assuming an oscillator frequency of 10 GHz, an incident 11.650 GHz signal gives rise to a 'difference' i.f. of 1.650 GHz, an incident 11.674 GHz signal, an i.f. of 1.674 GHz, an 11.175 GHz signal, an i.f. of 1.175 GHz and so on. Thus the satellite transponders' signals are 'block converted' to a lower band and appear in reverse order on the new, lower-frequency carriers which pass down the cable to the indoor unit. There they are tuned by a second superhet unit with variable local oscillator and fixed i.f. as already described in Chapter 3. The basic principle is shown in Fig. 4.12, though in practice there is an r.f. amplifier between the pick-up probe and the mixer diode.

SHF front end

The signal radiation reflected from the dish is collected by a waveguide at its focal point. The open end of the waveguide is fluted to provide an approximate match between its characteristic impedance and that of 'free space'; the front end of the horn thus formed is protected against water and other ingress by a sealed cap, transparent to SHF radiation. The shape of the waveguide horn is a matter of careful design since it determines not only the efficiency with which signals are collected, but also the shape and amplitude of the side-lobes in the directivity diagram (Fig. 4.6), and the bandwidth and noise performance of the ensemble. In commercial kits the dish, feedhorn and LNB are all matched, but care must be

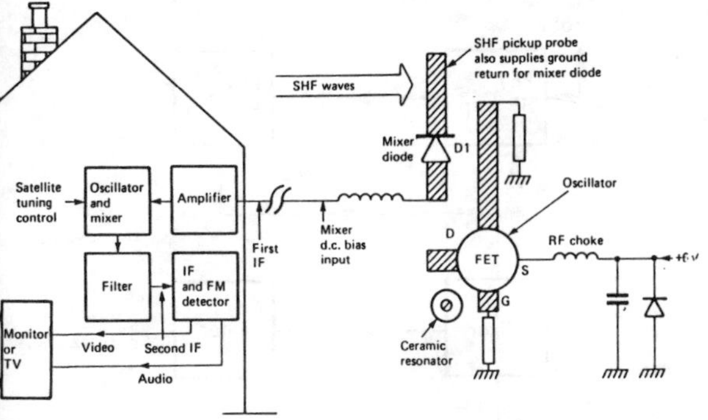

Fig. 4.12 *Essentials of a satellite receiving system. The components on the right are mounted at the focal point of the pick-up dish*

taken when assembling a head-end unit from unrelated components.

The feedhorn/waveguide is bolted to the front of the LNB, which contains the pick-up device in which the SHF magnetic energy is converted to an electrical signal current. It is at this point that provision must be made for selecting the required polarisation of radiation, and rejecting signals arriving in the wrong polarisation. The two most common methods of selection involve no moving parts. One design has (printed on a glass fibre board) a *micropatch* on which the SHF signal is intercepted, with two adjacent printed 'probes' set at 90°. Each has its own r.f. amplifier which also acts as an electronic switch to select the required vertical or horizontal mode.

The alternative system uses a needle-probe mounted vertically in the LNB's front aperture, capable only of intercepting vertically-polarised signals. In the feedhorn is an electromagnetic polariser consisting of a coil wound on a ferrite core through which the incoming r.f. wave passes. Depending on the current flowing in the coil the wave's polarisation is 'twisted' and at an optimum current exact alignment of the wave with the probe is achieved. Typically needing a d.c. current range of 70 mA to achieve 0–90° polarisation twist, these devices have low insertion loss but are frequency-dependent in their operation. A compromise setting can be made for a single narrow range of transponder frequencies, but where the system embraces a wide range of incoming signals – especially in a polar-mount system, where many satellites are addressed – provision must be made to optimise polariser current for each transponder.

DBS transmissions use circular polarisation, but all the transponders on each satellite have the same (either RH or LH) characteristic, so that LNBs designed for single-satellite use have fixed polarisation, and their design is simplified thereby.

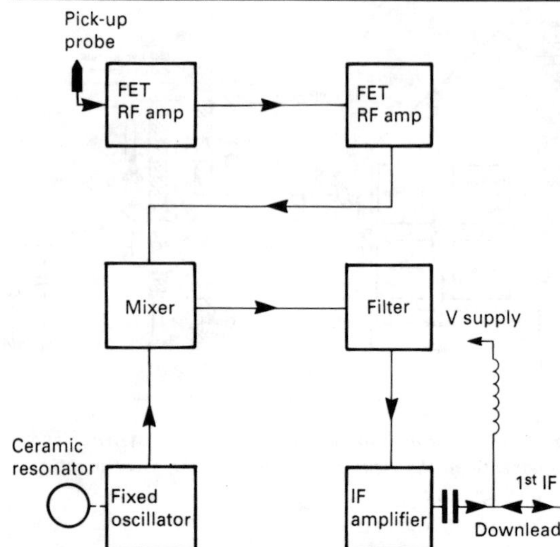

Fig. 4.13 *The functional blocks of the outdoor LNB*

LNB arrangement

Fig. 4.13 shows a functional diagram of a typical low-noise block. The pick-up probe is directly connected to an FET (Field Effect Transistor) made of gallium arsenide, GaAs, with tiny printed striplines 2–3 mm long as resonant circuits. One or two further stages of SHF amplification are provided to bring the signal level up to a point where it can be applied to a Schottky mixer diode, whose non-linearity ensures a strong beat signal, selected by filters and further amplified on its way to the output socket at the rear of the LNB module.

The local oscillator is also based on a GaAs FET: its output must be pure and noise-free and its frequency very stable with time and temperature. The tuned circuit is formed by a ceramic-based *dielectric resonator* mounted on the PCB between the drain and gate leadouts of the transistor, and not necessarily having any electrical connections to the circuit at all. The resonator may well have a screw-disc with which its frequency is preset at the factory.

The most important aspect of an LNB is its noise figure, normally quoted in dB, and indicating the relative amount of noise added to the signal in its passage through the device. Commercial LNBs for home use typically have a noise figure of around 1.6 dB, and current designs using HEMT (high electron mobility transistor) devices can achieve noise figures better than 1 dB. The overall gain of an LNB is about 60 dB, sufficient to launch the 1st i.f. signal into the downlead at a high enough level to overcome the losses in the cable.

The power requirement for an LNB is generally 15 V at about 200 mA, and is fed via the downlead, with signal and power separated at either end by L/C components.

SATELLITE RECEIVERS

There are two basic functions within a satellite receiver: to select the required channel and to demodulate it to produce video and audio signals. There are many secondary functions – powering the LNB, selecting polarisation, status indication, provision for descrambling, selection of sound carrier, remodulation to UHF and others – but most of them have counterparts in other home video equipment.

The first i.f. frequency, a block-converted group of channels containing the entire spectrum received by the dish ensemble and placed anywhere from 950 MHz to 1.7 GHz, enters the receiver and is amplified (Fig. 4.14) and a.g.c.-controlled. Image-rejection filtering is also carried out here. R.f. tuning is by lecher lines and varicap diodes, as in the conventional tuners examined in Chapter 3. The selected signal is applied to a mixer along with a second input from an oscillator whose frequency is varicap-controlled by a PLL tuning system of the type we have already met. The 2nd i.f., generally at about 480 MHz, is selected and extracted by a SAW filter with a bandwidth of 27 MHz. The filtered signal is amplified to overcome the SAW filter losses. After further amplification and close a.g.c. control the signal is brought to a level suitable for application to the vision i.f. demodulator. Before we leave this 'tuner-heart' section, note the prescaler and programmable divider within the dotted box. These are the essence of the tuning circuit: programme tuning data from the station memory enters the module at pins C, D, L (Clock, Data, Load/enable).

FM vision demodulator

There are several ways to demodulate f.m. signals. The quadrature detector has already been described in Chapter 3, and other forms of modern f.m. demodulators will be examined in videorecorder applications in Chapter 13. An IC-based technology for recovering f.m. signals is the phase-locked-loop (PLL) system, and this is commonly used in f.m. vision demodulators.

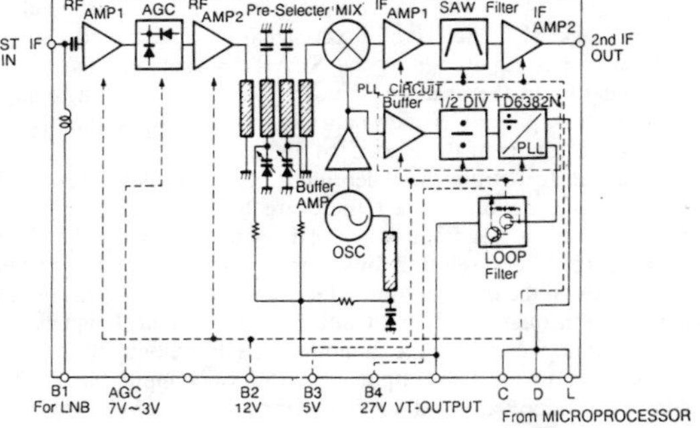

Fig. 4.14 *Satellite tuner front-end, the first indoor stage*

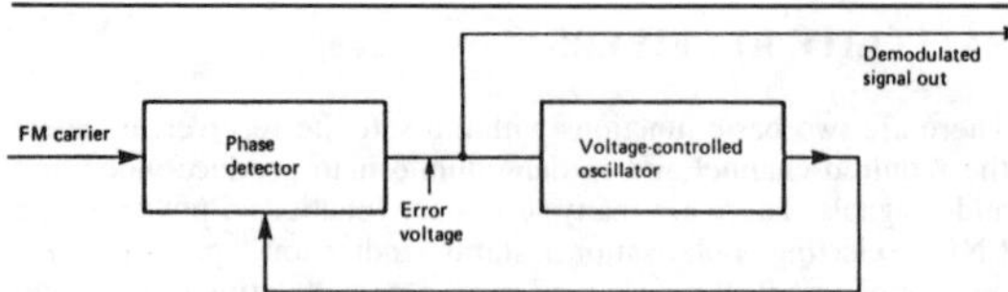

Fig. 4.15 *Phase-locked loop arranged as f.m. demodulator*

A simplified block diagram of a PLL demodulator appears in Fig. 4.15. The incoming carrier is applied as one input of a phase detector whose error output governs the frequency of a VCO (Voltage Controlled Oscillator). The second input of the phase detector is the VCO output, and since the phase detector's error voltage steers the VCO until its two inputs coincide in frequency and phase, the oscillator (provided a short enough time-constant is present in the error-voltage filter) exactly follows the frequency of the carrier signal, including its deviation due to the modulating (vision) signal. Thus the error – or correction – signal, in pulling the VCO continually in line with the f.m. carrier, reflects (in its amplitude and polarity respectively) the amount and direction of all excursions of the carrier from its nominal centre frequency. In doing so it forms a perfect facsimile of the original modulating signal, which is what we want from a demodulator: in this case a video waveform similar in form to that of Fig. 2.5. PLL demodulators are also used in f.m. radio sets for broadcast and communications reception, and in broadcast stereo decoders.

Integrated receiver/decoder

Fig. 4.16 shows a block diagram of an IRD (Integrated Receiver/Decoder) for reception of Astra transmissions. The tuner heart combines the functions of tuner, i.f. and vision demodulator, so that baseband video and sound signals are passed to the video input block, wherein is a de-emphasis circuit together with a clamp (to remove the energy-dispersal waveform), a sound-rejection trap, and output buffers. The main output goes from here to the video switch block which selects a direct signal or a decrypted one as necessary, passing it out to the SCART socket and the UHF remodulator. In the absence of a satellite carrier signal a tuning/identification pattern is automatically switched in, primarily to assist UHF tuning of the associated TV set.

A second feed from the video input block passes to the sound demodulator section. In fact there are four of these, tuned to different intercarrier frequencies. All operate continuously; their audio outputs are selected by a switching chip, working from commands on the internal control bus, to route stereo signals (when available) through the SCART interface. The L and R signals are mixed for application to the mono-only UHF remodulator.

There are two further outputs from the 'video input' block. The composite video/baseband out can be used to feed a MAC decoder or a special decoder for extra subscription programmes etc. A feed is also taken to the Videocrypt board, on which the scrambled (subscription) transmissions are restored to normal video signals – so long as the fee has been paid! The sync separator stage, IL01, is a simple processor from which line, field and coincidence

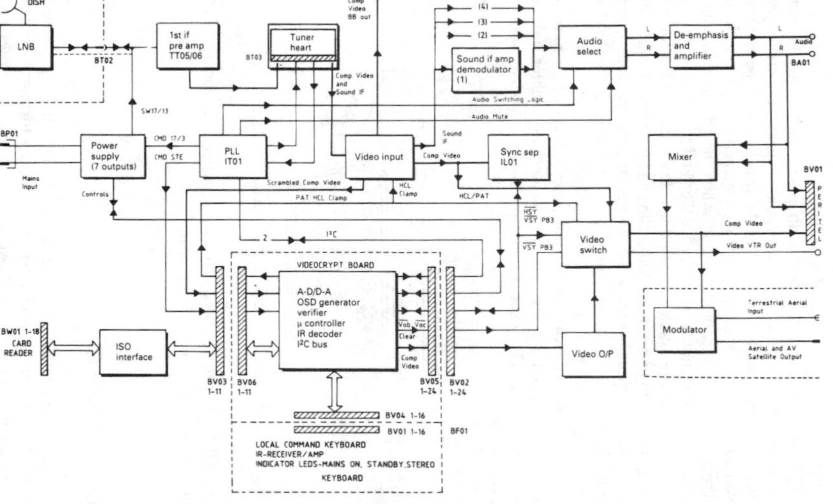

Fig. 4.16 *Block diagram of integrated satellite receiver decoder by Ferguson*

pulses are derived for use in the descrambler, which is digital in operation, and whose precise method of operation is a part of a confidentiality agreement between broadcaster and receiver manufacturer. A 'smart-card', purchased by the subscriber, is fed into the card reader, and so long as the data in the card is compatible with the transmission at the time, descrambling takes place. In this particular design the commands from the local and remote-control keyboards (the latter via an infra-red link) are also processed on the Videocrypt board – in the microcomputer control system, which governs all the functions of the receiver via the I^2C bus examined in Chapter 19.

The power supply section of a satellite receiver is similar to that of a TV or VCR, and will be dealt with in detail in Chapter 11. For cool running and efficiency, switch-mode types are increasingly being used. The PSU in Fig. 4.16 is of the switch-mode type and has seven output lines, not all of which are switched off by the control microprocessor during standby mode, when the r.f.-through amplifier, the remote control receiver/decoder and the display system must be kept in operation. Some designs leave the LNB powered during standby to prevent thermal cycling and maintain stability. In DBS/MAC receivers virtually the whole lot must be kept going during standby to receive and implement the authorisation codes transmitted at intervals to each individual set.

Satellite receivers without integral descramblers often have a connection socket for a separate card reader/descrambler, taking the form of a SCART socket or the 15-pin D-type connector system shown in Fig. 4.17.

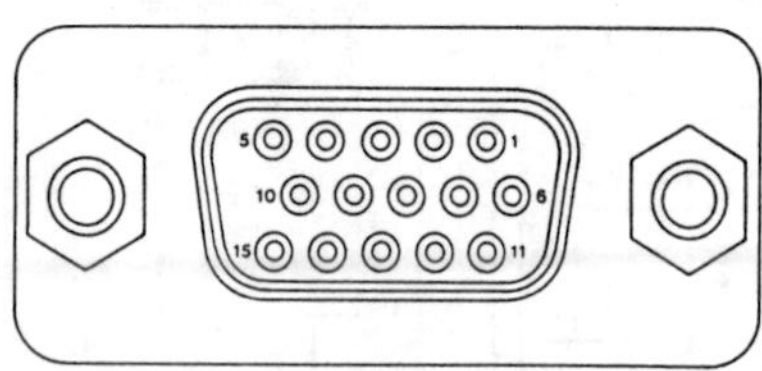

Fig. 4.17 *15-pin D-type decoder connection socket. Pin numbers are as viewed from front*

MAC ENCODING

The signal parameters, bandwidths and colour-encoding systems discussed in the previous chapter, and adopted for most satellite transmissions in the late 1980s, were developed in the fifties and sixties specifically for use with terrestrial transmissions and in bands and channels already in use for a.m. TV broadcasting. In those times the overriding requirement was to achieve compatibility and reverse-compatibility with black and white transmissions. Most of the constraints within which the NTSC committee, Henri de France (SECAM) and Walter Bruch (PAL) had to work have disappeared with the virtual demise of monochrome receivers and the advent of transmission media like spacecraft and fibre-optic cables. Developments in technology have been many and great in the intervening decades, and as TV screens get bigger and viewers more discerning, the shortcomings of existing systems have come sharply to the fore. Chief amongst them are cross-colour, in which spurious blue/yellow and red/green herringbone patterns appear superimposed on fine picture details; cross-luminance, where sharp transitions in the chrominance image are accompanied on screen by a moving luminance dot-pattern; and a shortfall of definition in both luminance and chrominance components of the picture due to the need for response filtering in both channels to avoid excessive mutual interference.

Several new encoding systems have been devised for picture transmission and recording, and where they are for exclusive or closed-circuit use there is freedom to tailor the system to suit the transmission or storage medium and the signal parameters in use. Where a *broadcast* system is involved, however, the requirements are very stringent: the receiving and decoding equipment must be cheap, non-critical and capable of good performance; the system must preferably be capable of evolution and upgrading without losing compatibility; it must take full account of current and future technology since it will be very long lived once entrenched in domestic receiver hardware; and the performance of the system must be the best possible within the constraints of currently available channel bandwidth, transmission and reception systems and picture-display techniques. The MAC (Multiplexed Analogue Components) system fulfils these requirements, and combines a digital sound system with an f.m. analogue picture transmission. These factors permit fault-free reception at much lower signal levels: whereas about 40 dB S/N ratio is required for good reception of a.m. TV transmissions, a C/N ratio of less than 11 dB suffices for MAC broadcasts from satellites and along cables.

The composition of a MAC signal is shown in Fig. 4.18. Its main difference from conventional (real-time) encoding and transmission systems is its use of time-compression, calling for memory banks at both ends of the signal link for short-term storage of audio, chrominance and luminance signals. In conveying a CCIR 625-line 50 field colour signal the overall time taken for one TV line must be 64 μs, but here this period is divided into four distinct time slots as Fig. 4.18 shows: a data period containing digital information on sound, teletext, identification and synchronisation; a clamping period at zero level for system stabilisation; a frequency-modulated chrominance signal conveying U and V information on alternate lines; and a long period of luminance information, also frequency

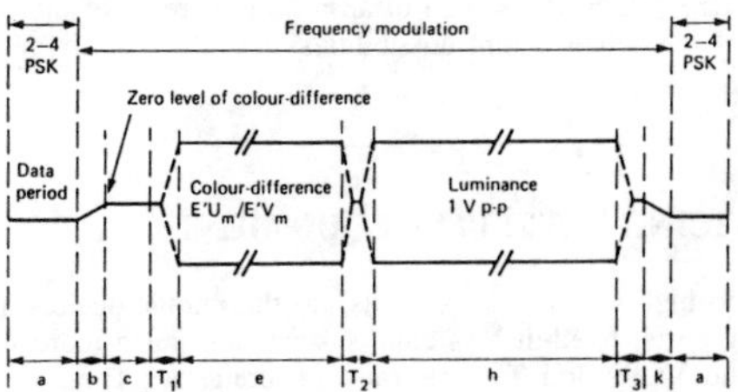

Fig. 4.18 *Line format of the EBU MAC TV signal*

modulated. The luminance signal is time-compressed in the ratio 3 : 2, and the chrominance signal in the ratio 3 : 1. Digital data is conveyed by PSK (Phase Shift Keying) in which logic 1 corresponds to a phase change of +90°, and logic 0 to a phase change of −90°.

The principle of PSK is fully explained in Chapter 9.

The sequence of the MAC line in Fig. 4.18 in detail is as follows:

(a) 206 bits for synchronisation, sound and data, made up of 1 run-in bit, 6 bits of line sync word, 198 bits of data (in two subframes of 99 bits each) and 1 spare bit.
(b) 4 clock periods as transition from end of data, including the leading edge of a pedestal added to the signal to provide energy dispersal.
(c) 15 clock periods at 500 mV for clamping purposes.
T1 10 clock periods, to include a weighted transition to colour-difference signal of 5 clock periods.
(e) 349 clock periods for f.m. colour-difference component, either U or V.
T2 5 clock periods for weighted transition between colour-difference and luminance signal.
(h) 697 clock periods for f.m. luminance component.
T3 6 clock periods for weighted transition from luminance signal.
(k) 4 clock periods for transition into data; includes trailing edge energy-dispersal pedestal signal.

MAC decoding

The MAC signal leaves the satellite transmitter as an f.m. carrier with a frequency around 12 GHz and a bandwidth of 27 MHz. At the receiver the digital data is gated to a PSK demodulator and thence to a decoder which produces sound, data, sync, text, conditional access and control information. The chrominance and luminance components are gated to line-stores, to be read out at normal scanning rates and recombined as part of the decoding process.

The MAC system lends itself to various enhancements, the implementation of which depends on receiver technology and price, and the viewer's requirements. Amongst these are an increase in definition to the 1250-line HDTV standard, and a widescreen presentation with an aspect ratio of 16 : 9 using a *digitally assisted* system which maintains compatibility with conventional 625-line 4 : 3 aspect ratio TV sets. The photo in Fig. 4.19 was taken direct from the screen of an advanced receiver, and shows some of the enhancement possibilities: note the high definition.

SERVICING SATELLITE EQUIPMENT

With no high voltages or currents, no thermionic devices and no moving parts, fixed-dish satellite systems are much more reliable than the VCRs and TV sets they sit alongside. The electronics within the receiver (Fig. 4.20) generally live a quiet and cool life, though in some early designs the internal temperature is much

Fig. 4.19 *Enhanced C-MAC picture photographed direct from monitor. Note wide aspect: ratio is 1.65 to 1*

higher than it need be, mainly because of inefficiency of the PSU section and its components. Indeed it is the power supply section which is most vulnerable to electrical breakdown. Most other faults are associated with the outdoor unit, and many of *them* arise through poor practice or false economy at the time of installation.

Fig. 4.20 *Internal view of basic satellite receiver. Tuner/i.f. at right, power-supply section at left. The two central presets are for magnetic polariser adjustment*

The majority of user problems, however, stem not from these, but from what is known in the trade as 'finger trouble' (mistuning, incorrect hook-up, random key-selection or twiddling of presets), or a lack of understanding of the operation of the equipment by its owner/user.

One of the most common troubles with a satellite home unit is sparklies, as shown in Fig. 4.7. This is due basically to a poor C/N ratio, and can stem from many causes, most of them associated with the outdoor unit. First check that the tuning is spot-on: when it is, there should be an equal mix of black and white sparklies. Next see whether both polarisation groups are affected (unless the system is a DBS type). If only one polarisation group is in trouble, check the polarisation-change arrangements in the receiver: generally a change of LNB supply voltage between 13 V and 17 V, or a change of ±35 mA through a magnetic polariser. In the former case, if the voltage *is* changing the LNB unit is suspect. With magnetic polarisers a marked change in sparklie-count should be seen as the current is altered by whatever means the receiver affords, or as the polariser cable connections are broken or reversed.

If the sparklies invade both polarities of signal, first carefully examine the whole outdoor unit and downlead for signs of damage, corrosion or ingress of water, foreign bodies etc.; then if necessary check the accuracy of the dish-pointing. With an accurately aligned dish the problem will be due to a faulty LNB, downlead or receiver unit. The most practical course now is a substitution test on each in turn.

Faulty LNBs cannot generally be repaired except by a specialist workshop with precision test equipment, some of which offer a repair/exchange facility to the trade, a cheaper solution than discarding the faulty unit and fitting a new one. Magnetic polarisers, together with the feedhorn of which they are a part, can be replaced separately from the LNB in their rare cases of failure.

Like the LNB, the tuner heart of the receiver, pre-aligned and enclosed in a screening can, is not usually regarded as a serviceable item and must be treated as a 'module' for service and repair purposes, though experience has shown that a careful examination inside (for dry joints and the like) can be worthwhile. Before condemning a suspect unit, carefully check its peripheral circuits, components and pin voltages/waveforms.

It is not usually difficult for an experienced TV engineer to discriminate between 'r.f.' (pre-demodulator) and baseband (post-demodulator) faults in both sound and vision sections of a satellite receiver. Such symptoms as sparklies and instability (vision), and hiss and sibilant distortion (sound), come into the first category, while in the second are low contrast, flicker (faulty clamp?) for vision, and incorrect level, hum or one stereo channel missing in sound. With an oscilloscope, multimeter (see Chapter 20) and the manufacturer's service manual such faults are easily tracked down. Very often what seems to be an internal fault has its origins in the connections, tuning or protocol of the associated TV, VCR or terrestrial aerial system.

Control systems rarely fail: where this appears to be the case the key checks, as with TV and VCR equipment, are for supply voltage (Vcc generally +5 V), clock oscillator operation, and reset pulse presence. If all these are correct, confirm that the data lines are not 'stuck' by some external cause, and that command data is reaching the microprocessor chip, before condemning it.

It has been suggested earlier that the power-supply section is the most prolific source of true electrical faults within a satellite receiver, and in the case of failure of any sort it is wise to start by checking all internal supply lines. PSUs are fully covered, with trouble-shooting advice, in Chapter 11.

5

Tubes for picture pick-up and display

Electron scanning tubes for image-gathering and display are the two essential ends of a TV or video system. They have much in common, especially at the back-end. In general, display tubes have large deflection angles, high-velocity electron beams and an electrostatic focusing system, whereas camera tubes have small deflection angles, and a low-velocity electron beam which is magnetically focused.

Fig. 5.1 shows the make-up of an electrostatically focused monochrome display tube. Electrons are emitted by a cathode (K) maintained at dull red heat by an internal heating element. The negatively charged electrons are attracted towards the first anode (A1) which is positive with respect to the cathode. The first anode consists of a skirted disc with a small central hole through which most of the electrons are accelerated. Closely surrounding the cathode is a cup-shaped electrode called the grid (G) which also has a small central hole. By varying the potential on the grid, typically within the range – 25 V to – 100 V with respect to the cathode, the density of electrons in the beam can be varied: phosphor brightness depends on beam density, so the instantaneous brightness of the scanning spot can be varied at fast rate by feeding a suitable modulating voltage between cathode and grid; this will normally be the video signal. Provided the scanning spot is in the right place on the screen at the right time a pattern of light and dark picture elements is built up to form a complete picture.

The second and fourth anodes are connected to a conductive layer (C) on the inside of the bowl of the tube, which itself forms a *wall anode*. Between anodes 2 and 4 comes the focus electrode A3, a cylindrical anode whose potential (typically variable between 0 and +800 V d.c. with respect to the cathode) determines the focusing point of the electron beam.

Anodes 2 and 4, the wall anode and the inner screen surface are together connected to a source of very high voltage (e.h.t.) which may vary between 5 kV in camera viewfinder tubes and 28 kV in very large-screen colour tubes. This voltage gives the screen-bound electrons tremendous acceleration.

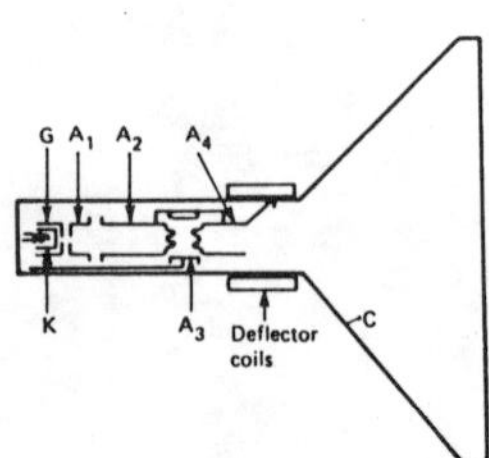

Fig. 5.1 *Basic black-and-white picture tube in cross section*

The screen in a monochrome tube is coated with a phosphor, usually composed of a mixture of blue-emitting zinc sulphide and yellow glowing zinc cadmium sulphide. The combination gives an approximation to white light emission when bombarded with electrons. The phosphor screen is backed by a film of aluminium which has three purposes: It acts as a barrier to heavy ions, preventing them burning the phosphor layer; it reflects phosphor-light forward into the viewing area; and it equalises the electrostatic charge over the entire screen area, preventing spurious local beam-deflection effects.

BEAM DEFLECTION

The square of light on which the picture is built up is called a raster, and to trace it out on the screen of a picture tube the electron beam must be deflected vertically and horizontally. The process is almost invariably a magnetic one in which deflection coils (Fig. 5.2) generate lines of magnetic flux in the tube neck. Note that vertical lines of force are responsible for horizontal deflection and vice versa. The angle through which the scanning beam is turned between opposite corners of the raster (i.e. across the diagonal) is the deflection angle. For medium and large monochrome tubes it is generally 110°. Many colour tubes also have 110° deflection, though 90° deflection is very common, and eases power-consumption and convergence problems. Very small screen tubes have much smaller deflection angles; 50° and even 23° may be encountered.

COLOUR PICTURE TUBES

To build up a colour picture three separate primary colours are used – red, green and blue. Combinations of these three can make almost any colour, including white; by adjusting the three colour intensities to obtain white and then regulating the brightness of all three *together* different brightnesses of white can be achieved, permitting the reproduction of a monochrome picture if required.

The construction of a modern colour tube is shown in Fig. 5.3. A single gun is used, working in similar fashion to the monochrome gun assembly already described, but containing three separate but closely-spaced cathodes. These cathodes are mounted in-line abreast, and the other electrodes in the gun assembly each have a row of three pinholes aligned with the electron beams emerging from the triple cathode array. As the three beams travel along the tube neck they are accelerated and focused by the anodes in the gun assembly, each to come to a sharp point of focus at the surface of the screen.

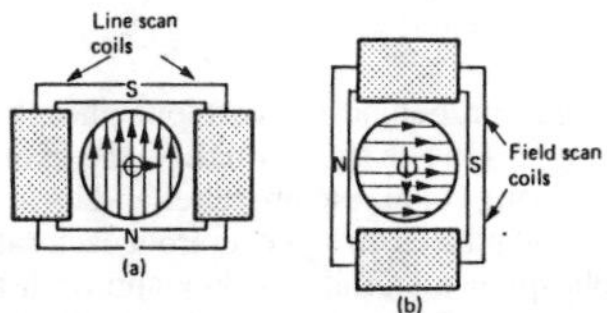

Fig. 5.2 *Beam deflection coils, lines of magnetic force and resulting beam movements*

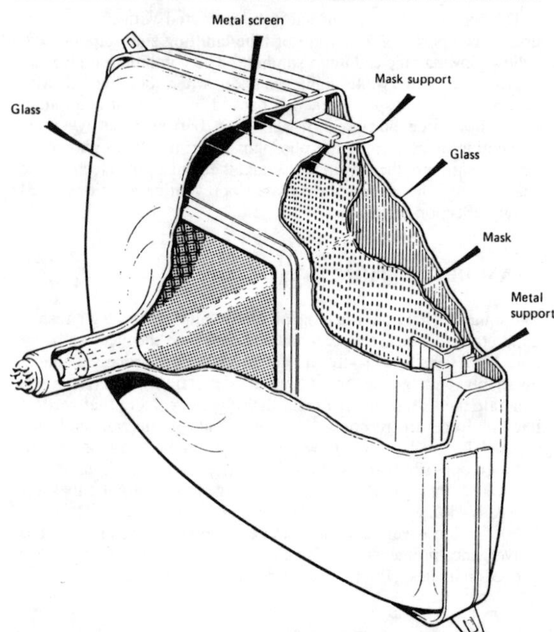

Fig. 5.3 *Overview of in-line-gun colour picture tube construction*

Colour screen

The rear of the screen of a colour picture tube is composed of a large number (typically 600 across the screen width of a large tube) of vertical stripes of phosphor material. The stripes are laid in the sequence RGBRGB etc. across the screen width. Red-emitting phosphors are made of a rare-earth material yttrium/oxysulphide/europium, while the other two are based on zinc sulphide with silver admix for blue and a copper/aluminium admix for green. The rear surface of the phosphor layer is *aluminised*, the thin coat of aluminium reflecting the phosphor light forward, equalising the electrical charge over the screen area, and preventing *ion burn* to the phosphors. The rear (gun side) of the aluminising layer is sprayed black to help in dissipating the heat developed by the shadowmask and screen.

Shadowmask

Mounted some 12 mm behind the tricolour phosphor layer is the shadowmask (Fig. 5.4). The shadowmask is the main feature of all current direct-viewing colour picture tubes and its function is to act as a filter, permitting the electron beam from each cathode to strike only its own phosphor material. As they approach the screen the three separate beams are on converging paths, with approach angles typically 1° apart. The beams cross over as they pass through

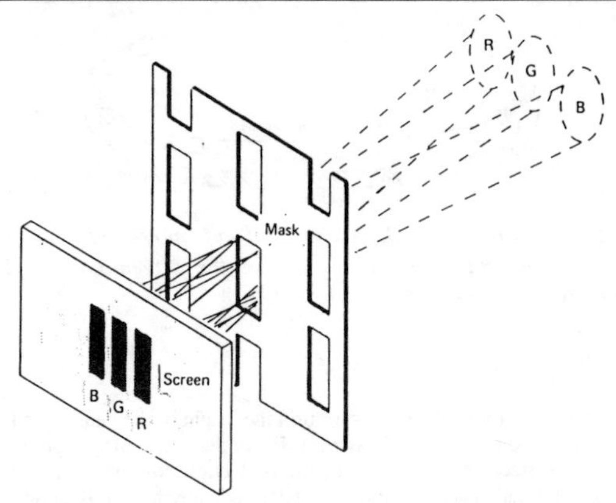

Fig. 5.4 *Shadowmask and screen structure*

the slots in the mask, and diverge beyond to impinge on their respective phosphor stripes. For each phosphor stripe the 'wrong' electron beams are shadowed by the mask, so that each beam (provided its approach angle is correct) can only see through the mask to its own phosphor stripe, and this applies regardless of the degree of deflection it suffers in its passage through the deflection field. Thus is set up the condition whereby three separate but super-imposed fields of primary colour, red, green and blue, can be produced on a single screen, each field being separately controlled by the bias applied to its own cathode with respect to the common grid plate.

The shadowmask is inherently inefficient in that most of the energy in the three beams is intercepted by the steel mask itself; only about 20% of the beams' energy reaches the phosphors, the rest being dissipated as heat in the mask itself. On very high brightness scenes the dissipation in the mask can exceed 20 W, and the effect of the resulting heat is to expand the mask. Any resulting buckling or distortion will upset beam landing accuracy and lead to impurity, in which the beams strike the wrong phosphor stripes, staining the picture with patches of incorrect colour. To prevent this the shadowmask is secured to the inside of the glass envelope by special mountings which permit the expansion to be taken up by moving the entire mask axially (i.e. towards or away from the screen) in such a way that beam landing accuracy is maintained. The mask mounting arrangement for the Philips/Mullard 45AX tube type is shown in Fig. 5.5

In the tube manufacturing process the mask and screen are aligned and fitted to a 'lighthouse' machine to fix the phosphors. In a three-stage process, phosphor material for each colour is coated over the entire screen area then 'fixed' in the correct shape, width and position by shining a powerful xenon lamp through the mask. Since the light source is in exactly the position subsequently occupied by the apparent beam origin for each phosphor in turn, provided that the beams are correctly positioned and angled during the operation of the tube, perfect purity will result.

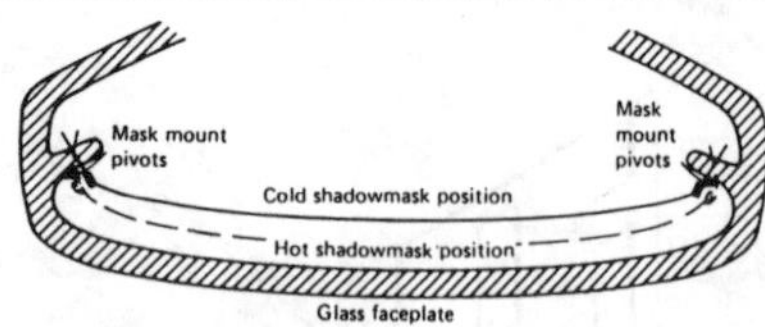

Fig. 5.5 *Shadowmask expansion and mounting, not to scale. The mask mountings are in the screen corners in the Mullard 45 AX design*

PURITY ADJUSTMENT

When the colour tube is in operation the origin of the beams (so far as the shadowmask is concerned) is the deflection centre, a point in the tube neck in the centre of the deflection coil assembly. The electron beams have to be manipulated to bring them to the correct deflection centre, and this is achieved by a pair of ring magnets (on the neck of the tube) whose *two-pole* field can move all three beams together sideways to correctly align the trajectories of the beams through the deflection centre. Adjustment of these purity ring magnets will give correct purity at screen centre, but at large deflection angles (i.e. towards screen edges) some impurity may be present. To eliminate this the deflection centre itself must be aligned axially by sliding the entire deflection yoke assembly along the tube neck, fixing it in position where full-screen purity is obtained. In practice there is a small 'sliding range' over which good purity obtains – for best tolerance and to provide for various drift influences the yoke should be fixed in the middle of this range.

CONVERGENCE

In setting up the purity, provision is made to reserve each phosphor for its own beam, but this does not mean that the patterns produced by the three beam/phosphor combinations will exactly overlay each other, an essential requirement when a composite picture is to be formed from three superimposed colour pictures. Any lack of *registration* will give rise to colour fringing on edges and outlines of picture features. In most modern colour tubes the green cathode is central in the gun and the green beam travels down the centre of the tube neck to trace out a square, central picture on the screen. Because the outer beams, red and blue, take a different path and angle through the deflection system their patterns suffer from *deflection distortion* preventing either from overlaying the green pattern. Steps must be taken to exactly register the three images on screen: they take two forms, static convergence and dynamic convergence.

Static convergence

Although the dimensional and alignment tolerances in electron-gun manufacture are very tight, it is not possible to fabricate and fix the gun accurately enough to ensure that the *centres* of their on-screen images coincide. Centre-screen registration is called static convergence, and depends on the position of each beam-path within the tube neck. To correctly align these, a series of ring-magnet pairs is fitted on the tube neck forward of the purity rings already described. Their magnetic fields are carefully tailored to cross the paths of the outer (red and blue) electron beams while having no effect (in fact, no magnetic field) on the axis of the tube neck where passes the central green beam's path. By means of a pair of 4-pole magnets whose field intensity and direction can be varied by co- and contra-adjustment, the outer beams' paths are moved horizontally and vertically so that their images coincide at screen centre to give a magenta (red plus blue) spot there. The position of this magenta spot will not necessarily coincide with that of the green spot, so a further ring-magnet pair, this time with six-pole field, is fitted to the tube neck.

The six-pole magnetic field set up by this third ring pair is again adjustable as to strength and direction, and because its flux patterns appear identical to the outer beams they are *together* moved in either a horizontal or a vertical plane so that the magenta and green images can be superimposed. Fig. 5.6 shows a typical neck magnet cluster with the effect of each ring-magnet pair on the paths of the beams. In some tube designs (Philips/Mullard 30AX and 45AX series) these neck magnet systems are not used. The required magnetic fields for tolerance correction in terms of purity and static convergence are permanently 'printed' into a single ring at the top of the gun assembly during the manufacturing process.

Dynamic convergence

Unfortunately the achievement of perfect convergence at screen centre will not alone ensure that the registration holds correct right out to the screen edges. As the beams are deflected away from screen centre the fact that the screen is flat rather than spherical means that the deflection-centre-to-screen path becomes longer. The beams converge at the image plane, an imaginary sphere centred on the deflection centre, and diverge beyond it to strike the screen at widely different points. A solution to this problem is to take advantage of the slightly different paths of the beams through the deflection centre, and carefully shape the latter's magnetic field to impart a corrective factor to the deflection force applied to individual beams. By very precise control of the physical position of each turn of wire in the line and field deflection coils, the shape of the flux-field each generates in the tube neck can be controlled. For a self-converging tube the vertical lines of force responsible for horizontal deflection need to conform to a pincushion shape, and the horizontal lines of force which deflect the beams vertically to a barrel shape, as shown in Fig. 5.7.

These field patterns, once only practical to produce with a toroidally-wound deflection yoke, can now be reliably generated with saddle-wound yokes broadly similar to those used with monochrome tubes. Except in very late designs of colour tube, yoke and tube tolerances are not sufficiently good to guarantee perfect convergence at the extreme edges and corners of the display. To take up these tolerances the front (flared) end of the deflection coil is made larger than the tube bulb flare, permitting the front of the yoke to be panned and tilted for optimum screen-edge convergence. When it is achieved the yoke is wedged and sealed in position. In a tube with green gun central, horizontal panning of the yoke has the effect of registering red and blue lines parallel to and adjacent to the screen edges, while vertical tilting of the yoke registers the extremities of the red and blue lines which pass through screen centre. In some deflection systems a four-pole

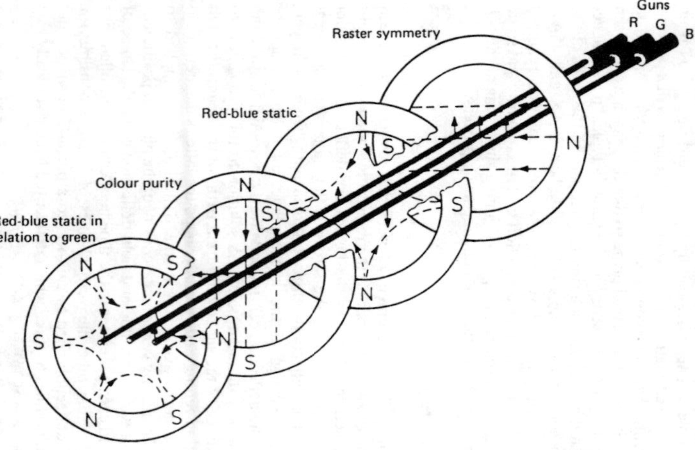

Fig. 5.6 *Beam trajectories through the neck-ring magnetic fields in an 'in-line' colour picture tube*

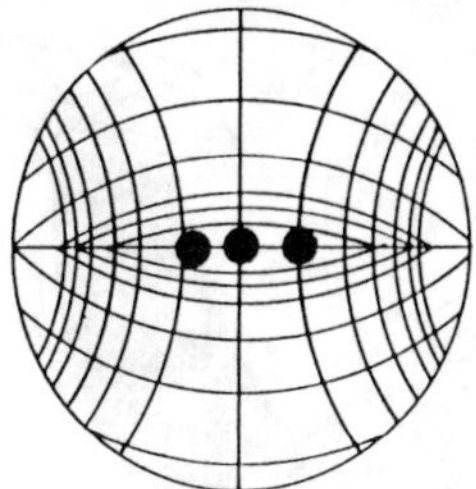

Fig. 5.7 *Shapes of magnetic deflection fields for a self-converging colour tube. The central spots depict the beams; the lines represent lines of magnetic force*

electromagnet is fitted to further assist with dynamic convergence. It carries sawtooth and parabola waveforms at line and field rate, whose amplitude and shape are adjustable by six or so resistive or inductive trimmers. Differential adjustment of the currents flowing in the two halves of each deflection coil pair (*scan balance* controls) may also be provided to correct crossover of red and blue horizontals on the screen centre-line.

TUBE SETTING UP

A typical set-up procedure for an in-line tube with green gun central, and adjustable neck rings and yoke is as follows: Allow 20 minutes for tube warm-up, then switch off red and blue guns and pull back the deflection yoke towards the guns. Adjust the two-pole purity ring magnets for a central green stripe on the screen, then push the yoke forward for a full pure green screen. Clamp the yoke securing band at the middle of the range over which there is no effect. Restore red and blue beams, switch off green and adjust the 4-pole rings to overlay blue and red images at screen centre. Restore green beam and manipulate the 6-pole ring pair to overlay green and magenta images to render a white cross or dot at screen centre. Finally tilt and pan the front end of the deflection yoke to achieve best possible convergence at screen edges, then fix and seal the yoke position with rubber wedges and silicon rubber compound.

TRINITRON TUBE

A variant of the in-line gun design is the Trinitron tube illustrated in Fig. 5.8. Its main difference from the tube already described is the omission of the tie-bars in the shadowmask to render an *aperture-grille* structure in place of the slot-mask; and the arrangement of the gun, in which the two outer beams cross over in the middle of the gun assembly. The focus anode and its adjacent electrodes form an *electron-lens*, and as in optical lens technology the larger the lens diameter the better its performance. The effect of the Trinitron gun assembly is to pass all three beams through the centre of a large lens assembly for less aberration and smaller spot

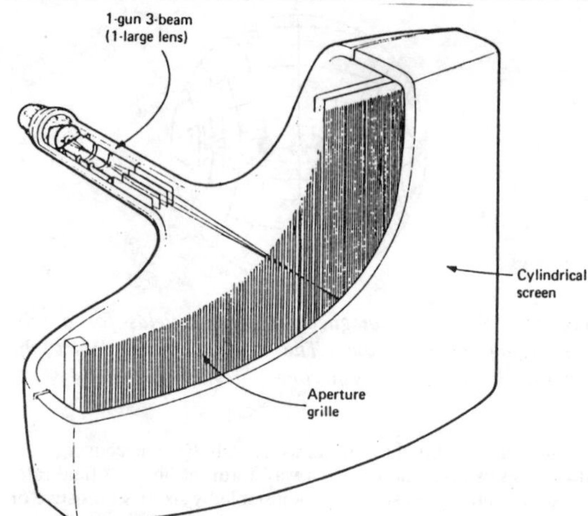

Fig. 5.8 *Principle and construction of the Sony Trinitron colour tube*

size than is easily possible with the small separate electron lenses of other types of gun assembly.

Static convergence is carried out in the Trinitron tube by means of concentric convergence electrodes which have a prism-like effect on the electron beams. The differential electrostatic deflection they introduce is adjusted by varying the potential between the plates, and since one set is connected to the final anode, the static convergence control is associated with the e.h.t. source itself, in the form of a highly insulated potentiometer whose output is passed into the picture tube via a co-axial connector let into the bowl of the glass envelope; the e.h.t. potential enters the tube by the same connector.

In other respects, Trinitron tube setting up is broadly similar to the procedure already given, except that wide-angle Trinitron tubes (114° deflection) sometimes require the use of self-adhesive button-magnets on the glass flare to correct minor areas of impurity.

PICTURE TUBE NOMENCLATURE

The type numbers assigned to different designs of picture tube have followed various formulae over the years. Tubemakers have now agreed on a worldwide type designation system which is detailed below:

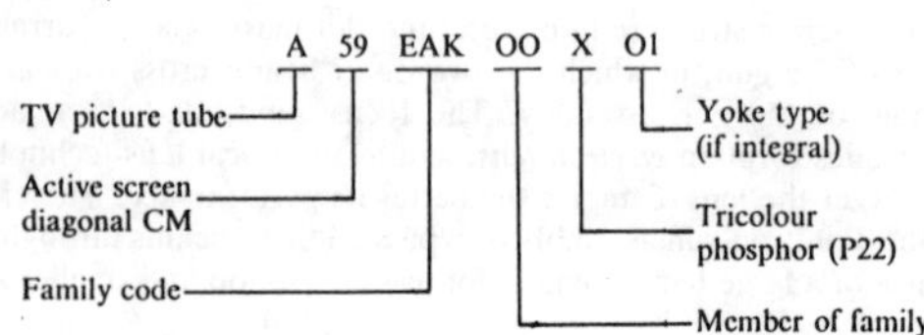

FACEPLATE DESIGN

The darkest parts of a TV picture have the same luminance value as the (unenergised) screen itself, and the darker the faceplate can be made, the greater the perceived brightness of the picture: the ideal viewing screen for a picture tube would be a flat matt-black surface. In practice the nearest approach to this is to minimise the *reflectivity* of the screen to ambient light and phosphor light reflected back from the viewers and viewing area.

To this end the spaces between phosphors on the rear of the faceplate are filled with a light-absorbent black pigment based on carbon or graphite, a technology called *black matrix*. The phosphor material itself is very light in colour, so dyes are added to make each absorb incident light of colours other than its own. The use of these pigmented phosphors, together with black matrixing, reduces the reflectivity of the tube face by 30% or more without any effect on brightness. The benefit can be reaped in terms of either enhanced brightness or contrast, depending on the light transmission characteristic of the faceplate glass.

The faceplate glass characteristic makes an important contribution to picture-tube performance. In effect the glass viewing panel acts as a neutral-density filter, having grey glass with a light transmission factor between 40% and 85%, depending on design. The basic idea of the dark-tinted faceplate, which inevitably reduces picture brightness, is to reduce the screen's reflectivity and thus increase picture contrast. Reflected light has to pass through the glass twice, while the phosphor-light passes through only once. Thus for a faceplate with 50% transmission a four-fold reduction in reflected light is traded for a halving of the available light from the phosphors. Fig. 5.9 shows the effect of two different glass densities on the contrast ratio; the screen reflectivity factor is based on a modern design with pigmented phosphors and black matrix.

Screen shape

The transmitted picture is rectangular, and the more nearly rectangular the viewing screen the better. As picture-tube design progresses the screen is becoming 'squarer' and 'flatter' though no conventional screen in sizes larger than a few centimetres can practically be made perfectly rectangular or completely flat due to the effect of atmospheric pressure on the glass envelope. The flatter the faceplate, the less 'capture area' it has for reflections from the viewing area, the wider its viewing angle, and the less distortion it gives to the picture.

TUBE REACTIVATION

The most common fault in picture tubes is low emission, where the emissive coating on the cathode cannot release sufficient electrons to provide a bright sharp picture. Very often a reactivation process can be successfully applied by overrunning the heater for a few minutes and applying a positive potential to the grid with respect to the faulty cathode. The resulting heavy current disrupts the surface of the cathode, cleaning it and exposing a new surface. Sophisticated machines (see Chapter 20) are able to give controlled reactivation. Other possible gun faults are short-circuits betwen electrodes – which will turn the afflicted gun hard on, very often on a sporadic basis; and (rarely) an open-circuit heater or electrode,

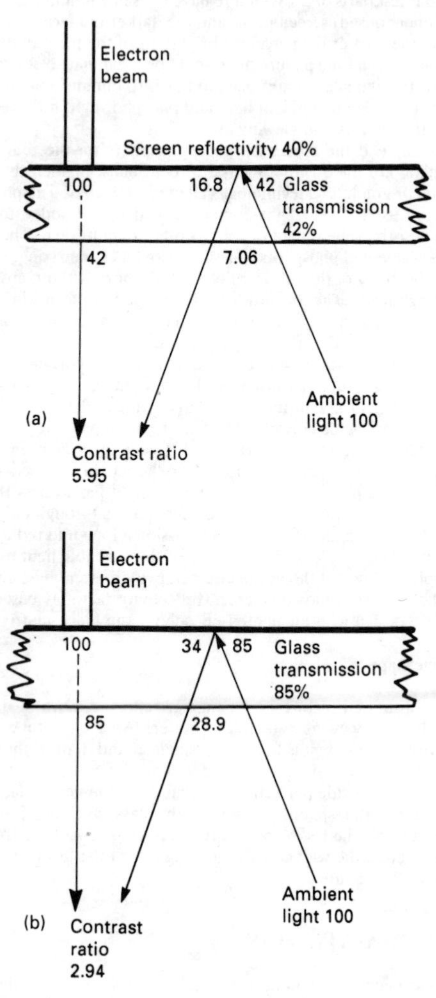

Fig. 5.9 *The effect of tinted screens on picture contrast. At (a) a dark faceplate with 42% transmission gives a contrast ratio of almost 6. At (b) a much lighter 85% transparent screen offers only half the contrast ratio, though picture brightness is greater*

which is not curable except by rebuilding the tube with a new gun assembly. Inter-electrode shorts not involving any heater can often be blown clear by application of high current and voltage, typically from a charged capacitor.

HANDLING PICTURE TUBES

The atmospheric pressure of the faceplate of a 51 cm tube is around 1600 kg, and over the total surface area is over 4000 kg. Sudden fracture of the glass results in very dangerous implosion, in which jagged fragments of glass can be hurled five metres or more if the tube is not fitted in its cabinet. Always wear protective goggles or a face mask and preferably gloves as well, when handling tubes. Hold the tube vertically screen down with both hands, one under the screen and one steadying the neck with small tubes, one hand on each side of large tubes. Place face down on a soft surface to avoid scratching, and always fit a shorting strap between anode connector, external graphite coating and rimband when removing or handling tubes: this avoids electric shock from the stored e.h.t. potential, particularly dangerous when carrying a tube. . . .

PICK-UP TUBES

Of the two 'live-image' pick up devices in current use the vacuum photoconductive tube was the first-comer; the more common solid-stage sensor will be described later. The generic term for photoconductive tubes is *vidicon*, the many other type names arising mainly from the use of different target materials.

A vidicon tube (Fig. 5.10) has an electron gun broadly similar to that described for display tubes, with the difference that the gun is designed for a very small beam current ($<1\ \mu A$) and very small spot size – around 20 micron diameter. It has electrostatic focusing, but this is supplemented by a magnetic focusing coil which is co-axial with the vidicon tube. The effect of the static magnetic focusing field is to impart to the individual electrons in the beam spiral paths, which at intervals along the beam length all cross through the same point. Adjustment of the strength of the axial

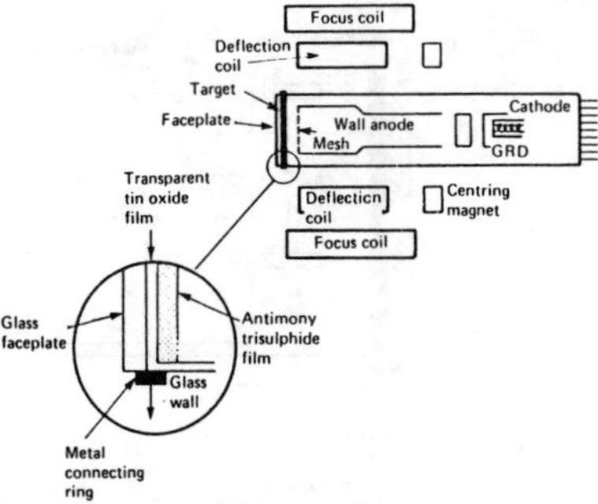

Fig. 5.10 *Cross-section of a vidicon pick-up tube: the inset shows detail construction of the target and faceplate*

magnetic field by varying the d.c. focus coil current enables one of these focal points to coincide with the *target* surface at the front of the tube. Another important effect of the magnetic focusing system is to alter the deflection characteristics of the scan yoke to those of *orthogonal* scanning, in which the scanning beam hits the target at right-angles to its surface regardless of the deflection angle involved.

In a vidicon tube the final gun electrode is a wall anode, and a mesh is fitted over its outer end. Between the high-voltage mesh and the low-voltage target layer exists a steep potential gradient, and the electrons travelling down this gradient are greatly decelerated to impinge on the rear of the target at low velocity. The rear surface of the target is now effectively connected to the cathode via the electron beam and is thereby charge-stabilised to the cathode potential.

Vidicon target

The electron beam in the vidicon is not modulated from the gun end of the tube save for blanking during field and line flyback intervals. Even so the beam current does become intensity-modulated as a result of the target's behaviour.

The image is focused on the front of the target which consists of two layers on the rear surface of the glass faceplate: first a transparent film of tin oxide on the glass, then a light-sensitive layer of semiconductor material as shown in the inset to Fig. 5.10. A low potential of say 30 V is applied to the tin oxide layer, setting up a potential difference across the thickness of the target. In effect we have a capacitor, and in total darkness its leakage resistance is very high. Where light is present on the faceplate, however, the resistance of the semiconductor layer becomes low, discharging the capacitor. Resistance is inversely proportional to light level so that a charge pattern is set up on the surface of the target to correspond with the pattern of light and shade focused on it.

As the electron beam scans out the interlaced raster of Fig. 2.1(b) on the target, it restores each picture element in turn to cathode potential, see Fig. 5.11. This obviously involves recharging the 'capacitor' represented by each picture element to a 'standard' charge – the potential difference between the target connection and the cathode. The charging current involved will depend on how

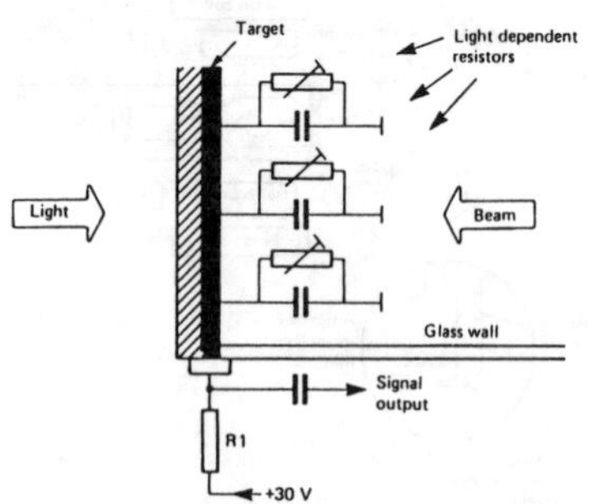

Fig. 5.11 *Operating principle of vidicon and allied photoconductive imaging tubes*

much charge has been lost due to illumination of the semiconductor layer, i.e. the incident light level. In total darkness, as when the lens is capped, virtually no beam current will flow; on any brightly lit area of the target a strong charging current will flow. This charge current necessarily flows back to the source of target voltage, and its fluctuations represent the patterns of light and shade being scanned and analysed by the vidicon's electron beam – in fact they form a video signal similar to that of Fig. 2.2. To convert this current (typically 200 nA) to a voltage we need only pass it through a resistor, represented by R1 in Fig. 5.11. Across R1, then, appears the video signal for amplification and processing.

DARK CURRENT AND LAG

The performance of the vidicon tube is limited by two main factors: its dark current and its lag. In theory no current should flow when no illumination is present at the target; in practice a small random current is present to cause shading and noise (grain) on the dark parts of the reproduced picture, and reduce the dynamic range (contrast gamut) of the picture. Other types of tube, notably the Plumbicon (lead-oxide target layer) and Saticon (selenium/arsenic/tellurium target layer) have very low dark current.

Image lag is a phenomenon whereby an 'image' is retained on the target when the light stimulus itself has gone. Its effect is to produce comet-tails on fast-moving objects or when the camera is panned across a scene, especially at low light levels. In this respect the true vidicon (antimony trisulphide target) is very poor, and the development of other types of tube, particularly the Plumbicon, improved lag performance by a factor of ten. For some types of tube a weak uniform background light applied to the target, typically from a red LED (Light Emitting Diode) in the optical system or communicating with the target via a lightpipe from the base region of the tube, gives an improvement in performance. It is used to establish a uniform reference dark current, maintaining beam/target contact at all times to avoid a 'detail drop-out' effect in the dark areas of the picture under all electron-beam conditions; and increasing the required target potential to a point where image lag is almost eliminated. The main features of several types of photoconductive pick-up tubes are given in Table 5.1.

COLOUR SENSING WITH A SINGLE TUBE

The photoconductive pick-up tube responds basically to the brightness (luminance) component of incoming light, and provided that the tube is reasonably panchromatic (sensitive to all colours) in its response the target's output signal is suitable, after amplification and insertion of sync pulses, for r.f. modulation or direct feed to a video monitor. To produce a colour picture more information must be generated by the image sensor – enough in fact to give details of the nature of all three of the primary colours, red, green and blue at every single picture element. Techniques have been developed to achieve this with a single photoconductive tube, involving some form of matrixed faceplate. In cameras intended for the domestic and enthusiast markets a popular variant is the colour striped faceplate drawn in Fig. 5.12.

In this form of striped faceplate the outer surface of the vidicon's front glass is covered with vertical stripes of translucent colour

Table 5.1 *Characteristics and performance of the main types of image pick-up device*

Type	Vidicon	Plumbicon	Saticon	Newvicon	CCD/CMOS
Target	Sb_2S3	PbO	SeAsTe	ZnSe/ZnCdTe	Si
Sensitivity, μA/1m	Varies	400	350	1200	700
Dark current, nA	20	<1	<1	6	5
Lag, relative	10	1	1.5	5	0.1
Target burn risk	High	Moderate	Moderate	Moderate	Zero
Warm-up			10 secs		Zero
Physical depth			100 mm		5 mm
Life, hours			4500		> 500 000
Max. safe temperature			40°C		80–100°C
Operating voltage			Up to 2 kV		9–12 V
Spurious effects			Shading		Fixed pattern noise

filters in the form green, cyan, clear, green, cyan, clear, and so on. The green filter will permit only the green (G) component of incoming light to pass; the adjacent cyan filter lets through both blue (B) and green (G) components; the clear stripes, of course, pass all light allowing red (R), G and B to reach the vidicon's photosensitive target. The basic video signal from the tube's target electrode produces a luminance signal, since the image being scanned still contains all brightness information for the scene being televised. Because of the presence of the stripes, however, an extra signal will now appear at the target, modulated with information concerning the colours in the scene.

As the faceplate is scanned, each line of picture information contains 'steps' as shown at the bottom of Fig. 5.12. The first step contains the G signal, the second a B + G signal, and the third an R + B + G signal. If we subtract the G signal from the B + G signal we have a B signal. Subtraction of the B + G signal from the R + B + G signal renders an R signal. Thus by a simple matrix circuit we can derive the three primary colour signals (RGB) required for a colour TV system, ultimately for the three guns of a shadowmask picture tube. While this simple explanation proves that three primary colours can be derived from a stripe-filter using only two colours, green and cyan, the way in which the chroma signal is derived and processed in a practical camera is different, making full use of the luminance signal produced at the target: these techniques will be described in the next chapter.

The pitch of the stripes in the colour filter is in the region of 40 μm, so the vidicon's beam focusing requirements are very stringent. As soon as the beam diameter exceeds the stripe width all colour is lost, and deterioration of beam focus will remove the colour (and in some cameras, substitute an overall green cast to the picture) long before any loss of fine detail (luminance response) is discernible.

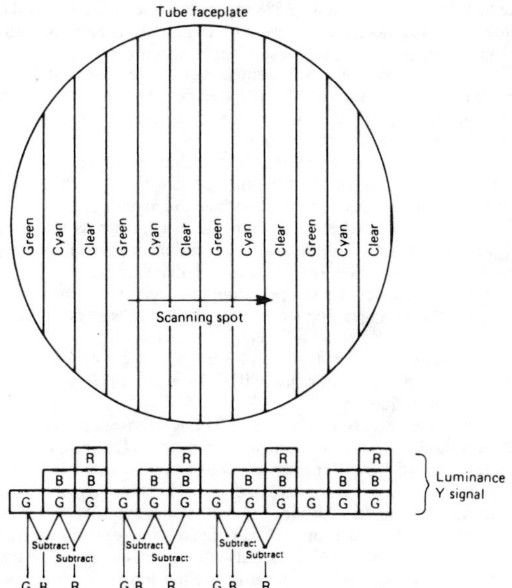

Fig. 5.12 *One form of single-tube colour-striping system. The stripes cover the outer glass faceplate, and are made of translucent gelatin-type material*

Fine detail in the picture being televised would cause a 'beat' pattern against the colour stripe gratings, so an optical filter (*crystal filter*) is present in the light path to remove it. This is one reason why very expensive lens systems are wasted on this type of camera. Because most types of vidicon tube – and particularly the Newvicon – are sensitive to infra-red radiation, an IR filter is also fitted: without this the colour rendering of an object would depend on its temperature as well as its natural colour.

SOLID-STATE IMAGE SENSORS

In the mid-eighties a new form of pick-up device appeared in commercial cameras and camcorders: the solid-state image sensor. This device needs no electron gun, deflection system or glass envelope. It is rugged and compact, with indefinite life and an ability to withstand mechanical shock and huge overloads of incident light – a direct view of the sun would write off any vidicon-type tube except the silicon-target variant, whereas a solid-state sensor would be unaffected.

In this 'flat-plate' system the photosensitive surface is not continuous; it is divided into hundreds of thousands of separate 'islands' of silicon photodiodes arranged in horizontal rows to conform with the television scanning lines themselves. In a typical consumer camera intended for use with a home video format recorder there are 577 lines, each containing 388 separate diodes to give a total of almost 224,000 picture elements. The right-hand column of Table 5.1 gives comparative data on solid-state imaging devices.

Each photodiode consists of a single picture element, and during the 20 ms field period it builds up a voltage charge proportional to the light falling on it. Each photodiode cathode has its own MOSFET transistor switch, as shown in Fig. 5.13. When a pulse is applied to the transistor gate the diode's charge is transferred to a shift register. Unlike a digital shift register the type used in a solid-state image sensor can deal with an analogue signal which in effect consists of 'packets' of electrons. It is known as a bucket-brigade device (BBD) and finds applications elsewhere in consumer electronics, primarily for analogue delay lines.

The charge packets are stepped along the register by sequentially changing the voltages applied to the BBD's cells. The electron charges readily fall into an adjacent 'potential well', and by setting up progressively deeper depletion layers in adjacent cells they can be stepped along the shift register/BBD by means of clock pulses in a four-phase sequence.

Fig. 5.14 represents a complete CCD photosensor; each column of photodiodes has its own vertical shift register. During each field blanking period a transfer pulse is applied to the gate of each FET to switch the charges accumulated in each photodiode into the adjacent shift register. All the FETs are simultaneously pulsed, so that once per TV field a complete set of pixel charges is transferred.

On the first change of V-clock pulse the charges in all the vertical shift registers hop one cell upwards. At the top of the array is a horizontal shift register, into which is now loaded the topmost line of the picture. This is another BBD, whose contents are continually and rapidly transferred towards the left by the same 'progressive well' technique as used in the vertical shift registers, using the same four-phase sequence of transfer pulses. For this register the pulse rate is much faster: the readthrough here is at picture-element rate, in practice about 8 MHz. The charge packets roll off the left-hand end of the horizontal shift register in the form of a series of pulses

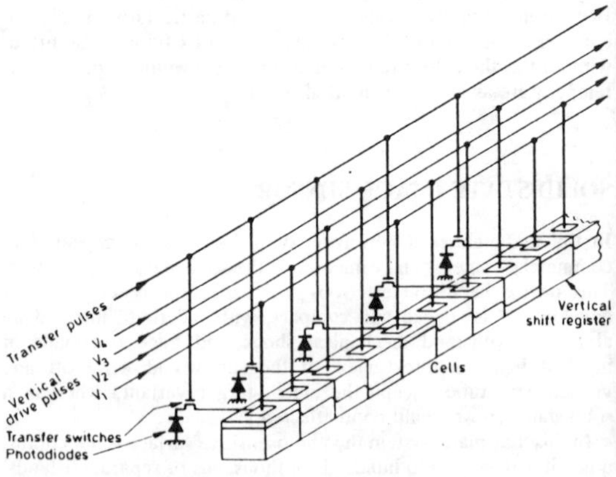

Fig. 5.13 *Basic principle of CCD image sensor. Operation is described in the text*

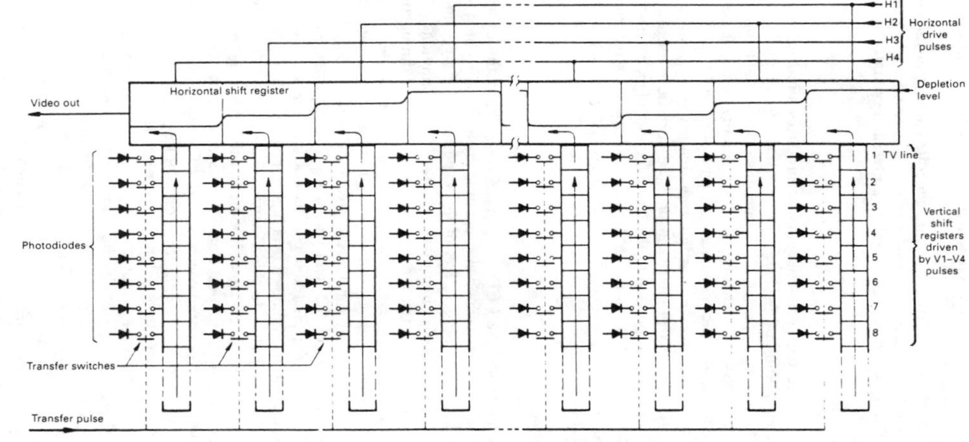

Fig. 5.14 *CCD image-sensor array, showing 'stepping' characteristic of charge packets. This simple representation has 8 × 8 = 64 pixels, while practical sensors have hundreds of thousands*

of varying height: an analogue video signal. Before it can be used the clock pulses and switching hash must be filtered out.

At each line blanking interval the vertical registers are pulsed to transfer complete picture lines into the horizontal BBD at 64 μs intervals, where each is clocked leftwards during the next line scan period. The serial information stream corresponds to the target output of a conventional vidicon tube. At the end of each field the charges from all the photodiodes have been read out, the vertical and horizontal BBDs are empty, and the whole sequence is repeated for the next field.

The CCD clock and drive pulses are generated in a timing/divider IC governed by the camera's master sync and subcarrier generator section (SSG), which is itself paced by a precision crystal.

Colour CCDs

The CCD image sensor described above produces a monochrome picture; each photodiode's charge is proportional to the luminance value of the pixel it represents. As with tubes, high-quality broadcast and professional cameras use three sensors, one for each primary colour, and the incoming light path is optically split and filtered. For consumer cameras this approach is too expensive, so single-array colour CCD image sensors have been developed with colour-filter matrices bonded to the faceplate and aligned with the photocell array. They work on similar principles to the ones described in this chapter (Fig. 5.12) and the next in connection with vidicon tubes.

Fast shutter

Like vidicon tubes, the CCD array builds up a charge throughout the field period, with each pixel integrating the light falling on it for about 19 ms. The storage effect of this exposure time gives good sensitivity, particularly important in low-light conditions. If, however, anything in the picture moves appreciably during this 19 ms period, it is displayed (during still-frame reproduction) as a blur. With a CCD image sensor it is possible to separate the 'scanning' and 'storage' functions to give a fast shutter effect.

Towards the end of the field period a special transfer pulse is applied to dump the photodiodes' charges into the vertical shift registers. It is shortly followed by a high-speed pulse train through all the vertical registers to 'flush' them. The effect of this is not visible because the video signal is muted at this time: the process takes place during the vertical blanking period. A short period (set by the user's shutter speed control) is afforded to the photodiodes to charge from incoming light, then once more a transfer pulse is applied to pass the charges into the vertical shift register. The brightness information acquired during this limited exposure is stepped along the registers in the normal way to form the video output signal, which appears continuous because of the storage capability of the cells in the BBD shift registers

The penalty for fast-shutter operation, as with conventional photography, is a loss of sensitivity, calling for an increase in light level or a large aperture setting. A range of shutter speeds is provided to trade off sensitivity against blur effects, the fastest of which is only suitable for use in bright outdoor situations. Even in good light, however, fast shutter settings should only be used when freeze-frame or slow-motion analysis of the event is likely to be needed.

6

TV cameras and colour encoding

Ultimately the transmission of a full colour TV picture requires three separate and simultaneous streams of information; those for the red, the blue and the green light components of the picture. Although these signals exist at each end of the chain (i.e. at the pick-up and display tubes) they are seldom conveyed along separate channels, even where the link is a short one consisting merely of cable. The reasons for this are many: much of the information in the three channels is identical, completely so on black-and-white scenes; the human eye is insensitive to *coloured* detail and discerns most fine detail as a black-and-white image; the channels available for transmission of a TV signal (whether in radio, cable or recording-media form) are not wide enough to handle three full-bandwidths signals; any differential treatment in regard to phase or amplitude response of the three would lead to degradation of the reproduced picture; and the system would not be compatible with pre-existing monochrome signals and equipment.

For these reasons colour TV signals are almost invariably coded at source and decoded only in the circuits immediately preceding the colour picture tube. There are four main encoding systems, NTSC, PAL, SECAM and MAC. The latter was dealt with briefly in Chapter 4; here the NTSC and particularly the PAL system will be described. The concept of these encoding systems is to start with the basic luminance waveform and add to it extra signals to describe the colours in the picture. A single *subcarrier* is added, along with a reference signal during the back-porch period of the line waveform. In the receiver's decoder the timing (phase) of this *chrominance* (chroma for short) signal is compared with that of the reference (burst) signal to indicate the hue of the colour being transmitted; and the amplitude of the chroma signal is compared with that of the burst signal to indicate the saturation of the colour being transmitted. The term hue distinguishes between different colours like yellow, green and red, while saturation describes the brightness of the colour – in practical terms, how much it is diluted by white light, or how different it is to a black-and-white reproduction of the same object.

The signals chosen for transmission of the chroma information are not primary-colour signals at all. It is more convenient to use colour-difference signals, each representing the *difference* between one primary-colour signal and the luminance signal. To arrive at a difference value a subtraction process is involved. Thus subtracting the luminance (Y) signal from each of the primary-colour signals renders the colour-difference signals G–Y, B–Y and R–Y. It is only necessary to send two of these signals; the third can be derived from them in an add-matrix at the receiver. Because the human eye is most sensitive to colours in the green region of the light spectrum, most of the G signal is conveyed in the Y channel, and of the three colour-difference signals (on an average scene, *not* a snooker table or a cricket field) G–Y is the smallest. For this reason the G–Y signal is chosen to be left out of the transmitted signal, and to be recovered from the other signals at the receiver. In effect, then, the full colour picture is sent in three 'packets', i.e. Y, R–Y and B–Y signals.

ENCODING

In an image pick-up system which renders RGB signals directly a Y signal must be derived from them; in accordance with the sensitivities of the human eye to each, 59% of the G signal, 30% of the R signal and 11% of the B signal are derived from the primary-colour signals by simple resistive potential dividers and then added together to form a properly-balanced Y signal, see left-hand side of Fig. 6.1. Further matrices add inverted Y (i.e. –Y) to each of R and B to produce separate R-Y and B-Y signals. These colour-difference signals are fed to modulators where each amplitude modulates a locally generated subcarrier signal at 4.433619 MHz (PAL) or 3.575611 MHz (NTSC), frequencies chosen to minimise the dot-pattern on the display due to the chroma signal. The local subcarrier feeds to the R-Y and B-Y balanced modulators have a phase difference of 90°, a timing delay of one quarter of one cycle. The effect of this is that one subcarrier's instantaneous value is at its zenith while the other is passing through zero – an important point in the subsequent decoding process, and the key to separating the encoded R-Y and B-Y signals.

The modulators used are special *suppressed carrier* types, in which the carrier itself is cancelled internally, leaving only the sideband products of the amplitude-modulation process. This *balanced-modulator* technique ensures that no chroma carrier is present to cause dot patterns in picture areas with low or zero colour content, and that only on highly saturated scenes do large subcarrier signals appear. The outputs of the R-Y and B-Y modulators are together added to the Y signal.

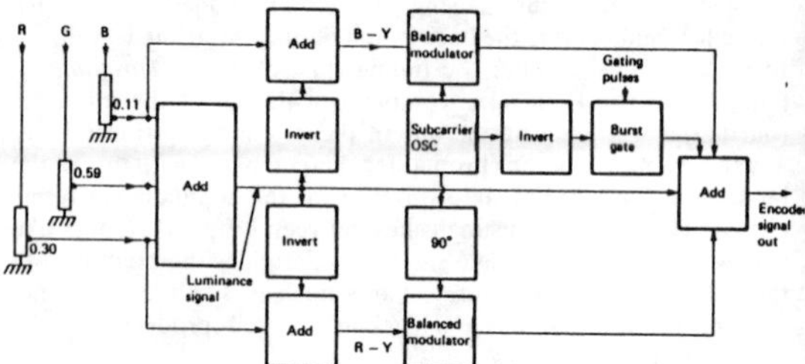

Fig. 6.1 *Basic form of colour encoding — the NTSC concept*

Burst insertion

A sample of subcarrier signal must also be added to the Y signal in the form of a colour burst, consisting of ten cycles of subcarrier with a phase corresponding to –(B-Y). Since B-Y phase is regarded as 0°, the burst is thus at 180°, and this sample signal is also derived from the subcarrier generator. It is passed to the Y amplifier via a gate whose opening coincides with the back porch: the *burst gating* pulse to operate it comes from a sync pulse generator which is also responsible for timing and forming sync and blanking pulses.

THE PAL VARIANT

The process so far described is a greatly simplified version of the first colour encoding system to be used, type NTSC. It works well, but has the drawback that if any level-dependent delay is present in the transmission chain – including any video tape machine used for 'storage' – the burst and signal-chroma components of the CVBS signal will, because they pass at different levels through the system, be treated differently. Since the correct reproduction of colour hue depends entirely on the maintenance of correct phase between these two, pictures transmitted over difficult paths by the NTSC process can suffer hue errors, necessitating a subcarrier phasing control (hue adjustment) at the receiver. To overcome this problem a modification of the basic NTSC system (PAL, Phase Alternation Line) was introduced, and has now become a standard in many countries.

In the PAL system the phase of the subcarrier conveying the R-Y signal is reversed on a line-by-line basis. This can be achieved by inverting either the subcarrier signal or the R-Y signal itself before entry to the suppressed carrier modulator. It offers the opportunity to cancel out hue errors due to differential phase distortion in the transmission path by means of a delay-line circuit in the receiver's decoder; more details will be given in the next chapter. To signal to the receiver's decoder which line carries the 'inverted' R-Y waveform an identification (*ident*) signal must now be added to the chroma signal for transmission. It is done by advancing the phase of the colour-burst cycles by 45° on 'PAL' (inverted R-Y) lines, and retarding their phase by 45° on the other ('normal') lines. The *mean* phase of the burst signal remains at 180°, corresponding to −(B-Y), but advances to 225° and retreats to 135° (see Fig. 6.2) on alternate lines – hence the expression 'swinging burst'.

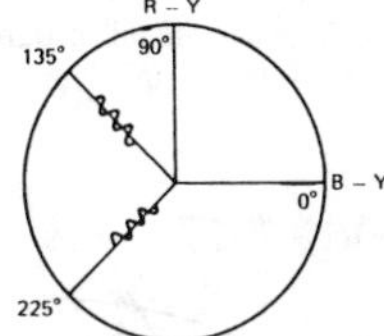

Fig. 6.2 *Vectorial representation of phases of colour sub-carrier signals. Here are shown R—Y, B—Y and burst axes*

CAMERA BASICS

A block diagram of the luminance chain of a simple colour TV camera is given in Fig. 6.3. This camera uses a segmented target, in which vertical stripes of translucent RGB light filters cover the entire faceplate surface of the vidicon tube. The target is likewise divided into vertical strips, one precisely aligned behind each primary-colour filter strip. By linking all the 'red' strips of target, all the 'blue' ones and all the green ones, and bringing them out to separate connections at the front of the tube, three separate primary-colour video signals are produced. They are amplified in low-noise FET preamplifiers and passed to attenuators as previously described for derivation of the correct proportions of Y

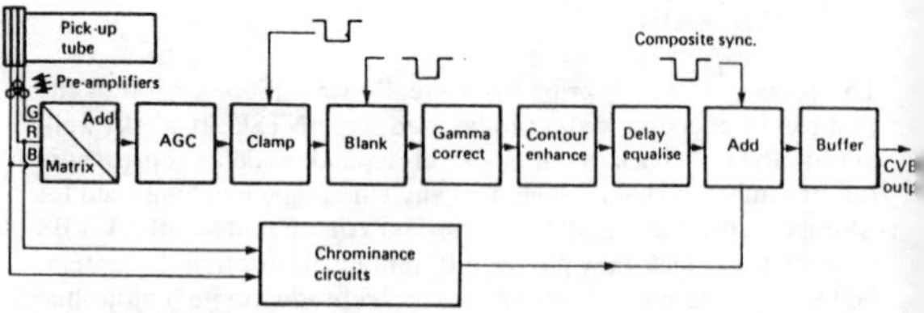

Fig. 6.3 *The main stages in Y-signal processing in a TV camera*

signal. An adder combines these into a Y signal for application to the video amplifier.

To prevent drift of the Y signal's black level with picture content, time, and temperature, a clamp is next encountered, in which the d.c. level of the waveform is returned to a fixed voltage during line and field blanking intervals. Spurious signals during the blanking intervals are suppressed by the blanking system at this point. Following further amplification the Y signal undergoes a gamma correction process. Whereas the most commonly-used image pick-up sensors render a voltage output proportional to light input (gamma value 1) the picture tube which will be used to reproduce the picture has a non-linear voltage input/light output curve (gamma value about 2.2, see Fig. 6.4(a)) which, if no compensating steps were taken, would result in a compression of contrast steps in the dark regions of the picture, and a 'stretching' of them in the lighter areas. Correct reproduction in monochrome and in colour requires the use in the camera of a non-linear amplifier called a gamma corrector, in which an equal-and-opposite input/gain characteristics(1/2.2) is introduced. The required curve (Fig. 6.4(a)) can be achieved with a ladder-network of diodes, resistors and reference voltages as in Fig. 6.4(b)). As new reference voltages V1, V2, V3 are attained by the video signal, progressively more diodes come into circuit to shunt away the signal and reduce its level – Fig. 6.4(c)).

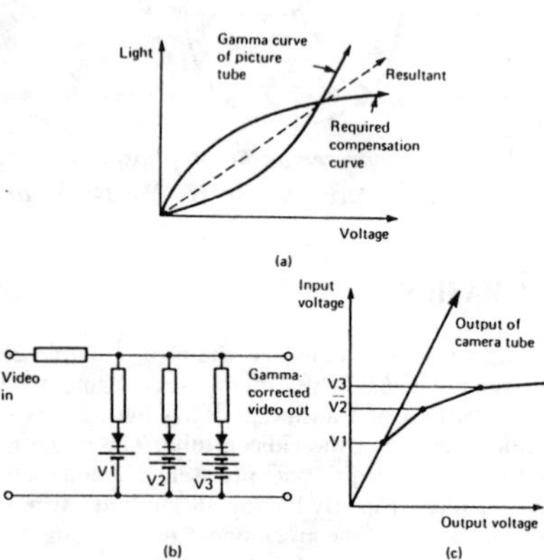

Fig. 6.4 *Gamma correction: (a) characteristic of picture tube and compensating amplitude-response curve; (b) principle of 'step' correction circuit: (c) the effect of the circuit of (b) – compare curve with that of (a)*

Next in the luminance circuit comes a contour enhancer or aperture corrector. Because the vidicon's scanning spot has a finite size its passage across a sharp black/white edge will give rise to a sloping edge in the video waveform rather than a step transition. To subjectively compensate for the 'softening' of the picture thus introduced, the start and finish points of each picture feature are emphasised by the addition to the video waveform of suitably polarised spikes to give both pre-shoot and overshoot. This is achieved by means of a short delay line, differentiators, inverters and adders. Although CCD pick-up sensors do not have scanning beams, the same sorts of 'crispening' circuits are used with them, now called *contour enhancers*. They give a useful sharpening effect to picture details.

The function of the next block is to delay the entire luminance signal by about 0.5 μs. As we shall shortly see, the bandwidth of the chrominance signal channel in the camera is restricted to about 500 kHz, which has the effect of delaying the chroma signals. To ensure that the edge-lines of both luma and chroma picture components coincide in the CVBS waveform and on the viewing screen this short delay is introduced in the Y signal path.

In the next blocks are added the composite sync pulses and the chroma signal, which already incorporates the swinging burst signal. The CVBS signal is now complete and passes to an emitter-follower buffer stage with an output impedance of 75 Ω for passage out of the camera to a videorecorder, monitor or r.f. modulator.

CHROMINANCE CIRCUITS

Fig. 6.5 shows in simplified form the colour circuits of the camera. The R and B preamplified chroma signals pass into a matrix where they are separately added to a – Y signal to render R–Y and B–Y components. Bandpass filters restrict these colour difference signals to a maximum frequency of 500 kHz on their way to be *weighted*. The weighting reduces the amplitude of R–Y and B–Y to prevent overloading of amplifiers and transmitters whose ratings are based on the standard 1 V pk-pk video signal. By reducing B–Y by a factor of 2.03 (becomes 0.493 B–Y, called *U signal*) and R–Y by a factor of 1.14 (becomes 0.877 R–Y, called *V signal*) the total excursion of the CVBS signal is limited to max. 1.23 V on bright highly-saturated colours, with the bottom tips of subcarrier cycles on highly-saturated dark colours (i.e. blue, colour-bar pattern) 230 mV below black-level, as in Fig. 2.5. The U and V signals are now ready for encoding. First comes a clamping stage, whence the U and V signals enter the suppressed-carrier modulators, whose

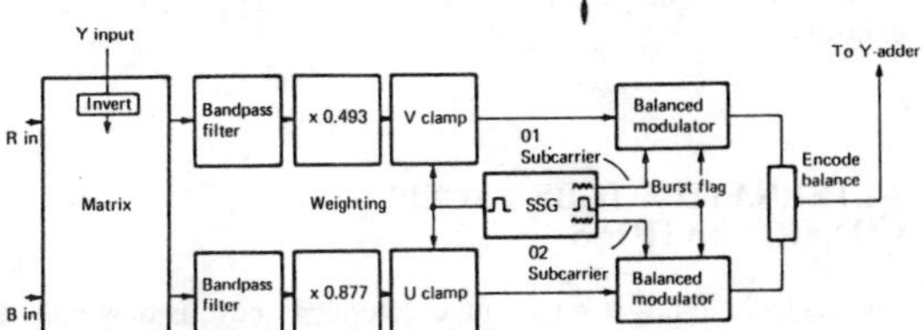

Fig. 6.5 *The simple chroma-processing circuit of a camera using a segmented-target pick-up tube*

carrier inputs are derived from an IC-based SSG (Sync and Subcarrier Generator). The emerging modulated U and V signals come together in an *encode balance* control from whose slider is tapped off the chrominance signal complete. After gain control and amplification the chroma signal is added to the Y signal.

Generation of the swinging burst

The V-axis subcarrier signal from the SSG already bears the required line-by-line phase reversals to conform with the PAL specification. The subcarrier feed to the U modulator is on the −U axis at all times, so that on line *n* the two available subcarrier feeds are as per Fig. 6.6(a), and on line *n* + 1 as per Fig. 6.6(b). If for the duration of the burst period the ordinarily-balanced U and V modulators are permitted to become *unbalanced*, 'carrier leaking' takes place, permitting some carrier output to appear from the modulators even when no chroma input (the R–Y and B–Y channels are blanked during the back porch) is present.

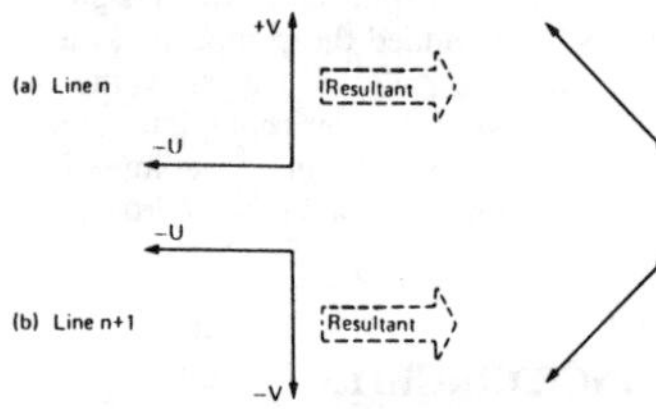

Fig. 6.6 *Generating a swinging burst by means of a flag pulse — operation is fully described in the text*

The balancing of the modulators (embodied in a d.c.-coupled IC) is governed by their d.c. conditions, so that if a *burst-flag* pulse is applied to the modulator IC to upset balance, pure carrier will be permitted to leak into the chrominance signal, the amplitude of which will depend on the height of the burst flag pulse. Equal amounts of −U and (alternating) ±V are thus produced for the duration of the burst flag pulse. In meeting at the slider of the encode balance control the vector-resultant of the two phases of the 4.43 MHz subcarrier are as shown by the phasors on the right-hand sides of Fig. 6.6(a) and (b). In fact these are the very vectors required for the swinging burst signal – ±45° centred on the 180° (−B–Y) axis. To maintain the required 90° swing it is important that the leak-signal amplitudes are equal for both modulators; and to ensure correct burst amplitude (0.3 V, equal to sync pulse height in the CVBS signal) the height of the burst flag pulse is carefully controlled.

ALTERNATIVE TUBE FACEPLATE CONFIGURATIONS

The segmented-target sensor tube described above is only one of several variants on the striped-faceplate theme. A more common arrangement is shown in Fig. 6.7. Here the stripes run slantwise across the sensor face, yellow stripes (passing R and G) alternating

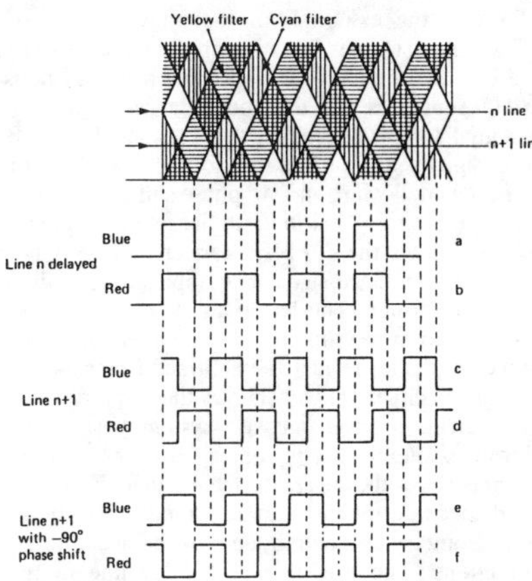

Fig. 6.7 *Slanted-stripe filters on tube faceplate. The time-related wave-forms below relate to the colour-recovery system*

with clear stripes in one direction, and cyan stripes (passing B and G) alternating with clear stripes in the other direction. At stripe crossover points only G light is permitted through to the faceplate. Consider the target signal during a random line *n*. Its output will consist, as the scanning spot traverses the target, of white (which is RGB), G, RGB, etc. On the line n + 1 below, the target output sequence will be yellow, cyan, yellow, cyan, yellow etc., which is R + G, B + G, R + G, B + G etc. as shown in Fig. 6.7. The angle of the stripes is arranged such that the resultant from the yellow stripes comes 90° *earlier* with each successive line scan, while the resultant from the cyan stripes comes 90° *later* with each successive line scan. This gives rise to the offset between rows a/b and c/d in Fig. 6.7. Row a is the blue ouput for line n, and row b the red output for line n. When this signal is passed through a 1-line delay it will be available at the same time as the signals for line n + 1, whose blue output is drawn in row c and whose red output is drawn in row d. Passing line n + 1 through a simple 90° phase shift network renders waveforms e and f for blue and red respectively. It can be seen that whereas the B and R signals are in phase (i.e. time-coincident) in the delayed line n signal (rows a and b) they are in antiphase at the output of the 90° phase shift network. Since the delay line has 'stored' row a/b for exactly one scanning line, it and row e/f are simultaneously available. Adding row a/b to row e/f will render 2 B (in-phase signals) while anti-phase R signals cancel out: at the adder output pure B appears. Subtracting row a/b from row e/f renders 2 R (R – [–R]) while B cancels out (B – B = 0): at the subtractor output pure R appears. A more detailed account of delay-line matrix systems appears in the next chapter.

Since green is present at all times (*no* colour filter in Fig. 6.7 stops G) it would appear that its presence would upset the B and R phase-recovery system. It does not, because whereas the B and R chroma signals appear at a high frequency of 3.9 MHz (the product of the line scanning rate and the stripe repetition frequency), the constant G signal has no such high frequency carrier, and is lost in a bandpass filter centred on 3.9 MHz.

Fig. 6.8 shows the essentials of the phase system of colour recovery. The target signal is first preamplified in a low-noise stage, then passed into two filters. A low-pass filter with response up to about 3 MHz separates off the mean target signal to give a luminance signal for processing in the Y channel. The B and R chrominance signals are picked off in the 3.9 MHz filter and applied to the 1 H delay line and 90° phase shifter for separation in the adder and subtractor. Their outputs are integrated in a low-pass filter which eliminates the 3.9 MHz carrier and renders smooth, pure B and R chrominance signals for application to the encoder section described earlier. The letters at circuit points in Fig. 6.8 relate to the waveform rows in Fig. 6.7. There is no true *subtractor* circuit artifice available; in fact the subtractor stage works on an invert-and-add principle, which achieves the same result.

The phase-detection colour recovery system works well, but the necessity for the scanning lines to coincide with the crossover of the stripe-filter matrix on the faceplate means that the tube must be designed and specified for the scanning standards to be used, and the scanning geometry and amplitude must be accurate and stable in both directions. The use of a 1 H delay line in the colour recovery circuit requires that the line scanning frequency be very closely maintained.

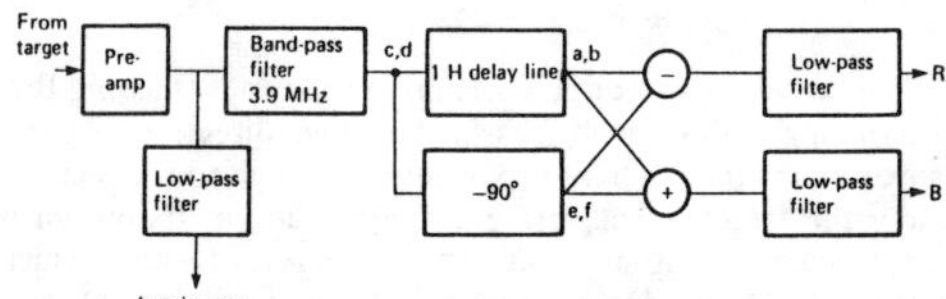

Fig. 6.8 *Colour recovery by the phase-discrimination process*

Step-energy colour recovery

The use of vertical RGB filter stripes in conjunction with a segmented target was described earlier in this chapter. An alternative vertical striping system was pictured in Fig. 5.12 with the primary-colour steps which appear in the output signal from the target. The combination of horizontal scanning rate and stripe spacing (hence repetition frequency) gives to the colour signals a carrier frequency about 4.1 MHz. There are two possible methods of recovering R and B baseband chroma signals from the step waveform. The first (Fig. 6.9(a)) requires opposite-polarity rectifiers working on the upper and lower envelope profiles followed by add/subtract matrices to recover R–Y and B–Y signals. The second (Fig. 6.9(b)) involves the use of 4.1 MHz (fundamental) and 8.2 MHz (2nd harmonic) bandpass filters; the 8.2 MHz signal is amplitude-limited and its *phase* compared with that of the fundamental (4.1 MHz) component. Further filtering takes place before application to add/subtract matrices, which render modulated R and B carrier signals, restored to baseband by a synchronous demodulator for each.

Frequency discrimination colour recovery

Another faceplate-filter stripe configuration is shown in Fig. 6.10(a). In this case the filter colours are red and blue, and their

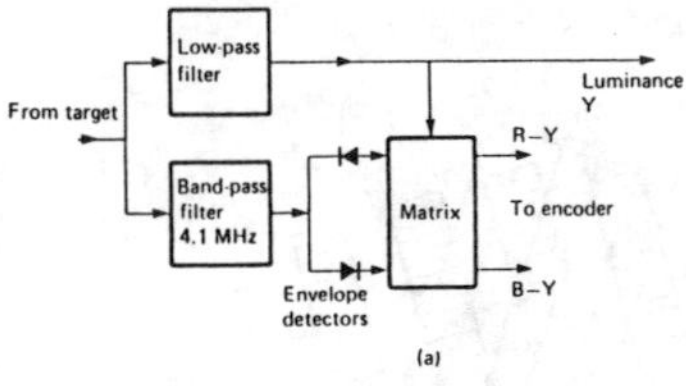

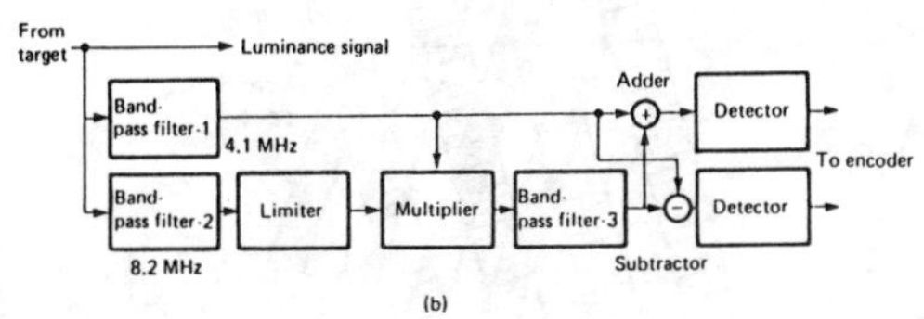

Fig. 6.9 *Colour recovery from the output of a vertically-striped mono-target pick-up tube as illustrated in Fig. 3.11: (a) using envelope detectors (b) using harmonic phase detection*

widths are typically 61 μm for red, 47 μm for blue. This gives rise to different carrier frequencies for R and B; to further reduce crosstalk between the two the angle from vertical is made +15° for R and −20° for B. The result, at 625-line scanning rate, is a carrier frequency of 3.9 MHz for R and 5.1 MHz for B. The colour-recovery circuits here are very simple as Fig. 6.10(b) shows, but the high B carrier frequency demands a very small spot size in the vidicon tube; any shortcomings here will upset picture hue by diminishing the blue signal with respect to the red.

DYNAMIC FOCUS AND SHADING CORRECTION

For the purpose of achieving adequate definition in the picture the focusing performance of the vidicon tube is not very critical. In stripe-filter pick-up tubes, however, very sharp focus is required for correct operation of the colour-discriminating systems; to avoid variations in colour-signal amplitudes over the picture area the focus must also be very uniform. To achieve this it is necessary in some camera types to modulate the vidicon's d.c. focus voltage with line- and field-rate waveforms of parabolic and sawtooth shape. Parabola and sawtooth waveforms are derived by integration of H-drive and V-drive pulses from the SSG, or from the timebase waveform generators themselves. In the complete camera block diagram of Fig. 6.11 the dynamic focus amplifer (bottom centre) takes adjustable parabola voltage waveforms at line and field rate. The presets are adjusted for optimum focus (maximum chroma carrier amplitude) throughout complete line and field periods respectively.

Even with dynamic focus correction within the vidicon, colour shading remains due to (a) imperfect linearity of vertical scanning velocity, causing stripe-colour errors and thus losses in the phase-recovery colour circuits; (b) poor linearity of horizontal scanning, giving rise to changes in stripe-colour carrier frequency over periods of 1 line; and (c) irregularities in the target and the

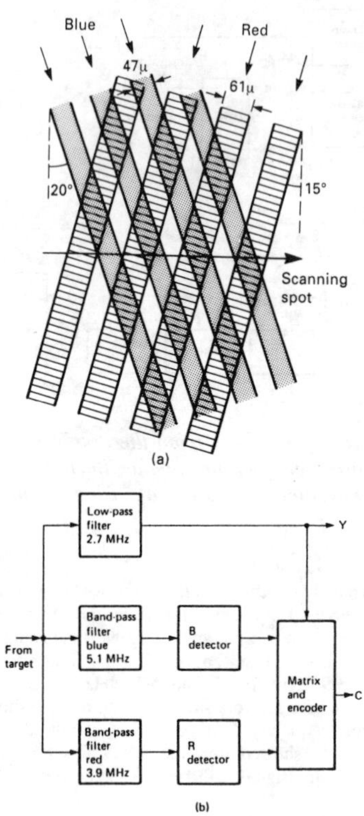

Fig. 6.10 *Frequency-discrimination of colour: (a) tube faceplate stripes; (b) simple recovery circuit*

electrical charge it carries. In Fig. 6.11 a horizontal-linearity generator adds an adjustable correction current to the line scanning waveform to mitigate condition (b) above. Still there remains the need to apply corrective waveforms to the R and B amplifiers to cancel out the shading effects on an equal-and-opposite basis. Hence the shading amplifiers and shading correctors in the centre of Fig. 6.11, each operating on tilted parabola waveforms controlled by banks of miniature pre-set potentiometers. The presets are manually adjusted for zero colour at all points on the monitor when the camera is scanning an evenly-illuminated white card.

Although not shown in the block diagram, it is also necessary to adjust the gains of the B and R channels according to the level of the Y signal: this maintains correct Y–C tracking.

The block diagram of a colour camera using a CCD image sensor is similar, but does not need the deflection circuits (whose function is taken over by the CCD-drive chip) or the shading correctors. While a CCD imager does not suffer from shading, production specimens can have faulty photodiodes in the diode array, leading

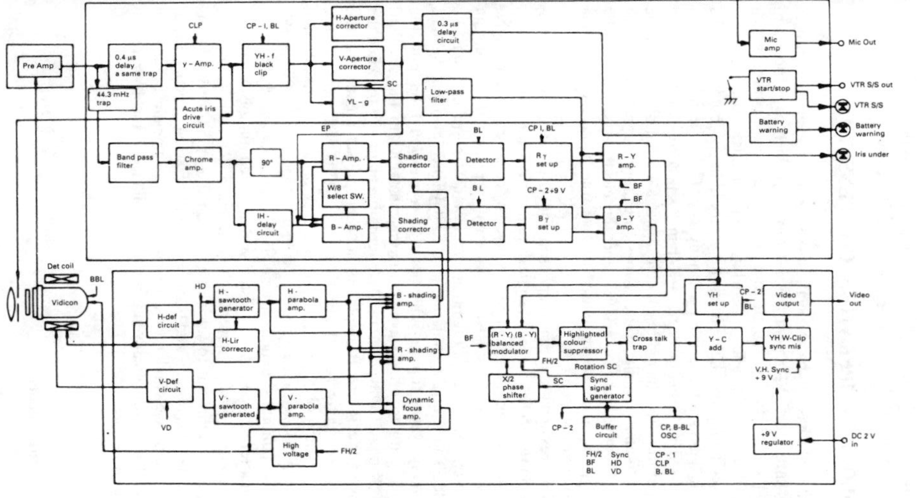

Fig. 6.11 *Complete block diagram of basic single-tube colour camera*

to blemishes and pinholes in the picture. To overcome this, a ROM (Read-Only-Memory) is supplied with the CCD chip, programmed to substitute an adjacent pixel for each missing or faulty one. The colour-process system varies with the type of faceplate matrix used, and is usually handled by purpose-designed ICs. Some late consumer-type camcorders use *digital* processing in the video/ chroma sections, wherein the signals are handled in binary-coded form.

COLOUR TEMPERATURE COMPENSATION

White light has two basic specifications, its luminance or brightness (measured for TV-camera purposes in *lux*) which corresponds to the level of the Y signal; and its colour temperature, which describes the 'shade' of white, in practice between the predominantly-red light from tungsten filament bulbs and the bluish light scattered from a cloudy sky. Colour temperature is expressed in terms of degrees Kelvin (°K), corresponding to the temperature to which a black object (i.e. a carbon block) must be raised to emit a similar white. Tungsten lighting has a characteristic colour temperature of 3200°K, and the electrical circuits of the camera are generally optimised to give true white (zero chroma signals) at this point.

Our eyes and brain can compensate for differing colour temperatures in the scenes we view, so flesh tones and white objects do not appear to change in hue whether viewed by electric or natural light. A TV camera does not have this inherent correction, so to maintain white balance under all lighting circumstances correction must be made. The simplest cameras have a 'daylight' lever on the lens assembly which flips a yellow-orange *conversion* filter into the optical path to bring daylight (average 6500°K) to the standard 3200°K point for the camera. An alternative method is to switch the gains of the R and B amplifiers between pre-set points, and the W/B select switch near the centre of Fig. 6.11 is of this type. It is a three position switch mounted on the back of the camera, offering tungsten/cloudy/sunny settings – colour temperature and lux ratings for familiar situations are given in Tables 6.1 and 6.2.

An alternative to the click-stop switch is a continuously-variable 'tint' control giving differential adjustment of R and B gain. This, however, is difficult to set without an on-site monitor to judge its effect; for this reason, and because it is not practical or economic to fit a colour viewfinder tube to inexpensive domestic cameras, a method of automatically setting white balance is incorporated in modern designs.

Auto-white balance

A sample of white at whatever colour-temperature is present on site can be obtained by fitting a white translucent lens cap or by pointing the camera at a white surface. For a true white output signal from the camera, both colour-difference signals R–Y and B–Y must be zero; alternatively, and amounting to the same thing: R = G = B. In cameras equipped with auto-white balance, pressing the set-white button starts an automatic process of gain adjustment in the R and B amplifier channels to achieve this status.

Table 6.1 *Colour-temperature characteristics of common light-emitters*

Blue	
10 000	Clear blue sky
9000	
8000	
	Overcast sky
7000	
	Illuminant 'D'
6000	Summer, noon
	Camera flash bulb
5000	Early morning, late afternoon
	Dusk and dawn
4000	White fluorescent tube
	Halogen bulbs 'normal' setting
3000	Tungsten bulbs (studio) for camera
	Tungsten bulbs (domestic)
2000	
	Candlelight
1000	Firelight
°K	
Red	

Table 6.2 *Lux ratings for commonly-encountered conditions. Above 100 000 lux a neutral-density filter is usually necessary*

100 000	Summer sunshine, midday
	Summer sunshine, 10 a.m.
	Cloudy noon
10 000	
	Indoors, daytime, near window
2000	Studio requirement
1000	
	Well-lit shop
500	
	Office, fluorescent lamp-lit
100	Living room, electrically lit
	Street lights at night
30	
10	Candlelight

The required offset voltage is noted by a microprocessor system which puts into store a number representing the plus or minus gain characteristic for each of R and B compared with the normal (i.e. 3200°K) setting. The stored numbers are subsequently allowed to control R and B gain via a D to A (Digital to Analogue) converter and an IC-based voltage controlled attenuator. The achievement of correct white balance is signalled by an LED indicator or an electronic symbol on the viewfinder screen. All pictures produced by the camera will now conform to the pre-set white point, and such subtle tints as flesh-tones and eye colours will be faithfully reproduced.

AUTO-IRIS AND AGC

The range of light levels over which a colour TV camera is required to work is indicated in Table 6.2, and can range beyond 1:10,000 between candlelight and a bright sunlit outdoor scene. Since the practical contrast range overall of a TV system is seldom more than 30:1, and since we wish to see reasonably normal brightness and contrast levels in all circumstances of lighting, a very wide-ranging automatic video level compensator must be fitted to the camera. It takes two forms – auto-iris control; and a.g.c. by electrical feedback circuits. The multi-bladed iris is driven by a moving-coil armature rotating against a spiral hair-spring – similar to the arrangement of a moving-coil meter. Iris opening is proportional to coil current, a useful feature in that when the camera is off the iris is fully closed to prevent accidental damage to the pick-up sensor in the event of its being pointed towards a strong light. To supplement the video a.g.c. circuit, then, a current proportional to light level (hence luminance signal voltage) is fed into the iris coil, forming a control loop which maintains video output level at 1 V pk-pk. There is a trade-off in auto-iris operation: for best video-signal-to-noise ratio maximum lens opening is required to get as much light as possible to the target; for optical reasons within the lens system best depth of focus-field is achieved at small iris openings. For these and other reasons the more light in the scene the better, and a level of 2000 lux should be aimed at for good results. Such a level can be achieved indoors easily with the aid of one or two 1 kW quartz-halogen lamps. Cameras fitted with sensitive pick-up sensors can produce acceptable pictures from a scene whose illuminance is as low as 4 lux. For very low-light situations most cameras have a 'sensitivity-up' switch which overrides a.g.c. operation to increase gain (at the expense of definition and video noise level) under these circumstances.

Since the auto-iris and a.g.c. systems work on the *average* level of the luminance signal a problem arises where the mean level of the light in the whole scene is such as to compress wanted detail down to or below black-level, e.g. a person standing indoors between the camera and a window. To overcome this the auto-iris system can be inhibited by a BLC (Black-Light Control) switch, whereby detail in foreground subjects can be maintained, even though the surrounding highlight areas are washed-out by overload of the vidicon target, caused by inability of the beam to recharge the target.

HIGHLIGHT CHROMA CLIPPING

In the situation just described, and on strong highlights in an otherwise low-level picture without the BLC circuit operating, the image sensor can reach light-saturation point. When it does (Fig. 6.12) the colour carrier signal from the target disappears, and the R and B signals disappear with it. Since the G signal, as part of the

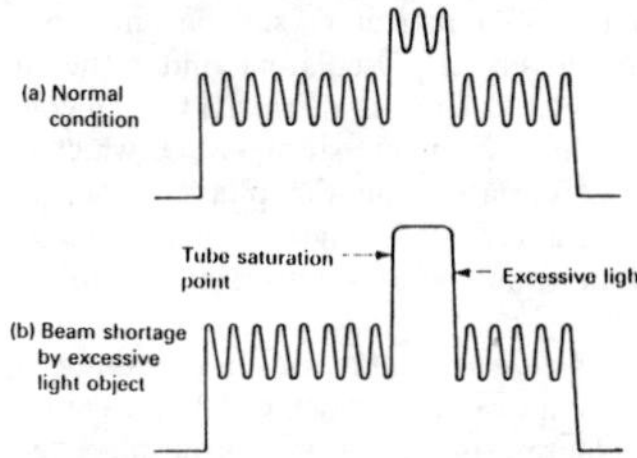

Fig. 6.12 *The effect of light-saturation in the target of a single colour-tube*

luminance component, is still present at high level the effect is to flood the saturated highlight areas with green, which is very objectionable to the viewer. Colourless highlight areas go virtually unnoticed, however, so the Y signal is monitored at a late stage in the luminance chain. When the 'flattened top' effect appears on the waveform a colour suppressor circuit comes into operation to effectively kill all colour, removing the bright green tint from the highlight areas. This function can be seen in the block between the subcarrier modulators and the Y–C adder in Fig. 6.11.

SSG AND TIMEBASE GENERATORS

The timing waveforms for use throughout the camera are generated in an LSI (Large Scale Integration) IC, with the fundamental clock pulses coming from a very stable quartz crystal reference, in most designs running at *f*sc × 4, which is 17.734 MHz. Use of a quadruple-frequency clock signal in conjunction with digital counters permits direct derivation of all required phases of subcarrier at 4.43 MHz; no recourse to drift-prone analogue (i.e. LC) phase-shift circuits is required. Further counting of *f*sc (set to exactly 4.433619 MHz by a trimming capacitor at the crystal) renders not only the line and field drive (sync) pulses at 15.625 kHz and 50 kHz respectively, but a half-line pulse at 7.8 kHz (ident) and the required blanking, clamping, gating and burst-flag pulses. A complex pulse train is required (Fig. 2.4) during the field sync interval, and a four-field-repeat sequence of burst phase and burst suppression during field blanking (*Bruch blanking*) is necessary to conform fully with the PAL specification. All these are generated within the SSG chip and distributed as required to all parts of the camera.

Genlock

Where the camera is required to operate with others in a 'studio' situation involving vision mixers or faders, the scan generators of all cameras involved must be synchronised so that their line and field scans are time-coincident. To ensure correct colour reproduction their colour subcarriers must also be locked together. Semi-professional (and a few 'consumer') camera types have facilities for this, in which the SSG master crystal becomes part of a VXO (Voltage-controlled crystal Oscillator) under the influence of a phase-lock-loop (PLL). This can be *slaved* to an incoming CVBS or burst-plus-syncs signal from an external SSG, which may be part of another camera. Variations in the phase response of electrical circuits, and in camera lead lengths usually necessitate a phase control preset at some point – it is trimmed to match the hue between cameras.

The advent of field-store memories in consumer equipment has opened the way to a form of genlock which does not depend on the SSGs of the cameras running in synchronism. The video output from one camera is digitised, one field at a time, then written into a large RAM (Random Access Memory). It is read out in accordance with the scan timings of the second camera to achieve the same result as true genlock. This system has the advantage of working with picture sources like VCRs and TV broadcasts.

SCAN DRIVE

The scan coils surrounding a vidicon tube operate at very low currents because the beam current is low and the deflection angle very small. At the 50 Hz field scan rate the vertical deflection coil may be regarded as purely resistive, and is fed with a true sawtooth current; feedback and correction artifices are employed to ensure very good linearity. The line scan coils equate to a pure inductance at 15.625 kHz horizontal frequency, and are 'switched' at line rate, their inductance performing most of the sawtooth-shaping function. In practice a very small line-scan transformer is used to couple the scan coil to the line output stage, but primarily as a convenient source of high voltage for the electrodes of the vidicon tube – the transformer forms part of a *d.c. to d.c. converter*. The techniques of field and line scan generator and flyback-conversion systems will be fully covered in Chapter 10. Suffice it here to say that the vidicon tube requires a grid potential of about −40 V, accelerating potentials of 350 V (A1 and A3) and 1.5 kV (mesh), and focusing potentials of 300 V and 750 V. All these are derived from rectifier/capacitor combinations on the line scan transformer – or a separate transformer (*converter transformer*) operating at line rate. Very little power is consumed since the electrode currents of the vidicon are minuscule.

Protection of the tube's target from burns caused by scan failure must be provided. It takes the form of a scan-current detector which cuts off the beam when necessary; where the line scan current and tube-operating voltages are both derived from the same transformer only field-scan protection is required.

CAMERA POWER SUPPLIES

A great deal of the design effort for a domestic TV camera is concerned with minimising its power consumption, since it is required to run (in conjunction with its videorecorder section) from a small rechargeable battery. In general the voltage requirement is 6V, 7.2 V or 9.6 V. Inside the machine, d.c–d.c. converters (see Chapter 11) furnish stabilised supply lines for the various electrical, control, and mechanical sections.

LENS ASSEMBLY AND AUTO-FOCUS

Normally the lens assembly on the front of the camera has two functions – zoom and focus. The zoom function is carried out by a complex assembly of individual lenses, moved along the axis of the barrel at different rates when the zoom lever is rotated. A small electric motor, driving through a clutch, is incorporated to zoom the lens through its range of typically 8:1.

Focusing is manually adjusted by a ring at the front of the barrel and ranges from infinity down to about 0.5 m. Many cameras have a *macro* facility available in a click-stop at one end of the zoom control, permitting focusing down to a few millimetres.

All domestic cameras have an auto-focus system in which the focus ring is driven by a small electric motor built into the lens barrel assembly. The motor and lens form part of a servo system, a closed-loop in which the image at picture centre is continually checked and adjusted for correct focus. Some use infra-red or ultrasonic beams to measure the distance between camera and subject. An advanced system of automatic focus is outlined in Fig. 6.13. The incoming light is split by a semi-transparent prism, and a small percentage is passed to an array of sensors which examine the centre portion of the picture. Twenty-four such sensors are present, each consisting of a micro-lens containing two CCD photodiodes. The information from these is analysed by a microprocessor which produces 'drive lens in' and 'drive lens out' commands to the focus ring drive motor depending on whether the focus plane is before or behind the subject. This technique, which *includes the subject in the servo loop* will work through closed windows and via mirrors. Not all scenes are amenable to auto-focusing; sometimes the main picture feature is not central in the frame, and sometimes a degree of defocusing of some or all of the televised scene is required for production or artistic effects. For these reasons, and to conserve battery power where applicable, the auto-focus facility can be switched off.

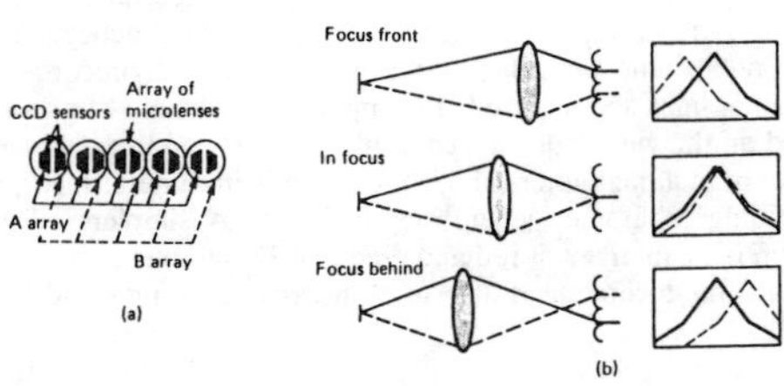

Fig. 6.13 *One form of auto-focus sensing: (a) sensor array; (b) principle of operation*

VIEWFINDERS

Some cameras employ an optical TTL (Through The Lens) viewfinder in which about 25% of the light from the incoming scene is deflected by a prism or mirror via relay lenses to a viewfinder lens.

This simple system has the disadvantages of wasting some of the available light; giving no indication to the operator of what is happening within the pick-up sensor or the camera's electronic circuits; offering less accurate focusing; and being unable to act as display device for instant review of recorded pictures. While a colour viewfinder tube would be ideal, it is difficult to manufacture in very small sizes with good resolution, is expensive and power-hungry; very small beam indexing (single-gun; RGB colour-switching from vertical stripe phosphor matrix) tubes have been developed for this purpose but colour VF displays are not yet common. Those which are offered have LCD display panels 2–5 cm diagonal, usually with magnifying eyepieces. Their definition is inferior to that of a monochrome picture tube of the same display size, and their colour rendering not as accurate as that of a conventional colour picture tube.

The norm, then, is a black-and-white viewfinder tube of about 2.5 cm diagonal mounted inside the upper section of the camera parallel to the image pick-up tube, or (more commonly) in a separate detachable EVF (Electronic ViewFinder) which clips to the camera body. The display tube is necessarily a low-energy device with small deflection angle. As in larger picture tubes, magnetic deflection and electrostatic focus systems are used. The VF tube is operated by what amounts to a complete monitor-circuit, including video amplifier and output stage; sync separator; timebases; and high-voltage supplies, the whole being miniaturised and designed to operate from its own 9 V or 10 V supply rail, derived from the camera's d.c. supply by an inbuilt stabiliser/regulator circuit. No external controls are needed, though brightness and contrast controls are provided as semi-accessible presets. This complete independence of the camera electronics is necessary to enable the viewfinder to perform its second role as video monitor for tape replay when the camera section is switched off. Although physically very small, the components and techniques of the EVF are just the same as are used in the TV receiver and monitor circuits to be described in following chapters. The basic connections required by the EVF in the camera-body mounted plug, then, are merely ground–supply voltage–video signal. In practice, various viewfinder indications for status of camera, videorecorder and incoming light are required. In some cameras, these are superimposed on the viewfinder *screen* display as dots and lines in black or white, or in alphanumerical form, especially in cameras incorporating titling (character-generation) facilities. A simpler indication system uses an array of red and green LEDs mounted near the VF screen; this technique is also used in cameras using optical viewfinders.

VIEWFINDER INDICATIONS

The status and warning indications relayed via the viewfinder vary with the cost and complexity of the camera. Three essential ones are incorporated in the basic camera of Fig. 6.11. These are (a) Iris Under, (low light) which comes on when incident light is so low that the auto-iris system has fully opened the lens and the risk of under-exposure is present; (b) Battery Warning, invoked when the battery is discharged to the point where the camera's internal voltage stabiliser has a small margin of operation: some designs flash an on-off LED indication when the battery is becoming discharged, and almost all will shut down (as will the partnering videorecorder) at a pre-determined point of battery exhaustion; (c) VTR start/stop indicator: this is associated with a trigger-switch mounted on the camera's body or handle which controls the pause function of the recorder.

With increasing camera sophistication and price more indications are provided in the viewfinder for the operator's guidance and information: auto-white balance complete, analogue exposure indicator, colour-temperature setting, etc.

CAMCORDERS

Camcorders combine the camera principles described in this chapter with the videorecorder systems described in Chapters 12–17 of this book, and use miniature deck assemblies and (often) small head drums. They use either low- or high-band formats (see Chapter 13) and small cassettes of the Video 8 or VHS-C type. Hi-Fi stereo sound, either in f.m. or pulse-code form, is also incorporated in some models.

The requirements of small size, light weight and minimum power consumption, together with competition between makers and formats for the best performance and greatest sophistication, has put camcorders in the forefront of electronic technology. Surface-mounted components, multilayer and flexible PCBs, LSI chips, advanced data-bus systems, and digital techniques are used in this equipment, together with tiny close-tolerance mechanical components. Reliability is good, due in part to the low power levels required and the absence of energy (heat)-dissipating components. The disadvantage is that dismantling is difficult, and access for diagnosis and repair is hampered by the tightly-packed compo-

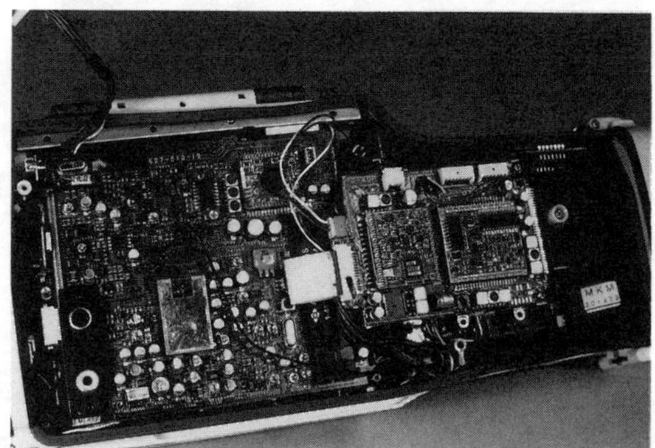

Fig. 6.14 *Tightly-packed electronics in portable equipment*

nents: special connecting-lead kits are needed to get the machine operational while dismantled. Servicing aspects will be more fully discussed in Chapter 20. Fig. 6.14 shows an internal view of a home-use camcorder.

7

TV signal processing

In TV receivers and monitors the final recipient of the video signal is the picture tube, be it a monochrome or colour type. The tube requires a modulating voltage between its grid and cathode; normally the grid is clamped at some fixed potential and the modulating signal applied to the cathode. In a monochrome system that signal will be the video waveform in *inverted* form – to produce white the cathode must be driven down towards grid potential. In a colour-tube the grid is common to all three beams (Chapter 5) and the cathodes are fed by RGB video signals, negative-going for white.

TUBE-DRIVE AMPLIFIERS

Large picture tubes require a peak to peak voltage drive approaching 100 V to produce a bright contrasted picture, small monochrome tubes 50–70 V. It is the job of the final video amplifier to provide this drive, and for full detail in the picture its frequency response should extend from d.c. to beyond 5 MHz. For data-monitors, and for sharp display of teletext and Prestel characters and graphics the video amplifier response must be better – to 10 MHz or more.

The stray capacitance of the video amplifier's load, represented by the tube cathode, base connections, transistor heat sink and associated wiring can exceed 10 pF, whose reactance at 5.5 MHz is 3 kΩ, and at 12 MHz is less than 1.5 kΩ. To avoid curtailment of h.f. response, then, the final video amplifier must have a very low output impedance to 'swamp' the capacitance of the load. Class A amplifiers have relatively high output impedance with practical values of collector load resistance and operating current, though they are used in domestic monochrome TVs and basic colour sets, where h.f. response is enhanced by the use of peaking coils in the collector circuit; and/or frequency-selective negative feedback by virtue of a suitable bypass capacitor across the emitter resistor. For more exacting requirements class AB video amplifiers are usually specified.

Fig. 7.1(a) shows the form of a commonly-used variant with two *npn* transistors. TR2 functions as a class A amplifier with R1 as collector load. When the transistor is being driven on (i.e. picture brightening) its low impedance to ground rapidly discharges stray capacitance C. For a picture transition towards black, however, TR2 c–e impedance rises, and stray C can only slowly charge via load R1, resulting in a blurred trailing edge on the picture feature. TR1 remedies the situation by conducting at this time via low-value resistor R2 to provide a shunt across R1 and a quick charge path for C. Fig. 7.1(b) gives a full circuit of one of the three primary-colour output stages in a commercial colour TV. TR208 forms an emitter-follower driver stage whose output is developed across R284. TR209 is the basic video amplifier with collector load consisting of the parallel combination R280 and TR210. The current flowing through this circuit remains fairly constant. HF signals are applied to TR210 base via C260. D204 and R258 provide bias for *pnp*

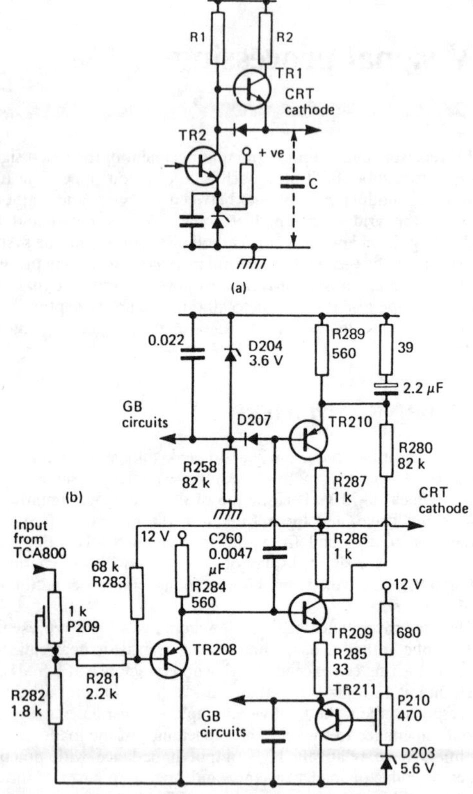

Fig. 7.1 *Examples of push-pull video output stages*

TR210, and D207 offers a degree of d.c. restoration. R289 and R285 equalise the current swings in the two transistors. R286 and R287 limit peak current, and hence power dissipation – and provide some protection in the event of short-circuits. The stage is stabilised by d.c. feedback via R283 to TR208 base, and the values of R281, 282 and 283 are chosen so that no current flows through P209 at black level.

The potentiometers P209 and 210 represent the difference between a video output stage in a good quality monochrome receiver or monitor, and one of the three matched RGB amplifiers driving the tube of a colour set. In the latter case it is necessary to equalise the light output of the three colour phosphors near black level by *background controls* – P210 and its equivalents in the other stages – which set the tube cathode voltages at black level; and also to provide separate contrast (*drive*) controls for each primary colour. These grey scale tracking controls are adjusted for true white (illuminant D) from the colour-tube display at all levels of video drive. The background controls are trimmed for neutral colours in the lowlights and then the drive controls (P209 in Fig. 7.1 and its equivalents) for true white in the highlight picture areas. Only when the grey-scale is correct will true colour reproduction be achieved. In sets incorporating auto-grey-scale tracking (see later, this chapter) the need for the background controls is removed.

CLAMPING AND BLANKING

In a monochrome monitor or TV the route from video input socket or detector to picture tube includes a low-level video amplifier as an interface between the source and the output stage. Here or at the output stage itself, two services are required. Because the response of the entire video path is unlikely to extend to d.c. and very low frequencies, the video signal must be *clamped*. At some known reference level in the waveform (i.e. back porch or line sync pulse tip) the signal is returned to a fixed voltage by a diode or transistor switch. DC restorers operate on a passive basis; *driven* clamps have better performance, using an electronic switch driven by a suitably-timed pulse from the line scan or sync separator stage of the set. Clamping ensures that picture black-level always coincides with the cut-off point of the picture tube, and remains stable with respect to time, temperature and picture content.

Blanking takes place at line and field scanning rate, and cuts off the video amplifier except when picture information is actually present. Thus spurious images from the flyback action of the scanning spot (during which burst, teletext and other signals are present) are suppressed.

What has been described so far in this chapter, and in Chapter 3, completes the signal processing arrangements for monochrome TV sets and monitors.

COLOUR DECODING

Most of the post-detector signal processing stages of a colour TV or monitor are concerned with recovering RGB video signals from the encoded CVBS signal coming from the receiver section, video-recorder or camera. The description which follows is based on the PAL system.

The CVBS signal is resolved into U and V colour difference signals by the first part of the decoder, illustrated in the block diagram of Fig. 7.2. The processes carried out here may be briefly summarised as follows:

1 Chroma amplifier with bandpass filtering based on 4.43 MHz to separate the chroma signal from the composite waveform and to provide initial amplification.
2 The output from the chrominance amplifier is fed to a *delay line and signal separating network* which separates the U and V signals by a process of adding and subtracting the direct (real-time) signals to and from those which have passed through the delay line. Here also is carried out the hue-averaging process between successive lines of chroma information.
3 The R–Y and B–Y outputs from the signal separation circuit are applied to synchronous demodulators which sample each at regular and short intervals according to the timing of their drive (reference) signals, derived from the *reference oscillator*. As there is a 90° phase difference between transmitted U and V signals the reference feeds to the synchronous demodulators are likewise in quadrature. In this

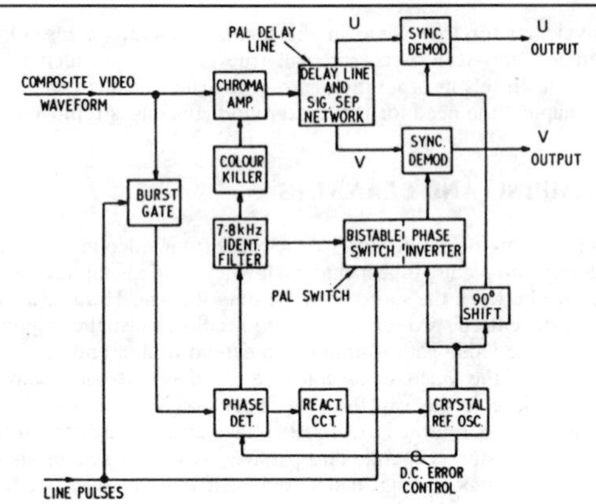

Fig. 7.2 *Simplified block diagram of a PAL decoder*

way the upper demodulator is made conductive only for U signals, and the lower only for V signals.

4 As the burst signal is required to synchronise the reference oscillator, a *burst gate* is needed to separate the colour burst from the rest of the chroma signal; this can be achieved by gating the stage with a pulse from the line timebase section so that it is switched on only during the back porch period when the burst signal is present.

5 As the subcarrier is suppressed at source it is necessary to provide a local oscillator as a source of reference carrier for the synchronous demodulators. This *reference oscillator* must operate at the same frequency and with the same phase relationship to the chroma signals as the subcarrier itself. For accuracy and stability a crystal oscillator is used; its phase – and its frequency within narrow limits – can be 'steered' by means of a phase detector and reactance control circuit.

6 The burst signal switches phase between ±45° on alternate lines, giving rise to a signal at 7.8 kHz (half line frequency) appearing as a 'ripple' at the output of the phase detector. This, the *ident signal*, is taken off by the 7.8 kHz acceptor filter and used to control the colour-killer and PAL switch phase-inverter circuits.

7 The colour killer circuit, controlled by the ident signal, operates to cut off the chroma signals during reception of monochrome pictures. This is necessary to prevent spurious signals (i.e. h.f. components of the luminance signal) and noise in the chroma circuits – whose gain in these circumstances will be at maximum under a.g.c. (a.c.c.) control – from generating cross-colour and confetti effects on the picture. When the ident signal disappears the colour killer shuts down the chroma amplifier.

8 Since the PAL system depends on phase reversal of the V chroma signal on alternate lines, it is necessary to incorporate a phase inverter (180° phase shift) controlled by a bistable switch which brings it into operation on alternate lines. The bistable switch is triggered by a pulse from the line oscillator, and is locked into the correct phase by the 7.8 kHz ident signal. The PAL switch may alternatively be incorporated in the V signal feed line, where it will have the same effect of restoring correct polarity to the V (hence R–Y, and finally R) chroma signal.

Many variations in decoder design are possible, as will be seen when IC decoders are investigated shortly.

Delay line and U/V separation

The line-by-line phase inversion of the V chroma signal in PAL-encoded transmissions was described in Chapter 6. The errors introduced by differential phase distortion in the signal path remain relatively constant so that they will have opposite effects according to which of the two V axes is in use for transmission. For instance if a blue area is being transmitted it may be shifted towards cyan during one line, but towards magenta on the succeeding line. If such a signal is displayed on a picture tube the human eye will tend to integrate and average out the opposing hues and see the correct blue hue. Large phase errors would give rise to a noticeable venetian blind effect, sometimes referred to as *Hanover bars*. The equal-and-opposite errors can be effectively cancelled out electronically by means of a one-line signal delay and associated matrixing circuits. Consider Fig. 7.3. Fig. 7.3(a) has a phasor A (solid line) transmitted on line n at 30°; phase distortion in the signal path causes it to be received as dotted phasor B at 40°. The same hue transmitted on line $n + 1$ now A′ at −30° with respect to the U axis, appears in Fig. 7.3(b) along with the phase-distorted resultant as a dotted line phasor B′ at −20°. After reversing diagram b's vector about its U axis, the two received signals B and B′ correspond to B and B″, (Fig. 7.3(c)) which when averaged give the correct hue A at 30°.

The essence of the decoder in a PAL receiver, then, is in the separation of the chroma signals modulated on the subcarrier, and in so processing them that the electrical average between each successive pair of lines is applied to the synchronous demodulators. It depends on the use of a delay line with which a one-line-old chroma signal can be made simultaneously available with a real-time signal. The delay line is made of glass; an input transducer converts the electrical subcarrier signal to an acoustic (mechanical) one, whence it is propagated relatively slowly through the body of the glass block in a zig-zag path, being reflected, snooker-ball style, whenever it encounters the glass wall. The path length is such that the transition time is exactly 63.943 μs ±3ns. At path-end the mechanical wave is reconverted to an electric one by a piezo microphone. The 63.943 μs delay time corresponds to 283½ cycles of reference subcarrier: the odd half-cycle is very important, ensuring that the emerging signal is in opposite phase to that of the undelayed (real-time) subcarrier signal. Since the U signal is always

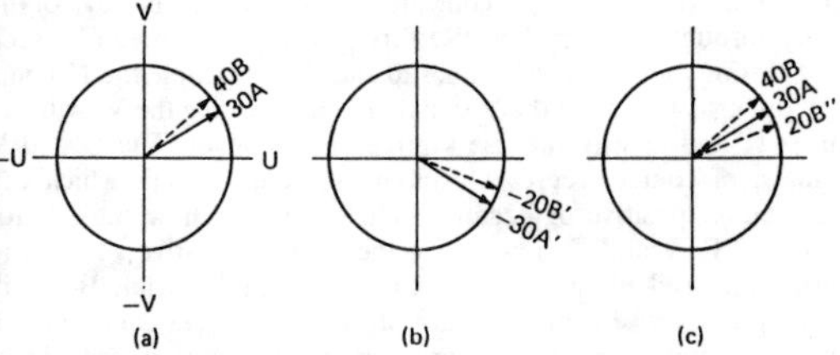

Fig. 7.3 *Principle of PAL automatic hue correction by two-line averaging*

transmitted in the same phase, addition of these direct and delayed signals (Fig. 7.4(a)) will cancel out U components altogether. V signals will be present however, because the phase reversal introduced during encoding will effectively cancel out the phase reversal due to the half-cycle offset at the delay line's output. The time-coincident V subcarrier cycles, then, will sit on each other's shoulders in the adder to render a pure 2 V output. Now consider the subtractor in Fig. 7.4(a). It receives the same two signals as the adder, but here the subtraction of each V subcarrier cycle from its identical and time-coincident fellow will render zero V output. Antiphase U cycles, however, when subtracted will reinforce each other to render 2U as sole output. An earlier chapter revealed a subtractor to be a combination of inverter and adder, and they are thus drawn in Fig. 7.4(b), making clearer the separation of the U signal. Since the chroma signals of two consecutive lines contribute to all U and V outputs the required averaging outlined in Fig. 7.3 is achieved simultaneously with the separation process.

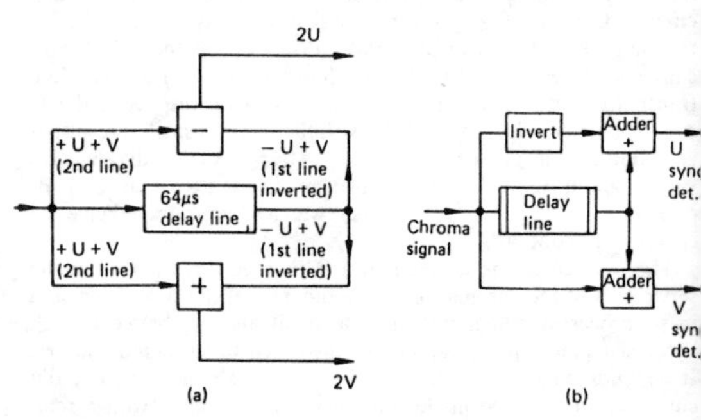

Fig. 7.4 *Delay line operation: (a) basic principle; (b) practical implementation*

Synchronous demodulation

Every NTSC or PAL decoder contains synchronous demodulators which are basically on-off switches, closed briefly once per subcarrier cycle by the reference waveform. The timing of the 'on' period is governed by the phasing of the local reference feed, which is locked in the required phase by the burst signal via a phase-locked-loop (PPL). Because the U and V subcarrier signals are in quadrature the peak of one coincides in time with the passage of the other through the zero line. Referring to Fig. 7.5, it can be seen that closing the U switch at times t0 and t2 will sample the U signal without crosstalk from the V signal, and that closing the V switch at times t1 and t3 will likewise sample only V level. The U and V signals, of course, represent colour-difference signals which can have either positive or negative values – on a yellow subject, for instance, R–Y and G–Y will take the form of positive voltages to turn on the red and green guns of the picture tube, while B–Y will take up a *negative* voltage to turn off the tube's blue gun. Study of Fig. 7.5 shows that the synchronous demodulator is capable of producing positive and negative outputs, and in practice each demodulator's output varies rapidly in terms of amplitude and polarity as the chroma subcarrier signal (there is only one in spite of

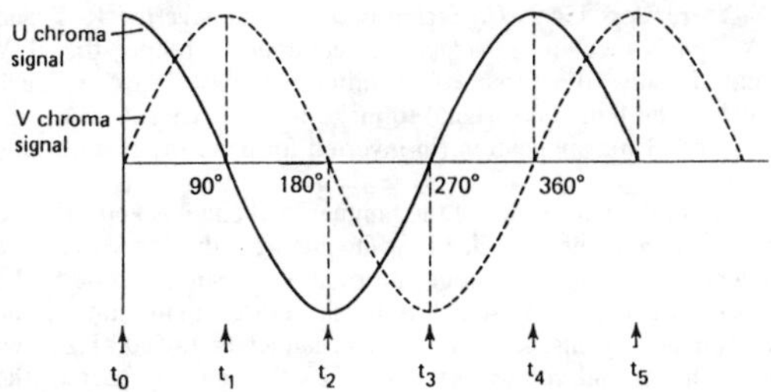

Fig. 7.5 *Principle of synchronous demodulation of signals in quadrature. Each carrier is modulated separately, and two demodulators — one synchronised with each carrier — sample the waves only at the times when one is at maximum and the other at null, thus separately recovering the two information streams. The solid-line (U) signal is sampled at times t0, t2, t4, and the broken-line waveform (V) at times t1, t3, t5*

the diagrams of Figs 7.4 and 7.5) changes its phase and amplitude to describe the hue and saturation of the picture elements in turn.

Crystal oscillator

A resonant crystal consists basically of a tiny slice of quartz mounted between metallic plates, and enclosed in a sealed envelope. Like a tuning fork the quartz slice has a mechanical resonant frequency; unlike the fork, it is barely affected by temperature variations, and behaves like an extremely high-Q tuned electrical circuit. While its stability is very good, it cannot by itself provide a reference signal of correct frequency *and phase*. Fortunately the resonant frequency of a suitable crystal can be slightly 'pulled' by capacitive loading; the use of a varicap diode for this purpose permits *voltage control* of oscillator frequency. This combination forms a voltage-controlled crystal oscillator (VXO) and is used in combination with a phase detector to make a much-used building block in electronic circuits – the phase-locked loop. Its principle was described in Chapter 3, and here the PLL is used to lock the local crystal to the mean phase of the transmitted burst signal. To prevent the local reference crystal trying to follow the swinging phase alternations of the PAL burst signal a suitably long time constant is present in the error voltage path.

G–Y and RGB matrixing

Before a G–Y signal can be made from the red and blue colour-difference signals the transmitted U and V chroma components must be de-weighted. It was explained in the last chapter that a reduction in amplitudes of R–Y and B–Y signals is made to prevent them from overdriving the transmission system. After passing through an amplifier with a gain of 1.14 the V signal is 'normalised' to R–Y. Similarly, B–Y appears at the output of a ×2.03 amplifier fed from the U signal.

Recovery of the G–Y signal depends on the basic equation given earlier: Y = 0.59G + 0.3R + 0.11B. In fact, G–Y can be directly derived from R–Y and B–Y. Adding 0.508 of (–R–Y) to 0.186 of

(–B–Y) renders G–Y. Correct proportions of *inverted* R–Y and B–Y signals meet in an adder and combine to render the G–Y signal. Finally, the three colour-difference waveforms are each added to the luminance signal to make the primary-colour signals R, G and B for application (in inverted form) to the picture-tube cathodes.

Because the bandwidth of the luminance channel is kept wide to ensure that a detailed black and white picture is displayed as a base on which the coarser colour information is superimposed, the transit time of the Y signal is much shorter than that of the chrominance signals, constrained in a channel about 500 kHz wide. When the Y and colour-difference signals come together in the RGB matrix this would result in them being out of step to cause misregistration on the screen. To prevent this a short delay line (*t* about 500ns) is provided in the low-level luminance path. The glass delay line described previously is not suitable for a wideband signal; the type used here has series inductance and parallel capacitance distributed along it, and takes the form of a low-inductance coil wound over a grounded foil. Alternatively, a bucket-brigade device (of the type described in connection with CCD image sensors in the previous chapter) is used, with its advantages of small size and IC construction.

Subcarrier trap

On highly saturated colours a large amplitude subcarrier signal is present and appears on the screen as a fine dot-pattern. Although the pattern itself is barely distinguishable at normal viewing distances the non-linearity (gamma) of the tube will have the effect of partially 'rectifying' this subcarrier signal, artificially brightening up highly coloured parts of the picture. A notch filter, sharply tuned to 4.43 MHz, forms a trap in the luminance signal path; in some decoder designs provision is made to switch off this trap during reception of monochrome transmissions, thus realising the full definition capability of the shadow-mask tube. The trap-switching is carried out by the colour-killer line.

BRIGHTNESS, CONTRAST AND COLOUR CONTROL

Provided that the black areas of the picture can be made to drive the picture-tube *just* to beam cut-off (and this can be achieved automatically, see later), and if viewing were always in low or zero ambient light, the only picture control necessary would be a contrast control, with a link to the colour (saturation) control line. Because viewing conditions vary greatly, as do viewers' tastes, all three controls are generally provided, though often relegated to semi-accessible presets. For brightness control, the d.c. level on which the entire picture sits is raised and lowered, generally by altering the pedestal clamp reference voltage. For control of contrast the gain of the Y-signal amplifier must be varied while maintaining correct black-level; because any adjustment of contrast requires a proportional adjustment of colour level, the user contrast control will generally influence the chroma gain by means of an electrical 'tracking link' between the two. Colour level (user control) and colour/contrast tracking are carried out by varying the gain of the chrominance amplifier.

There are several internal influences on these analogue control lines. Excessive beam current in the picture tube is detected by a sensing circuit which pulls down brightness, contrast or both to prevent excessive dissipation in the picture-tube's shadowmask. Some sets have ambient light sensors to adjust contrast to suit the viewing conditions. As an internal loop in the decoder, an a.c.c. (automatic colour control) circuit monitors the amplitude of the burst signal and adjusts chroma gain accordingly; this maintains correct saturation level in the face of chroma signal amplitude variations due to propagation conditions, mistuning, etc.

SINGLE-CHIP DECODER

The low-level signal processing stages in a colour decoder are ideally suited to IC technology. Early decoders used a single IC for synchronous demodulation and colour matrixing, with discrete reference and chroma-amplifier sections. Next came 3- and 4-IC decoders; as chip fabrication techniques improved, single-chip decoders became commonplace. An internal diagram of a typical one is illustrated in Fig. 7.6.

The luminance signal is applied at pin 8, having passed through the delay line and subcarrier trap. The input coupling capacitor also serves as reservoir for the black level clamping carried out within the chip. Luminance black level is referred to an internally-generated voltage pulse. Thus conditioned, the Y signal passes on to the R, G and B primary-colour matrices.

The chroma-separating bandpass filter feeds 4.43 MHz chroma signal and burst to IC pin 4. The first function within the chip is a.c.c., whereby chroma signal amplitude is regulated according to received burst level as seen by the peak detector – the control potential reservoir is the capacitor at IC pin 3. Regulated chroma signal now enters a voltage-controlled attenuator to come under the influence of the d.c. voltage coming in to pin 5 from the user control – this may be cabinet-mounted or part of a cordless remote control. The effect of the saturation control is removed once per TV line – for the duration of the burst signal. Thus the amplitude of the burst is unaffected by the setting of the colour control, and it travels, along with whatever level of chroma signal has been set, through the chrominance amplifier and buffer stages and out of the chip on pin 28 for application to the external glass delay line and matrix circuit. Separated and averaged U and V signals re-enter the chip on pins 22 and 23 respectively, for passage to the de-weighting circuits and synchronous demodulators. Once demodulated, the B–Y and R–Y signals take two paths – to the G–Y matrix and to the primary-colour matrices, where each colour-difference signal is recombined with the luminance signal to make R, G and B signals for onward progress towards the picture tube.

Because the burst signal has a ±90° phase shift, it does not get 'averaged' in the delay line matrix. It is input to the phase-locked-loop for subcarrier regeneration and services the entire 'reference' circuitry in the lower left-hand section of the chip diagram. It first encounters the burst gate where signal chroma is eliminated.

The subcarrier oscillator in this circuit runs at twice subcarrier frequency, 8.867238 MHz. Its frequency is divided by two and 90° phase shifted on its way to a phase detector wherein it is compared with incoming burst: the RC network between pins 24 and 25 form a low-pass filter whose long time-constant keeps the PLL steady at mean burst phase. Thus is the loop completed, with the advantage that the $2 \times f\text{sc}$ locked oscillator can render, via ÷2 circuits, correctly phased quadrature reference feeds to the two

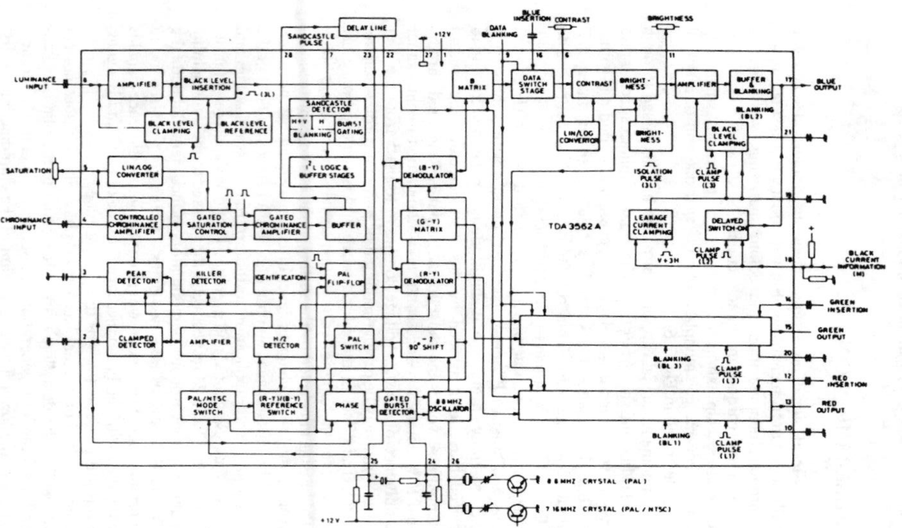
DELAY LINE
SANDCASTLE PULSE
+12V
DATA BLANKING
BLUE INSERTION
CONTRAST
BRIGHTNESS
LUMINANCE INPUT
AMPLIFIER
BLACK LEVEL INSERTION
(3L)
BLACK LEVEL CLAMPING
BLACK LEVEL REFERENCE
SANDCASTLE DETECTOR
H+V
H
BURST GATING
BLANKING
I²L LOGIC & BUFFER STAGES
B MATRIX
DATA SWITCH STAGE
CONTRAST
BRIGHT-NESS
AMPLIFIER
BUFFER & BLANKING
BLUE OUTPUT
BLANKING (BL2)
LIN/LOG CONVERTOR
BRIGHT-NESS
BLACK LEVEL CLAMPING
ISOLATION PULSE (3L)
CLAMP PULSE (L3)
SATURATION
LIN/LOG CONVERTER
(B-Y) DEMODULATOR
CHROMINANCE INPUT
CONTROLLED CHROMINANCE AMPLIFIER
GATED SATURATION CONTROL
GATED CHROMINANCE AMPLIFIER
BUFFER
(G-Y) MATRIX
TDA 3562 A
LEAKAGE CURRENT CLAMPING
DELAYED SWITCH-ON
V+3H
CLAMP PULSE (L2)
BLACK CURRENT INFORMATION (M)
PEAK DETECTOR
KILLER DETECTOR
IDENTIFICATION
PAL FLIP-FLOP
(R-Y) DEMODULATOR
GREEN INSERTION
GREEN OUTPUT
CLAMPED DETECTOR
AMPLIFIER
H/2 DETECTOR
PAL SWITCH
-2 90° SHIFT
BLANKING (BL 3)
CLAMP PULSE (L3)
RED INSERTION
PAL/NTSC MODE SWITCH
(R-Y)/(B-Y) REFERENCE SWITCH
PHASE
GATED BURST DETECTOR
8.8MHZ OSCILLATOR
RED OUTPUT
BLANKING (BL1)
CLAMP PULSE (L1)
8.8MHZ CRYSTAL (PAL)
7.16MHZ CRYSTAL (PAL/NTSC)
+12V

demodulators. En route to the V (R-Y) demodulator the reference feed is inverted on a line-by-line basis by the PAL switch, driven in turn by a bistable flip-flop circuit.

The flip-flop acts as a ÷2 stage on line-rate trigger pulses, but must be steered by an ident detector to ensure that the PAL switch phase is correct. Ident monitoring is carried out in the H/2 detector, which compares V *signal* polarity with V demodulator drive phase. When the two disagree a reset pulse is passed to the ident stage, thence to the flip-flop. The latter misses one beat, thus 'phasing up' to the incoming PAL signal. Once PAL ident has been corrected, the colour killer block opens the synchronous demodulators permitting colour to reach the screen.

A second function of the H/2 detector is that of a.c.c. control element. Its output is proportional to burst amplitude and is turned into a control voltage by a peak detector for application to the controlled chroma amplifier. This loop maintains constant burst amplitude, hence correct saturation level in the picture.

The crystals and transistors at the bottom of the diagram indicate the dual-standard capabilities of this IC. A switching voltage introduced at pin 25 will put the chip into NTSC mode, with PAL switch disabled, time-constant removed from the PLL error voltage line, and 3.58 MHz or 4.43 MHz reference selected by turning on the appropriate crystal-switching transistor. The necessary tint control is switched in across pins 24 and 25.

From the Y matrices the RGB signals (only B shown in full detail in Fig.7.6) each enter a data switch. At a command from pin 9 this changes state, passing to the output stages locally-generated RGB signals applied to pins 12, 14 and 16; they may typically come from an inbuilt teletext decoder or from a personal computer via a rear-mounted multipin plug/socket. These signals come under the influence of the contrast and brightness control stages next downstream in each channel. According to the d.c. voltages presented on pins 6 and 11 of the chip, these adjust the gain and d.c. operating points of all three RGB channels in parallel. These stages are necessarily perfectly matched by virtue of their simultaneous fabrication on a single silicon substrate. The controlled signals now pass through a clamping amplifier, blanker and buffer stage before passing out of the chip on pins 13(R) 15(G) and 17(B) to the high-level tube drive amplifier stage described at the beginning of this chapter.

The penultimate clamping amplifier has the special function of automatically setting up the black levels for each colour according to the gun cut-off characteristic of the picture tube in use. During the field blanking interval each gun of the tube in turn is driven just to cut-off point by a specially shaped and timed pulse from the IC. The measured cathode current is fed back into the IC on its pin 18 (black current information input); three pulses are received in quick succession, one for each gun, and are directed to the appropriate clamps in the IC. The measured currents are in each case converted to a clamp reference voltage, stored for R, G and B on the capacitors at pins 10, 20 and 19 respectively. By this means the three colours on the screen are made to cut off at exactly the same point on the reproduced grey-scale, regardless of ageing or manufacturing tolerances in the tube, and with no need for manual adjustment. The less commonly required (and less noticeable on viewing) need for drive adjustment to neutralise highlight tinting must still be provided – and made when gun emission or phosphor efficiency drops.

All control pulses for blanking, keying, clamping and gating enter the IC on pin 7. The waveform here is a 'sandcastle' shape, whose lower level contains line and field-rate blanking pulses, and whose upper level contains a short line-rate pulse coinciding with the period of the colour burst. It is sorted out by level detectors within the IC, and generated by the horizontal sync processing chip in the set's timebase section.

SECAM AND TRANSCODING

An alternative method of colour encoding, used in France, USSR and elsewhere, involves a similar subcarrier system to NTSC and PAL, but here the colour-difference signals *frequency-modulate* the subcarrier whose centre frequency is 4.437 MHz. The R–Y and B–Y signals are sent sequentially, i.e. R–Y on line n and B–Y on line $n + 1$ etc. To identify which chroma line is which, special ident signals are transmitted during the field blanking period (original system: France, USSR, Luxembourg) or the line blanking period (Albania and the Middle East).

To decode SECAM signals the chrominance subcarrier is filtered out in a tuned trap centred on 4.437 MHz, then applied to a *re-shaping* ('bell') filter (see Fig. 7.7) to compensate for the characteristic of an opposite-law filter introduced at the transmitter – their object is to improve chrominance S/N ratio. A pre-emphasis system is also used to the same end. The SECAM chroma signal now takes two paths – one direct and one via a one-line (64 μs) delay system. For any given TV line, then, both R–Y and B–Y signals will be available: one at the delay line output and one via the direct path. The double-pole, double-throw switch S1 is toggled at half-line rate (7.8 kHz) and steered by the SECAM-ident signal.

The now continuous R–Y and B–Y f.m. signals next pass through separate limiters on their way to f.m. demodulators, whose base-band output signals are then de-emphasised in the final noise reduction process. As for NTSC and PAL colour-difference signals, they are now de-weighted and matrixed with the (delayed) Y signal to make up R, G and B signals for driving the display tube.

The advent of multi-standard TV sets and videorecorders for direct reception of terrestrial SECAM transmitters, and particularly for use with satellite broadcasts, has brought with it the need for SECAM signal handling even in countries whose own broadcast system is otherwise. Although videorecorders do not decode the chroma signal, their colour-under circuits vary with the encoding system in use, and in the particular case of Video-8 format

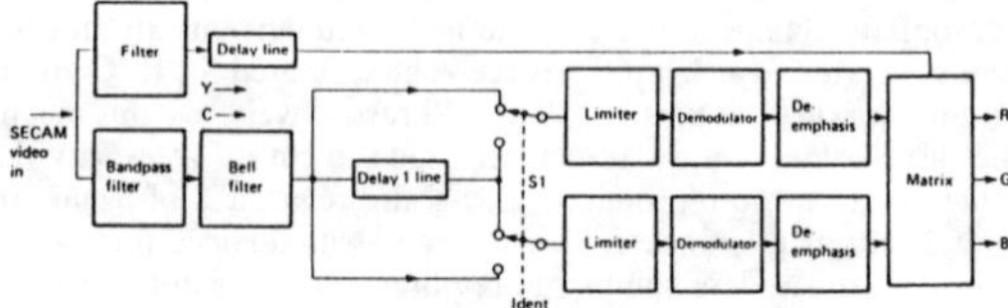

Fig. 7.7 *Principle of SECAM decoder — the ident signal is derived from the broadcast signal once per field (SECAM V) or once per line (SECAM H)*

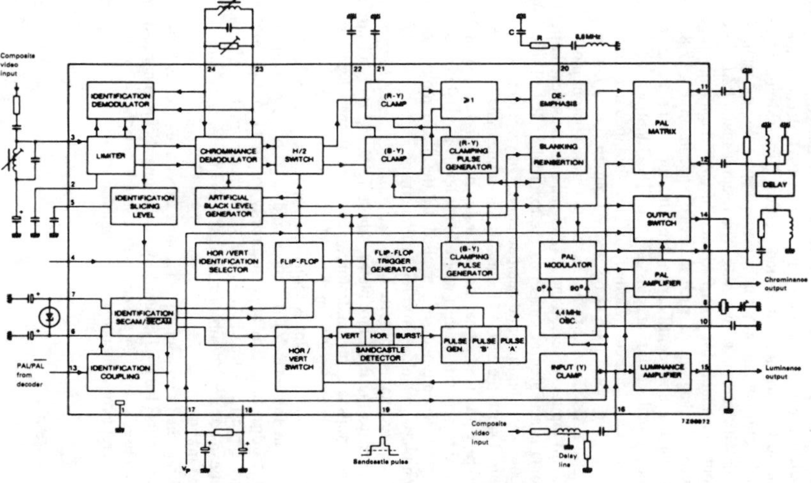

Fig. 7.8 *SECAM–PAL transcoder chip*

machines, SECAM signals have to be transcoded to PAL before commitment to the tape, and recoded to SECAM during playback.

Two approaches to the problem are possible in a colour decoder for use in a TV set or monitor. An early one was to use a dual-standard decoder in which the signal routing is switched between two ICs, the R-Y and B-Y outputs from the SECAM decoder entering the RGB matrix stages at the 'back-end' of the PAL-processing chip. Role-switching of the chrominance delay line is also necessary in this configuration, making fast automatic switching between colour standards difficult to arrange.

For use with videorecorder systems, and in multistandard TV sets and monitors the requirement is for a *transcoder* system to convert SECAM signals into PAL specification. Types are available which can be used with all types of PAL decoder, automatically adapt to horizontal and vertical SECAM identification signals, and contain a 'straight-through' path for incoming PAL signals with automatic switching. The result is that a PAL-encoded output is available for both PAL and SECAM input signals.

A block diagram of such a device appears in Fig. 7.8. The chrominance and identification demodulators share the same reference tuned circuit at pins 23, 24. The identification circuit automatically detects whether or not the incoming signal is SECAM – if not a path is opened via pin 16 (delay line here to equalise PAL/SECAM transit times) to chroma output pin 14. If a SECAM input is detected the PAL signal path is switched off, and chroma is accepted at pin 3 (via the external LCR bell filter) for amplification, limiting and demodulation. Only one demodulator is required since the SECAM signal is line-sequential. The demodulated B–Y and R–Y signals are separated by a 7.8 kHz switch, then applied to separate clamps where black levels are stabilised. They are then recombined and applied to the PAL modulator via de-emphasis, blanking and reinsertion circuits.

A burst signal is reinserted into the combined SECAM signal at the input to the PAL modulator, whose R–Y and B–Y subcarrier input signals are in quadrature, and come from a local crystal oscillator. The output from the PAL modulator leaves the chip on pin 9, and at this point is sequentially modulated with R–Y burst phased in the +(R–Y) direction; and B–Y burst phased in the –(B–Y) direction. It is applied directly to pin 11 and via a 64 μs delay to pin 12. A true PAL signal is constructed in the PAL matrix by means of an add/subtract process using the delayed and undelayed inputs.

While the transcoder system is more expensive in terms of special components (1 crystal, 1 luminance delay line, 1 chrominance delay line) it uses a single 24-pin chip with a simple peripheral circuit, and offers great convenience and versatility in use.

8

Teletext and viewdata

As suggested in Chapter 2 there are several 'free' TV lines in the field blanking interval of the broadcast vision signal. For many years these have been used to carry VITS (Vertical Interval Test Signals) in the form of pulse-and-bar and chroma signals: they are used for engineering tests on transmission lines and r.f. links. Other TV lines are used to convey data in the form of alphanumeric characters and graphics in coded form. A suitably-equipped receiver can display pages of text and graphics, either alone or superimposed on the broadcast picture. Regularly-updated magazine items such as news, travel information and share prices are transmitted, along with programme schedules, simple games, and on the commercial channels, advertisements. An invaluable service to deaf viewers is the transmission of subtitles for superimposition on the picture.

The BBC and ITV have each developed their own teletext systems which are now standardised, but retain their own individual names: Oracle for the ITV, and Ceefax for BBC 1 and BBC 2. It is possible to transmit many hundreds of pages of information on each of the four networks. LSI IC techniques and the economies of scale that result from mass-production permit the complex data decoding function to be added quite cheaply to the basic receiver, at the time of manufacture or afterwards. The decoded data consists of 'printing instructions' for a *character generator* whose RGB outputs are fed to the three tube-drive amplifiers via a data-switch like that shown in the TDA3562A IC of Fig. 7.6. Each primary colour output from the decoder has only two states – on or off – but permutations of these offer white, black, the three primaries red, green and blue, and their complementary colours cyan, magenta and yellow.

PRINCIPLES

The teletext specification allows for the use of 16 lines per field for data transmission. The more lines used, the more information can be sent, and/or the shorter the access time for the viewer.

Each page of teletext contains up to 24 rows of text, each having up to 40 alphanumeric characters. The active part of the line scan is divided up into 45 equal portions each containing a pattern of eight pulses. The first five portions contain synchronising signals for the decoder; the remaining 40 designate the symbols making one line of text (Fig. 8.1). To minimise the bandwidth required, the widely used NRZ (Non-Return to Zero) system is adopted, whereby the signal voltage during a logic 1 bit period is high (66% of white level) and during logic 0 it is low at black level. The bit rate of the data is 444 times line frequency: 6.9375 MHz.

The viewer can key-in the page number required on a remote control handset. In order to enable the decoder to locate a requested page, an identification code is broadcast on the top or *header row* of the page being sent. Unlike the other rows, this contains only 32 displayed characters, the first eight character code groups being used for page number and control codes. Since each

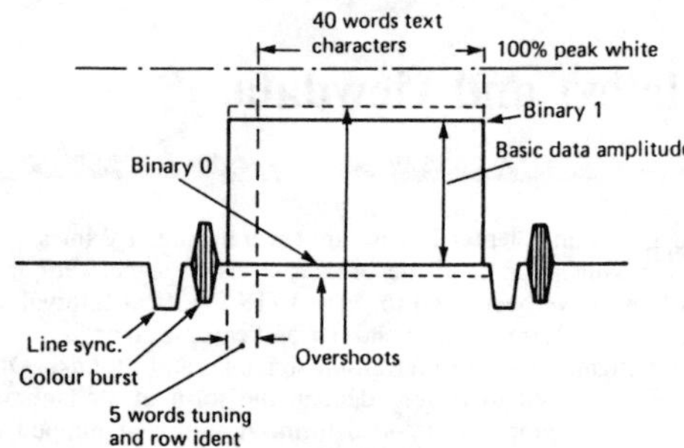

Fig. 8.1 *Data levels in the text signal. '1' is transmitted at 66% of peak white level*

transmitted line of data containing the 40 characters (32 for header rows) is transmitted in sequence, it takes about 0.06 s to broadcast each page. The whole sequence of pages is recycled at regular intervals on a 'rotating' basis.

For correct operation of the text decoder its internal clock must be locked to received bit-rate at 6.9375 MHz. At the beginning of each line the first two words are used to provide a clock 'run-in' for synchronisation purposes – not unlike the way in which the colour burst synchronises the reference oscillator in a chroma decoder. Once the clock has been synchronised the start of the data word must be located. Thus the next piece of data needed is the *framing code* which corresponds to 11100100 (Fig. 8.2) without which the decoder cannot locate the start of a line of text. The framing code is chosen so that even if (due to interference or other corruption) one bit were missing, this line of text could still be detected. Normally a *shift register*, a sort of electronic queue, is used for framing code identification. As each new bit arrives it pushes its predecessor one place forward in the register, which has a capacity of eight bits. When all eight have been received the first bit arrives at the output, when the entire framing code should be present in the register. The next data word starts to enter the register, and it is possible that sometimes the bits used in this may match the framing code. During the first eight clock cycles a maximum of five bits should match the prescribed framing code. On the ninth and subsequent clock periods, provided the shift register contains at least six matching bits, the code can be detected.

Each pair of bits is examined and if they match the code the condition is termed true; if one or more is incorrect it is termed error.

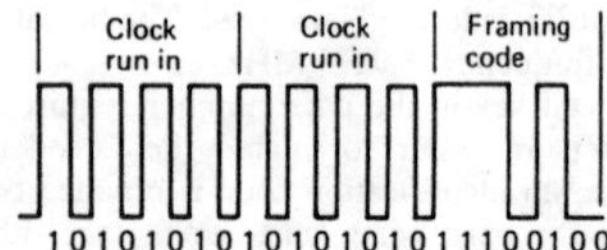

Fig. 8.2 *Clock run-in and framing code sequence*

Page memory

Th heart of the decoder is the memory unit in which the selected page is stored to be read out as the screen display. It consists of a RAM (Random Access Memory), a large array of cells, rather like bistables, which can have two states and can be set to be either high or low, corresponding to 0 and 1. This unit typically has about 7000 cells.

Character generator

The desired page of data must be converted into a display of rows of characters. These are produced by generating a pattern of dots in each character space on the screen. Another memory system is used, called ROM (Read-Only Memory). During manufacture this is pre-programmed with the required picture-element information for a whole range of alphanumerical characters as well as 'building-blocks' for graphics displays like maps and diagrams. Each of these has its own input code, the key to which is given in Fig. 8.3. As shown there, data is transmitted not only for the characters, but also for characteristics like colour, boxed, flashing, concealed and

BITS b_7 b_6 b_5				0 0 0	0 0 1	0 1 0		0 1 1		1 0 0	1 0 1	1 1 0		1 1 1	
				CONTROL											
b_4	b_3	b_2	b_1	0	1	2	2a	3	3a	4	5	6	6a	7	7a
0	0	0	0	NUL	DLE			0		@	P	—		p	
0	0	0	1	Alpha[n] Red	Graphics Red	!		1		A	Q	a		q	
0	0	1	0	Alpha[n] Green	Graphics Green	"		2		B	R	b		r	
0	0	1	1	Alpha[n] Yellow	Graphics Yellow	£		3		C	S	c		s	
0	1	0	0	Alpha[n] Blue	Graphics Blue	$		4		D	T	d		t	
0	1	0	1	Alpha[n] Magenta	Graphics Magenta	%		5		E	U	e		u	
0	1	1	0	Alpha[n] Cyan	Graphics Cyan	&		6		F	V	f		v	
0	1	1	1	Alpha[n] White	Graphics White	'		7		G	W	g		w	
1	0	0	0	Flash	Conceal Display	(		8		H	X	h		x	
1	0	0	1	Steady	Contiguous Graphics	)		9		I	Y	i		y	
1	0	1	0	End Box	Separate Graphics	•		:		J	Z	j		z	
1	0	1	1	Start Box	ESC	+		;		K	←	k		¼	
1	1	0	0	Normal Height	Black Background	,		<		L	½	l		‖	
1	1	0	1	Double Height	New Background	–		=		M	→	m		¾	
1	1	1	0	S0	Hold Graphics	.		>		N	↑	n		–	
1	1	1	1	S1	Release Graphics	/		?		O	#	o		■	

Fig. 8.3 *ASCII code as used in videotext digital transmission*

double height. Fig. 8.4 shows the formation of the letter A in a 5 × 7 dot matrix. To avoid the 'coarseness' at the top of this and similar letters character generator chips incorporate *character rounding*, in which half-elements are added in the corners and angles to give a smoother outline.

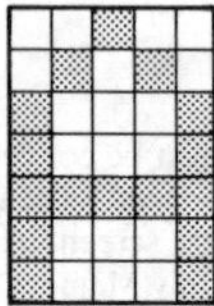

Fig. 8.4 *Character format on screen*

Data corruption

Very short term reflections in the path of the received broadcast picture due to ringing and ghosting may not noticeably affect reproduction of ordinary pictures, but can severely upset teletext reproduction. The standard of receiver alignment, accuracy of tuning and integrity of the aerial and its feeder becomes important if error-free displays are to be consistently reproduced. Since teletext uses a digital mode, the strength and S/N ratio of the signal is less important than for analogue applications – perfect text is receivable down to r.f. input levels of 200 μV, when TV pictures have deteriorated to an almost unwatchable point of snow and grain.

Within the active line period depicted in Figs 8.1 and 8.2, the actual waveform shape is rounded and not a true square wave at all. Having passed through the various transmission links and the receiver, some of the data at the input to the decoder will be below the specified 66% of peak white. Within the constraints of the transmission system, the ideal representation of a pulse train is as shown in Fig. 8.5. By taking two complementary test lines, i.e. one carrying 0101001 and the other 1010110, and displaying them on an oscilloscope, either superimposed or as a Lissajous figure with 'scope X' deflection operating from the teletext reference clock, the degree of distortion present can be directly viewed. The shape of the waveform produced is rather like an eye with a continuously moving thick outline. The upper ellipse represents all the '1' signals and the lower ellipse all the '0' signals. The distance between them is termed eyeheight, and the clear area therein (between the lowest '1' and the highest '0') is termed 'worst eyeheight' and represents the margin within which the decoder must differentiate between logic levels 0 and 1 in the received signal.

Fig. 8.5 *Theoretically ideal rounded text data waveform*

TELETEXT DECODER

Fig. 8.6 shows the essentials of a teletext decoder, and Fig. 8.7 a practical decoder by Mullard, based on purpose-designed LSI chips. The video input processor (VIP) consists of a data retrieval gate and a display clock generator. Fig. 8.8 is a block diagram of the SAA5030 VIP IC. A data slicer sets the level (half peak eyeheight) at which the decision between 0 and 1 is made. Some measure of immunity to noise and interference is thus accomplished. A clock signal is regenerated from the incoming data at 6.9375 MHz by the external tuned circuit L1/C1.

A quartz crystal is the reference for a 6 MHz display clock generator within the chip; this is passed to IC3 (SAA5020) for division to give one clock pulse every 64 μs. This re-enters the VIP for comparison with the incoming 64 μs line sync signals in a PLL which locks the text timing system to the transmission. A 'corruption detector' unlocks the loop and permits the crystal to free run in the event of existing data being displayed during transmission breaks or after closedown – it also prevents noise from interfering with data already held.

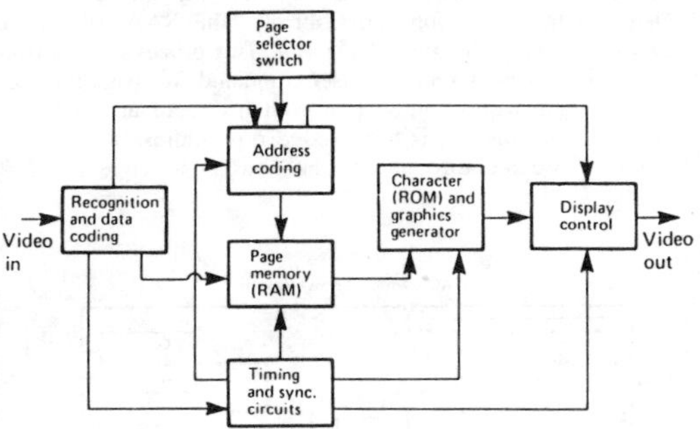

Fig. 8.6 *Teletext decoder block diagram*

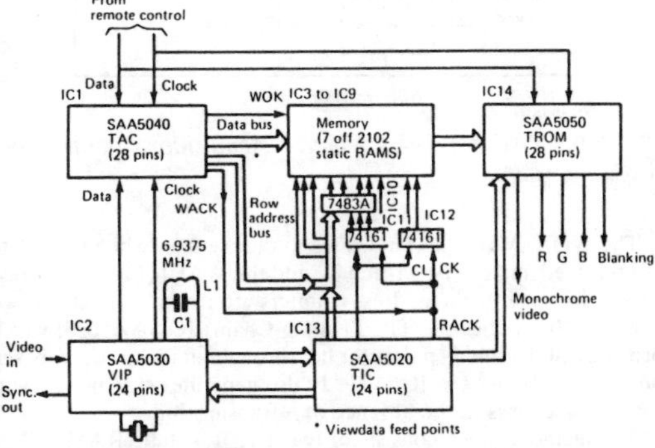

Fig. 8.7 *IC configuration for LSI text decoder*

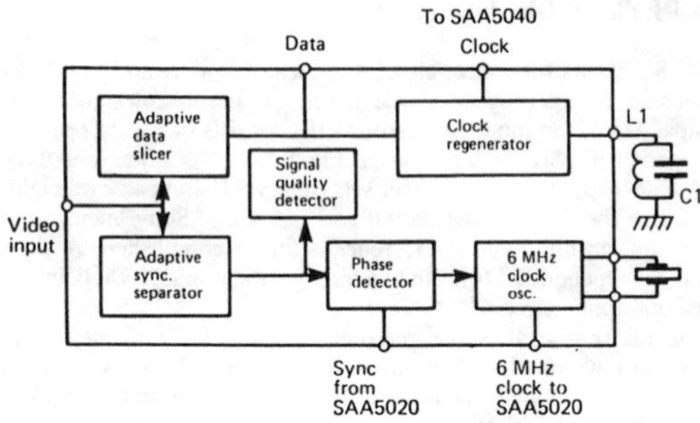

Fig. 8.8 *Video input processor SAA5030*

The adaptive sync separator extracts sync from the video information for the receiver timebases, although when displaying a 'solo' teletext page the sync pulses are derived from IC3.

Clock and data pulses are fed from the VIP into IC2, TAC (Teletext data Acquisition and Control). This SAA5040 chip is shown in the block diagram of Fig. 8.9. This processes data from the remote control system, i.e. user commands re. page no. etc., whilst its data acquisition section contains the Hamming code circuitry whose function is to reject corrupt address words. Character data are fed through the data bus as a sequence of 40 seven-bit words.

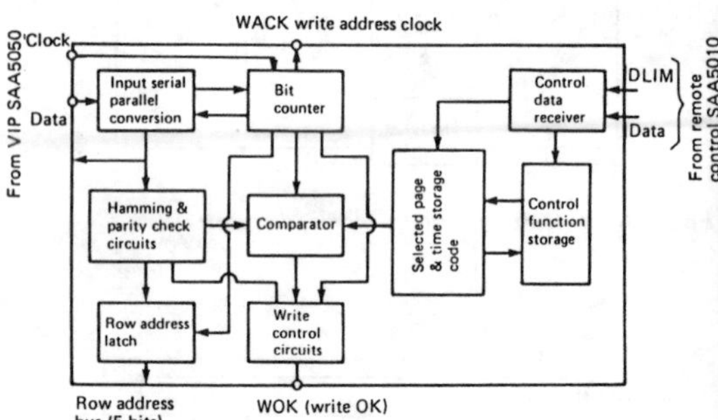

Fig. 8.9 *TAC – Teletext data Acquisition and Control – SAA540*

The WOK (Write OK) indicates to the memory when valid data are received and can be written in, and the WACK (Write Address Clock) increments the address counters after each character.

Fig. 8.10 outlines the TIC (Timing Chain) IC SAA5020, which provides all the timing pulses for use throughout the decoder, based on the 6 MHz clock in IC1 VIP. It also generates sync pulse trains for the timebases in the absence of a transmission.

The memory block consists of two 1 K × 4 static RAMs. They are arranged as four 32 by 32 matrices with each storage location

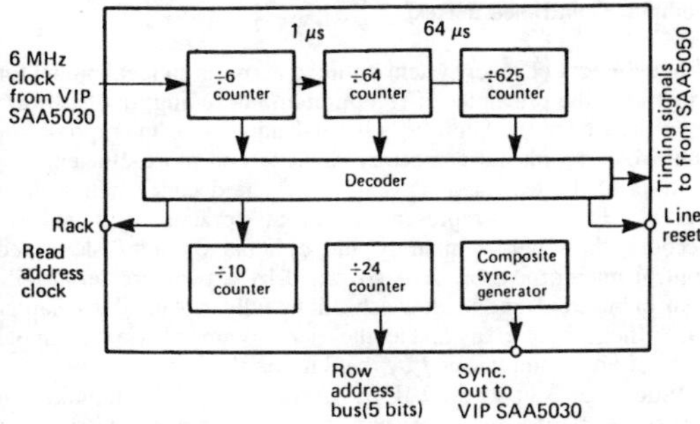

Fig. 8.10 *TIC – Timing Chain IC type SAA5020*

being selected by means of a binary code on 10 address lines. The teletext display is set up as a 40 × 24 matrix (24 rows of 40 characters) with a five-bit row and six-bit column address. A 74LS83A adder converts the eleven bits of display address into a 10-bit address code for the selection of one of the 960 locations in the RAMs. Fig. 8.11 shows the SAA5050 TROM (Teletext Read Only Memory) character generator IC which converts the seven-bit character data into a dot-matrix pattern in a 7 × 5 format. It has a character-rounding facility which effectively increases this matrix to 14 × 10 dots for improved presentation of the characters.

Outputs from the TROM are RGB signals; a blanking signal to permit the setting up of 'boxes' in the picture for newsflash and subtitle surrounds; and a monochrome teletext signal without background information. This would be applied to the PAL decoder chip's blanking pin (no. 9 on the TDA3562A chip of Fig. 7.6) as a 'fast blanking' signal to permit inlaying of characters during 'TV/text mix' mode, rather than superimposition, which gives poor legibility.

Decoder features

The decoder described offers the following features: timed pages; subtitles and newsflash updates; flashing characters; concealed display; double-height characters; graphics hold; contiguous graphics; background colour.

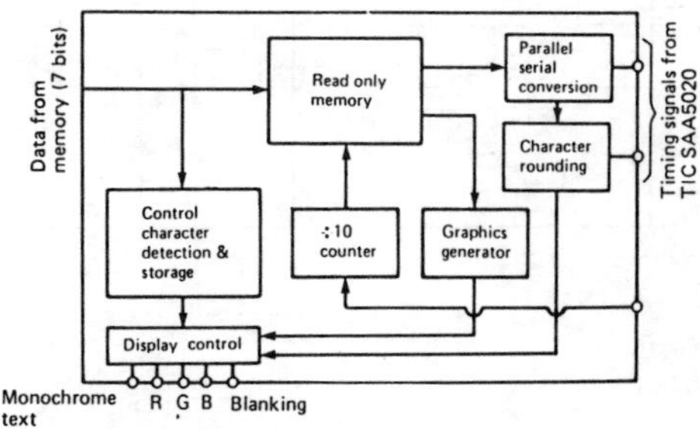

Fig. 8.11 *Character generator IC – TROM, SAA5050*

Computer controlled teletext

While the text decoder system outlined above is an ideal model for explaining the principles of reception and decoding, the hardware used has been updated to take advantage of microprocessor control, ICs with more memory capacity and more efficient formatting of the text data transmissions. The decoder system illustrated in Fig. 8.12 is representative of later practice, and uses two decoder chips plus a memory and optional on-board dedicated control microprocessor. It is governed by a two-wire serial data control bus SDA and SCL, which will be fully explained in Chapter 19. Suffice it here to say that all the user's commands via the remote handset are communicated by the data on the bus.

Video signals enter the VIP IC SAA5230 at pin 27 and take two routes: to a sync separator, and via conditioning circuitry to an adaptive data slicer similar to that already described. Taking the former path first, off-air sync pulses form one input to a phase detector; the other is in the form of a sandcastle pulse from a divider in the CCT chip SAA5240. The output of the phase detector steers the frequency and phase of a 6 MHz dot oscillator which drives both the divider chain (to complete the PLL) and the display generator in the CCT chip.

The second function of the VIP IC is to produce a 6.9 MHz text clock for the synchronous detector inside the CCT chip: it is generated by the phase-controlled 13.8 MHz crystal at pin 11, and passed out of the IC on pin 14.

The second IC of the main pair in Fig. 8.12 combines the functions of TIC, TAC and TROM in the older design, and is closely tied to the RAM store, whose capacity depends on the facilities offered by the set: 2K for 'manual' text and 8K for Fastext with 8-page storage. The inclusion of a dedicated teletext pro-

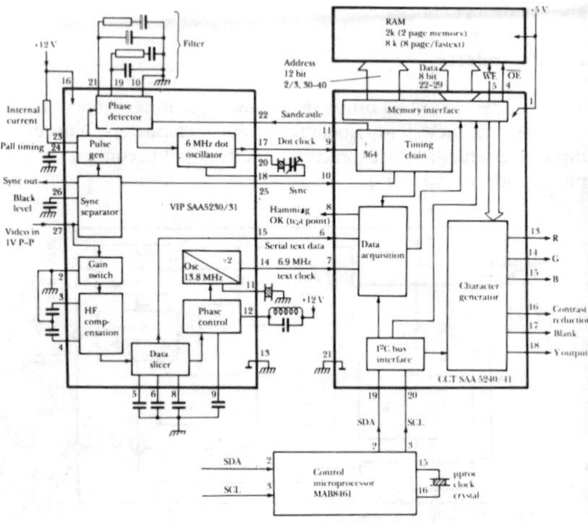

Fig. 8.12 *CCT teletext decoder chip functions*

cessor, as shown here, partially automates the page acquisition process. The character generator section is basically the same as that in the TROM previously described.

VIEWDATA

Viewdata is the generic term for systems which disseminate and retrieve computer-based information and interactive services using a telephone line for communication and a television receiver or monitor-type VDU (Visual Display Unit) for display. Prestel is the name given to the British Telecom system.

The displayed page format is the same as for Teletext, i.e. 40 characters per row, 24 rows to a page. Unlike teletext, the Prestel data is arranged, access-wise, in a tree-and-branch configuration rather than a magazine style presentation. Having called up the Prestel main index, one of many categories of information or service can be chosen; a subject index is then displayed and selection continues until the desired page is found. Unlike teletext, two-way communication with the data-base computer is possible, and question-and-answer exchanges are possible. Communication with such services as retail shops, travel agents, brokers and banks is also possible, along with the transfer of funds, making electronic shopping and business a practical reality.

The system is based on an LSI receiver/decoder IC which is purpose-designed. As Fig. 8.13 shows, in conjunction with a telephone interface system, microprocessor, memory and standard teletext components a complete system is made up. Facilities are also provided for data input from an alphanumeric keyboard, permanent recording by a printer, and data storage on a simple cassette recorder. Fig. 8.14 gives an idea of system architecture, with extra features in shaded blocks. The features and facilities of the chip are as follows:

1 Microprocessor interface
2 Modem (MODulator-DEModulator) for 1200/75 baud and 1200/1200 baud

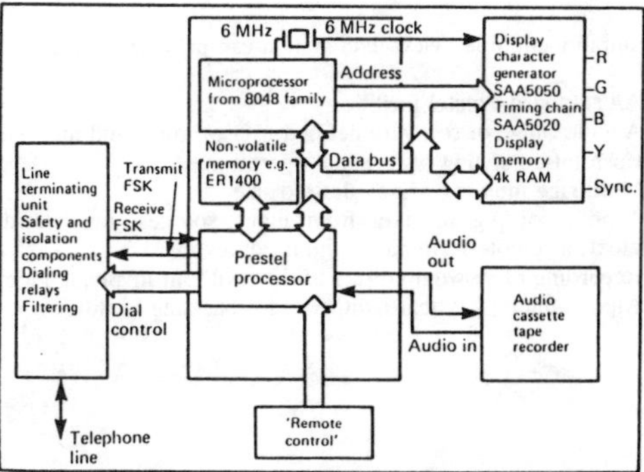

Fig. 8.13 *Prestel basic system*

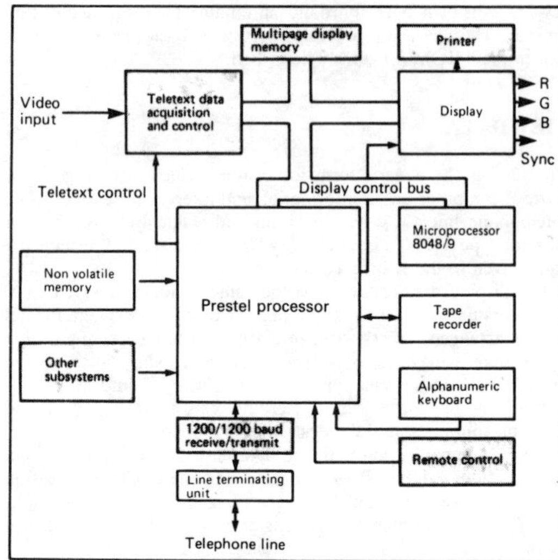

Fig. 8.14 *Processor and peripherals. Some extra features are shown shaded*

3 UART (Universal Asynchronous Receiver-Transmitter) with software parity control
4 Autodialler for British Telecom and continental requirements
5 Tape recorder modem (1300 Kansas City Standard)
6 Tape recorder UART with software parity
7 Non-volatile memory interface
8 I-bus receiver and transmitter for remote control recording and interfacing with other ICs and sub-systems
9 Timer circuits (60s and 1.5s timeouts)
10 Output ports for other sub-systems
11 Provision for connection of any external modem through V24 interface

A suitably-equipped view data system can provide:

1 All standard Prestel facilities
2 A wide range of software-defined user prompts and messages
3 Customised styling of terminal operation
4 Multipage memory of any desired size
5 Tape recording of data from many sources, i.e. viewdata, teletext, a remote terminal or the local keyboard
6 Recording of viewdata direct off-line without involving memory
7 Alphanumeric keyboard with word-processing facilities

9

Nicam stereo sound

The standard sound system for TV broadcasting is single-channel (monaural) f.m., with a carrier spaced 6 MHz (system I) or 5.5 MHz (systems B,G) above the vision carrier. As other audio systems have progressed into Hi-Fi, stereo and digital technology, the sound part of TV transmissions has steadily fallen behind them performance-wise, even though Germany and Japan have introduced stereo systems using analogue techniques. In 1986 a new proposal for TV sound broadcast was made by the BBC and IBA: Nicam 728. It is now in widespread use, alongside the conventional f.m. mono sound carrier, retained for compatibility.

OVERVIEW

The Nicam system is a digital one, with data conveyed in phase modulation of a low-level carrier, spaced for system I at 6.552 MHz above the vision carrier. The modulation system adopted is DQPSK (Differentially encoded Quadrature Phase-Shift Keying). The baseband signal (e.g. L and R) is sampled at 32 kHz rate with an initial resolution of 14 bits per sample. A *companding* system is used, with compression to 10 bits per sample in 32-sample (1 ms) blocks. For immunity to interference, parity bits are added and 45 × 16-bit interleaving is used. The frame format for this system is 728-bit frame length per 1 ms with 8-bit lumped frame-alignment word. The Nicam carrier is radiated at a level 20 dB below the peak vision carrier level.

At the receiver the Nicam carrier emerges from the tuner at a frequency of 32.95 MHz. It is selected by a filter for passage to the Nicam decoder, whose first section is a DQPSK demodulator. Emerging from that as a data-stream, the Nicam signal is progressively descrambled, de-interleaved, error-corrected, D-A converted and filtered. The baseband signals thus derived are amplified and passed out to loudspeakers.

ENCODING AND TRANSMISSION

Most of the cost of providing a Nicam stereo service is in the studio and control room, where new high-performance equipment must be provided, and much closer attention paid to acoustics, noise level, balancing and mixing. The actual Nicam encoding equipment consists of a handful of ICs, and the relatively low-level carrier is not difficult to accommodate at transmitters, especially those using modern designs of r.f. amplifier.

D-A conversion

The two sound channels of the Nicam system are completely independent and have total immunity from crosstalk. They can therefore be used for two monaural (i.e. dual-language) transmissions or for data signals, and provision is made for these in the specification. The most common application is the conveyance of L and R stereo sound signals, however, and it is this that we shall examine.

The baseband L and R signals coming from the studio are first pre-emphasised according to the CCITT J17 recommendation, which boosts the level of higher-frequency components for noise-reduction purposes.

Each is then sampled at 31.25 μs intervals, corresponding to 32 kHz rate, and offering a maximum response of 16 kHz. Input frequencies are in fact limited to 15 kHz in sharp cut-off filters at the D-A converter inputs to prevent *aliasing* and consequent distortion. Each sample is now quantised to 14 bits, which gives 16,238 possible sound signal levels. L and R sampling is carried out simultaneously in separate D-A convertors, after which L-channel signals are called A samples and R-channel signals are called B samples.

Digital compression

It is not possible, within the constraints of an already tightly-packed TV channel allocation, to transmit the full 14-bit data, so the rate is reduced to 10-bit for its passage over the air. The reduction is carried out in such a way, however, that most of the advantage of 14-bit resolution is retained. This is done by moving the sampling baseline, in effect, according to the status of the audio signal being sampled; during quiet and delicate passages, equal-to-14-bit resolution is achieved. At sharp transitions in signal level, and for very loud sounds, the resolution falls to 10-bit standard, but in the circumstances this is not discernible by the listener. Normally a 10-bit system offers a signal-to-noise ratio of about 60 dB. With the dynamic compression system used here, the subjective effect of an 80 dB S/N ratio is achieved.

The principle of digital compression used for Nicam is shown in Fig. 9.1. Running across the diagram are all possible combinations which could make up a 14-bit word. For transmission all the bits in the shaded blocks are retained. The most significant bit (MSB) at left passes through regardless. The 13th bit is discarded if it is the same as the 14th; the 12th bit is discarded if it is the same as nos 13 and 14, and the same is done with nos 11 and 10. If at the end of this process any word has more than 10 bits, sufficient bits are trimmed from the least significant bit (LSB) end to reduce it to 10 bits, as shown at the right top and bottom of the diagram.

So long as the decoder is continuously fed with information on which of the five possible coding ranges is in use at the compressor from moment to moment, it can reconstitute a very close approximation to the original signal. This *scale factor* is conveyed by a 3-bit data signal as shown in Fig. 9.1. The various scale factors require different levels of protection against data corruption in transmission, as shown in the right-hand column of the diagram.

Data protection

Because of the risk of data corruption or distortion in the transmission path, protection must be provided in the form of a check- or *parity*-bit added to the end of each word. Here even parity is used to check on the word's 6 most significant bits. At the encoder the 6 MSB are added together, modulo-two, to give a result of 1 or 0. The parity bit is given the same value so that the modulo-two

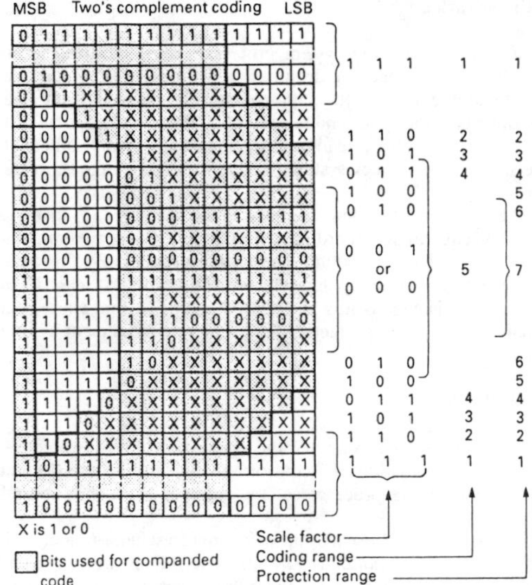

Fig. 9.1 *Bit-reduction code table for Nicam digital compression*

addition of the 6 MSB and the parity bit should always be 0. At the decoder, parity checking detects simple errors and permits correction.

The parity bits are also used to signal scale factor information to the decoder. They are modified in accordance with a look-up table held in memory at both ends of the chain. The 3-bit scale factor word is extracted at the decoder by majority-decision logic, while retaining (except during circumstances of heavy data corruption) the parity-check facility. The scale factor information enables the decoder to recreate any bit in the left half of the block of Fig. 9.1 which was removed during the digital compression process. Any bits removed from the LSB side of the word (right-hand top and bottom in the diagram) cannot be restored, but their loss is masked by the fact that their samples are not crucial ones noise-wise.

Thus full 14-bit resolution is given to the small vulnerable signals corresponding to range 5, falling in four steps to 10-bit resolution in range 1, which corresponds to the largest audio signals. This economy in bit-rate has little or no subjective effect on the listener.

For scale factor signalling purposes the protected 11-bit words are grouped together in blocks of 32, each block lasting for 1 ms. A 3-bit code word is sent with each block to indicate scale factor as shown in Fig. 9.1. Since only one such word has to cover 32 consecutive data words there is some inaccuracy here: not all words receive optimum expansion. In practice the decoder gets reliable information on the magnitude of the largest signal in each block, at a rate sufficient to track the fastest perceptible changes in loudness, and this achieves a subjectively high S/N ratio.

Bit interleaving

In a data transmission system protection must be given against impulsive interference or drop-out, which otherwise would make an irreparable 'hole' in the data-stream. It is achieved by interleaving the bits at the coder and reassembling them in the correct order at the decoder. This spreads and fragments any errors and enables the simple parity-check system to cope with quite large short-term errors.

The data is written into memory at the sending end, then read out non-sequentially according to a ROM address- sequencer which has a complementary counterpart in the decoder. By this means bits which were initially adjacent are transmitted at least 15 bits apart. Any damage is now distributed among several words, each repairable by parity protection and/or error concealment by interpolation.

Control data

So far we have only examined the signal data, that which conveys the audio information. To control and synchronise the decoding and signal-routing processes at the receiver extra data must be added.

Fig. 9.2 shows the make-up of a broadcast data-frame, which occupies 1 ms and contains 728 bits. The frames are sent continuously, with no gaps between them. First comes a frame alignment word (FAW) to initiate and synchronise the decoding sequence. It consists of 8 bits and always has the sequence 01001110. Following this is the application control word consisting of 5 bits, Co to C4. Co is the frame flag bit, which alternates between 0 and 1 at eight-frame intervals. It defines a 16-frame sequence, and is used to synchronise changes in the type of data being sent. Bits C1, C2 and C3 indicate the nature of the data broadcast according to Table 9.1 – it operates indication lights and route-switches at the receiver. C3 remains unchanged for all these options, but provides spare capacity which may be used in future for other sound and data coding options. C4 is a reserve sound switching flag, set to 1 when the Nicam system carries the same sound programme as the conventional f.m. sound carrier, and to 0 otherwise. It is used to mute the audio amplifier/loudspeaker when data other than TV sound is being sent, and for switching between f.m. and Nicam sound systems as circumstances and users require.

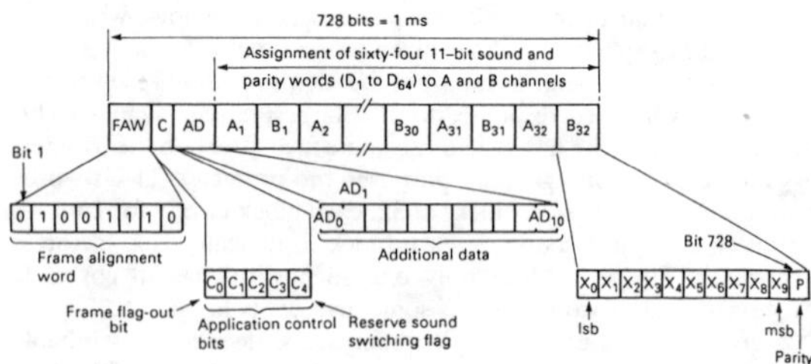

Fig. 9.2 *Structure of a stereo-signal Nicam frame, before interleaving*

Table 9.1 *Control-bit codes for signal-routing and user-indications*

Control bits			*Contents of sound/data block*
C1	*C2*	*C3*	
0	0	0	Stereo signal with alternate L and R samples
0	1	0	Two independent mono signals in alternate frames, e.g. bi-lingual sound
1	0	0	Mono sound signal and data stream, in alternate frames
1	1	0	One data channel

Following the application control bits come 11 AD (additional data) bits whose use and contents have yet to be defined. The rest of the frame is given over to the sound data whose conditioning we have already examined.

Audio data

The sound data bits are arranged in 64 11-bit words as shown in Fig. 9.2. For a stereo programme the A samples (L channel) and B samples (R channel) are sent alternately: 32 of each. In a monaural transmission the frame is arranged with two 32-word blocks (n and n + 1) placed end-to-end in a single frame, as shown in Fig. 9.3. The sound signal is carried in odd-numbered frames, leaving gaps which can be used if required for a second monaural (e.g. bi-lingual) sound track or for the transmission of other forms of data: for downloading into a computer, for instance. For mono sound, Table 9.1 indicates that the control code would be 100 (switches receiver to mono mode); for two independent mono signals the code changes to 010, and M1 or M2 can be selected by the user.

Scrambling

The data will be used to modulate a carrier, and fixed patterns in the data-stream set up fixed sideband patterns around the carrier.

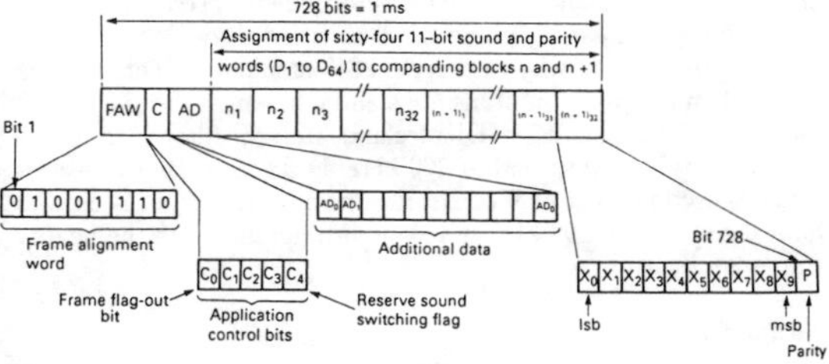

Fig. 9.3 *Nicam frame structure for a mono signal, before interleaving*

This is undesirable from the point of view of interference to co-channels and adjacent channels in the broadcast band, so the data-stream must be scrambled to make it appear random and noise-like. The frame alignment words are not scrambled because they initiate the descrambling process at the decoder.

At each end of the chain is a PRSG (pseudo-random sequence generator) which generates a sequence of binary digits in a fixed and repeatable pattern. Each PRSG is reset on the last bit of the frame alignment word, and its output is added modulo-two to the data bits. The effect is of a completely random bit-stream in the transmission channel.

Modulation

The data is now ready for transmission and must be modulated onto an r.f. carrier. The system used is four-phase modulation, which is economical of bandwidth. The carrier has four possible rest states – 0°, 90°, 180° and 270° – and is switched between them by the Nicam data. A serial to 2-bit parallel converter changes the serial data into a series of 2-bit pairs, which can only be 00, 01, 10 or 11. Each of these alters the carrier phase by a different amount, as shown in Fig. 9.4, *from its previous rest state*. Only a 00 bit pair will have no effect on carrier phase.

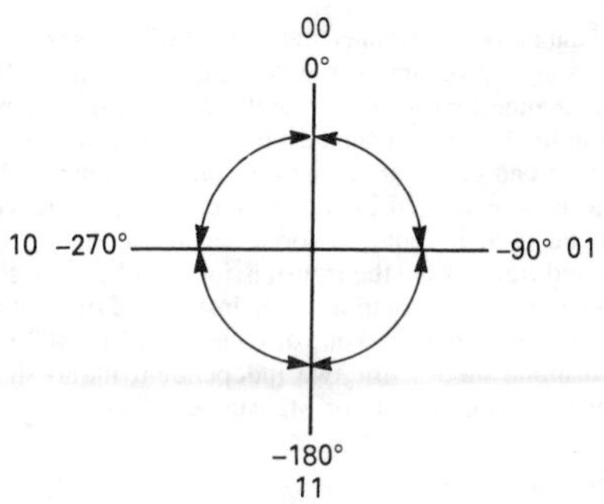

Fig. 9.4 *DQPSK modulation of carrier by bit-pairs*

Carrier phase changes, then, take place at 2-bit intervals with a maximum shift of half a cycle of carrier frequency. To avoid sudden sharp changes of carrier phase the data is fed through a spectrum shaping filter on its way to the DQPSK modulator. This has the effect of 'smoothing' the transitions and quietening the sidebands. For system I transmissions (UK, Ireland, etc.) the filter used gives a maximum sideband spread of 700 kHz. For system B/G transmissions as used in most of Western Europe a sharper filter is used to limit the spread to 500 kHz and avoid interference with the nearby f.m. sound carrier.

Nicam carrier

In system I the f.m. sound carrier is 6 MHz above the vision carrier at a relative level of –10 dB. The Nicam carrier is spaced 6.552 MHz (nine times bit rate) above vision carrier at a level of

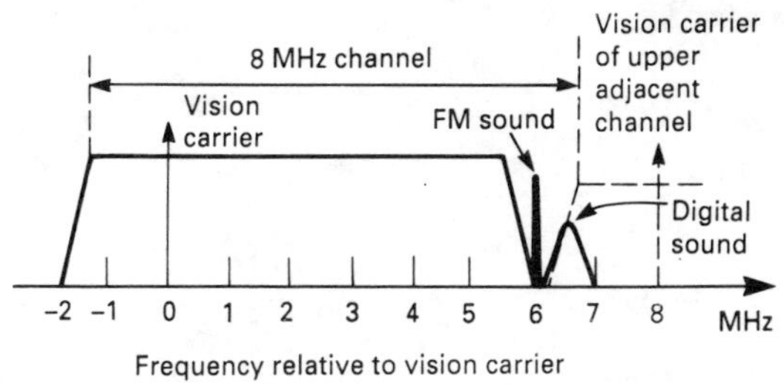

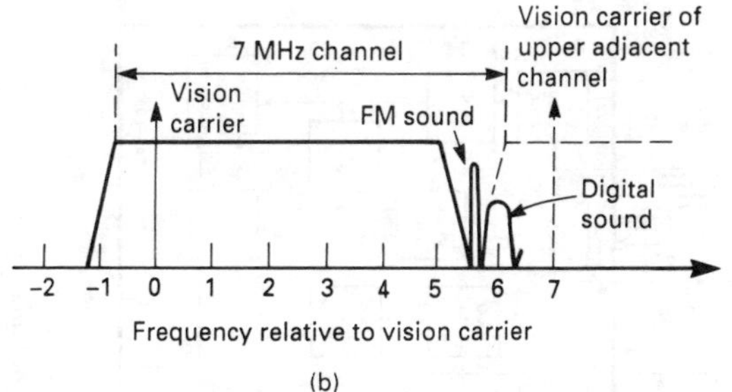

Fig. 9.5 *Vision, f.m. sound and Nicam carriers: (a) system I; (b) system B/G*

−20 dB, see Fig. 9.5(a). For system B/G transmitters the Nicam carrier is at +5.85 MHz as shown in Fig. 9.5(b).

The Nicam format is compatible with the MAC/packet system used for DBS transmissions so that chip sets developed for the one can be used for the other.

RECEPTION AND DECODING

The processes at the receiving end are the inverse of those carried out by the Nicam encoder, applied in reverse order to recreate the L and R baseband audio signals which were present at the studio microphones. The take-off point for the Nicam carrier is at the output of the tuner of the TV set or videorecorder, where it appears as an i.f., typically at 32.95 MHz. This frequency is beat against the vision i.f. to produce an intercarrier frequency at Nicam carrier rate: 6.552 MHz for system I, 5.85 MHz for system B/G.

DQPSK demodulation

Fig. 9.6 shows an internal block diagram for a commercial DQPSK demodulator IC as used in domestic receivers. The Nicam carrier enters at pin 4 at a level of about 60 mV r.m.s. It passes through an a.g.c. control stage to maintain a reasonably constant input level to

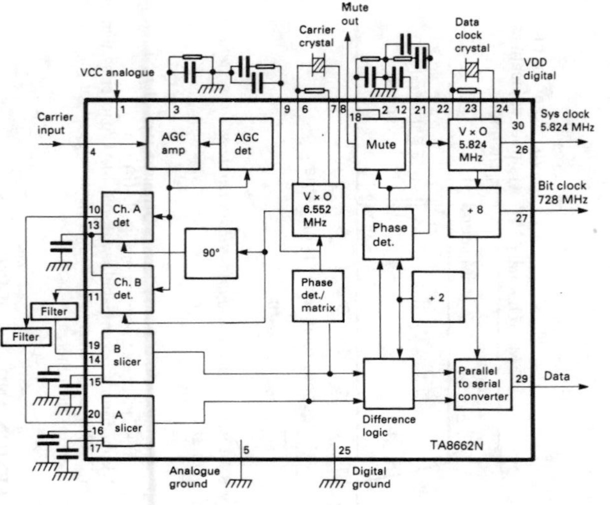

Fig. 9.6 *Toshiba DQPSK demodulation chip functions*

a pair of detectors, A and B. They are arranged as synchronous demodulators working in quadrature, rather like the U and V detectors of the PAL decoder described in Chapter 7. Emerging from these are in-phase (cosine) and quadrature (sine) components of the phase-modulated carrier signal. They leave the IC on pins 10 and 11 for passage through separate but identical shaping filters whose characteristic is the same as those used at the DQPSK modulator at the transmitter. They remove harmonics and optimise the noise performance of the decoder.

The filtered quadrature signal components re-enter the chip on pins 19 and 20 for application to a pair of adaptive data slicers, A and B, whose operating points are held symmetrically about the signal's mid-point. The data outputs from the slicers are applied to a matrix and phase-locked loop, PLL, to generate a synchronous c.w. feed for the detectors already described. The main path for the data signals is to a differential decoder, which uses a second PLL for sampling. It is here that 0 or 1 decisions are taken. The decoder output contains the bit-pairs into which the data was grouped at the transmitter's modulator. After passage through a 2-bit parallel to serial converter, the demodulated data-stream emerges on IC pin 29 for application to the Nicam decoder proper.

The crystal oscillator in the second PLL in this IC runs at 5.824 MHz, eight times the bit rate of 728 kHz. Its output is divided by eight to provide: a bit clock drive for the following demultiplexer chip via pin 27; an internal drive for the P–S converter stage; and via a ÷2 stage a drive at 364 kHz for the differential decoder and the phase detector which steers the PLL. If the loop comes out of lock no coherent data can be detected and the mute output goes low on IC pin 18.

Demultiplex

The second main IC in the Nicam decoder is called a demultiplexer; it descrambles, de-interleaves and reformats the sound data to present an output suitable for application to a conventional D-A converter system, along with the necessary clock and ident outputs. A typical demultiplexer IC is shown in block diagram form in Fig. 9.7. It has provision for fall-back switching to f.m., language selection, and control by direct line or serial data bus.

Data enters the IC on pin 23 wherefrom it takes two routes, one for signal and one for control. The latter starts with the FAW detector, consisting of an 8-bit serial register and comparator. Once the 01001110 FAW sequence is detected the PRSG generator is reset and started. Its synchronised output is added to the data-stream to descramble all the bits which follow the FAW. The control bits are now routed to their own decoders to provide audio route switching and status indications for the user. The data proper passes outside the chip (pins 7/15) for interception if required, then to a serial to parallel converter whose 64 outputs consist of all the bits in two blocks of data. They are loaded into 64 × 11-bit memories in order to carry out the de-interleaving process, which consists of reading out from memory in the required order, controlled by an address sequencer governed in turn by the ROM-based interleaving code. Two memory banks are used, one being written as the other is read to render alternate A and B samples for stereo use. A third memory is incorporated for use with M1 and M2 (two mono, bi-lingual) transmissions where both are present in alternate blocks as shown in Fig. 9.3.

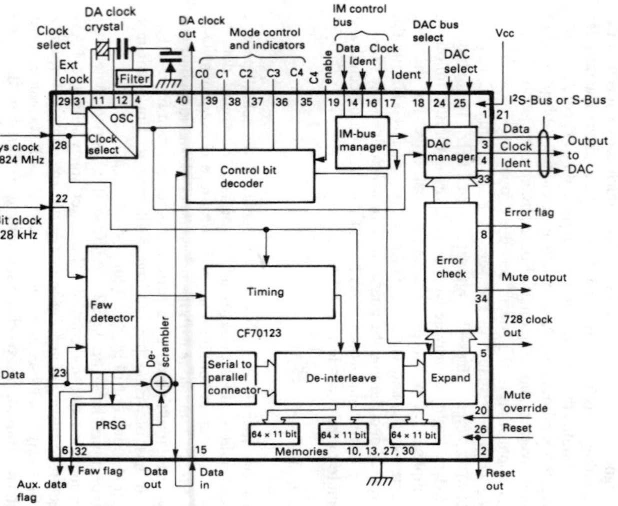

Fig. 9.7 *Texas Nicam demultiplex chip*

The 11-bit protected words, now descrambled and de-interleaved (but not yet error-corrected) must now be expanded back to 14-bit form. The scale factor information held in the parity bits is extracted, assembled and interrogated to control the data-expand stage, from which emerge 14-bit data words ready for error-correction and repair. This is carried out in the error-check block with reference to the parity bits for simple correction; and to the protection range data (conveyed by the range code) for more sophisticated error-*concealment* using interpolation, a process of replacing suspect data with locally generated samples derived by 'averaging' adjacent known-good samples.

Data leaves the IC on pin 3. It consists of alternate bursts of A and B (stereo L/R) information, defined by an ident (flip-flop) signal at pin 33, and a clock drive at pin 4. These three feeds go to the D-A converter stage from which the baseband signals will be reconsitituted.

The bit clock signal from the demodulator chip enters at pin 22 for use in the FAW detector. The main clock within the demux IC runs at 5.824 MHz and is also derived from the demodulator chip via pin 28: it is used throughout the Nicam decoding sections. A third clock signal, derived from the crystal at IC pins 11 and 12, provides a 16.384 MHz drive to the D-A converter.

Early designs of demultiplexer IC use external RAM for data interleaving, but all current types have on-board memories for this purpose, and work in broadly similar fashion to that described here.

D-A conversion

Conversion of the data back into analogue form is the final process in the Nicam decoder. The circuits and principles used are the same as those in audio CD players. In both cases the L and R audio information is contained in the same data-stream, which alternates between the two.

Generally an *integrating* type of D-A converter is used. Its principle of operation is to charge a precision capacitor from a constant-current source for a period set by the data in each 14-bit word. A hold circuit is used to maintain the charge level between samples. Separate integrating capacitors are used for L and R channels, selected in turn by the L/R switching feed from the demultiplex chip. The outputs from the D-A converter now undergo filtering to remove sampling components and smooth the 'stepped' output waveform. In simple decoders the filters cut off sharply above 15 kHz; more sophisticated designs use *oversampling* with a smoother roll-off in the analogue filter, another technique widely used in CD players. This prevents distortion and coloration of audio signal components between 12 kHz and 15 kHz.

At the outset the L and R signals underwent pre-emphasis and now the complementary de-emphasis is applied to restore correct balance throughout the frequency spectrum and reduce noise. The L and R signals are now ready for audio amplification and application to loudspeakers in the case of a TV set, or processing for Hi-Fi recording in a VCR. All Nicam-fitted equipment has audio output sockets to facilitate connection to other units, most commonly a separate Hi-Fi system with good performance and high-class loudspeakers.

SERVICING NICAM DECODERS

Because Nicam circuits are largely digital in operation, and because they dissipate little power, they are amongst the most reliable sections of TVs and videorecorders.

Alignment

Some DQSPK demodulator ICs have external trimmers for adjustment. The type shown in Fig. 9.6 has one associated with pin 6 for setting the carrier clock. It should be adjusted for 6.55185 MHz ±50 Hz with an accurate frequency counter and no Nicam signal applied. Alternatively an oscilloscope can be used, synchronised externally from IC pin 22 and displaying the waveform at pin 20. With a Nicam signal present adjust for maximum eye-height in the pattern shown in Fig. 9.8.

The data clock frequency also has an external adjustment in this type of chip, in the form of a trimmer at pin 22. Adjust for zero volts ±30 mV on a digital voltmeter connected between pins 12 and 21 (Nicam signal present) or alternatively for 5.824 MHz ±20 Hz at pin 26 with no Nicam signal present.

In the demux chip illustrated in Fig. 9.7 provision is made for setting the DACLK frequency: adjust the trimmer at pin 12 for a frequency of 16.384 MHz at pin 11. Other types of demux IC have no need for manual adjustment.

Some decoder designs have an adjustable bandpass filter in the 6.552 MHz feed to the DQSPK demodulator IC. It is set for best eye-pattern at the spectrum-shaping filter, e.g. pin 20 of the IC in Fig. 9.6. Setmakers usually give specific alignment instructions for this filter.

Fault tracing

Seldom to Nicam decoder faults give rise to 'borderline' symptoms. As with most digital processors the device tends to either work perfectly or not at all, due to the various mute systems which come into operation when a PLL unlocks or in the presence of heavy data corruption. In that event the receiver will generally fall back to conventional f.m. (mono) operation, signalled by front-panel or on-screen indications.

Fig. 9.8 *Nicam eye-pattern during set-up. The larger the clear areas the greater the error-margin*

If there is no Nicam reception first ensure that the TV transmission is in fact Nicam-encoded, and that any system switch is correctly set. After checking that the ICs are getting correct Vcc supplies, examine the level of the signal at the mute pin of the first IC: in Fig. 9.6 this is no. 18. If it is low (mute on) check that the Nicam carrier is reaching the chip input, and then that the PLLs are locked, here indicated by correct clock rates as described above. If the mute line is high (mute off) the fault lies further downstream in the decoder, probably around the demux chip.

In these circumstances the first tests should be at the data and clock signal inputs to the demux chip, and the outputs from the IC to the D-A converter; clock, data and ident. If the latter are missing or incorrect, check that the PLL within the IC is working and locked up before suspecting the peripheral components, and then the chip itself, in that order. Most Nicam ICs have test/switching pins which can be identified from the IC manufacturer's (or setmaker's) data and used in fault diagnosis.

If the Nicam sound is distorted the cause is unlikely to lie in the digital sections of the decoder: as a general rule they will automatically mute before operating conditions deteriorate to the point where sound reproduction is impaired. For distortion, then, the starting point for tests should be the D-A converter IC if both channels are affected and supply voltage levels are correct. Any fault which is confined to *one* of the L/R sound channels will not arise from the digital section of the decoder because both are handled together there. Using an oscilloscope, check the output signals from the low-pass filters immediately following the D-A converter, and then continue downstream in the faulty channel until the trouble is located. The fact that two identical channels, one working correctly, are present is a great help in diagnosis because comparison tests can easily be made.

10

Timebase circuits

Every picture tube, be it for image pick-up or display, must have a means of deflecting its scanning spot to all parts of the screen or target. Except in oscilloscope displays and a very few vidicon-type tubes the electron beam is deflected by magnetic fields in the neck of the tube. These are generated by deflection coils wound on a ferrite former and securely fitted to the tube neck. One pair of coils is used for vertical spot deflection, and between them make *horizontal* lines of magnetic flux in the tube neck: these deflect the beam vertically, in a direction determined by the polarity of the flux lines, and to a degree proportional to the intensity (or number of lines) of flux. For horizontal deflection of the electron beam a second pair of coils is used, this time generating *vertical* lines of force through the tube neck. Again beam deflection is proportional to strength and direction of the magnetic field. The complete assembly of coils and moulded ferrite former is called a *scan yoke*. Each yoke is manufactured specifically to match, physically and magnetically, the tube type with which it is intended to be used; this is particularly true of colour tubes, as was made clear in Chapter 5.

The intensity of magnetic field developed by an electromagnet is proportional to the current flowing in it. Since beam deflection is exactly proportional to field strength, the basic requirement for linear image scan is a sawtooth *current* waveform in each pair of deflection coils. Unless the coils behave as a pure resistor, the voltage appearing across them will not be in sawtooth form – in fact, to create a sawtooth (linearly-rising) current in a *pure* inductor, a constant d.c. voltage must be applied to it.

At very small deflection angles such as those used in vidicon tubes a linear deflecting current for line and field scans will result in the required constant velocity of the scanning spot over the target. In large flat-faced display tubes, especially 110° deflection types, a linear deflection characteristic will not impart constant scanning speed over the screen however: the differing beam path lengths between screen centre and screen edges tends to speed up the 'linear' progress of the beam towards picture extremities, and correction must be made for this in the shape of the scanning current waveform passed through the deflection coils.

At field frequency (50 Hz) the scanning coils behave almost as a resistance during the forward stroke, so the required voltage drive approximates to a sawtooth, with compensatory shaping to correct for scan coil inductance and where applicable the 'flat-face' effect. Here the scan output stage acts in similar fashion to a conventional amplifier, e.g. an audio output stage. On the other hand, the line scan-coil pair represent almost pure inductance at the much higher (15625 Hz) horizontal scanning rate; to correctly drive these, then, a constant voltage in one direction must be applied for the 52 μs of the active picture period, then a higher constant voltage in the opposite direction for 12 μs to achieve a complete reversal of magnetic field and a complete traverse of the screen by the scanning spot on its flyback stroke.

Timebases, then, consist of three basic sections: a timing source (in practice some form of oscillator, locked to incoming sync pulses); a shaping stage, consisting of ramp generator for field applications or a pulse generator for line timebases; and a power output stage as a means of driving rapidly-changing currents through the scan coils.

RAMP GENERATORS

The sawtooth drive waveform required by a field timebase is called a ramp, and of several possible methods of generating it, the simplest is to use a series RC charging circuit. Fig. 10.1 shows the principle, in which capacitor C is allowed to charge towards HT potential via series resistor R. Each time the switch across the capacitor is closed the capacitor rapidly discharges to form the flyback stroke of the scanning spot. As the waveform in Fig. 10.1 shows, however, the sawtooth's forward stroke is not linear. As the capacitor charges the voltage across the resistor diminishes, with a corresponding reduction of current. In this series circuit the reducing resistor current flows also into the capacitor, and this diminution of charging current with time is responsible for the curvature in the waveform. It can be overcome by charging the capacitor from a *constant-current source*. In its simplest form this may consist of a very high HT potential and very large resistor R; provided the charging process has not advanced far towards V_{HT} before the flyback switch closes the charging current is substantially constant, and the resulting ramp substantially linear. This configuration is inconvenient for modern IC circuit design, where a constant-current generator is easily arranged in the emitter circuit of an internal transistor.

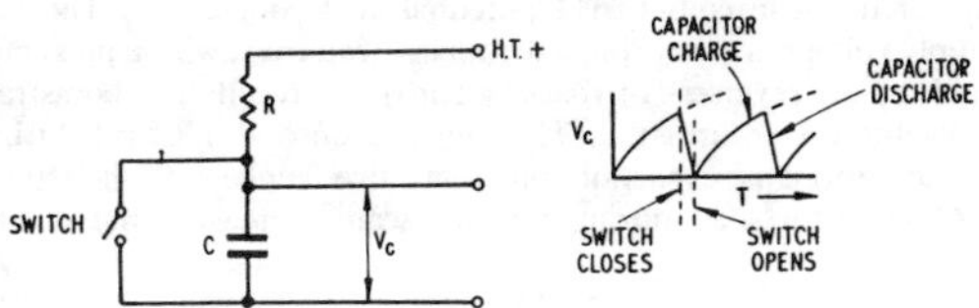

Fig. 10.1 *Sawtooth generation: RC charging circuit*

FIELD OSCILLATOR

Since the ramp-generator function is performed by a capacitor-charging circuit, the only requirements of the field oscillator are that (a) it closes an electronic switch once per 20 ms to discharge the ramp capacitor; and (b) that its free-running frequency be just *below* 50 Hz to enable it to be synchronised, or triggered, by incoming sync pulses. Many oscillator configurations are possible, though the oscillator must run free in the absence of sync pulses to prevent damage to the picture-tube's screen when tuning, or during breaks in transmission. All modern receivers use IC-based field oscillators, in which a form of multivibrator (astable) oscillator is most commonly used. Where a field hold control is provided this adjusts the time-constant of the RC timing network.

An alternative technology is to count line synchronising pulses, triggering the field flyback after $312\frac{1}{2}$ of them. A representative system will be described later in this chapter.

FIELD OUTPUT STAGE

The most common configuration for a field output stage in current practice is the class B type, in which a pair of transistors are connected in series across the d.c. supply line with the scan-coil load connected (via a d.c. blocking capacitor) to their mid-point. The circuit design is similar to that of an audio output amplifier, with both transistor bases being driven together by the sawtooth; each output transistor conducts for half the scanning stroke, the crossover point taking place at screen centre. A typical circuit (simplified) is shown in Fig. 10.2, where the incoming sawtooth waveform comes to TR1 base via C1 and R1. TR1 collector load consists of split resistor R4/R5, across which appears an amplified sawtooth for application to the commoned bases of complementary-symmetrical output pair TR2/TR3. At the commencement of scan TR1 collector voltage is high, and TR2 fully conductive as a result. As forward scan progresses TR2 turns gradually off, reducing current in the scan coil via R7, C4 and low-value resistor R11. At the mid-point of scan TR2 is almost off, and TR3 beginning to be driven into conduction – a smooth changeover is ensured by the base-voltage offset introduced by preset R2 and temperature-compensating thermistor R3. For the second half of field scan TR3 is driven progressively harder into conduction by the falling ramp at TR1 collector, to the point where the former is almost saturated at scan-end.

Flyback is initiated by a sharp drop in drive voltage at TR1 base, rapidly turning it and TR3 off. The upper plate of scan-coil coupler C4 is at almost ground potential, and this large capacitor cannot quickly charge. TR2 saturates and D1 conducts, clamping the top end of the scan coils to HT potential at decoupler C2. The full supply voltage is now present across the scan coils, whose magnetic field rapidly reverses (t flyback = 1 ms) as a result. The bootstrap capacitor C3 ensures that TR2 remains on and TR3 off during flyback; the same capacitor applies positive feedback to the tap on TR1 collector load during forward scan, increasing the circuit efficiency.

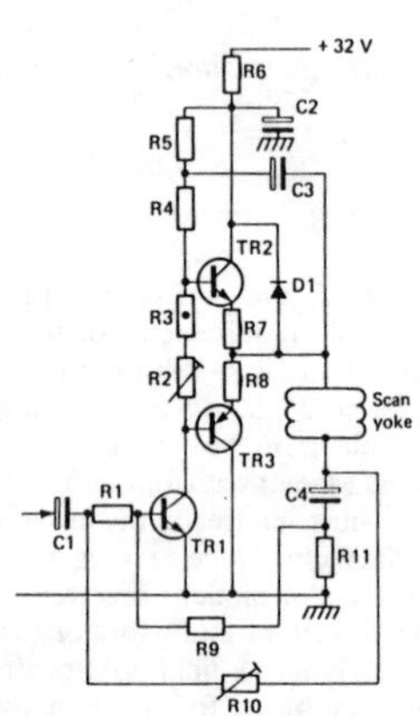

Fig. 10.2 *One form of field output amplifier. Here a complementary-symmetrical pair of transistors are used in class B configuration*

The low-value sampling resistor R11 develops a sawtooth voltage proportional to yoke current, passed via R9 as a.c. negative feedback to TR1 base to improve the scanning linearity. A second feedback path, this time with d.c. continuity, comes from the lower end of the scan coils to TR1 base via preset R10. Its purpose is to stabilise the mid-point voltage of the output stage, permitting the output voltage swing to be symmetrical between supply rail and ground. Any rise in mid-point voltage increases conduction in TR1, which pulls down the base voltage of the output pair (and hence their emitters' voltage) to compensate. Balance is set by adjustment of R10. The second preset R2 sets a small standing (quiescent) current in the output pair to avoid crossover distortion at the point where TR2 hands over to TR3.

The circuit described above is but one variant of many which have been used as field output stages. In most cases the class B output stage is incorporated in an IC which directly drives the yoke via a coupling capacitor; some large-screen receivers and monitors use a class B 'power booster' downstream of the ICs output stage. For camera applications a small IC is adequate for the low energy requirement.

IC FIELD TIMEBASE

The field timebase, with its maximum internal power dissipation (in the case of a large-screen colour TV) of about 5 W, is amenable to encapsulation within a single heat-sinked IC. The TDA1170 in Fig. 10.3 is a good model for illustrative purposes. The oscillator is triggered by field sync pulses coming into pin 8 via C321, and runs

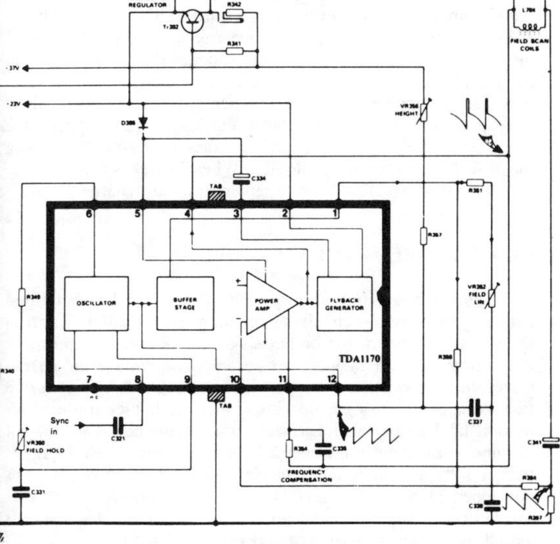

Fig. 10.3 *Complete field timebase based on the TDA1170 chip – Decca*

at a frequency determined by the RC time constant of R349, field hold control VR350 and C331. The 'switching' output from pin 12 is a negative pulse of 100 μs duration; it rapidly discharges the ramp-forming capacitor C337/338, which subsequently charges towards supply rail potential via R357 and height control VR356. The sawtooth wave thus formed is buffered within the chip to emerge at pin 1, where it is applied via R361 and linearity adjustment pot VR362 to the tap on the ramp-charging capacitor as a source of linearising feedback.

Pin 1 output passes through R358 to re-enter the IC on pin 10 as an input signal to the internal class B power amplifier. Its output, in the form of a ramp-down, appears at pin 4 and is applied directly to the field scan coils whose bottom end is grounded (a.c.-wise) by a large capacitor C341. R367 (1 Ω) samples coil current to produce a sawtooth voltage for re-application to IC pin 10 as negative feedback. The gain of the output stage is determined by the ratio of input resistor R358 to feedback resistor R364.

The frequency response of this type of IC can extend well into the r.f. range, and to prevent instability and parasitic oscillation the RC combination R354/C336 is included as a frequency-selective negative-feedback path to curtail h.f. response.

Flyback booster

During field flyback a high supply voltage is required for direct application to the scan coils in order to effect a complete reversal of current during the 1 ms flyback time available. A typical pair of field scan coils may have an L/R time constant around 2 ms, calling for a supply voltage *during flyback* of roughly double that required for scan-period drive. To avoid the excessive dissipation in the upper half of the power output stage which would result from the provision of a 'double voltage' d.c. supply line, the *flyback generator* technique is used. During the forward scan pin 3 of the chip is at low potential, permitting C334 to charge to supply rail potential (about +20 V) via D305, which also supplies the output stage via pin 5. At the commencement of flyback a switch within the IC links pins 2 and 3, applying +20 V to the negative plate of C334. Since the capacitor cannot instantaneously alter its charge its upper plate now rises to 2 × 20 V = 40 V, reverse-biasing D305 and doubling the available supply voltage at pin 5. When flyback is complete the switch reverts, enabling C334 to replenish its lost charge.

CLASS D FIELD TIMEBASE

Although the class B output stage is efficient, especially when fitted with a flyback booster circuit, some energy is dissipated as heat in the two transistors of the output stage. An alternative and more efficient method of building up an analogue voltage or current waveform is to switch a d.c. supply into an integrator by means of a fast-acting chopper-switch working at high (compared to the alternations of the basic analogue waveform) frequency. The ratio of on-time to off-time in the switch determines how much energy is built up by the integrator. A class D field timebase IC was developed along these lines. The TDA2600 contains a 150 kHz oscillator as chop-timer and an r.f. switch whose duty-cycle is varied according to a 20 ms ramp generated within the chip by conventional means.

A later approach to switch-mode field scan technology is illustrated in basic form in Fig. 10.4, where the vertical deflection coils

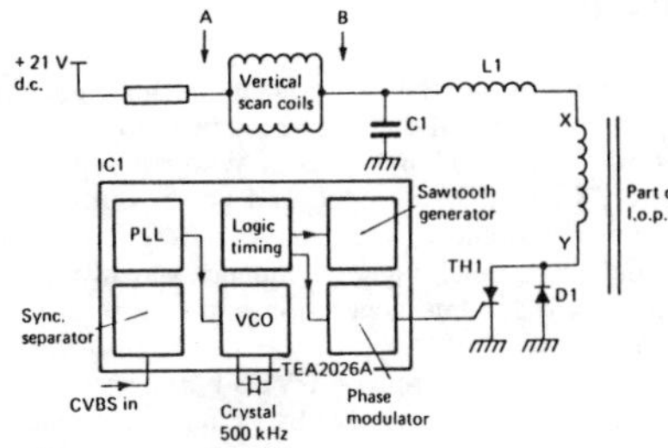

Fig. 10.4 *Working principle of the switched-pump field scan system*

(yoke) have one end (A) permanently connected to a source of +21 V d.c. By varying the charge on capacitor C1, current can be made to flow through the yoke in either direction. As an example, variation of C1 charge between +30 V and +10 V in linear fashion over a 20 ms period would build up a sawtooth scanning current, symmetrical about Izero, in the coil.

The charge on C1 comes from winding X–Y on the line output transformer, which is so phased that during each line flyback period pin X goes 190 V positive of pin Y. If thyristor TH1 remains permanently off, diode D1 will act as rectifier and C1 will become charged to +190 V via L1. If, however, TH1 stays permanently on, LOPT pin Y is fully grounded: the pulse voltage at pin X positions itself symmetrically about ground potential (d.c. zero line) and the charge on C1 falls to zero. By varying the conduction period of TH1 the charge on C1 can be varied throughout the 20 ms field period. Since TH1 is always turned off at the beginning of *line* flyback by the negative pulse from LOPT pin Y, its conduction period depends on the timing (phasing) of its positive gate turn-on pulse.

In this circuit, at the start of each field scan the TH1 trigger pulse comes late in each line, so a high voltage develops across C1; current flows from B to A (*conventional* current flow) through the scan yoke. As field scan continues, TH1 trigger pulse timing (during each line period) is progressively advanced to linearly reduce C1 charge. Halfway through field scan (t = 10 ms) C1 charge equals +21 V and no current flows in the yoke; continuing advancement of TH1 gate pulse phase reduces C1 charge below +21 V, and an increasing current flows through the yoke from A to B. This reaches its maximum at the end of field scan (screen bottom) when TH1 gate pulses are cut off, C1 charge rapidly reverts to +190 V and a large current passes through the yoke in direction BA to give rapid flyback.

As Fig. 10.4 shows, the pulse generation and timing are carried out in IC1, type TEA2026A. The basic field scan timing is governed by a quartz crystal oscillator and phased to incoming field sync. To control the timing of the line-rate thyristor drive pulses a field-rate ramp is generated within the IC; its level is sampled at line rate in the field logic timing section. The sample level is processed in the field phase-modulator to form thyristor triggering pulses. This same IC is also responsible for sync separation; line flywheel synchronisation; line pulse generation; and control of the switch-mode power supply circuit.

LINE TIMEBASE

As for the field section, the function of the line timebase is to deflect the scanning spot of the picture- or pick-up-tube, and it has the same three basic building blocks of synchronised oscillator as timing source, shaping/driver stage and power output amplifier. Line timebase circuit designs are quite different to field ones, however, due to the much higher frequencies involved. Discrete-component designs for line generation and synchronisation have long disappeared.

All line timebases which rely on CVBS-borne syncs incorporate *flywheel* synchronisation. Instead of using individual sync pulses to trigger each line scan, the frequency and phase of the locally-generated line drive pulses are compared with those of the incoming sync pulses in a phase detector. Its error signal acts on the local oscillator to pull the two streams of pulses into phase-coincidence. This is another example of a phase-locked-loop, and here the time-constant is chosen to be long compared with the period of one line; by this means the effect of interference or noise on incoming sync is minimised, since the triggering of any one scanning line is determined by the *mean* timing of many preceding line sync pulses.

The arrangement of a representative IC containing sync separator, flywheel sync, line oscillator and noise suppression gate is shown in Fig. 10.5. The sync separator section contains a 'slicing' stage to strip away the video signal component of the CVBS waveform applied to pin 8. Pure sync signals emerge on pin 7, whence the field components (long-duration pulses) are separated out by an integrator for application to the field oscillator. The short-duration line sync pulses alone are picked out by a differentiator feeding IC pin 6, where begins the business of line synchronisation. The IC has three control loops, each containing a phase comparator; the first is part of a PLL providing flywheel sync by comparing timings of line oscillator pulses and incoming sync pulses from pin 6. The error-output voltage from this first comparator (pin 12) passes through an external low-pass (flywheel) RC filter to re-enter the chip on pin 15 where it finely controls the oscillator

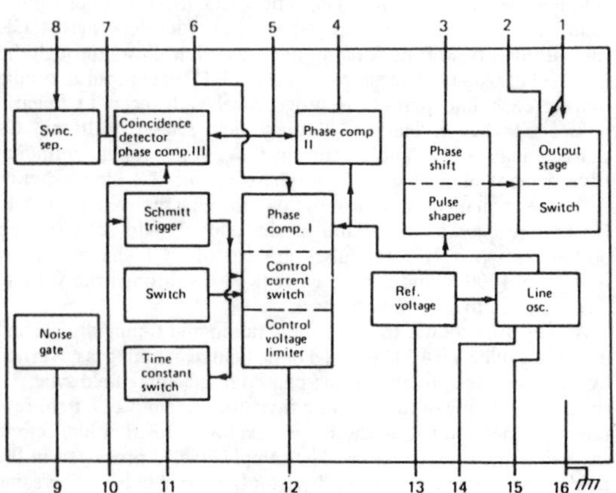

Fig. 10.5 *Block diagram of a typical line oscillator IC*

frequency. Free-running oscillator frequency is governed by a close-tolerance capacitor at pin 14 and a potentiometer network (line hold control) at pin 15.

The second comparator examines the timing difference between flyback pulses from the line output transformer (applied at pin 5) and oscillator pulses. Its error output represents unwanted phase shift in the driver and output stage, which may vary with picture brightness etc., and is externally low-pass filtered between IC pins 4 and 3. At IC pin 3 this second control voltage operates on a phase shift/pulse shaper section which corrects the phase of the oscillator output pulses. Phase-locked drive pulses emanate from pin 2 for onward passage to the line driver stage, to be examined shortly. At this point the waveform is square, switching cleanly between two voltage levels and completing one cycle every 64 μs. Sawtooth waveshaping for the line scan coils is carried out further downstream – the function of this waveform is purely a switching one.

Mention must be made of the third comparator within the IC. This simply changes the characteristic time constant of the flywheel loop from a long duration – which gives best noise-immunity in situations of high interference or weak received signal strength – to short duration, to facilitate rapid lock-in from the unsynchronised condition, as when changing r.f. channel. Provision is made for connection of an 'AV' switch to pin 10 to hold on the short time-constant mode for use with local signal sources whose CVBS signals contain timing jitter. This arises mainly in mechanically-driven replay systems like videocassette machines and disc players; a short time constant in the line PLL enables the line oscillator to follow instantaneous variations in signal timing, and maintains correct positioning of the simultaneously-jittering picture elements along each scanning line. The AV switch is electrically linked to an 'AV-dedicated' channel selector button for automatic switchover. Many sets have a 'standard' flywheel time-constant short enough to permit good tape/disc reproduction without the necessity for switching.

Multifunction IC

The functions of timebase generation, as well as many of the other sections examined in this and previous chapters, are embodied in the TDA4501 IC shown in Fig. 10.6.

A differential i.f. feed is taken at pins 8/9 from the SAW filter, a.g.c.-controlled and demodulated with reference to the tuned circuit at pins 20/21. The resulting video signal passes out of the chip on pin 17. After passage through an intercarrier filter FL1 the sound carrier re-enters the IC on pin 15 for quadrature demodulation (tuned circuit L2) and amplification of the baseband audio signal. An electronic volume control, governed by the voltage at pin 11, passes this signal on to a buffer stage whose output appears at pin 12.

The output from the vision detector takes a second path through a noise-reduction stage to the sync separator, whence line pulses are counted down in a synchronised divider to give a field-rate switching action at pin 2, where the vertical ramp is generated. The divider system has three modes of working, selected by an internal check on the quality and stability of the incoming sync pulses, to give optimum stability and protection from interference. The system automatically adapts to 50 or 60 Hz incoming field rates.

The line generator circuit works on similar principles to those already described. There are two phase detectors, one for the basic

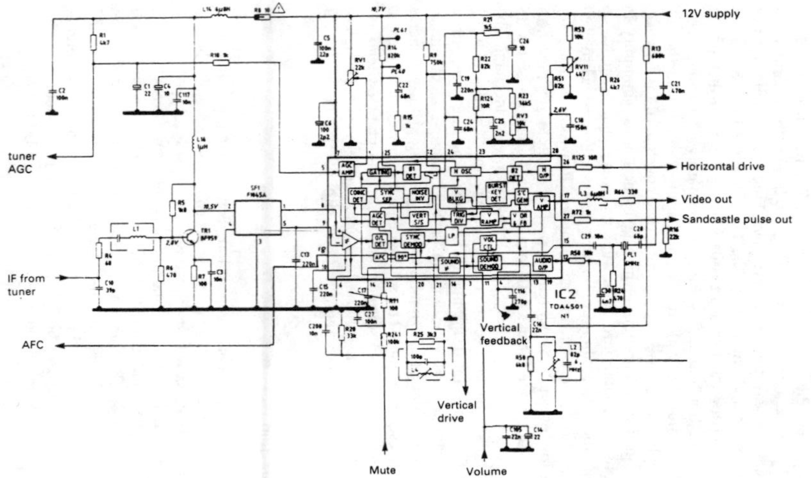

Fig. 10.6 *'Jungle' IC for signal processing and timebase generation (Ferguson)*

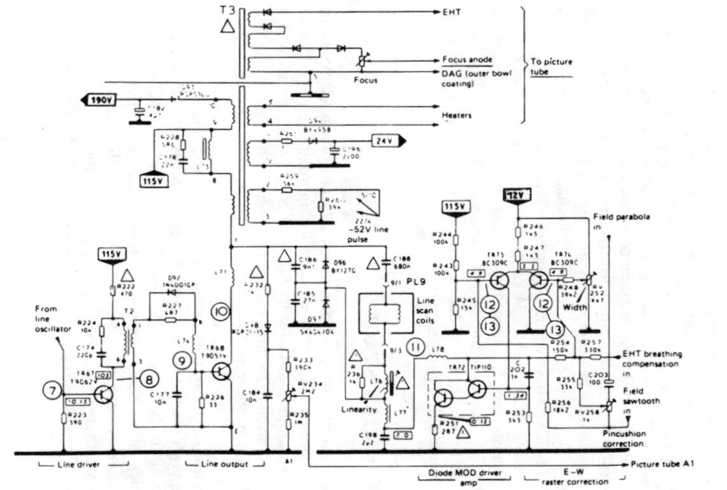

Fig. 10.7 *Line scan output and driver stages with peripheral circuits by Ferguson*

flywheel synchronisation function, and one to optimise the timing of the horizontal drive pulse emerging at pin 26.

Other modern timebase chips combine similar artifices to the TDA4501 shown here with the thyristor field-scan switching system of the IC in Fig. 10.4, and with double-frequency (31.25 kHz) line oscillators, which have no need for frequency-trimming presets.

LINE DRIVER

Interposed between the line oscillator and output stages is a matching stage. Where the output device consists of an ordinary npn transistor (as opposed to Darlington types, or thyristor line output systems) this *driver* section takes the form of a transistor pulse amplifier with a step-down transformer as collector load. The functions of the line driver are twofold: it isolates the line generator stage from the switching impedance of the output transistor; and provides power amplification to drive the required considerable base current into the output transistor. Fig. 10.7 shows a typical line output stage for a colour receiver. The line drive square wave is applied to TR67 base where it switches TR67 fully on and off. The components R224 and C174 damp the primary winding of line driver transformer T2; its secondary winding drives current through the base of TR68, the line output transistor. D92 and L74 prevent spurious turn on of TR68 due to 'ringing' in the transformer, while R227 limits TR68 base current.

LINE OUTPUT STAGE

The line output transistor acts purely as a fast switch, clamping an inductor across a d.c. power source for approximately one-half of the line scan period. Consider Fig. 10.8(a), in which a line output stage is reduced to its most basic form. Initially the transistor switch is off, and no current flows in L. Passage of a turn-on current through the transistor base links point A directly to ground, placing the entire supply voltage across inductor L. As a result, a linearly-rising sawtooth current (t1 to t2 in Fig. 10.8(b)) flows in the coil. Some 26 μs later at t2 the line drive ceases and the transistor switches off. The collapsing magnetic field about L causes an immediate reverse in the direction of magnetic flux and coil-current flow, which now reverses to charge capacitor C; this charging current flows via large capacitor Cres, which effectively links point

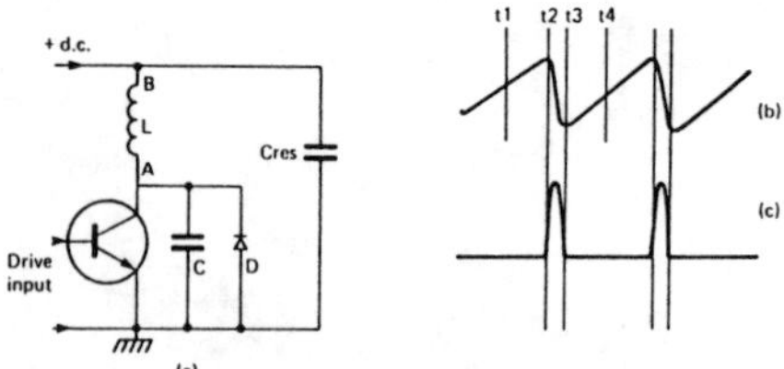

Fig. 10.8 *(a) Essentials of a line-scanning output stage; (b) current and (c) voltage waveforms; t1 to t4 represents one 64 μs period*

B to ground for a.c. purposes. At a time t3 determined by the LC time-constant, one half-cycle of oscillation has taken place, and the energy in the capacitor is ready to feed rapidly back into L. Since point B in the circuit is effectively grounded by Cres, this would involve point A going below ground potential: it is prevented from doing so by the action of clamp diode D. The result is that the charge on capacitor C effectively becomes a d.c. voltage source, whose energy is linearly discharged to zero between times t3 and t4. At t4 the circuit is at rest, with no energy left in L or C. This corresponds to the situation at t1, and the transistor is at this point switched on once more to repeat the sequence – at 64 μs intervals. In this way a sawtooth current is built up in L, which represents the line scanning coils themselves. In practice L is a multi-winding transformer (line output transformer, l.o.p.t.) to which the scan coils are coupled.

The voltage across an inductor is proportional to the rate of change of current in it. Since this *rate* of change is constant during the forward scanning stroke, but fast and varying during the retrace (flyback period), the voltage waveform across the l.o.p.t. and scan coils is a series of pulses about 12 μs wide recurring at 64 μs intervals – see Fig. 10.8(c). Plainly the flyback period is determined purely by the LC time-constant rather than any characteristic of the line drive waveform.

Translating line output stage theory into practical terms, the transistor switch in Fig. 10.7 is TR68, L is formed between pins 7 and 8 of l.o.p.t. T3, D corresponds to D96, and C to C186; the bottom ends of the latter two may be regarded as grounded – D97 and C185 will be discussed shortly. The line scan coils themselves are in effect connected across the l.o.p.t. primary: their bottom end is grounded, and their top end linked to l.o.p.t. pin 7 by C188.

Line scan correction

The circuit of Fig. 10.7 is somewhat complicated by the need to introduce various shaping influences on the line scan waveform – these will now be explained in turn. L76 is the line linearity corrector, acting as a *saturable reactance*. Its magnetic field embraces a small permanent magnet which at some point in the sawtooth current cycle will cause the ferrite core to saturate, whereupon the coil's characteristic changes from an inductive to a resistive one, with marked effect on scanning current. The onset of saturation is adjusted by rotation of the permanent magnet which thus sets up horizontal picture linearity.

The flat face of the picture tube would show a picture somewhat cramped in the centre and stretched at the sides if a truly linear scanning current were used. To compensate, the rate-of-change of line (and field, incidentally) scan current is slowed down at beginning and end of each sweep, giving a characteristic S-shape to the current waveform. For line scan it is easily achieved by a careful choice of yoke-coupling capacitor – in Fig. 10.7 the 680 n component C188.

Some picture tubes use deflection yokes which cannot themselves compensate for a geometrical distortion of the raster which results from scanning a virtually-flat tube face, especially in wide deflection-angle types. To correct the resulting cushion-shaped raster, a diode-modulator is used as a controller of picture width – when fed with a field rate parabolic waveform it provides dynamic correction of cushion distortion: adjustment of the d.c. working point of this E–W control system sets up the picture width.

In Fig. 10.7 the action is based on the elements L77 and C198 in the scan coils' ground return path.

During the flyback time the magnetic field around the line scanning coils collapses and energy is transferred to C188, the S-correction capacitor. C188 obtains a charge from this energy, and it is this charge which is held across the scan coils via D96 which contributes towards the first half of scan. Any variation in this charge will modify the current in the scan coils, and hence picture width. During line flyback the energy lost in this scanning circuit is replenished from the energy stored in the l.o.p.t. This replacement energy is divided between yoke-series capacitors C188 and C198 during flyback. If C198 were shorted to ground the charge across it would be zero and that across C188 at a maximum: the result is maximum picture width. With the short removed from C198, minimum width would result. By varying the impedance of a circuit connected across C198 picture width can be varied without altering the tuning or flyback time of the stage, thus keeping e.h.t. voltage (see later) constant. The 'variable-impedance circuit' in Fig. 10.7 is in fact the Darlington transistor TR72. Its base is fed by (a) a field-rate parabolic waveform obtained by double integration of the field scanning current waveform; (b) a standing d.c. current to set picture width; (c) a small correction current derived from a beam current sensor – it compensates for picture 'breathing' effects due to imperfect e.h.t. regulation, and is also applied to the height control circuit for the same reason; and (d) in some sets, a sawtooth waveform at field rate, with which any *keystone* distortion of the raster can be corrected.

EHT and auxiliary voltage supplies

The l.o.p.t. is a useful source of the many auxiliary voltages and power supplies required elsewhere in the receiver, monitor or camera. Fig. 10.7 shows a secondary winding between l.o.p.t. pins 4 and 6 which generates 6.3 V r.m.s. to energise the picture-tube heaters. During flyback a pulse voltage (Fig. 10.8(c)) appears across the l.o.p.t. windings and this can be caught and held by a diode and reservoir capacitor (i.e. D98 in Fig. 10.7) to provide a high-voltage supply. Approximately 1000 V is built up across C184 by this means, and after 'potting down' in the resistive divider network R233, R235 and preset RV234 is used to provide accelerating voltage on the A1 electrode of the picture tube.

The flyback-rectification system of D98 does not give good regulation of the secondary supply it provides – the flyback pulse is present for less than 20% of the total time. For low-current requirements like accelerating anodes in tubes this presents no problem, since the reservoir capacitor (here C184) can be made large enough to sustain the supply between flyback pulses. For feeding more energy-hungry circuits like field timebases and audio power-output amplifiers, better regulation is secured by *scan-rectification* in which the l.o.p.t.-fed rectifier is so polarised as to block the flyback pulse and charge a reservoir capacitor from the much lower (but longer-sustained) voltage present during the scan period. Fig. 10.7 shows two such scan-rectified supplies – D94 and C196, fed by safety/surge limiter resistor R261 from l.o.p.t. secondary winding 1–12 and providing a +24 V supply for the field timebase; and D93/C182, which, fed from l.o.p.t. winding 9–10, add a +75 V 'boost' to the 115 V line output stage supply rail to render a 190 V potential as operating voltage for the RGB video output stages.

E.h.t. voltages, too, can be obtained by rectifying l.o.p.t. pulses. Flyback pulses are invariably used to obtain the very high final anode voltages needed for modern tubes – ranging from 10 kV for a small monochrome type to 30 kV for the largest colour tubes. Some sets, particularly small portables, have a large secondary winding with many turns (*overwind*) producing full-e.h.t. voltage pulses for application to a single well-insulated diode, often encapsulated within the sealed l.o.p.t. moulding. A more common technique is the use of a separate diode/capacitor voltage multiplier assembly in the form of an insulated moulded block, use of which requires a smaller (lower-voltage) overwind on the l.o.p.t. Fig. 10.9(a) shows a typical doubler circuit. The load, or smoothing, capacitance is normally provided by the conductive inner and outer coatings on the picture tube bowl. It mode of operation is similar to the more common *tripler* arrangement in Fig. 10.9(b). On the positive flyback input pulse from the transformer overwind, D1 conducts to charge C2 to the peak value of the pulse. During the subsequent scan period the input voltage falls almost to ground potential and the high voltage present on C2 turns on D2 to charge C1 to the peak value of the original pulse. At the next line flyback another pulse appears at the input, 'jacking up' the left plate of charged C1: its right plate is thus pushed to *twice* the peak voltage of the input pulse. D3 charges both C4 and (via D4 and D5) the load capacitance to this voltage. A third flyback input pulse pushes the right plate of C3 up to three times the pulse input voltage for passage via D5 to the load. Thus the ladder-network of diodes and capacitors has tripled the input voltage – typically producing 25 kV from an input pulse train of 8.5 kV peak. In practical tripler circuits, C4 can be returned to D1 cathode instead of ground to reduce the voltage stress upon it. Very often the bottom end of C2 is brought out to a separate insulated lead-out from the assembly; by returning it to various pulse-points (positive and negative) on the l.o.p.t., the e.h.t. voltage can be adjusted as required to match correct picture width.

A second source of e.h.t. is required as a focusing voltage in bi-potential tube types, and in some cases around 8 kV must be made available to give an adequate range of adjustment. It can be

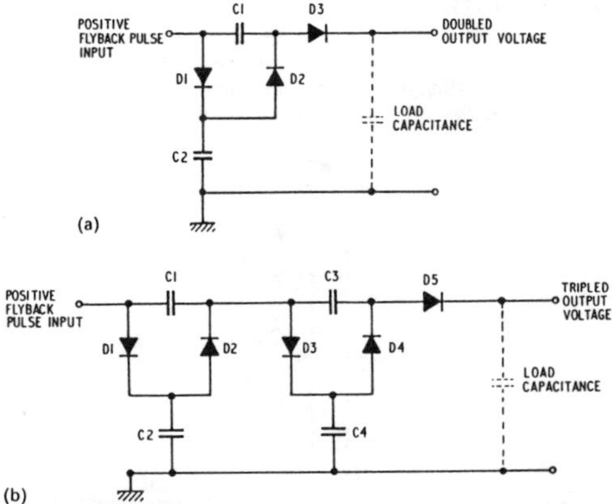

Fig. 10.9 *Voltage multipliers: (a) doubler; (b) tripler*

derived by a tap from the first diode multiplier stage in the tripler, or by a potential divider chain from the full e.h.t. voltage supply.

Diode-split e.h.t. system

E.h.t. triplers are not very reliable, and most failures in them can be attributed to breakdown of the internal high-voltage capacitors. An alternative and more reliable way of assembling an e.h.t. voltage generator is to build rectifiers into a sectionalised overwind assembly as shown in Fig. 10.10. Here three separate 'cells' are present, each consisting of an 8.3 kV secondary winding, an encapsulated rectifier and a capacitor, the latter formed by the windings themselves and with insulating layers acting as dielectric. Each cell has only a d.c. potential with respect to its neighbours, and they are connected in series to render the required e.h.t. voltage. The l.o.p.t. in Fig. 10.7 is of the diode-split type, using three L/C cells and three rectifiers. The fourth diode is provided as a source of focusing voltage. Early diode-split l.o.p.t. designs had primary and overwind assemblies on different limbs, necessitating the provision of a 'link' winding underneath the overwind, connected in parallel with the primary – this eliminated the characteristic high leakage inductance. More recent l.o.p.t.s have all windings on a single limb, and often incorporate both focus and A1 (background) control potentiometers in the moulding, greatly reducing assembly costs, and increasing reliability.

An alternative method of deriving auxiliary and e.h.t. supplies is to rectify pulses at the secondary windings of a *chopper* transformer, which forms the heart of most modern power supply stages – to be examined in detail in the next chapter. In such sub-miniature circuits as are used in TV cameras, the auxiliary high-voltage supplies for pick-up and viewfinder display tubes are drawn from very tiny multipliers and rectifier/capacitor sets associated with the miniature l.o.p.t.s used; the techniques of line and field timebase and l.o.p.t. secondary functions are the same as described above, though the very small energy demands in such equipment scales down the currents and voltages involved.

PULSE FEEDS

Many sections of the receiver or monitor require pulse feeds at line rate for gating, clamping and keying. In the luminance stage the signal must be black-level clamped; the line flywheel sync circuit

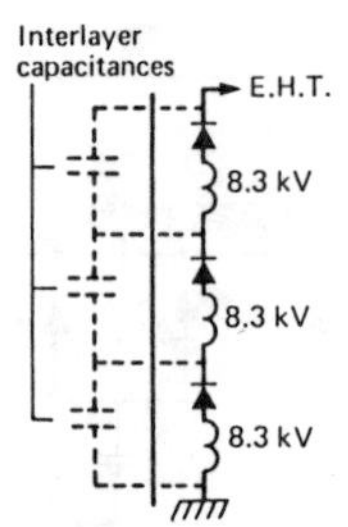

Fig. 10.10 *Internal construction of HV secondary of diode-split line output transformer*

needs a timing reference pulse; the decoder requires gating pulses for extraction of the colour burst and for triggering the PAL switch; some i.f. a.g.c. systems are keyed by line-rate pulses; the scanning spot must be extinguished during flyback; many switch-mode power supply units work synchronously with the line timebase and must be triggered; and so on. Many of these pulses are derived from the line oscillator chip in late designs, but the l.o.p.t. itself is often the main source of reference pulses throughout the set. In Fig. 10.7, l.o.p.t. winding 2–3 and the divider R259/R260 provide – 52 V line-rate pulses for use elsewhere – other functions are catered for by a sandcastle pulse assembled in the line oscillator IC.

SUPPLY VOLTAGE STABILISATION

The amplitude of the line and field scanning waveform is directly related to the supply voltage to the timebase. While a degree of internal stabilisation is possible within the negative feedback loop of a field timebase, and via the E–W correction circuit of a line timebase, close stabilisation of supply voltage is necessary. This is the function of the power supply circuit, which can be integrated into the line output stage. More commonly, a quite separate PSU (power supply unit) is provided to cope with the greatly varying load presented by a line timebase, whose energy demand depends largely on tube beam current, which in turn depends from moment to moment on picture content. It may vary in a large-screen colour set from 40 W at zero beam current to 65 W when a very bright contrasty picture is being displayed. Where the operating voltage for the field timebase is obtained from the l.o.p.t. it will be indirectly stabilised by the action of the main PSU.

THYRISTOR LINE OUTPUT STAGE

The thyristor is a more efficient switch than a transistor, and has found uses in both power supply circuits and line timebase output stages. In its line-output switcher role, the thyristor circuit is not so dependent on a stabilised supply voltage, since stabilisation can be built-in locally, as it were. The circuit is more complex, however, because a thyristor is less easy to turn off than a transistor – the anode voltage must be arranged to fall to that of the cathode to turn off the device. Fig. 10.11(a) shows the basic concept of the RCA design. TH2/D2 form a bidirectional switch similar to a transistor, but with the tuning capacitor Ct returned to ground via the left-hand circuit – there is no d.c. path between the two. D2 conducts during the first half of forward scan, giving way to TH2 to move the beam from screen centre to the right-hand side. L1 provides a load.

TH1/D1 form another bidirectional switch which together with L2 and the timing capacitor Ct switches off TH2 and provides the flyback stroke. A short pulse from the line oscillator triggers TH1 gate at the end of scan, switching it on and instigating flyback. This connects the left-hand side of L2 to ground and discharges Ct which had previously charged to h.t. potential. L2 thus forms with Ct a resonant circuit; L2 is called the commutating coil.

Fig. 10.11(b) shows a secondary winding added to L1 to furnish the trigger pulse for TH2. L4, C4 and R1 provide pulse shaping. To reduce the stress on individual capacitors (and save component costs) a T-network is used for Ct in the form of C1, C2 and C3. A

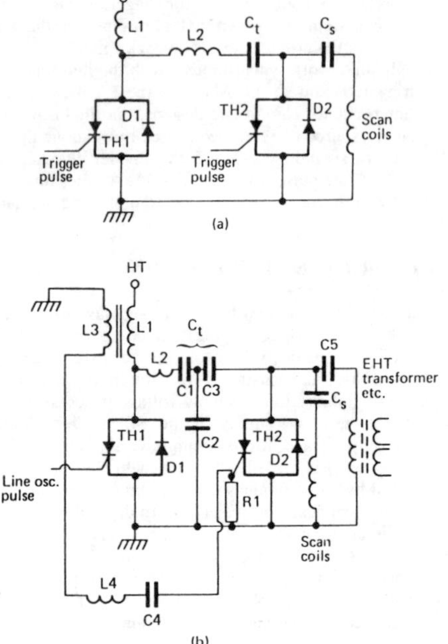

Fig. 10.11 *(a) Basic concept of RCA thyristor line output circuit; (b) a secondary winding on input choke L1 provides a trigger pulse*

line output transformer takes the place of the scan coils in order to utilise the flyback energy for generation of e.h.t. and other auxiliary supplies.

Fig. 10.12 traces the current waveforms during the scanning sequence and is related to Fig. 10.11(a). Prior to flyback, TH1 is triggered by a pulse from the line oscillator. The energy stored in the deflection coils collapses and the decaying current flows via the coils, Cs, Ct, L2 and TH1 to zero. The charge on Ct reverses, providing the negative pulse required to turn TH1 off. This completes the first part of flyback. At this point the left-hand plate of Ct is negatively charged and its right-hand plate positive. D1 is now biased on, providing a discharge path for Ct via the deflection coils to give the second part of flyback. At the end of flyback the current flowing via D1, L2, Ct and Cs will have stored energy as a magnetic field around the scan coils. With the electron beam now at the left edge of the screen and Ct discharged, D1 switches off. The oscillation tries to continue in a negative direction but the clamping action of D2 prevents this. The magnetic field surrounding the scanning coils diminishes and a linear decaying current flows via the coils, Cs and D2. The first part of the forward scan has begun again, and towards screen centre TH2 is once more switched on by the pulse from L3. The current in the coils smoothly reverses and continues to complete the scan.

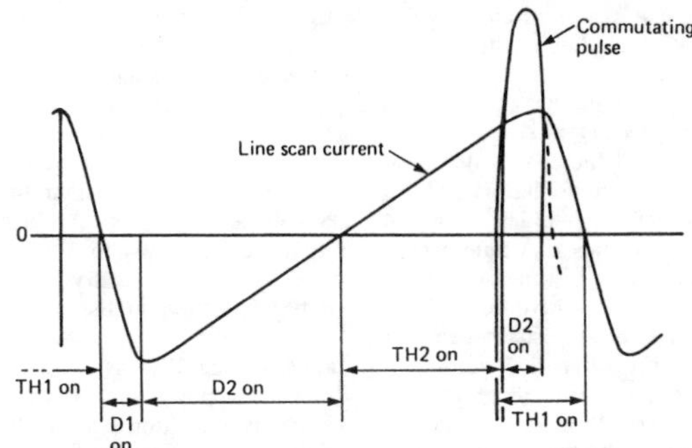

Fig. 10.12 *Thyristor current waveforms for the circuit of Fig. 10.11*

At completion of scan, thyristor TH2 must be switched off. Since TH1 is switched on by the line oscillator about 3 μs before flyback, both thyristors will be conducting simultaneously for this brief period. Current therefore flows via TH1, L2, Ct and TH2 and, because of the tuned circuit formed by L2 and Ct, the current builds up rapidly to give the commutating pulse. This current flows through TH2 in a direction opposite to the scan current; when it exceeds the scan current TH2 switches off.

In this circuit, TH1 is called the flyback thyristor and TH2 the scan thyristor. Late designs use integrated thyristor/diodes, with the parallel diode incorporated in the same package as the thyristor. By applying a variable resistive damping influence (in practice a transistor) across inductor L1, the power to the output stage can be controlled by a feedback loop incorporating a pre-set width control.

TIMEBASE SERVICING

In field timebases where the fault is complete lack of output (single horizontal line across the screen) the first essential is to reduce screen brightness to prevent damage to the phosphor layer. Once it is established that the operating voltages for all sections of the timebase are present, the next step is to ascertain which section – oscillator, driver or output stage – has failed, for which the oscilloscope is the best tool. Where the entire time-base or amplifier is embodied in a single IC which is proved faulty, check for destructive conditions before fitting and powering a new one. Typical of these are a shorted flyback diode (D305 in Fig. 10.3), excessive supply voltage, shorted capacitors or heavy output loading due to a leakage or short-path to ground.

More often, field faults will take the form of various kinds of raster-shape distortion. Low supply voltage, faulty electrolytic capacitors or incorrect feedback conditions are the most common causes of these. A top foldover effect with teletext lines superimposed is due to slow flyback. A cramping at picture bottom is generally due to an inability of the supply line or the output stage to furnish sufficient current to drive the scan coils fully; this may well be due to a dried-up or ageing electrolytic decoupling capacitor on the supply line to the field output stage.

Where the line oscillator, driver and output stages are not involved in the generation and control of power supplies (see Chapter 11) the diagnosis of a 'no-go' fault follows the same pattern of signal (here, pulse) tracing from oscillator via driver to output stage. Line oscillators and drivers are much more reliable than the output stage, which works with relatively heavy currents and high pulse voltages. A quiescent line output section is easy to troubleshoot with test-meter and oscilloscope – such things as dry joints, faulty base drive resistor or open base junction in the output transistor are usually responsible.

More often line output stage faults are manifest as excessive loading, leading to a high current drain on the power supply, which will usually invoke the latter's overcurrent protection system; the end-result, then, will often be a 'pumping' symptom, as will be described in the next chapter. First the e.h.t. rectifier or multiplier (if external to the l.o.p.t.) should be disconnected from the overwind. If the set now bursts into life replace the e.h.t. rectifier. Should the stage still not function, the output transistor and efficiency (where relevant, EW modulator) diodes should now be checked for leakage. The l.o.p.t. can also be loaded by leakage in any other rectifier diodes it may feed, or by heavy loading of their outputs, e.g. a leaky or shorted A1 reservoir capacitor. If after exhaustive testing, and unloading of suspect components like shift chokes, the stage remains heavily loaded, the l.o.p.t. itself is suspect for short-circuit turns or (in diode-split types) faulty internal multiplier components. Shorting turns in the line scanning coils can give rise to similar symptoms, but this is rare; it can be checked by disconnecting the yoke.

During fault-finding it is often prudent to work with reduced voltages and currents in the line output stage to prevent damage, and this can be arranged by fitting a suitably heavy wire-wound resistor in the h.t. feed line to the stage, or by feeding the set from a *variac* – details in the next chapter.

In thyristor line scanning circuits a very common cause of trouble is dry-joints at the leadouts of the heavy wound components or the large capacitors. If all joints are intact, 'cold' ohmmeter checking of the thyristors and other semi-conductors will locate leaky or shorted devices. For testing purposes the set can be safely switched on with a shorting link across the anode and cathode of the *scan* thyristor. This will remove the drive from the line output transformer and tripler, though the latter should already have been eliminated as a suspect by disconnecting it. If with drive thus stopped the overload disappears the l.o.p.t.-loading possibilities already outlined should be investigated.

Excessive e.h.t., sometimes leading to the destruction of tripler, one or both thyristors and their parallel diodes, is commonly caused by a problem with the gating pulse to the flyback thyristor. It may be missing, wrong frequency or intermittent, and again dry-joints are often responsible. A second and less common cause of excessive e.h.t. and flyback voltage is an open line-scan coil circuit; the connections are more likely to be in trouble than the scan yoke itself.

11

Power supply systems

In strict terminology, the power supply for operating such things as TVs, videorecorders and cameras is a *primary energy source* like domestic mains electricity, a battery or a generating set. In our context, the power supply unit (PSU) is not a generator but a controller of energy; the less energy it dissipates within itself (manifest as heating of components) the better. All the above-mentioned energy sources are subject to fluctuation: mains supplies can vary ±6% of nominal voltage due to load and distribution factors; batteries have a falling output voltage throughout their discharge cycle; and the voltage supplied by a generator depends on engine speed and the load imposed, both mechanical and electrical. Natural sources of energy such as windpower and sunlight (both are used for powering electronic and transmitting equipment, sunlight being the sole source of energy in geostationary TV satellites) are even more erratic, calling not only for stabilisation, but even for a back-up supply if they fail altogether.

Nor are supply fluctuations the only factor. Unless the *source impedance* of the electrical energy supply is zero – impossible to achieve in practice – variations in current demand (load) in the equipment have an effect on the line voltage. As electronic devices become more efficient their current consumption follows more closely the demand made upon them – a TV set's requirement may vary over 2:1 with beam current changes; the current required by a portable videorecorder depends on the function (i.e. standby, rewind, pause) in use, and different sections of a TV camera (zoom, viewfinder, or built-in cassette recorder) will come in and out of use as occasion demands. For any equipment, then, the stabilised power supply section has several functions; some or all of the following may be required:

1. Maintenance of constant output voltage against supply fluctuations.
2. Maintenance of constant output voltage against varying load
3. Transformation of supply voltage to required load-operating voltage; usually down, sometimes up
4. Rectification of a.c. supplies to render d.c. operating line
5. Facility for adjustment of stabilised output voltage to set correct conditions and take up tolerances in load
6. Provision of safety cut-outs to prevent damage and overheating in the event of an internal fault or malfunction in the load
7. In the case of mains-powered PSUs an even, low and equal demand on both half-cycles of the domestic a.c. supply
8. A minimum absorption of power in the stabilising circuits themselves, crucial where primary energy is at a premium, and a significant contribution to reliability by keeping operating temperatures low
9. Low ripple voltage on stabilised lines
10. Low internal impedance for good decoupling between different sections of the equipment using the same supply line

ZENER STABILISATION

The simplest form of voltage stabiliser is shown in Fig. 11.1(a), and consists of a series resistor and zener diode, which device has a sharp knee in its reverse voltage/current characteristic. Output voltage remains at this *zener* point for a wide range of diode currents. If the load is so great that the diode runs out of current, stabilisation breaks down. The most common application of this simple principle is in the provision of a stabilised tuning voltage for varicap tuners. Here the zener diode takes the form of a two-terminal IC (example ZTK33B) with built-in thermal compensation; unlike a simple zener, these devices have virtually zero temperature coefficient.

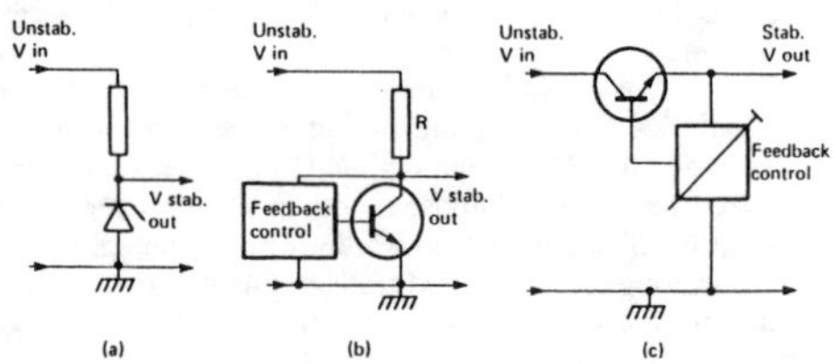

Fig. 11.1 *Three forms of simple voltage stabiliser: (a) zener diode; (b) shunt regulator; (c) series regulator*

SERIES- AND SHUNT-REGULATORS

In situations of varying load and/or supply voltage it is easy to arrange an absorption circuit to fully compensate for variations in supply and demand. The shunt regulator (Fig. 11.1(b)) is connected *across* the load and this combination is fed from the unstabilised supply; the series resistor R may be a ballast resistor, but more usually is formed by the source impedance of the supply. The current flowing in the shunt transistor is regulated at its base to maintain constant voltage across its c–e terminals.

Less wasteful of energy is the series regulator, outlined in Fig. 11.1(c). Here the control transistor is in series with the load and alters its resistance to match the demand of the load, again maintaining constant output voltage.

A practical circuit for a series regulator, as typically used in a monochrome portable TV, is given in Fig. 11.2. The regulator element is *pnp* power transistor VT201. Its voltage source is the dotted box, representing a mains transformer/rectifier/capacitor ensemble, or a 12 V car battery. At switch-on conduction in VT201 is established by c–e current via VT202, itself turned on by base current from VT203 and 'kick-start' components C201 and W201. Voltage appears on the collector of VT201 then, and is potted down in R204/205/206 for application to the base of comparator transistor VT203. This transistor's emitter is held at a steady voltage of 4.7 by zener W202 and resistor R207. VT203 collector provides an error voltage to drive a proportional current into VT202 base. This latter device behaves as a current amplifier, steering the base current in regulator VT201. Output voltage is trimmed by preset R205.

Imagine a bright picture tending to pull down the 11.3 V supply line. As it falls, VT203 (*pnp*) base voltage falls to *increase* its

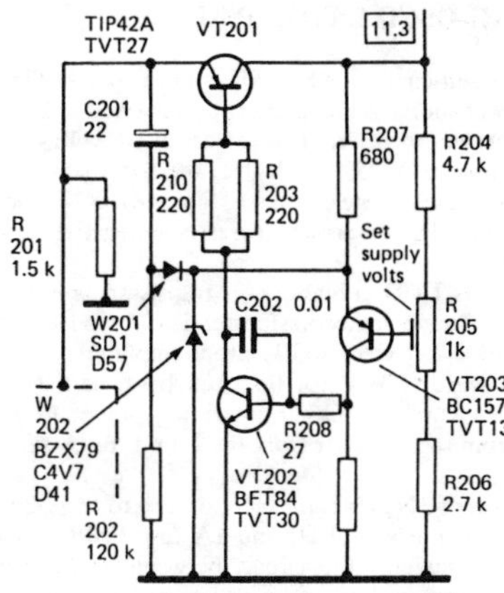

Fig. 11.2 *Practical commercial series regulator circuit*

collector current, which increases VT202 base current. VT202 collector current increases as a result, and since all of it flows through the base of regulator VT201, the latter is turned harder on to supply the extra current demand and restore the correct 11.3 V line voltage. Many such d.c. regulator circuits can respond up to and beyond 100 Hz rate, and the regulating mechanism described above can work on a 'sawtooth' basis to eliminate hum-ripple from a 'coarse' mains-derived supply. By the same token, it can absorb ripple induced on the supply line by timebase or audio output stages.

SWITCH-MODE CONCEPT

The types of regulator so far described have the advantage of simplicity but are wasteful of energy, which is dissipated as heat in the regulating device itself and in any associated ballast resistor. A more efficient method of regulating power uses a control element which itself absorbs virtually no power – a switch. The principle of switching energy into an integrator was described in Chapter 10, where a field-scan sawtooth waveform at 50 Hz was built up by feeding 15 kHz pulses into an LC store. Control was effected by varying the 'on' period of the switch, i.e. the *duty-cycle* or *mark-space ratio*. In a switch-mode power supply unit (SMPSU) the mark-space ratio of a chopper switch (which may be one or more thyristors, but is more commonly an *npn* transistor) is varied to suit the requirements of the load. When little energy is required the switch dwells only a short time in the on position, briefly dumping a charge into an inductive or capacitive reservoir to be drawn on throughout the 'off' period of the chopper switch. When the energy requirement in the load is large a monitor circuit automatically opens up the mark-space ratio to increase the charge-dumping period. In this way the energy drawn from the primary power source exactly matches the energy required by the load. There are many ways in which chopper power supplies can be arranged.

BLOCKING-OSCILLATOR PSU

One form of self-contained SMPSU is illustrated in Fig. 11.3. The primary power source is mains energy, converted to 290 V d.c. in a full-wave bridge rectifier. This unstabilised voltage enters the regulator circuit at XQ53 and XQ51, the latter point (+ve) being connected to receiver metal chassis (ground). RN04 act as surge-limiter and CN03 as reservoir to render a negative supply line at choke LN01.

The switch is TN03, a high-power transistor, and the secondary windings of chopper autotransformer LN03 feed diode/capacitor sets to render +250 V for RGB output amplifiers; +160 V for the line output stage; +34 V for field timebase; and +22 V for the audio power amplifier. Other operating potentials are derived indirectly from these, either from the l.o.p.t. or by separate series regulator circuits.

The emitter of TN03 is connected directly to the −290 V rail via sampling resistor RN09 (1 Ω) and 1A fuse FN01. LN03 primary (pins 2–12) completes the circuit between TN03 collector and ground, so that when the transistor turns on TN03 primary winding is connected directly across the 290 V rail. A secondary winding between pins 5 and 7 provides positive feedback to TN03 base, so that once started by a positive 'kick' pulse from the mains rectifier via RN11 and CN09, self-oscillation takes place in TN03, LN03 and CN12. Each time TN03 cuts off, the collapsing magnetic field in LN03 induces voltages at the output taps for rectification and storage in reservoirs CN13–CN16. It remains to regulate these output voltages by varying the duty-cycle of TN03.

Regulation

For the purpose of the regulation circuit, the 'ground' line may be taken as that connected to TN03 emitter. With respect to this ground line transformer winding 1–3, DN03 and CN04 set up a sample voltage of about +22 V. This is used to control the regulator via sampling transistor TN01. DN01 and RN07 set up a steady voltage on its emitter for comparison with the 'potted down' (RN01/2, PN01) sample applied to its base. TN01 collector is connected to the mid-point of potential divider RN05/RN06, the latter fed by a −5.5 V potential from DN04 and CN05. TN01 collector, then, takes up a potential negative of 'ground' depending on the sample voltage across CN04. This is applied to the gate of thyristor TN02.

Sampling resistor RN09 is in series with the switch, and its upper end develops a *negative* sawtooth voltage corresponding to LN03 current. TN02 cathode is connected here, and as the negative ramp reaches and passes the standing gate voltage the thyristor conducts to ground TN03 base via CN08 – TN03 switches off as a result. When TN03 goes off, CN08 is charged through DN02. The regulating action, then, is based on turning off TN03 at an earlier point in each cycle than it would if left to free-run.

A rise in output voltage increases the voltage across CN04 and increases the current in TN01, causing the negative potential at TN02 gate to fall. TN02 conducts earlier in its cathode ramp cycle; TN03 conduction is terminated earlier and the secondary voltages reduce to cancel the original rise. The converse is also true. The stabilised output voltages depend on the d.c. operating point of TN02 gate, set up by adjustment of PN01.

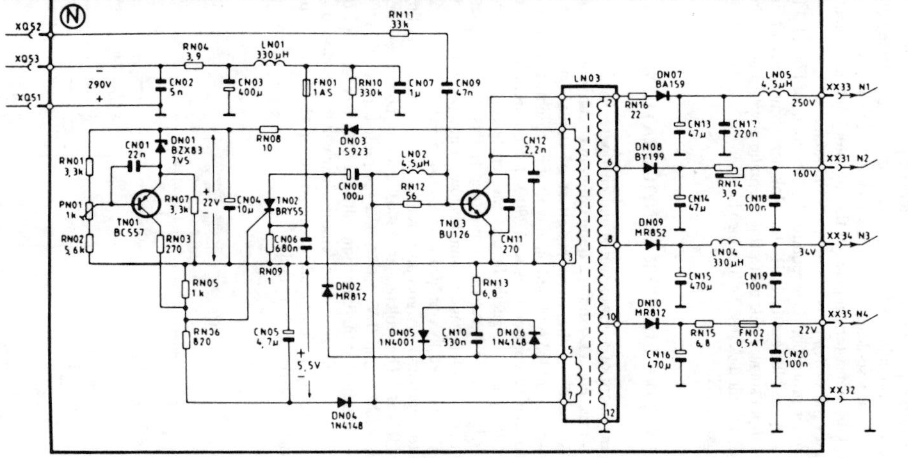

Fig. 11.3 *An early, discrete form of switch-mode PSU. Many manufacturers used almost identical circuits*

Two unique characteristics of this PSU system are a variable free-running frequency – which ranges between 22 kHz and 42 kHz with load requirements; and an inherent immunity to overload in the form of heavy damping of LN03, i.e. in the event of one of the secondary rectifiers shorting, or a short-circuit elsewhere in the receiver. Under these circumstances the chopper frequency falls to a very low rate, limiting current to safe levels and calling attention to the problem by a characteristic purring sound. Late variants of self-oscillating SMPSUs have different arrangements: some use a purpose-designed power-switching/regulating IC; some use switching transistors in place of the thyristor control element. In all cases the switch principle remains the same.

Such other protection as is required by the circuit of Fig. 11.3 is provided by fusible resistor RN14 to break heavy fault currents in the line output stage; FN02 protecting the audio power stage on the 22 V rail; and the 1 A fuse FN01 which blows in the event of a short or leakage in TN03.

ALTERNATIVE CHOPPER CONFIGURATION

The arrangement of a power switch and energy reservoir can take several forms. Fig. 11.4 shows a quite different circuit in which the action is based on the clamping effect of diode D1464. The chopper-switch T1463 is turned on and off at its base by the control circuit so that its emitter rises to +290 V for the duration of t1, storing energy as a magnetic field in the ferrite core of inductor L1465. When T1463 is cut off during time t2 this field collapses, tending to push its left-hand terminal below ground potential. Such a move is prevented by conduction in D1464, which clamps T1463 emitter to approximately ground potential via low-value sampling resistor R1461. The voltage at T1463 emitter now alternates between +290 V and 0 V. L1465 and reservoir capacitor C1406 form an integrator: at their junction will appear an average value of the square wave voltage at T1463 emitter. The voltage developed at L1466 is directly proportional to the ratio of t1 to the 64 μs (line-synchronous) switching cycle.

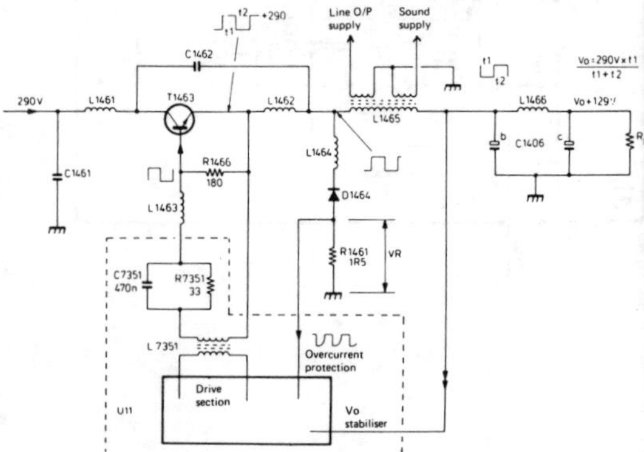

Fig. 11.4 *Switch-mode PSU using clamping diode (Philips)*

To stabilise the output voltage at C1406c against variations of input voltage and load, the 129 V output line is sampled against a reference voltage. When the drive section senses a rise in output voltage the duty-cycle of T1463 is reduced; if the output voltage falls the duty-cycle is increased. A protection function is provided by the sampling resistor R1461 as follows: an increase in current through the load increases the ripple current in D1464 and the corresponding ripple voltage across R1461. If this voltage (negative of ground) exceeds a pre-determined level an overload is indicated and the drive section cuts off, switching off chopper T1463.

For T1463 to switch cleanly and enjoy low power dissipation its base drive current must be carefully controlled. In Fig. 11.4 drive transformer L7351 isolates the pulse-forming circuits from the 0–290 V switched emitter of T1463. Choke L1463 produces a negative pulse at the end of each base drive period to ensure fast turn-off. C1462 limits T1463 dissipation at that moment by its charging pulse from the +290 V line. Coupling capacitor C7351 ensures a sharp 'attack' in chopper base drive, speeding up switch-on and minimising dissipation in T1463. R7351 limits base current to a safe level thereafter.

The secondary winding on L1465 is a convenient point from which to derive (via a rectifier and reservoir capacitor) a supply voltage for the audio amplifier section. A 20 V line is provided in this way. The other section of the secondary winding directly drives the base of the line output transistor, taking the place of the line drive transformer circuitry described in the previous chapter. It will now be obvious that the frequency and phase of the PSU drive section is critical, and must be flywheel-phased to incoming line sync pulses. In fact the switch-mode control IC (TDA2581) contains all the elements of a line oscillator/sync section. In other designs the line output transistor is driven from a winding on the chopper transformer in the same way, but the SMPSU chip is synchronised to the output of a conventional line sync/oscillator IC. The use of a line-synchronous SMPSU avoids the risk of beat frequencies between line timebase and power switch, which could give rise to spurious beat patterns on the picture.

Another approach to the design of the switch-pulse integrating system is depicted at the right of Fig. 11.5. Here the chopper transistor T12 switches a *minus* 320 V line to the bottom end of transformer winding L11 during each *on* period – the top end of L11 is grounded. The magnetic field built up in the core of L11 at this time is released when T12 turns off. Its liberation induces a reverse voltage across L11, whose bottom end now goes positive of ground, to turn on rectifier diode D18 and charge reservoir capacitors C51 and C52. This arrangement has the advantage over the configuration of Fig. 11.4 that high voltages are not developed on the line output line in the event of the chopper transistor remaining turned on, i.e. due to an internal short-circuit or a fault in its drive circuit.

Some peripheral circuits in Fig. 11.5 are worthy of mention: Secondary winding L13 generates a +20 V line via D17 and C50; secondary L12 is the source of the d.c. feedback voltage by which the control IC monitors PSU output voltage. D19, D20 and associated components protect T12 from breakdown by excessive reverse-voltage. The emitter-series resistor R89 samples the current in T12, developing a sawtooth voltage whose amplitude reflects the degree of loading on the +125 V and +20 V output lines. As with R1461 in Fig. 11.4 it is monitored by the over-current protection circuit in the control IC. The chopper transistor's base

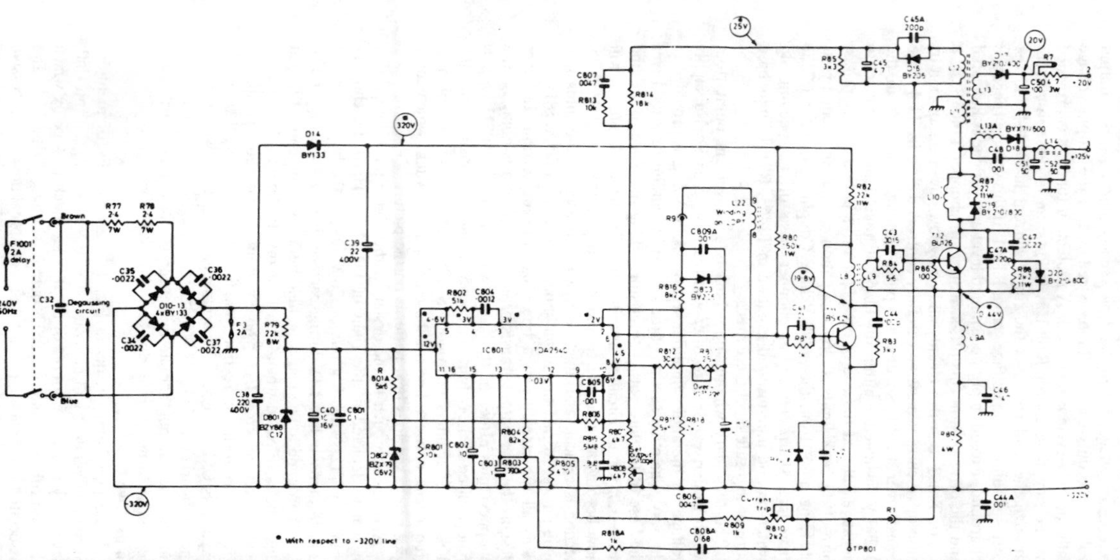

240V 50Hz
Brown
Blue
Degaussing circuit
IC801
TDA2540
Current trip
• With respect to -320V line

feed circuit components are similar in arrangement and function to their counterparts in Fig. 11.4.

IC-BASED SMPSU

Modern stabilised power supply units almost invariably use an IC in the chopper control circuit. Within the chip is incorporated a square-wave oscillator, a means of varying its mark-space ratio (duty-cycle) according to feedback information and a facility to lock it to incoming line syncs. Also present are sophisticated protection and cut-out circuits to limit energy dissipation in the event of faults within the PSU itself or the circuits fed from it. Fig. 11.6 shows the individual functions within the TDA2640 chip, the heart of the power supply system of Fig. 11.5. This IC has a built-in oscillator whose free-running frequency is determined by the components connected to pins 3, 4 and 5. These are chosen to give a frequency slightly below 15.625 kHz, permitting the oscillator to be synchronised to the (separate) line oscillator via a pulse feed to pin 2. The oscillator drives a pulse-width modulator (PWM) which provides a 12 V p–p output on pin 6. The operation of the PWM is governed by a comparator which compares a zener-derived reference voltage at pin 9 (refer also to Fig. 11.5) with a potted-down sample of output voltage entering on pin 10. The sample division ratio is variable by set-HT preset control R808.

The rest of the blocks within the TDA2640 are concerned with protection functions. A sample of l.o.p.t. flyback voltage (hence e.h.t. voltage) is fed to pin 8, and a voltage corresponding to load current between pins 11 and 12. If either is excessive the duty-cycle of the output waveform drops to zero to cut off the PSU and the TV. Some overloads are transient events due to flashover or momentarily-high beam currents. To cater for these, the IC is designed to sample conditions a few hundred milliseconds later, driving the chopper with an increasing duty-cycle via the *soft-start* circuit. If an overload is still present the off-on cycle will repeat, but

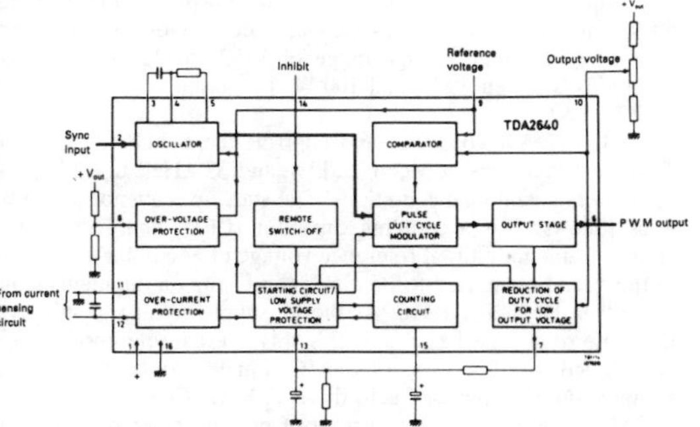

Fig. 11.6 *Internal block diagram of the TDA2640 chip used in Fig. 11.5*

not indefinitely: the IC shuts off after a number of resets determined by the size of the capacitor at pin 15, typically chosen to permit six trip-cycles.

The block connected to pin 7 is provided to prevent danger if the feedback loop goes open-circuit. In a closed-loop stabilisation circuit failure of the feedback signal will cause the system to go to full gain in an attempt to restore the 'missing' input. Should this happen in a PSU system output voltages could rise to an excessive level. The loop fault protection block ensures that immediate shutdown results if the feedback voltage to pin 10 drops to zero as a result of an open or shorted feedback loop. Another protection facility is embodied in the IC: if the supply voltage to pin 1 falls below 66% of normal the output duty-cycle is reduced. This prevents damaging surges in the chopper transistor if the mains supply is momentarily interrupted. Without this protection, the IC would go to maximum duty-cycle in an attempt to restore the falling output line voltage, and a high current could flow at the moment of mains power restoration.

Some final points on the drive section of the complete PSU of Fig. 11.5: IC operating potential of +12 V (with respect to PSU 'earth' at −320 V) is provided by dropper resistor R79 and 12 V zener diode D801. The PWM output from IC pin 6 passes into the base of chopper driver T11 whose operating voltage comes from D14 and C39, and whose base bias current is provided by R80. Over-current and excess-voltage trip thresholds are set by variable resistors R810 and R817 respectively. Line-rate synchronisation of the chopper-switch is conveniently taken from the same l.o.p.t. winding as the over-voltage monitor, and is applied to pin 2 via potential divider R816/R811.

Direct-drive PSU IC

In the circuits so far examined, the output of the control IC has needed a power amplifier, in the form of the chopper driver stage, in order to drive sufficient current into the base of the main switching transistor. A later design of switch-mode control IC, the TDA4600, has heat-sinking facilities and is capable of direct drive of the switching transistor. The circuit is given in Fig. 11.7. In essence it consists of a self-oscillating non-synchronous blocking converter whose frequency and duty-cycle automatically adjust to variations in mains supply voltage and loading of the output supply lines. The secondary voltages are stabilised to within 1 part in 200 over a mains input voltage range of 185 V to 265 V. For load variations between 30 W and 100 W the output voltages will not vary beyond ±1%.

IC631 (TDA4600) drives and controls the switching transistor T634 at frequencies between 22 kHz and 35 kHz, depending on input voltage and load conditions. The start-up sequence of the IC is as follows: first a coupling capacitor (C631) charge circuit is enabled, and an internal reference voltage of about 4 V is built up in the circuit connected to IC pin 1; this draws on the mains input supply via D616 and R616. As the IC supply voltage, coming via the same route, reaches about 12 V this internal reference voltage is switched to all sections of the IC. Finally the control logic is enabled and the chip begins to drive T634 via C631.

R621 limits the charging current of primary reservoir capacitor C626 at switch-on. IC631 starts from mains voltage via D616 and R616 at switch-on, but once PSU operation is stabilised it is powered from chopper transformer secondary winding 11–13 via D633 and C633; the action of D616 ensures that R616 current then

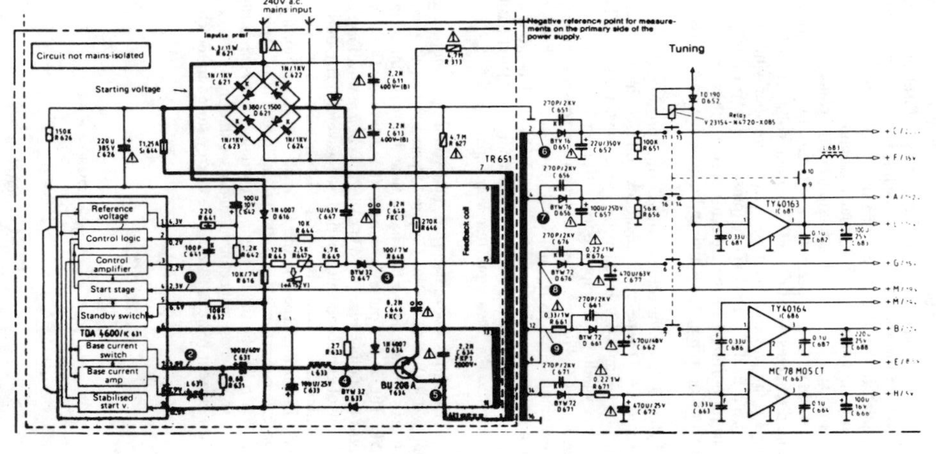

Fig. 11.7 *Chopper power supply based on TDA4600 IC " Grundig design*

falls. The IC is now held on by a bleed via R632 to pin 5 where a stand-by switch facility is provided: grounding this point will shut down the chopper supply, typically for use with a remote-control system incorporating stand-by facility. The shut-down/stand-by block within the IC also comes into action in the event of mains-supply undervoltage.

The 50 Hz a.c. supply voltage is full-wave rectified in diode bridge D621, smoothed by C626 and passed through protection fuse Si644 to form a +305 V operating line for the chopper system. It is applied to the primary winding (pin 7) of transformer TR651 whose bottom end (pin 1) is regularly grounded by main switcher T634. R646 and C646 provide a facsimile of the collector current to the IC at pin 4. C646 is permitted to charge whilst the transistor is on, and discharges whilst it is off. The ramp voltage thus formed at IC pin 4 is impressed on the base current amplifier within the chip and is used to drive T634 via IC pins 7 and 8, providing a base current proportional to the collector current, thus improving the transistor's operating conditions and minimising power dissipation within it.

Winding 9–15 on the chopper transformer provides (by means of D647 and C647) a reference feedback voltage which reflects the actual line voltages developed by the diode-capacitor sets on TR651 secondary windings. It is applied to control pin 3 via set-voltage pot R647. R648/C648 prevent over-oscillation and consequent peaks on the switching edges. R644 and C641 feeds back to the IC information on zero-crossing conditions in TR651 so that the chopper transistor is not switched on until all the energy in TR651 has been transferred to the five output reservoir capacitors C652, 657, 662, 672 and 677.

Fig. 11.8 shows relevant current and voltage waveforms in the circuit. At (a) appears the chopper transistor collector current which rises linearly during the charge time due to the inductance of TR651. The initial pulse is due to the action of C634, which smooths the falling edge of T634 collector *voltage* waveform at the beginning of each conduction period, see waveform (b); during the charge time T634 collector voltage is virtually zero. The base current driven into T634 by the IC is shown in waveform (c); it follows collector current due to the facsimile feed into IC pin 4. At a time controlled by the IC the base current is reversed to rapidly turn off T634, whose collector voltage rises sharply as a result. As collector current reduces to zero the energy stored in the chopper

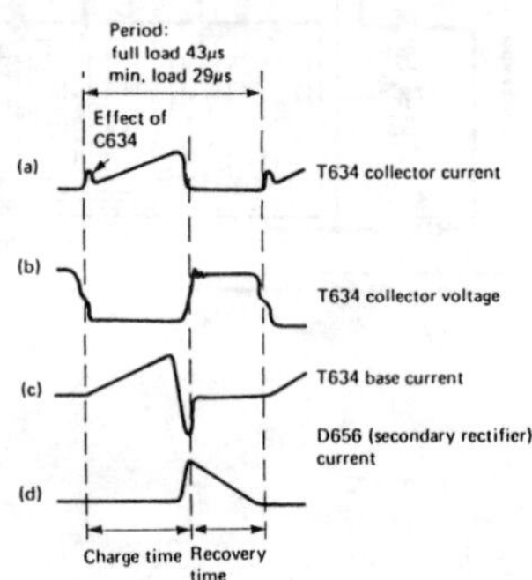

Fig. 11.8 *Voltage and current waveforms in the switching stage of a PSU incorporating the TD A4600*

transformer TR651 is transferred into the various reservoir capacitors via the rectifier diodes on TR651 secondary windings. Waveform (d) shows the current waveform through main rectifier D656, which decays linearly to zero as the charge in C657 is fully replenished.

The diode current reaches zero when all the stored energy in TR651 has been transferred to the secondary reservoir capacitors and loads. At this point all the voltages across TR651 windings are at zero, and T634 collector is at primary supply voltage, +305 V, see Fig. 11.8(b). This condition is noted at IC pin 3, whose decay to 0.6 V triggers the chopper transistor on once more to repeat the cycle. This 'stop-before-proceeding' characteristic accounts for the fact that operating frequency depends on supply and demand conditions. The circuit runs at about 23 kHz under normal circumstances, rising to some 35 kHz under zero beam-current conditions. Inductors L633, L634 and capacitor C641 are included to prevent any tendency to self-oscillation at r.f., which would upset T634 operation and could cause spurious pattern pickup at i.f., v.h.f. or u.h.f. frequencies.

The 12 V '+B' line (and others) in Fig. 11.7 is provided by a series regulator of the type discussed earlier in this chapter. It is fed from the +M 19 V line, and takes the form of a three-legged IC. As with most such semiconductors its response reaches up to r.f. so decoupling capacitors C686 and C687 are used to ensure stability. LF decoupling thereafter is catered for by large capacitor C688, as it is for the other supply lines by capacitors C652, C657, C662, C672 and C677.

Internal overload protection is embodied in the TDA4600 IC in the form of an overload ident circuit connected to pin 3. This operates on the start stage and control logic to reduce drive to T634 in the event of abnormal conditions within the PSU or on the controlled output lines.

Mains isolation

Provided the chopper transformer is a well-insulated and high quality component capable of withstanding a peak voltage of 5 kV between primary and secondary windings, it can fulfil a mains-isolating role, with the mains-live primary circuits (including the control IC itself) in a screened and protected section of the circuit board – or on a separate panel. The ground line of the TV or monitor itself can then be safely connected to true earth, exposed metalwork or other video/TV equipment. This is an essential feature of any piece of equipment to which direct connection of *baseband* audio and video signal feeds are to be made, and saves the provision and maintenance of special high working voltage isolating components in the aerial socket assembly. The circuit of Fig. 11.7 provides this mains isolation, the safety barrier being represented by the dotted line around the heavily-shaded portion. The only link between the two is formed by the two small high-grade capacitors C611 and C613 which prevent the isolated chassis from drifting to some high potential with respect to true earth and mains neutral potential as a result of static charges.

STEP-UP SWITCH-MODE PSU

Except where they drive very small picture tubes, TV chassis need a main supply line voltage around 110–170 V to satisfy the requirements of the line output stage. Where operation from a mobile power source such as 12 V and 24 V vehicle and marine batteries is required a step-up converter is used. Fig. 11.9 shows the circuit of a switch-mode d.c.–d.c. converter designed by Ferguson for this purpose. This circuit (shown in simplified form) uses a T9005 V transistor TR407 in a blocking oscillator configuration. The oscillator/output transformer T401 has a pre-set switching arrangement in its primary winding to cater for 12 V or 24 V inputs. The voltage induced across secondary winding 2–4 is rectified and smoothed to form the 115 V stabilised output. Secondary winding 3–5 supplies positive feedback to the transistor's base, whose operating voltage sits on a pedestal of 0.5 V set up by diodes D408 and D409 to ensure correct start-up conditions via resistors R410 and R413. R427 and C413 protect TR407 from voltage surges.

The regulating action is based on the collector-current sampling transformer T402 and a two-transistor regenerative switch TR405/TR406. TR406 base is biased from the junction of R419 and R422 (via T402 secondary) such that when the voltage across R425 (corresponding to TR407 collector current) reaches a predetermined level TR406 conducts, turning on TR405 and rapidly latching the pair into hard conduction. A grounding path for the positive plate of C407 is thus established. This point previously carried about 6 V, so the negative plate of C407 tries to move 6 V negative likewise. The effect is to divert TR407 base current into C407, as a result of which TR407 turns off; its base is now driven into reverse bias by T401's feedback winding.

A further circuit (not shown) compares a sample voltage derived from secondary winding 2–7 with a zener reference potential; an error voltage is developed for application to the junction of R419 and R422 where it influences TR407 base bias to complete a voltage stabilisation loop. Further circuit sections cater for low supply voltage and overcurrent trip functions; the latter operates on any load current exceeding 650 mA. The low supply voltage protection device shuts down the converter if the battery voltage falls below 10.9 V (21.8 V in 24 V mode). Other specifications are: Input voltage 11 V–14.4 V and 23–28 V; input current 4–5 A (depending on beam current) in 12 V mode, 2–2.5 A in 24 V mode; reverse-input voltage protection by diode and fuse.

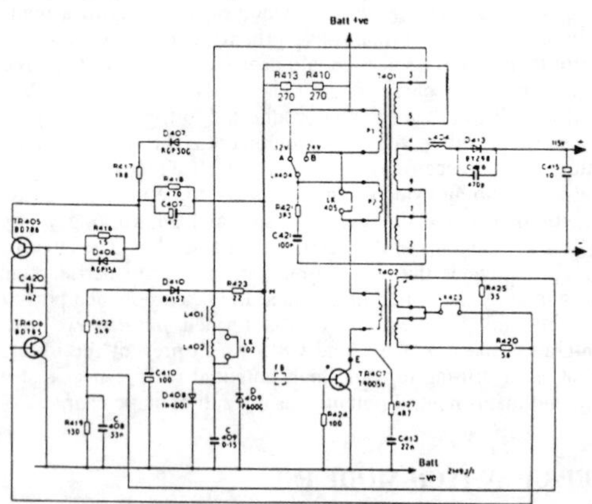

Fig. 11.9 *Voltage step-up SMPSU designed by Ferguson to operate a small-sceen colour TV from vehicle or boat batteries*

INTEGRATION OF POWER SUPPLY AND LINE OUTPUT STAGE

Fig. 11.10 shows the outline of a combined power supply and line timebase by Salora. Since the majority of chopper PSUs operate at line frequency a combination of the two sections is a logical step. The Salora design shown here features very low power consumption (38 W for a 41 cm tube, 45 W for a 56 cm tube), making more practical its operation from battery power.

Thyristors THB1 and THB2 operate at line frequency. THB1 forms the start-up circuit which also acts as an electronic fuse, cutting off if the voltage on either the 20 V or 28 V rail rises abnormally. If the rise is a short-term one THB1 switches on again; if the fault is sustained THB1 continues to interrupt the PSU's operation.

THB2 is switched on during the line scan period and off during the flyback period, behaving as a chopper with its parallel diode acting as efficiency/clamping diode. HB1 is a thick-film hybrid assembly akin to an IC, in a 28-pin ceramic-based package, type LF0015. It contains the soft-start, voltage limiting and electronic fuse functions. Start-up supplies come from the DB40–43 bridge rectifier at mains transformer MM1, which with line-pulse transformers MB4, MB5 and l.o.p.t. MB1 provide complete mains isolation of the receiver. The sample pulse for regulation control comes from MB1 winding 5–17; a sample mains feed to the control circuit comes via DB38. Operation of the line output stage is conventional, using a BU208 output transistor; all auxiliary supplies for the operation of the picture tube and other electronic stages of the TV/monitor are derived from l.o.p.t. MB1.

VIDEORECORDER PSUs

TV and monitor PSU systems operate at relatively high power, and so are more vulnerable to breakdown than other sections of the set. For this reason, and because of the great diversity of circuit designs encountered, much of this chapter has been devoted to them. In general the circuits of videorecorders require low-voltage supplies in the 9–12 V region, with some exceptions such as varicap tuning voltage sources and screen/accelerating potentials for florescent status/display panels, both low-energy devices.

To derive the low stabilised voltages required from mains power, two approaches are possible: a double-wound 50 Hz mains transformer with secondary windings feeding rectifier sets and series regulators as required; or a switch-mode PSU with (typically) a closely-regulated 12 V output. Both give the necessary full mains isolation, and the manufacturer's decision rests upon weight, cost and reliability factors. Most mains-powered home-based machines adopt the former option. In a mains-driven unit intended to power portable video machines and cameras, weight and bulk are saved by using switch-mode techniques – essential where, as is sometimes the case, the mains power unit is the same size and shape as the Ni-Cad or lead-acid battery whose place it takes.

Videorecorders have special requirements of their power supplies; in many cases regulators are switched by the system control section, and during standby mode power has to be maintained to clock-display, timer and system-control circuits. In portable equipment, power supplies are provided and withdrawn as the

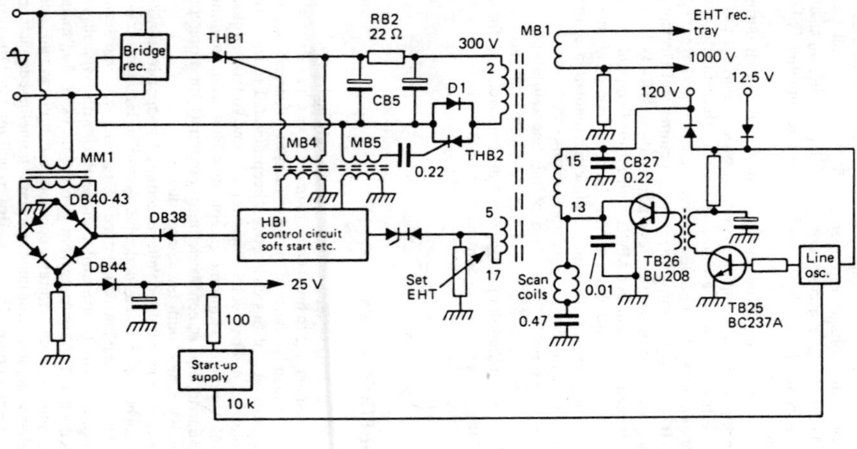

Fig. 11.10 *Integrated line output stage and power supply by Salora*

mode and user's requirements dictate in order to minimise power consumption and prolong battery life.

Tiny d.c.–d.c. converters are often found in the midst of videorecorder operating circuits. To provide a low-current unstabilised supply a postage-stamp sized screening can conceals a miniature ferrite transformer, blocking oscillator transistor and rectifier diode, working into an external reservoir capacitor. Apart from the absence of a stabilising circuit, these devices work on just the same principles as high-power SMPSUs, and have high conversion efficiency. They are particularly useful where a negative line is required, as where a fluorescent display panel is to be fed directly from a microprocessor or display-driver IC.

SERVICING POWER SUPPLY UNITS

The power-supply section of a TV or monitor vies with the line timebase section for the distinction of being the most troublesome area of operation, and as such the one most likely to need service attention when breakdown occurs.

The approach to servicing a faulty PSU depends very much on its design and vintage, and whether the fault is destructive of components. The first point to bear in mind is the safety aspect, especially where the chassis is not isolated from mains potential. In the workshop a double-wound isolating transformer is essential to reduce risk of electric shock to the technician. It should ideally be rated at 500 VA and protected on the secondary side by a 2.5 A anti-surge fuse; and on the primary side by a 5 A HRC fuse. While this will eliminate the risk of a mains-to-earth shock, it will not protect the operator if he completes a path between its secondary terminals or across any derived a.c. or d.c. voltages. This is particularly relevant where PSU 'ground' is at a different potential from signal 'ground' – in Fig. 11.5 the two are 320 V apart, for instance. PSU fault diagnosis is generally done with test instrument's 'low' line connected to the common return line within the circuit – 'PSU ground', see, for instance, the top of Fig. 11.7.

Where the PSU is dead, normal voltage- and oscillogram-testing will trace the root of the fault; it is important to bear in mind the presence and effect of the various cut-out and trip circuits, however. A completely dead PSU may be the result of a short-circuit line output transistor, secondary rectifier or efficiency diode; so ohmmeter checks of such vulnerable components may solve the problem without an in-depth investigation of the PSU. If no overload is present, the lack of results will generally be due to failure of the switch-transistor or thyristor to turn on; the drive pulses can be checked back to source.

In cases where a trip circuit is obviously operating (indicated by a pulsing, ticking or initial burst of energy from the PSU) it is very unwise to disable the trip circuit itself – without protection, the fault currents and voltages can damage components. Much can be gleaned by carefully observing and evaluating the effects on each pump-cycle where relevant – the appearance of a burst of sound and expanding flash of picture, for instance, suggests that the timebases and PSU are working, but that the overvoltage trip is operating. In that particular case, monitoring the PSU output voltage with a d.c.-coupled oscilloscope (the response of a meter, analogue or digital, is too slow) will show it to rise slightly above normal on each pump-cycle, leading to an investigation of the PSU reference-voltage zener diode and the resistive network associated with the 'set voltage' pre-set control. Other 'pump-cycle' effects may be a squawk or arc from the l.o.p.t. (insulation breakdown or incorrect line frequency) or a low-frequency 'thump' with no activity in the timebase or audio stage (heavy loading on PSU-derived line; l.o.p.t. or tripler failure, etc.).

The most difficult PSU faults to deal with are those which cause damage to components – within or external to the PSU itself – at the moment of switch-on. Very often cold-checking of relevant semiconductors will reveal the culprit. If not, and where the cause of a trip coming into action is not obvious, an almost indispensible aid is a variac, a variable mains transformer. With this device, applied mains input voltage can be 'wound up' from zero while voltages and currents are monitored by test instruments. Where kick-start circuits are employed, especially those incorporating a charging capacitor, it will be necessary to override them by means of an external supply, or a suitable bypass resistor.

The application of an external voltage (i.e. from a low-voltage battery or stabilised power supply unit) is a useful aid to diagnosis, applicable to both discrete and IC-based SMPSU control circuits. With an appropriate operating voltage applied, the oscillator, control section and sometimes the driver stage can be made to run for study of drive waveforms and voltages. Since the chopper device is unpowered at this time there is no risk of damage; with correct drive established (and still in the presence of the low-voltage external supply) the variac can be used to judiciously turn up the 'mains' voltage; the set-up for this is outlined in Fig. 11.11.

The capacitors used in SMPSUs work hard, and sometimes fail with various effects: trouble in the *primary* reservoir capacitors may cause heavy 100 Hz modulation of supply lines, with a moving wasp-waist travelling vertically over the picture; drying up of the secondary (PSU output) reservoir capacitors may cause line-rate modulation of their supply line, leading to shading effects or operation of the over-volts trip on ripple-peaks. The same fault in PSU-internal capacitors used for smoothing the sampling voltage or the control-system operating voltage often gives rise to a tearing of the picture and/or a squawking noise from the chopper transformer. The latter effect is often dependent on tube beam-current, when it will vary with adjustment of brightness and contrast controls.

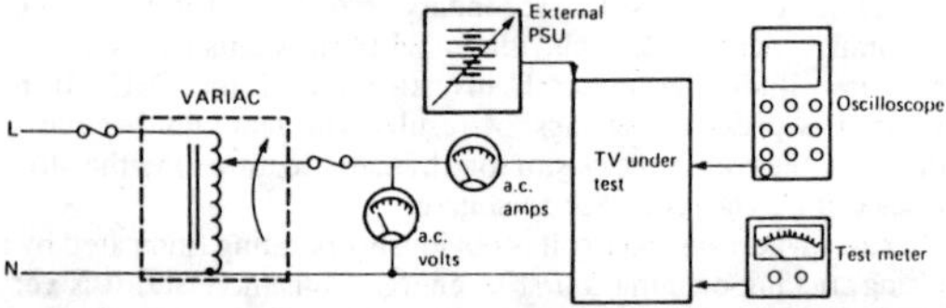

Fig. 11.11 *Set-up for diagnosis of power-supply circuit faults. Note: An isolating transformer is not shown here; the initial current surge into a large variac will generally blow a correctly-rated isolating-transformer fuse. Unless the variac is operated from a 'floating' supply the mains-to-earth shock hazard must be taken into account during servicing*

12

Video on magnetic tape

The use of magnetic tape to record and replay video signals is now commonplace, but the techniques involved are not so straightforward as for audio recording. The main problem is the relatively large bandwidth of the video signal, which for a broadcast-standard signal extends from d.c. (about 25 Hz in practice) to 5.5 MHz. For domestic video-recorders a more limited response is adequate – the h.f. roll-off occurs at about 2.5 MHz, permitting a more sparing use of the tape.

A magnetic tape system's output level is proportional to the *rate of change* of the magnetic flux, so that output is directly geared to frequency. Thus each halving of frequency (octave) halves the output signal, giving the tape/head interface a characteristic 6 dB/octave curve. Because the difference in levels between magnetic saturation of the tape's coating and the inherent noise of the system is about 1000:1, corresponding to 60 dB, it is plain that the 6 dB/octave will permit a maximum of ten octaves to be fitted between the noise floor and the overload point, so long as massive compensation is provided to equalise replay levels across the frequency spectrum.

FM MODULATION

A television signal, even the bandwidth-restricted one described above, occupies fifteen or sixteen octaves, and so cannot be directly recorded on tape by any means. *Indirect* methods of recording are possible, however, and they involve modulation of the video signal onto a carrier. Invariably an f.m. carrier is chosen for this purpose: the use of f.m. increases noise immunity, masks shortfall in signal strength stemming from slight tracking errors and imperfect head/tape contact, and permits either (a) its use as recording bias for a second signal carrying the chroma information or (b) the facility to drive the tape coating into magnetic saturation on each f.m. carrier cycle to further improve S/N ratio.

The way in which the f.m. carrier technique reduces the octave range is shown in Fig. 12.1. Carrier frequencies are assigned for both extremes of the luminance signal waveform, typically 3.8 MHz for sync tip and 4.8 MHz for peak white. This actually permits the recording of d.c. (zero frequency) video signals since a constant level of white or grey will give a constant f.m. carrier frequency. During each line sync pulse the carrier falls to 3.8 MHz for its 4.7 μs duration, and during the 52 μs active line period the carrier frequency rapidly deviates between 4.1 and 4.8 MHz to describe the levels of light and shade in the TV picture.

In deviating in this way the f.m. modulator produces sidebands, and the *modulation index* (the relationship between video and f.m. frequencies) is chosen so that virtually all the sideband energy is confined to the first pair of sidebands above and below the carrier frequency itself. In the VHS system, for instance, enough sideband energy is recovered to properly demodulate the f.m. signal when the record and replay frequency response extends from about 1 MHz to about 7 MHz, which embraces the entire lower sideband

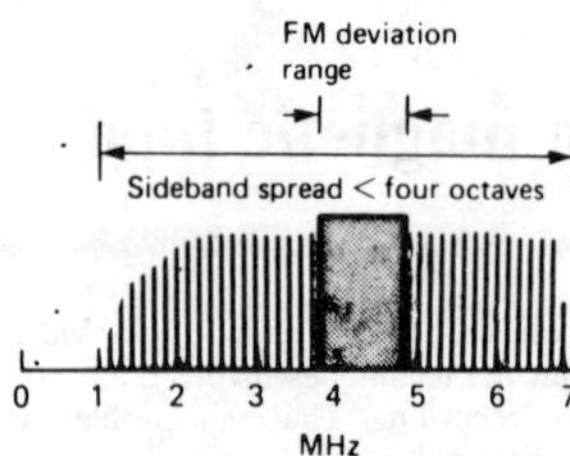

Fig. 12.1 *Reduction of octave range of signal by f.m. modulation: the solid block represents carrier deviation range, and the lined areas the first-order sidebands*

and a portion of the upper one – balance is restored by careful shaping of the frequency response of the playback amplifier. An operating range of frequencies between 1 and 7 MHz represents an octave range of less than four – well within the capability of the magnetic tape system.

HEAD GAP AND WRITING SPEED

Although the octave range has necessarily been reduced by using an f.m. carrier system, the maximum frequency required to be recorded has greatly increased. Peak white occurs at 4.8 MHz, and the upper sideband signal – most extensive when sharply-defined detail is being recorded – extends towards 8 MHz. The head/tape transfer system must be capable of passing such frequencies, and the magnetic surface of the tape capable of retaining them. The period of an 8 MHz signal is 125 ns, and during this short time enough tape must traverse the video head gap to adequately imprint the entire cycle as a magnetic pattern in the tape coating. With a typical headgap of 0.5 micron ($= 5 \times 10^{-7}$m) the tape-to-head speed needs to be around 5 metres/second: this is called writing speed.

The achievement of such a high writing speed is very difficult in a 'direct' transport system, where extremely high spool and capstan speeds would be required. A solution is to rotate the heads themselves against the tape; the heads are mounted on a spinning head-drum, and protrude beyond its surface to make intimate contact with the tape ribbon which itself is wrapped around the drum. For domestic (and many professional) video formats the arrangement takes the form of a *helical-scan* setup, illustrated in basic form in Fig. 12.2.

HELICAL TAPE SCAN

The tape is wrapped around approximately 180° of the drum's periphery and takes a helical path due to the tilting of the head drum and a precision-machined guide rabbet on the lower (stationary) part of the head drum. The head assembly spins anticlockwise at 1500 r.p.m. which confers the required high writing speed. All that is required of the tape transport system now is that it moves the tape along by one track-width per head scan in order that successive tracks are laid down side by side and just abutting each other during record. At playback the same tape-transport system ensures that as each new head sweep presents itself to the tape wrap a fresh track is

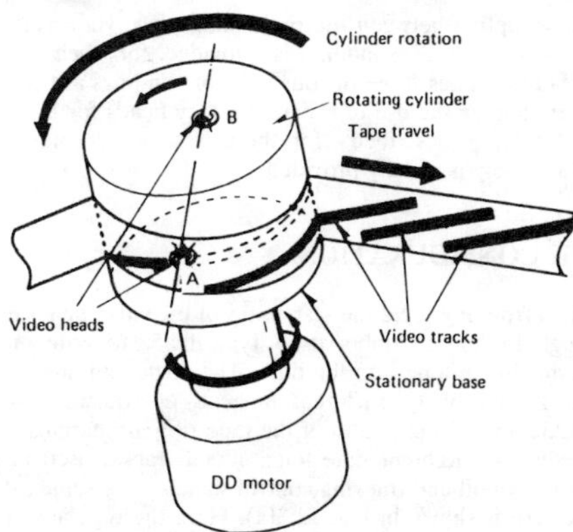

Fig. 12.2 *Basic principle of helical tape scanning*

lined up in its path for readout. In a typical system using 49 μm-wide video tracks the tape progresses through the deck at 2.34 cm/s, pulled around the head drum by a downstream capstan/pinchwheel assembly. At the entry and exit points of the tape's head-drum wrap are positioned guides which precisely align the path of the tape around the drum; these and other mechanical aspects of the desk will be examined in detail in Chapter 17.

The head-tips must maintain intimate contact with the magnetic surface of the tape. In audio-recorder practice this is achieved by the use of pressure-pads which hold the tape tight against the heads. That is obviously impractical in a helical-scan system, where a degree of lateral tension is imparted to the tape in its head-wrap by (a) a *back*-tension brake on the feed spool; and (b) the friction of the tape against the surfaces of the upper and lower head drum sections. Against the taut tape ribbon the rotating videohead-tips, which project about 50 μm from the drum face surface, push out a moving 'stretch-spot' in which the required head-tape pressure is set up.

TWO-HEAD SCANNING

Because the tape wrap only covers half the circumference of the head drum, and signal transfer must take place all the time, conventional domestic head drums are fitted with two video heads. As one leaves the tape wrap at the end of a scan, another (diametrically opposite) begins a new scan of the tape. The signals from each head are routed in turn into the replay amplifiers by a switch during playback – the switch is synchronised by a head-position sensor associated with the head drum. During record both heads are driven with writing signals, though only the one traversing the tape is recording at any one moment.

Rotating transformer

The transfer of video signals to and from the spinning video heads is accomplished by a rotating transformer whose ferrite core is arranged as two shallow discs concentric with the head drum itself. One half is stationary and the other rotates with the head disc, magnetic coupling between the two taking place via a very small air-gap. One pair of windings is provided for each head; in multi-head machines three or four pairs of windings are required. In a later chapter the use of separate rotary heads for hi-fi sound signal transfer is described – for these a separate rotary transformer assembly is usually provided.

TRACK CONFIGURATION

As is plain from Fig. 12.2 the scan paths of the video heads make a small angle to the tape ribbon itself, typically 5°, to write a narrow track some 10 cm long into the tape. The angle and alignment of the head-guide rabbet is such that the heads do not sweep over the entire 12.65 mm (½ in) width of the tape ribbon; margins are left at the edges to accommodate longitudinal tracks, used in some formats for sound and tracking-control signals. The standard VHS track pattern is shown in Fig. 12.3(a). Here the tape advances at 2.34 cm/s to give tracks 49 microns wide. They are scanned from bottom to top of the tape. The upper tape edge is reserved for a conventional sound track 1 mm wide, which for stereo is split into two 0.35 mm tracks separated by a 0.3 mm guard band. The lower tape edge carries the control track, which provides a positioning reference for the video tracks themselves, and is used to guide the head sweeps during replay. This topic will be examined in more detail later.

Fig. 12.3(b) gives the Betamax track pattern. The tape width is 12.65 mm again, but video tracks are narrower at 33 microns with a correspondingly lower linear tape speed of 1.87 cm/s. The larger Beta head drum of 74.5 cm diameter is responsible for this format's high writing speed of 5.83 m/s compared with VHS format's 62 mm drum and 4.86 m/s writing speed.

Tape parameters for Video 8 are given in Fig. 12.3(c). A major difference from other formats is the tape width. This narrow tape lends itself well to portable, mobile and lightweight video applications, especially since its cassette package (95 × 62.5 × 15 mm) is little bigger than an audio type. Except for special applications like programme indexing/cueing and other auxiliary signals, the V8 format has no need of longitudinally-recorded tracks. Tracking-control signals in an ATF (Automatic Track Finding, see later) system are recorded along with the video signals themselves, and sound is also carried in the narrow helical tracks – this technique of sound-with-vision (hi-fi) record and playback will be examined in Chapter 16, and is essential in the V8 system since the linear tape speed – approximately 2 cm/s in standard-play mode and 1 cm/s in LP mode – would render very low quality sound from a stationary-head system.

Other features of V8 technology are a facility for PCM (Pulse Code Modulation) audio recording on a 30° extension of the video track; a relatively low writing speed of 3.1 m/s, due to the conveniently-small head drum diameter of 40 mm; and a 34.5 micron track width, which in LP mode reduces to 17.2 micron.

Format parameters

Table 12.1 gives a comparison of the main physical features of each format in current use. In comparing the data and dimensions in Fig. 12.2 and Table 12.1 the following general points should be borne in mind: (a) Narrow video tracks give high recording density

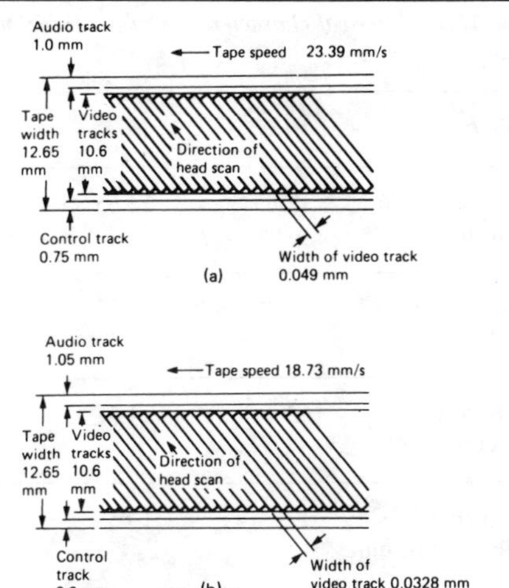

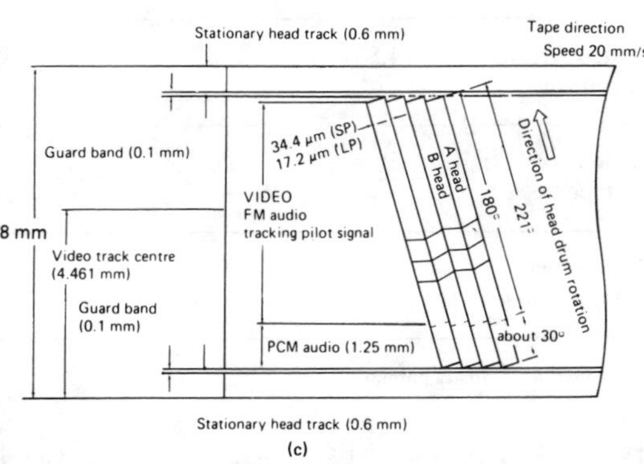

Fig. 12.3 *Tape track configurations: (a) VHS; (b) Betamax; (c) Video 8. All are drawn for standard-play (SP) mode*

on tape but an inferior noise performance; at track widths below 25 micron good tracking is difficult to achieve without an ATF system. (b) Head drum diameter is directly related to video-track writing speed; the larger the drum (for a given wrap angle, i.e. 180°) the greater the writing speed and the wider the frequency response. (c) Linear tape speed determines the sound-channel frequency response where longitudinal tracks are used – the higher the speed the greater the frequency range. (d) Longitudinal-track audio S/N ratio depends on track-width; the half-width stereo tracks for use with stationary audio heads have the worst S/N ratio. (e) All half-wrap head drums for use with 50 field/s TV systems rotate at 1500 r.p.m. in order that one half-revolution occupies exactly the period of one

Table 12.1 *Physical characteristics of the three main videotape formats*

Format	*VHS*	*Beta*	*Video 8*
Tape width, mm	12.65	12.65	8
SP linear tape speed, cm/s	2.339	1.873	2.051
Standard drum diameter, mm	62	74.5	40
Audio track width, mono, mm	1.0	1.05	0.5*
SP video track width, μm	49	32.8	34.4
Video writing speed, m/s	4.86	5.83	3.12
Video track angle to tape	5°57′	5°01′	4°54′
Video head azimuth offset	±6°	±7°	±10°

*only used for auxiliary purposes

TV field; in 60 Hz systems (USA, Canada, etc.) the head-drum speed is 1800 r.p.m.

AZIMUTH OFFSET

As the diagrams of Fig. 12.3 show, in all current formats the video tracks are laid directly alongside each other, with no intervening guard band. When a track is being read out during playback the adjacent tracks give rise to spurious signals in the video head, even when it is correctly 'tracked' and exactly centred on the wanted track. These *crosstalk* signals can cause patterning and interference on the reproduced picture. Since adjacent tracks are scanned by different heads (i.e. the two heads' tracks are interleaved) the problem of crosstalk can be reduced by making each video head insensitive to the tracks recorded by the other. It is done by the *azimuth-offset* technique.

Conventional (i.e. audio) tape recorders use heads whose magnetic gap is at right-angles to the direction of travel of the tape; this may be regarded as 'normal' azimuth. If a tape recorded by a normal-azimuth head is replayed in a machine whose head-gap is not at right angles to the tape's travel the signal developed in that replay head will be very deficient in h.f. response, and the greater the azimuth offset the more will high frequencies be attenuated; indeed a high-frequency tone on a test tape is used to set up the azimuth angle of stationary audio heads in video and audio tape machines. By cutting the gaps on the two video heads on the drum at opposite angles from normal, the magnetic patterns written into adjacent tracks will have offset azimuth characteristics as shown in Fig. 12.4: azimuth angles are generally about ±6°. Crosstalk will still take place at low frequencies but from 1 MHz upwards a significant and increasing immunity will be manifest. As we shall shortly see, the colour, and where applicable the ATF signals occupy the vulnerable l.f. end of the tape frequency spectrum. Special circuitry eliminates the effects of crosstalk from the colour signal, while the ATF system *depends* on crosstalk for its operation. Each will be examined in due course.

COLOUR RECORDING

What has been described so far is only concerned with the luminance and audio components of the TV signal. The space between zero and 1 MHz in the tape-frequency spectrum (Fig. 12.1) is reserved for the chroma signal, and to prevent it being encroached upon by the lower sideband of the luminance f.m. signal, the rise-time and frequency range of the latter are reduced in the pre-modulator luminance processing stages; any shortcomings in this bandpass filter will permit luminance and chroma signals to cross-modulate, with consequent patterning in the played-back picture.

The colour signal is recorded direct onto the tape without any form of modulation system. It is already encoded and based on a 4.43 MHz subcarrier whose phase and amplitude relative to the accompanying burst signal describe the colours in the picture. To interfere in any way with the chroma signal would be to invite hue and saturation errors; to decode and demodulate it to baseband for recording and encode/modulate it during replay would be a complex

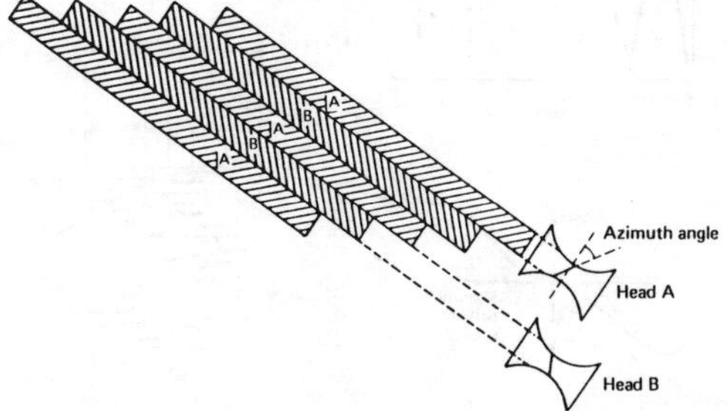

Fig. 12.4 *Azimuth patterns in tape tracks and corresponding head-gap cuts*

and unpredictable business. The PAL (or other) colour signal cannot be recorded in its 4.43 MHz form as broadcast, however: it is above the frequency range of the baseband signals that the system can handle; the timing jitter introduced by the mechanics of the recording/playback process would play havoc with the phasing of the subcarrier signal and hence the hue; and the bandwidth demand would be too great to accommodate in the limited tape spectrum. Two processes are carried out on the chroma signal to slot it into the 0–1 MHz space assigned to it. It is bandwidth-restricted in a bandpass filter which limits its sideband excursions to ±500 kHz on each side of the carrier frequency; and it is frequency-shifted by a heterodyne process to a new base frequency around 600 kHz. Thus is formed a lower-definition, lower-frequency chrominance signal with all characteristics of phase, amplitude and burst features intact. This new frequency allocation and 'clipping of wings' tailors it for the position it occupies in the tape-frequency spectrum: it is added to the f.m. luminance signal and passed to the heads for recording. Fig. 12.5(a) shows the complete signal spectrum on tape.

FM carrier as recording bias

Because the transfer characteristic of magnetic tape is not linear, Fig. 12.5(b), a recording *bias* must be provided and added to the signal to be recorded if severe distortion is not to take place. It is normal practice in audio tape recorders to add a relatively high frequency (say 40 kHz) switching signal to the audio waveform before it is applied to the recording head; the locally-generated bias signal is very carefully controlled in amplitude so that its peaks sit in the centres of the linear sections A–B and C–D in Fig. 12.5(b). As the record signal is rapidly switched between these two centrepoints by the bias signal, it is printed *in linear fashion* as magnetic patterns in the tape, as Fig. 12.5(c) shows. The ability to work on both sections of the tape transfer curve increases the replay level and improves S/N ratio.

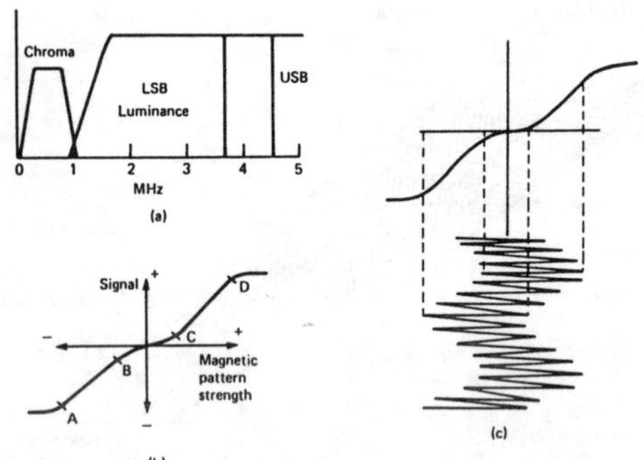

Fig. 12.5 *Video signals on tape: (a) frequency spectrum; (b) transfer curve; (c) effect of recording (hf) bias*

In the *colour-under* recording system used in domestic videorecorders the f.m. luminance carrier acts as a.c. bias source for the low-frequency chrominance signal. The two are added in the recording amplifier, and the variations in 'bias' frequency matter not at all – during replay a low-pass filter in the chrominance amplifier removes all signal components above 1 MHz.

For the scheme to work the levels of both f.m. luminance carrier and chrominance signal must be closely controlled, and their pre-set amplitudes depend very much on the characteristics of the tape to be used. The level of the f.m. carrier (*luminance writing current*) must be set to take the tape's magnetic coating halfway to saturation in each direction; the chrominance record level then must be trimmed so that the largest expected colour-signal amplitude (fully-saturated cyan or red) drives the magnetic surface of the tape to just short of saturation in the positive direction, and just short of non-linearity in the negative direction. Correct settings of these levels ensure low signal distortion and maximum S/N ratio. In the audio world, different tape materials (oxide, metal, chrome, etc.) are available, and need different bias and drive settings for optimum performance; for videorecorders (as yet) the levels are pre-set to the type of tape available for that format. The metal and metal-evaporated tapes used with Video-8 format have very different bias, coercitivity and saturation characteristics to conventional tape as used in other formats. Where colour is not present in the signal to be recorded (mainly vintage films) a useful gain in noise performance can be achieved by increasing the gain of the luminance recording amplifier; a 6 dB boost in writing current drives the tape into magnetic saturation in both directions on each cycle of f.m. carrier.

HEAD TRACKING

Although the tape guides and the lower-drum rabbet ensure that the head sweeps are in the right plane to align with the videotape tracks during replay (and to record standardised patterns on the tape during record) the earlier formats such as VHS and Beta do not incorporate any replay-head guidance system *within the recorded track* itself. For these systems a track-position indicator must also be recorded on tape. It takes the form of a marker pulse recorded on the control track by a stationary head downstream of the head-drum scanner. This control-pulse head is incorporated into the audio head assembly, and during record is fed with one pulse per 40 ms, marking the tape at alternate video tracks. The control pulse is derived from the incoming video signal itself, to which the head drum speed and phase are also locked; this ensures correct phasing between video tracks and control-track pulses and establishes a fixed *physical* relationship on tape between the two. The control track pulses are used during replay to establish and hold the head-sweep paths in line with the video tracks on the tape.

At playback the head sweeps will be in the correct plane, but without tracking control there is no reason why they should be aligned with the pre-recorded tracks. As alternate tracks are recorded with offset azimuths, correct and noise-free replay can only be assured by means of a control loop based on the off-tape control-track pulses, referencing head-sweep positions to the actual tracks on tape. Videorecorders using this system have a tracking control with which tolerances can be taken up: the tracking control acts as a phasing control with which the 'head-aiming path' can be rocked about the nominally-correct position. Optimum setting of the tracking control is when the head sweep is centred on the track and the reproduced picture shows minimum noise.

AUTOMATIC TRACKING SYSTEM

The Video 8 format uses a more advanced form of head-tracking control called Automatic Track Finding (ATF). This system relies on the fact that at relatively low recording frequencies the azimuth offset of the two video heads is not effective in preventing crosstalk from tracks adjacent to the one being scanned.

The principle is to add to the video signal being recorded a pilot tone at the very low end of the tape-frequency spectrum. A different pilot tone is used on successive tracks in a carefully-chosen sequence: 101 kHz, 117 kHz, 163 kHz and 147 kHz. The sequence then repeats over successive groups of four tracks – frequencies given here are approximate. The track layout is shown in Fig. 12.6(a). During replay the ATF tones are read off the tape and separated from the video signals in a low-pass filter. When the correct track is being scanned by the appropriate head the most prominent ATF frequency is that coming from the track being read. There are, however, vestiges of crosstalk signals from *both* adjacent tracks, and each of these beats with the main ATF signal to give two new frequencies: examination of Fig. 12.6(a) shows that for any given track the beat frequencies are either (in round figures) 46 kHz (e.g. crosstalk appearing on track 3 output from adjacent track 4) or 16 kHz (i.e. crosstalk appearing on track 3 output from adjacent track 2). The ATF frequencies are carefully chosen to ensure that this is so, see Fig. 12.6(b). Continuing with track 3 as our example, an increase in 46 kHz beat output indicates that the head-scan is straying too high, whereas an increase in 16 kHz beat output indicates that the head-scan is too low. When the 16 kHz and 46 kHz beat products are balanced in level the replay head must be exactly centred on its intended track. The situation is reversed for line 2: a predominance of 16 kHz output warns of too high a head-path, a predominance of 46 kHz output is the result of too low a head-path. Again, when both crosstalk signals are equal the head is correctly aligned on track 2.

Processing of the ATF replay signals is illustrated, in basic form, in Fig. 12.7. The heads' output signals, after low-pass filtering, are applied to two sharply-tuned acceptor circuits, one resonant at 16 kHz, the other at 46 kHz. Each feeds its own amplitude detector, whose outputs are in proportion to the respective cross-talk levels. Adding the outputs gives an error signal whose polarity indicates the direction of the tracking error, and whose amplitude indicates the magnitude of the tracking error. After amplification the error signal is applied as a phase-control to the capstan or head-drum motors to maintain accurate tracking.

The loop works continuously to maintain equal crosstalk signals from both adjacent tracks, thus ensuring optimum tracking without the need for any form of user-control; tolerances due to non-standard recordings, tape-tension, temperature and ageing are automatically taken up. In Video 8 LP mode the video tracks are a mere 17 microns wide, and such a narrow track can only be reliably scanned with the aid of an ATF system. In VHS systems a simpler form of auto-tracking is used in many machines: the level of off-tape f.m. signal is continuously monitored, or sampled at the

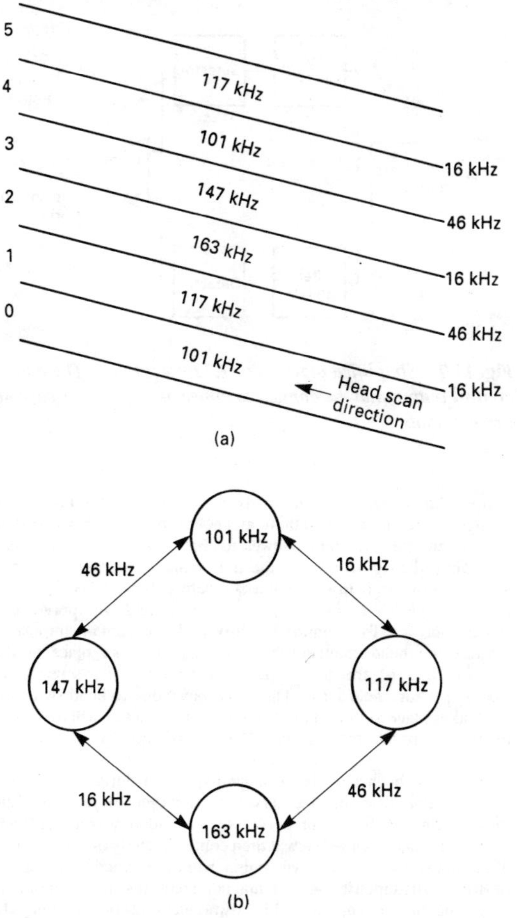

Fig. 12.6 *Video 8 automatic track finding: (a) pilot-tone sequence on tape tracks; (b) formation of beat-tones*

touch of a key. Tracking is adjusted electronically to maximise the replay signal. In this closed-loop system a continuously-variable user tracking control is thus unnecessary.

HEAD-SWEEP PHASING

The use of two heads to record a continuous picture means that at some point a switch must be made between the two. To facilitate this the head-wrap is a little more than one half-turn around the drum – typically it is made 186°. The 'spare' 6° permits an overlap

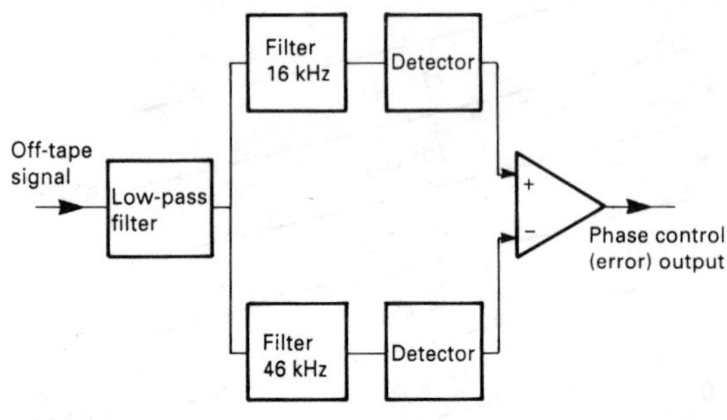

Fig. 12.7 *Simplified diagram of ATF electronics. The phase-control output may be applied to either head-drum or capstan drive circuits*

period during which both heads are scanning the tape. The changeover point will inevitably make a visible disturbance on the picture, and this cannot be allowed to appear on the screen. It must take place during or close to the field blanking period, and since continuity of the field sync pulse is essential for correct field scan timing in the TV or monitor, and the post-field-sync period is a crucial one for TV monitor stability and can contain important signals, the head changeover is arranged to take place at the extreme end of the active field period – typically seven lines (450 μs) before field syncs. The disturbance due to head-switching now takes place at the very bottom of the picture and will be hidden by the slight overscan for which TVs and monitors are usually adjusted.

Although the heads are not signal-switched during record it is essential that each head enters onto the tape at just the right moment in the field-scan period of the video waveform being recorded – each head-scan will then contain exactly one TV field of 312½ lines, and the field sync pulses will all be lined up along the bottom of the tape ribbon. The magnetic patterns corresponding to each line in turn will then be positioned end-to-end along the slanting track, as depicted in Fig. 12.8, which also shows the control track pulses referred to earlier. This correlation of tape tracks and TV lines and fields is achieved by phasing-up a drum (hence head) position indicating pulse (*tacho pulse*) with the incoming field sync pulse in a phase-locked-loop. In fact this PLL is the head-drum servo, to be examined in detail in Chapter 14. The exact phase relationship between field sync pulse and head tacho pulse is adjustable in the *record switch point* preset, with which the seven-lines-before-field-sync condition is set up.

LONG-PLAY VARIANTS

As new formats were introduced over the years, each capable of achieving a higher density of signal-information on tape than its predecessors, attention was turned to the possibility of increasing

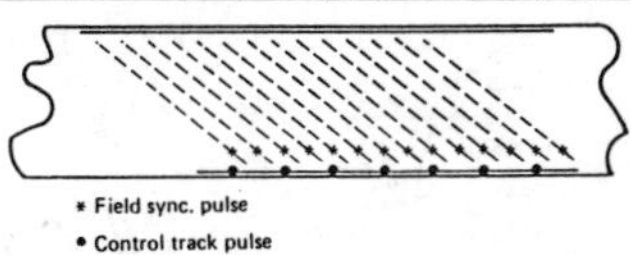

Fig. 12.8 *Position of field syncs and control-track pulses on tape*

the playing time of the established formats. Thinner tapes were introduced to pack four hours recording time into a standard VHS cassette (E240 package) and Beta cassette (L830 type). These thin tapes led to mechanical problems with some (especially older) deck mechanisms, and an alternative approach was adopted: reducing the forward speed of the tape and narrowing the video tracks. In countries using 60 Hz NTSC signals, Beta II and Beta III – progressive reductions of tape speed – became established as standards; in the UK and Europe only the standard Beta speed of 1.873 cm/s was offered.

The greatest progress in long play technology was made with the VHS format, whose double-speed variant VHS-LP has become widely established. Here the rate of forward progress of the tape is halved to 1.17 cm/s and special, separate narrow heads on the drum write video tracks of half width: 24.5 microns. The track layout for this system differs only in this respect from that given in Fig. 12.3(a). The picture quality suffers surprisingly little, though the slow forward tape speed limits longitudinally-recorded audio response to about 6 kHz. To overcome the degradation of vision S/N ratio on VHS-LP special noise-reduction systems are used in the luminance signal-processing circuits. To satisfy the one-field-per-head sweep requirement, the head-drum rotation speed remains at 1500 r.p.m. The narrow LP video heads are usually incorporated on the same ferrite chips as the standard-play heads, and have the same azimuth-offset characteristics.

SMALL HEAD DRUMS

In order to produce very compact VCRs and camcorders, ways were found to record standard Beta, Video 8 and VHS track-patterns on tape by means of smaller than standard head drums. In Betamovie (Fig. 12.9(a)) the drum is 44.67 mm diameter (normal Beta drum is 74.49 mm across) around which the tape is wrapped 313° by a special tape-loading mechanism. A single head-chip is active over 300° of the tape wrap; it contains two head gaps with opposing azimuth angles and separate windings, alternately switched in on successive head-scans to maintain the correct recording-azimuth angles on adjacent tracks. To cover 300° per TV field the drum neccessarily rotates faster than the 1500 r.p.m. of the conventional Beta head drum, but the linear tape speed is of course the Beta standard of 1.873 cm/s.

The operation of Betamovie is based on the concept of recording only, and fulfils the requirements to write onto the tape tracks corresponding to standard Beta formation for subsequent replay in a conventional Beta VCR. To achieve this the video signal, over 1 field period, must be time compressed at 1.2 times normal speed, and the line scanning and colour subcarrier frequencies are correspondingly increased, to 18.75 kHz and 5.32 MHz respectively, though the latter frequency does not appear *as such* in the

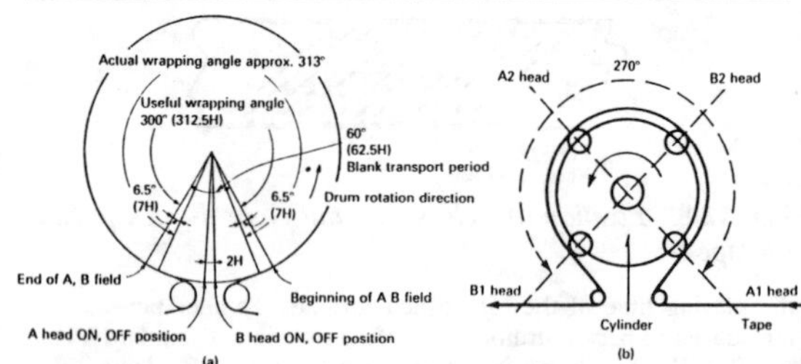

Fig. 12.9 *Small head drums for standard formats: (a) Betamovie, with one head chip; (b) compact VHS, with four heads*

camcorder; the recorded colour-under frequencies are directly derived from the pick-up tube's colour processing circuits. The Y signal's f.m. carrier frequency must also be increased to lay down the correct magnetic pattern on tape in the shorter available period: the 3.8–5.2 MHz deviation range for playback is achieved with a record range of 4.56–6.24 MHz. All this is only made possible by the fact that the incorporated camera circuitry is specially designed to render these non-standard signals, with field scan being completed in 16.66 ms and 'resting' for the remaining 3.3 ms while the head traverses the gap in the tape wrap; a complete 'set' of 312.5 scanning lines being completed in the 16.66 ms period; and so on. It is obvious why the system cannot be used for replay – a 20% 'dead' period would occur once per field as the head traversed the tape-gap, and the 'time warp' tricks are not practical during real-time playback.

An alternative small-drum configuration is shown in Fig. 12.9(b). This is designed for the VHS system, and is suitable for recording and playback. It is used in portable equipment, often with a miniature cassette (VHS-C) containing a small (30 mins) reel of standard VHS tape: the mini-cassette fits into an adaptor of the shape and size of a standard cassette package for replay in a full-size machine. Some camcorders use the small-drum system with a full-size cassette.

The mini-VHS head drum is two-thirds the diameter of a conventional VHS head drum (41.3 mm and 62 mm respectively). Again, the essential requirement is to record standard track patterns, for which the tape must be wrapped around three-quarters of the drum's circumference, i.e. 270°. Four heads with suitable azimuth offset are mounted at 90° angles around the drum, which itself rotates at 1.5 times normal speed: 2250 r.p.m. Both tape and drum rotate anticlockwise.

Consider head A1 in Fig. 12.9(b). It is timed to enter onto the tape just as a field scan is finishing, and starts by recording the new field sync pulse on tape. At the end of the field, head A1 is running off the tape at the end of its 270° sweep, and head B2 is entering the tape wrap to record the next field. This is completed by head B2 270° and 20 ms later; as it leaves the tape wrap, head A2 is just entering the tape 90° further round to record TV field 3. Heads A2 and A1 have the same level and azimuth, and record identical tracks. Completion of head A2's sweep of the tape puts head B1 (identical to B2) at the starting point of the tape wrap to record field 4, at whose termination A1 takes over once more to repeat the head-sequencing cycle.

Thus by a four-field sequence of head-switching, standard VHS signal patterns can be laid into the tape; during replay the same switching sequence enables continuous replay of a standard VHS recording. The head-switching waveforms are derived from a drum tacho-pulse, and apart from the necessity for four replay head-preamplifiers the rest of the electronic circuits are similar to those of conventional machines.

In Video 8 technology, very tiny camcorders – *palmcorders* – are made possible by reducing the diameter of the (already comparatively small) head drum. The same techniques of long wrap and multi-head switching are used.

FREEZE-FRAME FACILITY

The concept of freeze-frame is a simple one: stop the tape transport and permit the spinning video heads to continually scan the now-stationary tape track, reading out continuously the same TV field complete with sync pulses. TV field scan continues to be triggered by the regularly-repeated 20 ms-interval sync pulses, and the reproduced picture should be a frozen image. In practice a problem arises: The angle of the video tracks laid down during record is not the same as that of the guide rabbet around the lower head drum – it is modified, made more shallow. During normal-speed replay the moving tape ensures that the head/track alignment is correct. When the tape is stopped, however, the effective head-scanning angle reverts to that of the guide rabbet. As Fig. 12.10(a) shows, the disagreement between head scan and tape track angles gives rise to mistracking and consequent noise bars at one or more points in the field scan. If the mistracking is bad at the beginning of head-scan the field sync pulses will be missing or distorted, leading to field tripping and picture rolling on the monitor screen. To overcome this problem wider heads are needed to scan a broad enough path to pick up sufficient f.m. carrier throughout their sweep of the tape, Fig. 12.10(b). Some videorecorders are fitted with wide *auxiliary* heads on the drum to be switched in during still-frame and other 'trick' modes.

A common approach to the problem of achieving noise-free still frame is to provide two wide heads to ensure that each head sees enough of its own (azimuth-tilted) track on freeze-frame operation to render a usable f.m. replay signal. Typically head A may be 59 microns wide, and head B 79 microns wide. Provided the tape is stopped at the right point (head A crossing symmetrically over an 'A' track) the still picture reproduced is noise-free. The stopping-point of the tape does not occur at random when the pause or still-frame mode is called up; the capstan motor comes under the influence of a circuit which examines the off-tape video signal for mistracking noise, and is braked at just the correct point to render a noise-free picture. The exact nature of this capstan-halt procedure varies with the design and vintage of the machine: in early types several 'shunts' were involved during which the noise bar was shuttled out of the picture, whereas later machines with more advanced circuitry achieve the correct stop-point almost instantaneously.

The extra-wide heads are used during *record* modes in machines where only two heads are provided for standard-play use. Since their bottom edges are on the same reference plane, however, each lays down its recorded video track 49 microns (standard VHS track-width) above the bottom edge of its predecessor's track, and

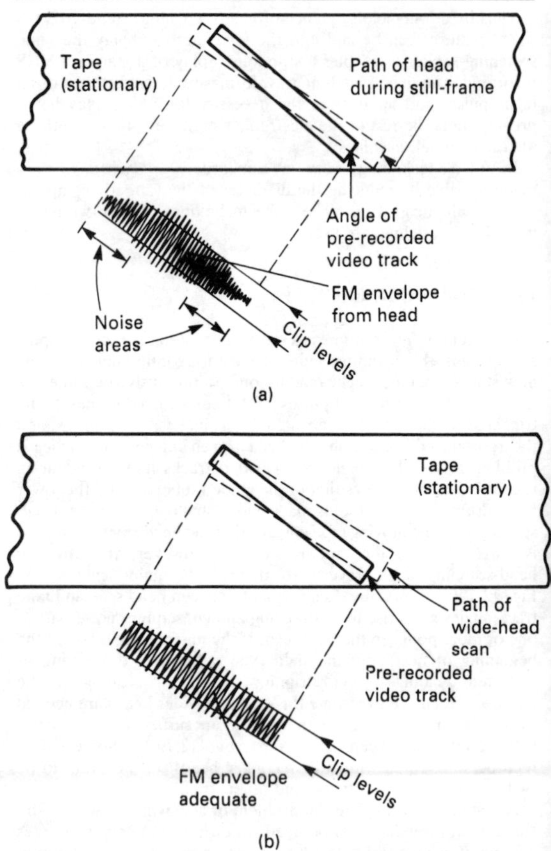

Fig. 12.10 *Still-frame tracking with (a) standard head, and (b) wide head*

for each head the excess track width is erased by the recording action of the next head sweep, a process called *overwriting*.

Artificial vertical syncs

It can happen that due to imperfect tracking the field sync pulse in still-frame mode is noisy or distorted. Even if not, the fact that both heads now have exactly the same path and starting point for their sweeps means that (due to the offset starting points of adjacent slanting video tracks) there will be a timing error of 1½ TV lines between the field sync pulses coming from alternate head sweeps. This would badly upset field triggering in the monitor, and cause vertical judder in the reproduced still frame. To prevent that, a circuit called a VD (Vertical Drive) synthesiser is added; it generates and inserts into the output waveform a specially-made vertical sync pulse whose timing is governed by a semi-accessible pre-set with which vertical judder can be eliminated on still-frame.

Repeat-field still frame

The freeze-pictures described above can eliminate still-frame problems due to the mechanics of the machine itself, but judder and blurring of the reproduced 'frozen' picture can still occur on fast-moving picture objects. If anything in the scene moves significantly during the 20 ms field period the alternately-reproduced interlaced fields will be quite different and their combination into a single frame unsuccessful; typical of this is a wobble effect on a player – or on the ball – in a fast-moving sport shot.

Fast-action wobble on still-frame can be overcome by reading out a *single* video track continuously, presenting it twice (with suitable half-line offset of the field sync pulse) as the two fields of a single frame. While some vertical definition is lost as a result, the still picture is *perfectly* still. The video head configuration to achieve it is relatively simple: One of the two head chips has two gaps with opposing azimuth angles, each with its own winding. If the chosen head is designated 'A' its auxiliary winding and gap (called head B2) will have the same azimuth angle as the 'B' head on the opposite side of the drum. The auxiliary head (wide type) is not used during record, being switched in only on still-frame reproduction.

An alternative and earlier arrangement is the provision of two completely separate wide heads on the drum, mounted 90° away from standard heads A and B. Both these auxiliary heads have B-type azimuth, and come into play only on still-frame and double-speed replay modes.

The increasing use of digital field stores in consumer electronics has led to *electronic* still-frame. Here a complete field of video information is captured before the tape stops, then digitised in 6-bit or 8-bit form for storage in a fast, high-capacity DRAM. The captured field is continually and repeatedly read out, according to newly-generated sync pulse trains, to give a noise- and jitter-free still picture image.

13

Videorecorder signal processing

Many processes have to be carried out on the CVBS signal in order to get it through the head/tape system in both directions while maintaining reasonable fidelity. The complete record/playback video signal system is outlined in Fig. 13.1, where it can be seen that luminance and chrominance signals are separately dealt with throughout the recording and replay circuits, only coming together at a late stage in the playback processing circuit.

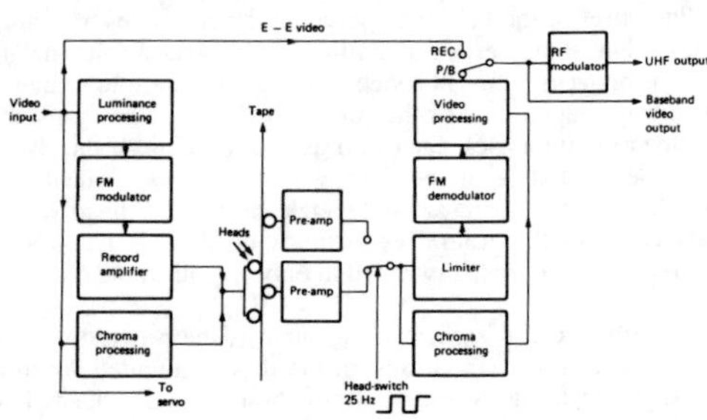

Fig. 13.1 *Overview of videorecorder signal system*

RECORD LUMINANCE SYSTEM

Fig. 13.2 gives a simplified block diagram of a typical luminance recording process. It is based on a single IC, here designated IC3001 – the numbers in rings denote chip pin numbers, and significant waveforms are annotated. The CVBS signal enters the IC on pin 1 where it passes through an a.g.c. stage. It operates on sync pulse amplitude (always 30% of a standard 1 V p-p video signal) to maintain a constant amplitude of output signal without affecting black level or mean level of the video signal.

Emerging from IC pin 24 and passing through the transistor 'record switch' Q3009, the CVBS signal enters low-pass filter FL 3001, whose response rolls off sharply at about 4 MHz to strip away all chroma signal – at TP 3002 appears a pure *luminance* signal. It is buffered in emitter-follower Q3011 and attenuated in the adjustable deviation preset R3012. It is the amplitude of the signal which determines the upper limit of f.m. modulator deviation, and R3012 is adjusted for 4.8 MHz f.m. output during peak-white.

To reduce noise in f.m. systems the high frequency components of the modulating signal are customarily boosted, a process called pre-emphasis. For optimum noise performance *non-linear emphasis* is used, in which small-amplitude h.f. components are given a greater boost than large-amplitude ones – the selection here is made by a diode level-detection circuit D3004, D3005. After buffering, the pre-emphasised luminance signal re-enters the chip on pin 16. Here the sync tip is clamped once per line to a fixed voltage which defines the f.m. modulator frequency for sync tip: in

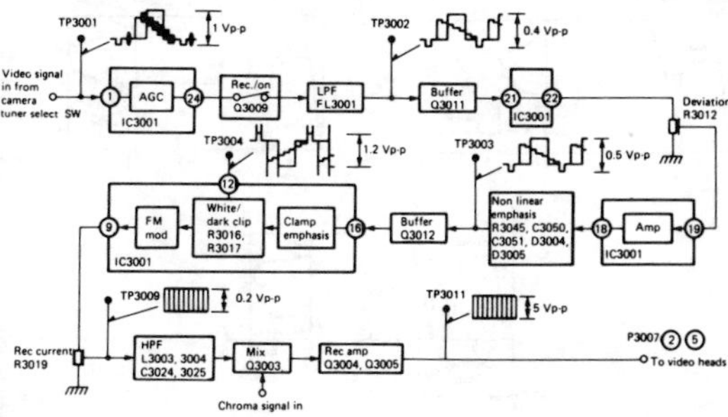

Fig. 13.2 *Luminance record signal processing – Panasonic*

this VHS machine it is 3.8 MHz. The associated emphasis stage has a rising frequency response, offering some 15 dB gain at luminance frequencies around 2 MHz, compared with 6 dB gain at 250 kHz.

The effect of pre-emphasis is to introduce overshoots at transitions in the luminance signal as the waveform for TP3004 shows. If these spikes extend too far above peak white or below sync tip levels there is a risk that the modulator will over-deviate to generate excessive sideband energy – it is prevented by amplitude limiters controlled by white and dark clip control pre-sets R3016/R3017. Finally the luminance signal is applied to the f.m. modulator, a form of voltage-controlled oscillator. Again this is incorporated in IC3001, and takes the form of an astable multivibrator; its charging capacitors have the luminance waveform as an *aiming voltage* so that the output squarewave frequency is governed by the level of the processed luminance waveform. The f.m. signal emerges at IC3001 pin 9 and is developed across record-current preset R3019: its slider taps off a suitable proportion (about 200 mV p-p) to set correct *luminance writing current*.

Since the colour-under signal will occupy the 0–1 MHz spectrum, it is important to remove any harmonics, beat frequencies and vestiges of sidebands in this region that may be present in the output of the modulator; the LC high-pass filter L3003 etc. traps out such l.f. components to prevent the risk of beat patterns during playback. The filtered f.m. signal is now added to the chroma record signal in Q3003 for onward passage to the recording amplifier, a two-transistor class B push-pull power amplifier section which drives around 5 V p-p into the rotating transformer and hence the video heads themselves. The frequency response of this amplifier is tailored to compensate for head response shape and the gain/frequency characteristic of the head/tape interface.

So far as recording f.m. and chroma frequencies are concerned, Fig. 13.3 gives the characteristics of the three main domestic formats.

High-band video recording

Both VHS and Video 8 formats have high-band variants known respectively as S-VHS and Hi-8. They differ from the standard systems described above in one main respect: the deviation of the carrier. Using high-grade small-particle tape and extra-narrow video head gaps, the usable frequency response has been pushed up to achieve a picture definition of more than 400 lines. For

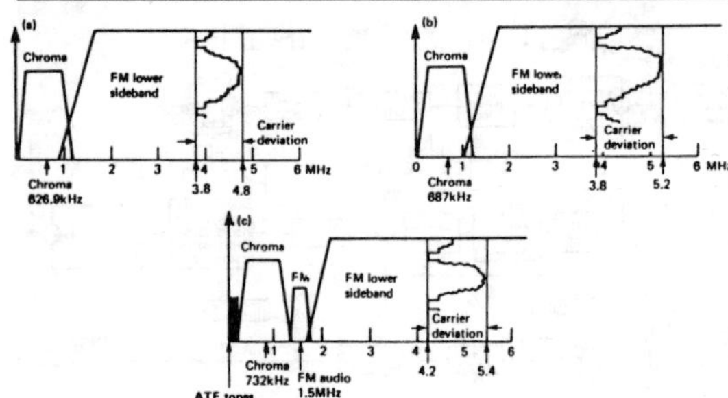

Fig. 13.3 *Signal spectra and key frequencies for three formats: (a) VHS; (b) Betamax; (c) Video 8*

S-VHS the carrier deviation is 5.4 MHz (sync tip) to 7 MHz (peak white), and for Hi-8, 5.7 MHz (sync tip) to 7.7 MHz (peak white). In the latter case the recorded wavelength is around 0.4 micron.

The second feature of high-band domestic videorecorders is provision for keeping the luminance and chrominance components of the video signal separate throughout the machine, and thus avoiding the cross-colour penalty of band-shared colour-encoding systems. It is not relevant to terrestrial and f.m. satellite broadcasts, but gives very good results from MAC broadcasts and high-band camcorders. In these systems the standard connector is the *S-terminal*, whose plug wiring details are given in Fig. 21.1(f).

PLAYBACK LUMINANCE SYSTEM

A simplified block diagram of the luminance playback process, taken from the same Panasonic machine as Fig. 13.2, is given in Fig.13.4. This circuit is preceded by the replay head-switcher which selects the output signal of each head in turn as it scans the tape. Again the entire replay process is based on a single chip, IC3004. The two heads each have their own preamplifier, with adjustable resonant circuits to equalise the heads' outputs and maximise them at about 4.9 MHz – any imbalance in their response (set by Q-trimmers) or amplitude (set by 'balance' pot) will give rise to some form of 25 Hz flicker in the replay picture. Correction for phase errors in the head-response shaping filters is provided by the phase-compensator block at the top left-hand corner. This is followed by a 627 kHz trap to remove all traces of the colour-under signal from the luminance f.m. waveform. Next comes the dropout compensator.

All videorecorders incorporate a dropout compensator. A dropout is a momentary loss of f.m. replay signal due to dirt at the tape/head contact point or a minute imperfection of the tape surface. If uncorrected it gives rise to white or black streaks and dots in the picture. The correction process consists of substituting good f.m. carrier signal from the previous line, which will usually be very similar in video content. The amplitude of the replay f.m. signal is examined by a level detector, which triggers a switch when signal level falls below a preset point. The f.m. replay signal is continuously fed to a 1-line delay (between pins 10 and 12 of

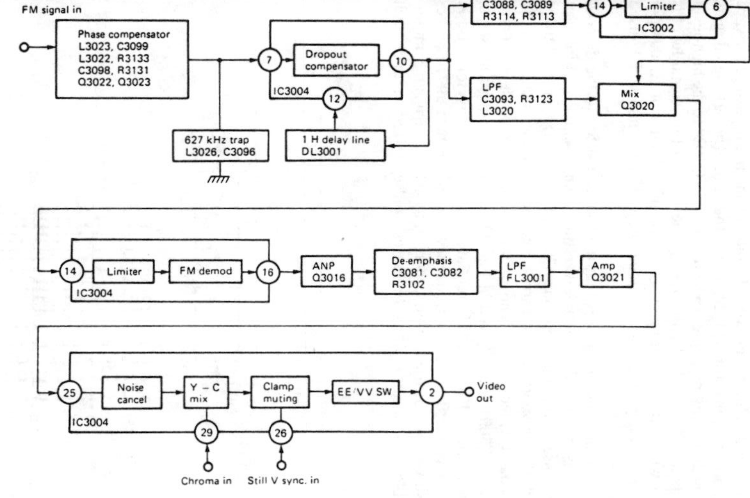

Fig. 13.4 *Luminance playback chain*

IC3004), and the switch changes over to the delay line output during a dropout. This delayed signal is recirculated through the line DL3001 and can be re-used several times if the duration of the dropout is great. The use of dropout compensation greatly improves picture appearance, especially when old or worn tapes are in use.

The blocks to the right of IC3004 pin 10 are concerned with noise and interference elimination during momentary periods of loss of f.m. carrier, or severe amplitude-modulation of it, which almost amounts to the same thing. The resulting noise will cause disturbances on picture, especially at white/black transitions. To prevent these effects, a *double-limiter* circuit is used: The signal is split into two paths by filters, the high frequencies passing to their own amplifier and limiter between IC pins 14 and 6, for passage forward via adder transistor Q3020. Only the a.m. (noise) signal gets through the low-pass filter to be re-added in Q3020 to the high-level clipped f.m. signals; by this means the wanted f.m. signal level is kept within the operating range of the main limiter at IC3004 pin 14. This double-limiter technique is an effective and widely-used one.

The main limiter ensures that the f.m. signal fed to the demodulator is free of all amplitude variations, an essential requirement for noise-free demodulation. The output voltage at pin 16 of IC3004 is proportional to carrier frequency, and as such forms the baseband video signal. The operation of the f.m. demodulator within IC3004 is illustrated in Fig. 13.5. The incoming f.m. signal (waveform A) is first differentiated to produce waveform B. A full-wave rectifier acts as frequency doubler to turn all the spikes positive – waveform C – in order that each can trigger a monostable multivibrator, which generates a pulse of fixed width on each

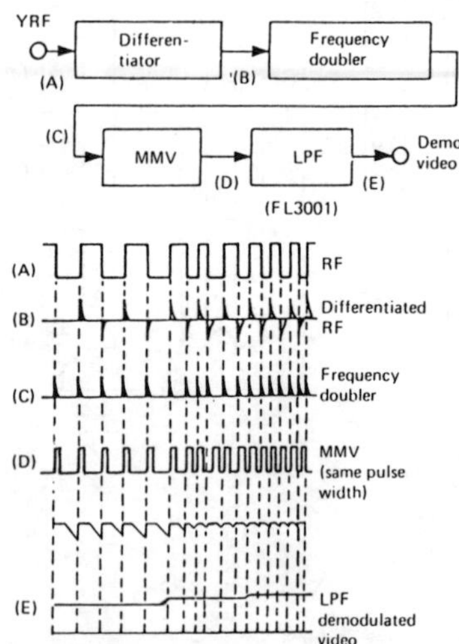

Fig. 13.5 *Operation of one form of f.m. video demodulator. It is built-into a purpose-designed IC*

spike, waveform D. As with the switch-mode field timebase and PSUs discussed in earlier chapters, we are now dealing with a waveform of varying duty-cycle, whose mark-space ratio reflects the amplitude of the required output signal. This is integrated (waveform E) to build up the output signal: as yet it is in somewhat 'spiky' form.

Returning to Fig. 13.4, the de-emphasis process follows demodulation, and is carried out in the blocks to the right of IC pin 16. During record the high frequencies of the luminance signal were boosted in a non-linear emphasis circuit (Fig. 10.2), and now balance is restored in a frequency-conscious replay network whose response, in terms of frequency versus amplitude, is the inverse of that used during record. In de-emphasising the video signal in an amplifier with falling h.f. response, much of the noise picked up during record and replay is eliminated – such noise is predominant in the upper frequency ranges.

Since the demodulator output is still in somewhat spiky form, and contains vestiges of the f.m. carrier waveform itself, the next process required is low-pass filtering to render a smooth luminance waveform. The filter is FL3001, whose response falls sharply at frequencies beyond 2.5 MHz. On emergence from this filter the luminance signal is fully balanced with regard to frequency distribution, but the reduced system bandwidth has degraded the rise and fall times of transients in the waveform, including the important sync pulse edges. The block marked Q3021, then, contains reactive components (or, in some videorecorder models, a complete delay-line-based crispener circuit as briefly described on page 95, Chapter 6) to sharpen up both picture transients and sync pulse edges.

After filtering and crispening, the processed luminance signal re-enters IC3004 on pin 25. Here it is applied to a noise cancelling circuit in which the high frequencies – containing most of the processing noise – are separated off and amplitude-limited. The limiter's output consists largely of unwanted noise, interference and other spurious components: these are inverted in a following stage then added to the direct signal. In the adder stage the equal-and-opposite noise components cancel to leave a clean luminance waveform.

The noise-reduced luminance signal is now passed to a Y–C adder stage where it is recombined with the playback chrominance signal to produce a complete CVBS output. The chroma signal enters IC3004 at pin 29, and the resulting composite waveform undergoes treatment in the clamp stage. Here its d.c. level is stabilised, and here the synthesised field sync pulses are inserted as substitute for the jittering 'real' sync signal during still and trick modes where applicable. Also present at this point is a muting stage, brought into play whenever a disordered picture may be displayed: while the servo systems are locking up, when no control track pulse is present (e.g. replay of blank tape), or when the machine changes speeds during playback; the circuit of Fig. 13.4 is taken from a dual-speed videorecorder. Finally the CVBS signal passes through a record/playback switch on its way to IC output pin 2.

Possible refinements not detailed in Fig. 13.4 are luminance crosstalk compensation by means of a delay line and second demodulator; provision of a front-panel 'sharpness' control in which the crispening action may be controlled by the user; and the special circuits used in LP playback mode, notably for trick speed reproduction. The arrangements described are applicable in principle to any of the home video formats.

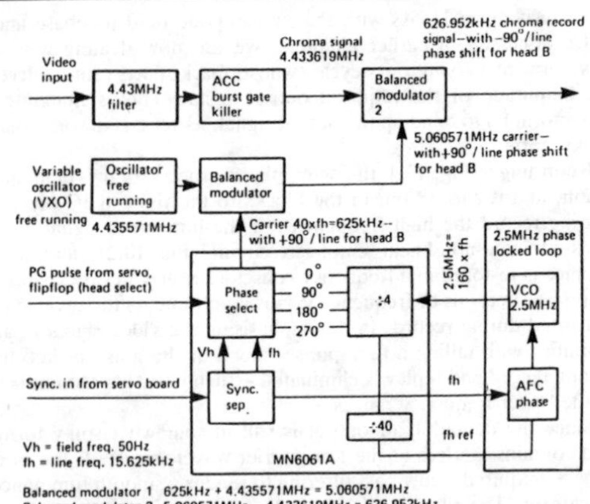

Fig. 13.6 *Main features of the VHS colour-under recording processor*

COLOUR-UNDER SYSTEM

The basic concept of colour-under video recording is a simple one: to translate the entire encoded chroma signal to a lower frequency around 700 kHz for recording by means of a heterodyne process with a local oscillator; and during replay to translate it back to its correct 4.43 MHz frequency by a second heterodyne process. If the tape were a perfect recording medium this would be all that were necessary. In practice there are three factors which prevent the use of such a simple system: the fact that at low colour-under frequencies the azimuth-offset of the recording heads does little to prevent inter-track crosstalk; an inability with conventional electronics to control replay speed within the very fine limits required to adequately maintain colour subcarrier frequency during replay; and, allied to this, the mechanical imperfections in the deck, transport system and tape ribbon which impart timing jitter to all video signals recorded and replayed on tape – or, indeed, on disc. Chapter 6 indicated how crucial is the timing and phase of the chroma signal, which must be held to within ±3 ns or so, representing a mere 5° of phase error tolerance. Such a requirement is far beyond the ability of a mechanically-driven system, so special artifices are necessary to maintain correct hue and saturation in the reproduced colours.

CHROMINANCE RECORDING

As Fig. 13.3 shows, all formats place the colour-under signal at around 700 kHz in the tape-frequency spectrum. Taking specifically the VHS system as example the recording arrangements are shown in simplified form in Fig. 13.6. Chroma signals are separated from the other components of the CVBS input signal in a composite filter based on 4.43 MHz. This filter has a bandwidth of about 1 MHz in order to limit each sideband of the chroma signal to approximately 500 kHz; in this way beating and interaction between taped luminance and chrominance components are avoided.

A following a.c.c. stage regulates chroma amplitude by maintaining constant burst signal level in a sample-and-feedback circuit. For this purpose it contains a burst-gating circuit keyed by a suitably-delayed line sync pulse. Here, too, is a colour killer to prevent the recording of 'coloured noise' on monochrome programmes.

Thus conditioned, the 4.43 MHz chroma signal enters a balanced modulator (mixer) where it is beat against a locally-derived 5.06 MHz c.w. signal. The difference frequency – 630 kHz in round terms – is selected by a suitable low-pass filter and added to the luminance f.m. signal for application to the recording heads. In fact the colour-under frequency is precisely 626.952 kHz, derived from the 4.433619 MHz and 5.060571 MHz inputs to balanced modulator 2. The derivation and characteristics of this latter frequency is the key to successful elimination of the problems outlined earlier. It is produced by balanced modulator 1, and is itself the result of additive mixing of a 4.435571 MHz wave from a crystal oscillator; and a 625 kHz signal from the MN6061 A IC. This chip is associated with a PLL wherein a 2.5 MHz oscillator is locked to 160 times incoming line frequency by virtue of the ÷4 and ÷40 counters within the chip. Outputs from the ÷4 stage of the counter derive four separate phases of 625 kHz signal for use in the *phase-select* section of the IC. During the tape-scanning period of video head A (as signalled by the PG pulse derived from a position-indicator on the head drum) the phase-select block passes 0° phase 625 kHz signal to balanced modulator 1. During the scanning period of head B, however, the phase-selector advances to the 90° position, effectively *retarding* the phase of the carrier of head B's colour-under signal by 90° due to the action of subtractive balanced modulator 2. Head A sweeps next with a 0° subcarrier signal. The second sweep of head B sees the phase selector 'step' forward to render a recording phase of −180°; 0° for head A follows, then −270° for head B. Again head A sees the phase select block at 0°, and for the duration of the following head B sweep its phase, too, is stepped backwards to 0°. The step-back-phase action retards the chroma record phase by 90° per TV line for head B, then, while keeping head A chroma constant. It is important to understand that the 90° phase retard per line for head B is achieved by a phase *advance* in the PLL.

In this recording system, then, we have manipulated the colour-under signal in two ways: the frequency of the colour-under carrier has been tied firmly to recorded line sync frequency by the PLL, and a line-stepped phase-retard characteristic has been given to the colour signals recorded by video head B. The resulting pattern of colour signals on tape is indicated in Fig. 13.7, which is drawn in respect of the burst phases recorded on tape. The top row, for head A, is recorded without phase modification, so the burst phasors follow the standard PAL pattern over the eight TV lines shown. The phase-retard feature given to head B, however, results in a two-by-two line pattern in its recorded burst phasors. We shall return shortly to examine the lower lines in the diagram.

CHROMINANCE PLAYBACK

An outline of the chroma replay system for VHS is given in Fig. 13.8. The chroma input from the replay heads is based on 626.952 kHz and selected by a low-pass filter. It contains crosstalk as well as frequency and phase errors. Three processes must be carried out on it: up-conversion, crosstalk cancellation and de-

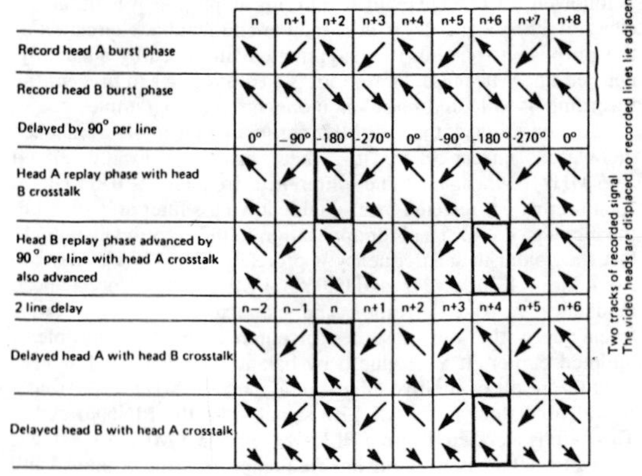

Fig. 13.7 *Phase-manipulation of the recorded chroma signal to facilitate chroma-crosstalk cancellation. Full explanation in the text*

jittering. These individual functions are somewhat mixed in the diagram. Up-conversion takes place in balanced modulator 2 whose second input is a locally-generated 5.060571 MHz wave. The frequency difference between these two inputs is 4.433619 MHz, as required for a standard CVBS signal, and this is selected by an output filter. As during record, it is this second input to balanced modulator 2 which steers the output colour signal in special ways to overcome the bad influences of crosstalk and timing jitter. As during record, too, the local signal is produced in balanced modulator 1, whose inputs are crystal oscillator VXO1 wave at 4.435571 MHz; and the 625 kHz (40 times line frequency) carrier derived from the same phase locked loop as before. The phase selection system works in identical fashion too: 625 kHz carrier for all head A sweeps are at zero phase, whereas those for head B sweeps step 90° forwards on each TV line.

The phase advance thus imparted to the heterodyne signal for head B's up-conversion process will, because both mixers are now operating in subtractive mode (*difference* beat output used in both cases), have the effect of *advancing* the phase of the upconverted head B colour signal. The original phase retard characteristic is thus cancelled out in the up-conversion process. Phase normality, then, is restored to the chroma output signal in which the burst (and hence chroma-signal) phases are now as transmitted – shown by the *large* arrows in the third and fourth rows of Fig. 13.7.

Timing correction

The timing jitter imparted to the chrominance signal during record and playback must now be eliminated. It can only be done by adding an equal jitter factor to the 'local' input to balanced modulator 2, such that even though the off-tape signal is varying in terms of frequency and phase, the difference between them is always precisely 4.433619 MHz.

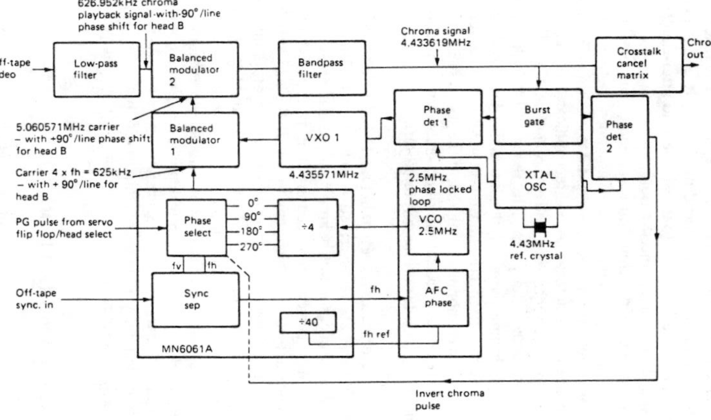

Fig. 13.8 *Block diagram of VHS colour replay processing. Up-conversion, phase correction and crosstalk cancellation is catered for*

The 625 kHz input to balanced modulator 1 is locked to off-tape line sync pulses by virtue of the 2.5 MHz PLL. All jitter influences (during record *and* playback) on the chroma signal are also applicable to the line sync pulse component of the composite luminance signal which accompanies it both on and off the tape; colour frequency errors are cancelled out, then, by the influence of the jitter signal present in the 625 kHz (and hence 5.06 MHz) heterodyne signals.

Frequency correction by itself is not adequate to fully stabilise the replay chroma signal however. Very short-term variations in timing of off-tape subcarrier upsets its phase in a random way between 'PLL updates' once per line. A second loop is therefore provided to cater for *phase* correction of replayed subcarrier. It is based on the second input to balanced modulator 1, and depends on 'steering' the phase of VXO1 to inject a second jitter-cancelling correction signal into the balanced modulators.

A sample of replayed colour burst is gated out of the up-converted chroma output and compared in a phase detector with a reference c.w. wave from a stable crystal oscillator. The error output from the phase detector is a direct indicator of the phase jitter in the replayed subcarrier, and is applied to VXO1 in the correct sense to cancel that jitter. This second PLL locks up the videorecorder's chroma output to the internal 4.433619 MHz reference crystal, which itself now 'masters' the subcarrier reference oscillator in the TV or monitor being fed. If the second PLL should come out of lock a playback colour killer shuts down the chrominance channel to prevent spurious colour patterns appearing on the screen.

A second phase detector is present in Fig. 13.8. Its function is not only to provide the above-described colour-killer action, but to monitor the degree of correction being provided via phase director 1. Whenever a large correction is required, it is reduced by the action of phase detector 2 which acts to invert the 625 kHz local signal either via the phase select section or by a separate inverting switch. The effect is that of a 180° phase change, and the operating range of phase detector 2 is thus reduced.

In addition to these artifices, some home video equipment incorporates *timebase correction*, in which jitter is ironed out by an electronic (digital) data store. The unstable signal is A–D converted and loaded into a memory chip, then read out almost instantaneously according to a new and stable set of sync pulses.

CROSSTALK CANCELLATION

The electronics in the chroma recording section had two separate influences on the phase of the colour-under signal recorded on tape. The purpose of locking the new low-frequency colour subcarrier to line sync has been fulfilled in the replay de-jittering loop just described. Considerable trouble was taken to rotate the phase of head B's subcarrier signals 'backwards' during record, and 'forwards' during replay in order to establish a specific pattern of chroma phases on tape. Its purpose is to facilitate a method of cancelling inter-track crosstalk.

In standard-play VHS format, the start-points of successive video tape tracks are offset by 1½ TV lines, but because of the shallow angle which they make to the tape ribbon itself, recorded TV lines lie side-by-side on tape, with all line sync pulses adjacent. The effect is that crosstalk picked up by either head consists of signals from the same line in the alternate field, and as such their signal content will be similar to that of the main signal read out by the head in question. The cancellation of crosstalk interference depends on this correlation of recorded TV lines on tape, and on the carefully contrived pattern of chroma phases on tape described earlier, and shown in Fig. 13.7. The third row of that diagram shows the burst phasors picked up by head A during replay – the long arrows represent the main signal (from the top row), and the short arrows the crosstalk interference from the adjacent track on either side written by head B.

The fourth row of Fig. 13.7 shows the final effect of head B's replay. In the up-conversion process its chroma phase is advanced by 90° per line to restore normality to the chroma signal; in doing so, the crosstalk signal picked up from adjacent 'A' tracks will also be advanced by 90° per line. Again, the large arrows represent the main signal and the small ones the crosstalk components. A two-line (128 μs) delay is now introduced. The direct and delayed signals made available represent a time-coincidence between line n and n + 2 as shown by the fifth and sixth rows of the diagram. The content of lines n and n + 2 are highlighted by the boxes drawn in rows three and five of the diagram. It can be seen that the main signals are phase-coincident so that they will reinforce when added, whereas the spurious crosstalk signals are in antiphase – adding these components will cause them to cancel to zero. The arrangement of the two-line delay and add-matrix is depicted in Fig. 13.9, along with a vectorial representation of the cross-talk cancellation process.

That the process works on every line is illustrated by the boxed examples in Fig. 13.7's rows four and six. These head B lines n + 4 and n + 6 are also brought into time-coincidence by the delay line, and their addition in the matrix will again double the amplitude of the wanted main signal while cancelling out the crosstalk components. For perfect cancellation the time delay must be exactly 128 μs with in-phase arrival of both direct and delayed signals at the adder; both signals must also have equal amplitude. Adjustment of phase and amplitude is made with an inductive and a resistive preset respectively. In practice they are trimmed for minimum crosstalk on replay of a colour-bar signal from a special alignment tape.

BETAMAX CHROMA RECORDING

The Sony Betamax video system uses the same principles as VHS in its colour-under system. Again the individual TV lines lie alongside in adjacent recorded tracks on tape; the frequency of the colour-

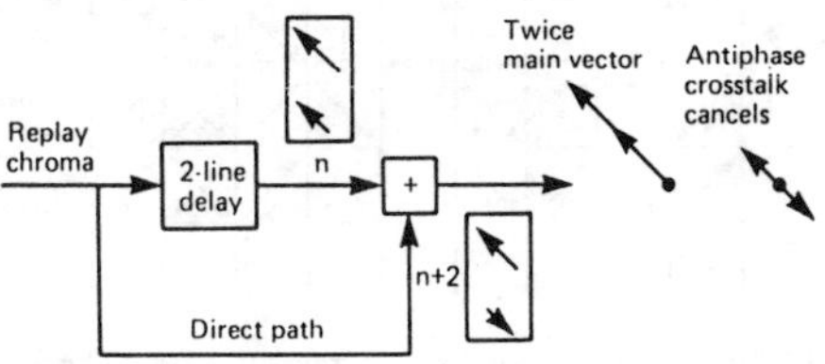

Fig. 13.9 *Operating principle of two-line delay-and-add matrix*

under carrier is tied to line sync for jitter elimination; and the phases of subcarrier signal are laid on tape on adjacent lines in such a way as to facilitate the use of a 2-line delay and add matrix to eliminate inter-track crosstalk. Beta differs mainly from the other systems in its choice of colour-under frequency at 687.5 kHz (44 times line frequency), and the way in which the two-line chroma phase pattern is achieved.

In effect the subcarriers for head A and head B are made to continually rotate in opposite directions. This is achieved by giving their subcarriers frequency offsets. Head A's subcarrier runs 1.953 kHz below nominal subcarrier frequency, and head B's subcarrier 1.953 kHz above it. The effect, when the line frequency of 15.625 kHz is taken into account, is a continual phase retard of 45° per line for head A and a continual phase advance of 45° per line for head B. This arises because the subcarrier offset frequency for each head is one-eighth of line frequency (15.625 ÷ 8 = 1.953) and one-eighth of a full 360° cycle is 45°. The resulting phases of PAL burst signals on tape are shown in Fig. 13.10. Here the dotted phasor-arrows represent those transmitted, and the solid lines those recorded on tape as a result of the subcarrier offsets imparted in the recording electronics. Comparisons of line-columns n and n + 8 show that the sequence indeed repeats at eight-line intervals.

During replay the same delay-line matrix as for VHS (Fig. 13.9) is used for crosstalk cancellation. Row three of Fig. 13.10 represents the up-converted and phase corrected 4.43 MHz subcarrier for head A, with spurious crosstalk signals also phase-advanced in the replay electronics. The lines n and n + 2 brought together by the delay line can be seen to have in-phase main signals (reinforce) and antiphase crosstalk signals (cancel) in the hatched squares in diagram row three. For head B, lines n + 5 and n + 7 have been selected at random as an example – again the main signals add while the crosstalk signals cancel, see the dotted squares in diagram row four.

The alternation in colour-under frequency between the two heads takes places at 25 Hz, corresponding to 20 ms intervals, and is triggered by a flip-flop signal derived from the video head tacho pulse. It is carried out by a programmable divider in the PLL which locks colour-under subcarrier to line syncs in this way: A VXO is alternately locked to 5.484375 MHz (351 times line frequency) and 5.515625 (353 times line frequency) by the 25 Hz head flip-flop squarewave. These alternating frequencies pass into an eight-

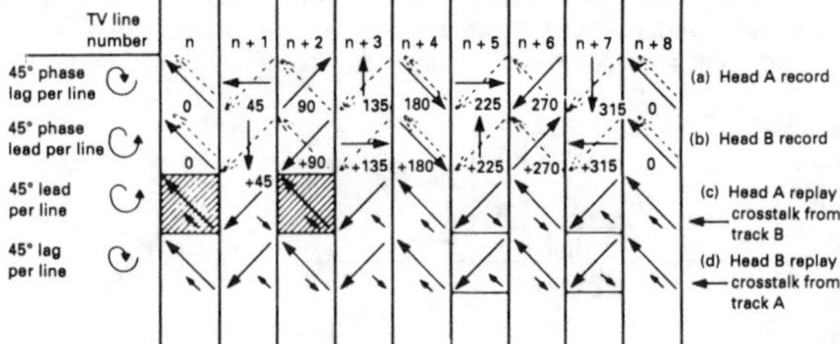

Fig. 13.10 *Bust phasors on Betamax tape. The shaded blocks in rows (c) and (d) illustrate the crosstalk cancellation process*

counter which renders 5.484375/8 = 685.547 kHz during head A's scan, and 5.515625/8 = 689.453 kHz during head B's sweep –these have the required offset frequencies to render the oppositely-rotating vector effects of the first two rows of Fig. 13.10.

During replay of Beta tapes the same programmable divider is used to lock the same VXO alternately to 351 and 353 times *off-tape* line frequency. As before, phase restoration and coarse de-jittering of the chrominance signal is thus achieved. Crosstalk cancellation takes place in a 2-line delay matrix as already described.

Pilot burst

The use of the inherent swinging PAL burst for subcarrier-rate de-jittering of the replayed chroma signal is not ideal. In Fig. 13.8 the PLL which locks replay chroma burst to the local 4.433619 MHz reference crystal must have a sufficiently long time constant to prevent too slavish a lock, otherwise the ±45° swing of burst phase (essential to the PAL concept) would be lost – all bursts would rigidly lock into phase with the master crystal. The necessarily slow response of the loop is not what is required for good de-jittering performance.

To overcome the problem a new constant-phase large-amplitude burst signal is generated in the colour record system of a Beta videorecorder and added to the colour-under signal in the position normally occupied by the line sync pulse in the CVBS waveform, and quite vacant in its chroma counterpart. On replay it is gated out of the up-converted chroma signal by off-tape separated line sync pulses, and used as a jittering sample for comparison with the reference subcarrier crystal in a circuit very similar to that of the right-hand side of Fig. 13.8, but with a short, 'tight' time constant for good performance in phase correction.

The pilot burst, having realised its usefulness in the de-jittering process, is removed from the chroma signal further downstream (and before its combination with the luminance signal) by a blanking (*pilot burst cleaning*) stage.

VIDEO 8 COLOUR PROCESSING

The Video 8 format uses another variation on the same theme in order to arrange for crosstalk signals to come off the tape in antiphase over a two-line period. Here the colour-under frequency is higher than in other formats at 732 kHz, corresponding to (47–⅛) *f* h. This frequency is locked to incoming line sync pulses by means of a PLL running at 5.86 MHz (375 *f* h) whose output is divided by eight in a counter to give 732 kHz. During head A's sweeps the phase of this colour-under carrier is advanced by 90° per line to give the phase pattern on tape shown in the top row of Fig. 13.11 – this simplified diagram takes no account of the swinging burst, though the crosstalk cancellation process to be described works in just the same fashion when the PAL burst is taken into account. Head B's sweep records constant-phase chroma shown by the black arrows in diagram row two. Rows three and four show the phases of the main and crosstalk signals during replay by head A, respectively before and after the necessary phase correction, effected by introducing a phase retard of 90°/line. The fifth row of the diagram represents the 2 h delayed signal – row four moved two places to the right. Comparison of the signal phases in rows four

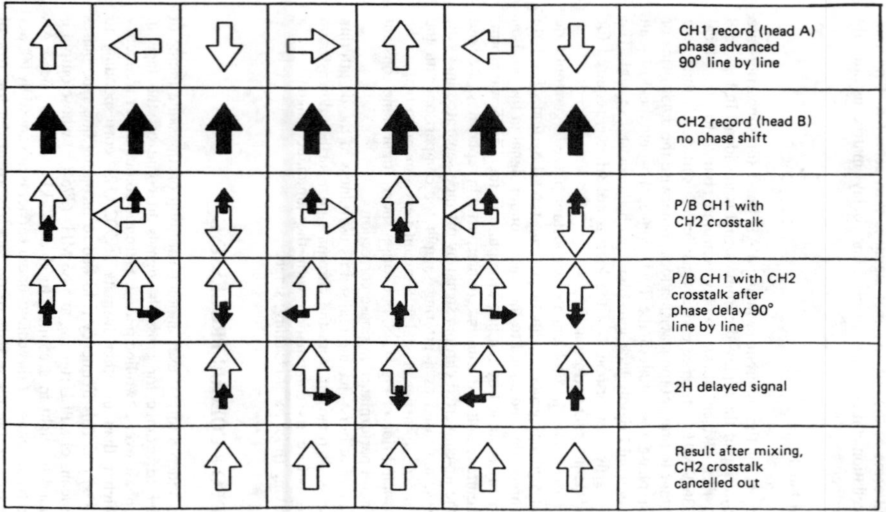

CH1 record (head A) phase advanced 90° line by line

CH2 record (head B) no phase shift

P/B CH1 with CH2 crosstalk

P/B CH1 with CH2 crosstalk after phase delay 90° line by line

2H delayed signal

Result after mixing, CH2 crosstalk cancelled out

Fig. 13.11 *Crosstalk cancellation for chroma signals in Video 8 format*

and five shows the now-familiar pattern of signal reinforcement and crosstalk cancellation when applied to the circuit of Fig. 13.9. Although the 'clean' signal on row 6 is drawn for head A signals, crosstalk on B channel is cancelled in just the same way, as study of the upper rows will prove.

In other respects V8 chrominance circuitry follows the same broad principles as the systems already discussed. No pilot burst is employed, but to minimise the effect of recording noise the crucial burst signal is doubled in amplitude (+6 dB) before recording, and restored to normal level by a gated 6 dB attenuator during playback. This raises the burst level to that of a fully-saturated colour on tape, and is called *burst emphasis*. It is used also in USA-standard NTSC VHS videorecorders.

Opportunity has been taken in V8 format to introduce two more refinements for the sake of better colour reproduction: a chroma emphasis network is provided in record, with corresponding de-emphasis in playback; this improves chroma S/N ratio, particularly for low-amplitude high-frequency components. Secondly the chroma crosstalk delay/matrix is attended by a correlation detector operating on a feedback loop – it acts to prevent distortion of the chroma signal on horizontal colour transitions in the picture where the direct and delayed main chroma signals are markedly different.

Video 8 format has no provision for SECAM-coded colour signals – they are converted to and from standard PAL by a transcoder IC like the one described at the end of Chapter 7.

FAULT-FINDING IN VIDEO SIGNAL CIRCUITS

With a reasonable working knowledge of circuit principles, a service manual and fairly simple test equipment, diagnosis of faults in the signal processing stages is not difficult. The first thing to establish is whether the fault is present during record, playback or both to check for record faults the suspect tape is played back in a known-good machine of the same format; to check for replay faults a known-good tape containing test patterns and colour bars on vision, and a 1 kHz tone on sound, is ideal. This test-tape need not be the very expensive alignment (*interchange*) tape produced by videorecorder manufacturers as a standard reference; to avoid wearing it unduly, it should be reserved for interchange and alignment testing, and used as seldom as possible. The test-tape can be recorded on a new well-aligned machine, and its characteristics checked against those of the precision alignment tape in the same machine.

Record luminance faults

Once it has been established that the input signal is of good quality, any shortcoming in record performance will be due to faults or misalignment in the record section. A noisy or 'streaky' recording suggests head wear; if the same effect is present after cleaning the video heads (see Chapter 17) the luminance writing current should be checked. Streaking or noise at vertical edges of picture features can also be due to worn heads, but may possibly have its origin in an incorrectly adjusted f.m. modulator (check frequency and deviation with a digital frequency counter) or too high an operating level of the white clipper. Incorrect modulator frequencies can also lead to a change in luminance levels generally or a 'gamma shift' in which one end of the grey-scale becomes stretched or compressed.

Maladjustment or faults in the clippers will also affect the extremes of the composite luminance signal: too low a white clip level will 'flatten off' highlights, and wrong dark-clip level foreshortens the sync pulses. A lack of detail in the recording suggests insufficient pre-emphasis. Further possibilities in the luminance record channel are too high a writing current, flattening off *large* chroma signal excursions; and faulty bandpass filters, allowing the modulator to overdeviate. This can create beat patterns with the chroma signal, especially at sharp transitions and in highly-detailed areas of the picture.

Playback luminance faults

Perhaps the most common replay fault is that of snowy, streaky picture with much dropout. If the video heads are clean, and confirmation of a low f.m. carrier level is made, head wear is almost always responsible. Any form of 25 Hz flicker in the picture means that the two head signals are unbalanced in some way: 'noise' flicker implicates head wear in *one* head or maladjustment of its preamplifier channel; flicker of high or low frequency gratings in the picture should direct attention to the peaking and damping controls at the input circuit of the affected pre-amp. These can only be set up properly during replay of the 'sweep' section of a factory-made alignment tape whose signal, over one TV field-scan period (one head sweep), ranges through all those normally handled by the video heads – a typical oscilloscope trace of a sweep-tape replay is shown in Fig. 13.12, and the pre-amps' frequency response is adjusted for head resonance and damping to achieve the pattern shown here.

Causes of poor resolution downstream of the head pre-amps can be: a maladjusted or faulty noise canceller; a defunct picture-sharpening circuit; or a faulty bandpass filter. Such things can be tracked down by oscilloscope signal tracing, with careful examination of test-pattern 'grating' amplitudes or rise/fall times of transients in stairstep or colour-bar waveforms. Spurious beat patterns on the monochrome picture, where recording problems are not responsible, will generally be due to failure of bandpass filters, or more commonly to vestiges of the f.m. carrier itself appearing on the output signal. Sometimes a faulty demodulator is responsible,

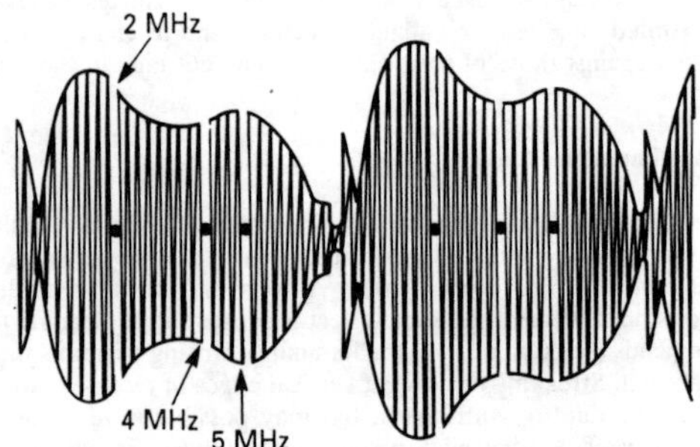

Fig. 13.12 *Sketch of typical oscilloscope trace during replay of sweep section of alignment tape. The gaps and centre dots are frequency markers*

but imbalance in limiters, demodulator etc. is a more likely cause; balancing is carried out by adjustment of *carrier leak* controls for minimum 'grass' on unmodulated sections of the waveform such as sync pulses, porches and the 'tread' sections of stairstep signals.

Chroma record faults

Because most of the colour-under circuitry is common to record and replay, there is little likelihood of a chroma-record fault which does not upset colour on playback. Cases of no- or poor colour record, then, can generally only arise from: failure of either the input (4.43 MHz) or colour-under output (620–680 etc. kHz) bandpass filters or the signal routing to and from them, e.g. record chroma add stage; failure of the 25 Hz flip-flop pulse (derived from incoming field sync) to the record phase (frequency) shifting block; problems in the record/playback switching circuits; or, in a Beta machine, failure of the pilot burst generator or insertion circuits.

Chroma replay faults

Most replay faults affect record too, but are easier to diagnose if dealt with in replay mode, where progress can be monitored on the TV screen and a convenient source of test signal is a known good tape containing stationary colour bars. Some important points to remember are (a) weak colour-under signals will, due to the action of the a.c.c. circuits, give rise to *noisy* colour signals rather than desaturation – the effect is of 'cotton-wool' in highly-saturated parts of the picture, colour-confetti elsewhere; (b) most colour-under problems invoke the action of a colour-killer circuit, which shuts down the chroma channel to render diagnosis more difficult; this particularly applies to frequency- or phase-errors, and the killer action cannot usually be easily overridden, necessitating oscilloscope investigation of the killer trigger circuits; and (c) the readout of a frequency counter or timer can be misleading in some sections of the circuit because it usually counts zero-crossings over a sampling period rather than *dominant* frequency. Thus erroneous readings would be given at the phase rotated 625 kHz input to balanced modulator 1 in Figs 13.6 and 13.8, unless the phase rotator is stopped by holding the flip-flop input high to simulate constant-phase head A condition. Similarly, no coherent counter reading will be obtained from the alternating-frequency colour-under carrier generator in Betamax machines unless similar steps are taken. Outputs from mixers and modulators contain many frequencies and will again give misleading readings from a digital counter.

A 25 Hz flicker in the coloured parts of the picture will almost certainly be due to a problem in *one* head or its associated circuit; if the luminance signal is unaffected, poor l.f. response is the obvious possibility. Complete loss of colour on every other field, if colour-under signals are emerging from the head preamplifiers, suggests a problem in the frequency/phase rotational circuit; it is always within an IC, but check pulse feeds and peripheral components before condemning the chip.

Poor colour lock, with horizontal bands of colour flashing on and off, or floating vertically on the picture, indicates that one of the colour phase correction loops (a.f.c., based on off-tape line sync, or a.p.c, based on a local 4.43 MHz crystal) has failed. A first step here should be a frequency-counter check of the free-running frequencies of both crystals used in the colour replay circuits. Most colour phase and frequency faults, however, are not visible on the TV or monitor screen because of the action of one or more colour-killer circuits either in the videorecorder or in the monitor TV.

No colour is the most common manifestation of chroma circuit faults. A quick first check is to ensure that the crystal oscillators are running and producing the correct frequencies. Many no-colour faults are due to an absence of an essential ancillary pulse feed; a check on head flip-flop pulses into the chroma frequency/phase rotator circuit, and for the presence of line-rate triggering and burst-gating pulses will often expedite the diagnosis. If all pulses are present and correct the oscilloscope must be used to trace the chroma signal itself. In colour-under form (i.e. based on 600–700 kHz) the standard colour bar waveform looks like the 'scope trace of Fig. 13.13. It should appear in this form as far as the input of the up-converting modulator or mixer, i.e. balanced modulator 2 in Fig. 13.8. If so, and no up-converted colour output appears from the mixer, it is likely (assuming that the output filter has signal-continuity) that one of the 'local' inputs to the mixers is faulty or missing.

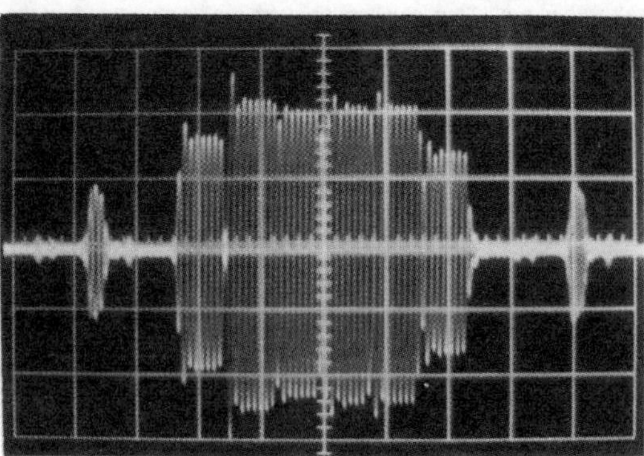

Fig. 13.13 *Off-screen oscilloscope trace of colour-under (626.9 kHz) waveform for standard colour bars. The 'double' nature of individual cycles is due to (a) the PAL phase alternations; and (b) the phase-rotation imparted by the chroma record system*

Each of the two mixer/modulators has two inputs, and all of these should be checked in turn with the 'scope. Most of the colour-under circuitry is contained in special ICs, and fault-finding here is largely confined to seeing that they have correct inputs, pulse-feeds and supply-line voltages; if all these, and such peripheral components as decoupling capacitors are correct, the IC must be replaced. A useful, if slow method of faultfinding is to follow the manufacturer's alignment and setting-up instructions until a problem is encountered – investigation of this will lead to the fault area. Block diagrams in service manuals are also very useful.

Occasionally coloured picture areas may be afflicted by a swirly- or herringbone-pattern which disappears when the colour is turned down. A local m.f. (medium-wave) radio transmitter may be responsible for breakthrough into the colour-under circuits, in which case a filter in the UHF aerial lead or additional head/circuit shielding may effect a cure. Other possible causes are faulty bandpass filters in the chroma *or* luminance sections, or a high degree of *luminance* (f.m.) carrier leak, whose frequency is near 4.43 MHz, and whose level will be excessive if the luminance circuits are not balanced at f.m. carrier frequency.

14

Servo systems

A servo system, in the context of domestic electronic equipment, consists in its simplest terms of a movable or rotating *load* and an electrical drive circuit with two inputs – reference and feedback – and one output. The reference input commands the system, and the feedback input conveys the state or position of the load; the output signal drives the load to the required position or speed such that reference and feedback signals agree; this is called a *closed-loop* system. The load is now positioned in accordance with the command/reference input, and correction ceases until either the command or feedback inputs change (e.g. motor slowed by additional friction or different speed/position required) when servo output will drive or steer the load to restore the status quo, or meet the new requirements.

Servomechanisms are finding many applications in consumer service: auto-iris and auto-focus in video cameras; steering and homing-in of satellite receiving dishes; turntable speed and tracking control in audio and video disc players; and the main concern of this chapter, the regulation of tape positioning and transport in a videocassette recorder. These are *velocity* types which control the speed and phase of a rotating shaft, as opposed to *positioning* servos which hold the controlled device in a position specified by the input-command signal, e.g. lens and antenna servos. The operation of the latter types is easy to understand when the principles of velocity servos are mastered.

VIDEORECORDER SERVOS

The basic function of the capstan servo is to maintain an even and correct speed of the tape through the video deck; that of the head-drum servo is to ensure that (a) during record the video tracks are laid down on tape according to the appropriate format specification; and (b) that during replay the video head scans are perfectly aligned with their appointed tracks. This latter function can be (and usually is) performed by the capstan servo, whereby the head-drum servo maintains correct video head speed while the capstan positions the tape such that the video tracks are correctly aligned under the head sweep-paths.

As Chapter 12 showed, it is fundamental to all helical-scan formats that each head enters its scan of the tape just before the arrival of the field sync pulse in the video waveform. This ensures that head changeover takes place at the correct point at the extreme bottom of the picture, and that all the recorded field sync pulses lie in a line across the bottom edge of the videotape ribbon. During record, then, the timing of a tacho pulse (head-position indicator) is compared in a phase detector with that of a 25 Hz (40 ms period) pulse derived from incoming field syncs in a ÷2 stage – the arrangement is depicted in Fig. 14.1. Here the magnet on the flywheel induces one pulse per revolution in the tacho coil – the PG pulse. The servo system drives the motor to the point where reference and feedback pulses are 'phased up', and maintains correct phase thereafter. The exact timing relationship between

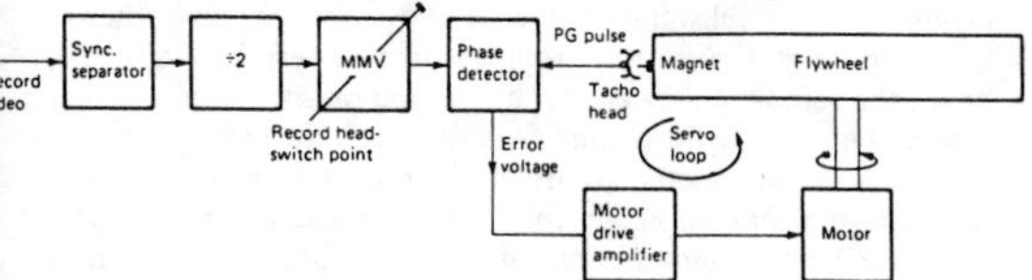

Fig. 14.1 *Basic videorecorder servo function*

head position and field sync pulses is determined by the *record switchpoint* preset, which is part of the RC time-constant of a monostable multivibrator (MMV). The MMV acts as a pulse delay circuit, and is adjusted to set the head changeover on record to take place seven TV lines before field sync. In practice a little overlap is permitted, and the head actually hits the tape about ten lines before the field sync pulse is written onto the tape.

Phase detector

There are several possible configurations for phase detectors, but the most common type in such low-frequency applications as video motor servos is the sample-and-hold circuit, the elements of which are shown in Fig. 14.2. Each reference pulse (a) triggers a ramp generator whose output voltage (b) rises linearly with time; the generation of a linear ramp was dealt with in the field timebase section of Chapter 10. Some short time later a feedback pulse (c) arrives to close the sampling switch, whereupon the storage capacitor charges to a level determined by the ramp amplitude at that moment, waveform (d). The ripple voltage developed across the storage capacitor is integrated and amplified in the blocks to the right to produce a steady d.c. *error* voltage output (e) whose level is proportional to elapsed time between the arrival of reference and feedback pulses. The early arrival of a feedback pulse indicates excessive motor speed, and samples the ramp at a low level, producing a low output voltage. Motor current is reduced as a result, slowing the motor to the point where reference and feedback pulses have the same time-interval; the controlled shaft is now 'phased-up' to incoming sync pulses.

For rapid and accurate control of head-drum phasing a steep ramp is required; small phase errors then have a large effect on error voltage for rapid correction. Such a steep ramp leads to

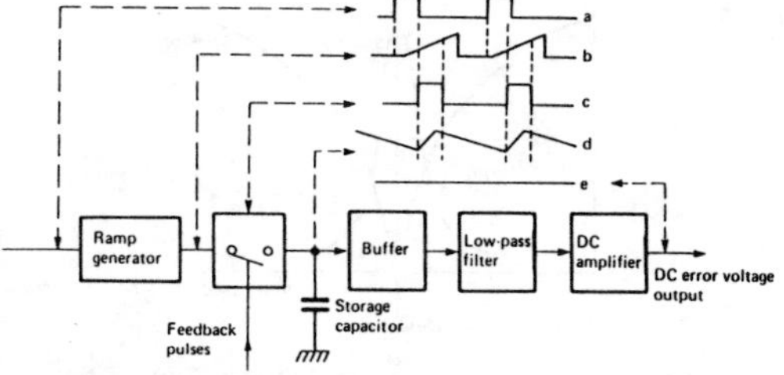

Fig. 14.2 *Working principle of sample-and-hold phase detection system*

problems in establishing correct *speed*, however, and when the controlled motor is starting from rest or recovering from a disturbance the sample pulses appear at random on the ramp to produce a jittering error voltage and 'hunting' and instability in motor speed. A second motor control influence (speed drive) is introduced to overcome this problem. It maintains motor speed at about the correct point, providing a small 'window' in which the above-described phase control system works.

Speed control loop

The speed of the motor is monitored by a frequency (tone)-generator (FG) built into the motor itself. It usually takes the form of a multi-toothed wheel passing over a capacitive or magnetic pickup device, the output frequency from which is proportional to motor speed. This output passes to a frequency-to-voltage convertor whose output is also applied to the motor as an error drive, forming a *dual-loop* servo with separate speed and phase sections as outlined in Fig. 14.3(a). The speed loop rapidly establishes correct rotational speed, then the phase loop takes over to hold the 'dynamic position' of the head-drum rigidly in accordance with the phase of the reference input. When the speed is incorrect, operation of the phase loop is not required since its error voltage output is disordered at this time; similarly the influence of the speed-correction loop is superfluous during the presence of a phase error.

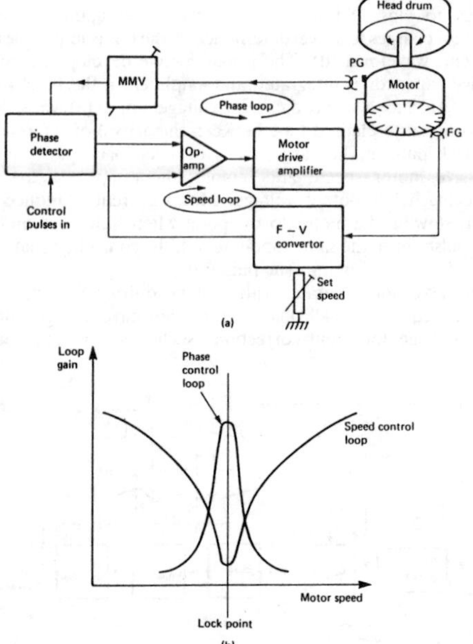

Fig. 14.3 *Dual-loop servo: (a) block diagram; (b) complementary speed/gain characteristics of the correction loops*

The gains of the two feedback loops are arranged to vary according to the motor speed, then, as shown in Fig. 14.3(b): this gives optimum correction performance.

FREQUENCY-TO-VOLTAGE CONVERTOR

Several forms of F–V convertor are possible; a widely-used one is illustrated in Fig. 14.4. Here the FG tone at correct motor speed is 100 Hz (waveform a) which after amplification and clipping becomes the sloped squarewave b. A form of full-wave recification now takes place in which the upper half of waveform b is inverted to give a series of triangular pulses c. A level detector and switch produces a clean pulse (d) for each spike. Waveform d is delayed for a short fixed period (e) before being made to trigger a ramp generator which has *constant-slope* characteristic. The ramp continues to rise until the arrival of the next trigger pulse, when it commences once more from zero as shown at waveform f. Because the slope, in terms of volts per second, is constant, the final voltage achieved depends on the *period* of the ramp, which is proportional to FG frequency. It only remains, then, to sample it *at its highest point* to derive a voltage proportional to motor speed. Because of the MMV delay in Fig. 14.4 the highest point on the ramp is always time-coincident with the pulses in waveform d, which open a gate in the sample-and-hold circuit to charge storage capacitor C1 to peak ramp voltage, waveform g. After filtering and amplification a ripple-free error voltage is produced which is *inversely* proportional to motor speed. As Fig. 14.3(a) shows, the F–V converter is associated with a pre-set pot which sets the 'free-run' speed of the motor. In the case of a conventional head-drum it will be 1500 r.p.m.

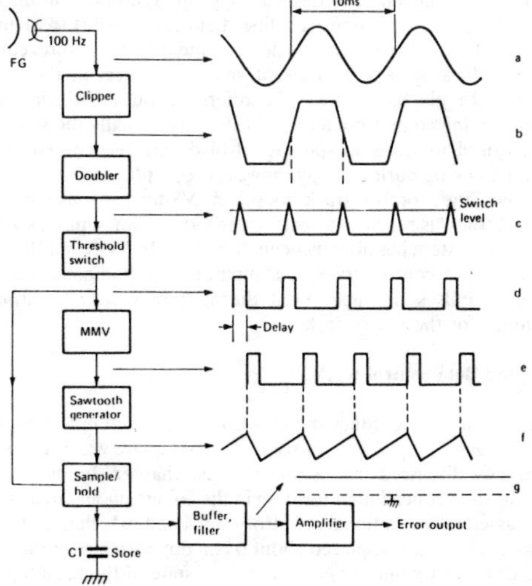

Fig. 14.4 *One system of frequency-to-voltage conversion for speed loop*

for a capstan motor it will depend on the diameter of the capstan shaft and the tape speed in use.

REFERENCE SOURCES

Since the angular position of the capstan shaft is not relevant in the same way as that of the head-drum, there is no intrinsic requirement for a PG on the capstan motor or shaft, and a PG is seldom provided here. For optimum performance of the capstan servo, however, a dual-loop system is often used, with both speed and phase loops working from the capstan FG output. In its most basic form the capstan servo is purely a speed regulator, and so may be 'paced' by a stable reference crystal during record, playback or both. It is common practice to use the 4.43 MHz chroma crystal as reference, and count-down its output frequency to a rate comparable with the FG frequency; alternatively a dedicated servo reference crystal running at 30–40 kHz may be found. Once locked to such a reference the tape speed is regulated with great accuracy, and any momentary speed variations due to changes in tape tension or other factors are rapidly nullified by the servo-feedback system. During record the capstan shaft speed is always locked to some local reference – on playback, capstan control may be more elaborate, as will be described shortly.

Coming to the drum servo, on record the invariable phasing reference (which also sets the speed, of course) is incoming field sync, in order to comply with the one-complete-field-per-head-sweep requirement as already described. During playback there is no external reference frequency to lock to, hence no *absolute* phasing requirement, unless the videorecorder output is required to lock to another source of video signals for use with a vision mixer or effects console – rare in domestic situations, and difficult to implement with a machine not designed for this *genlock* feature. In a stand-alone situation, however, line, field (and audio) frequencies must conform closely to broadcast standards to ensure correct timebase locking, and to prevent spurious effects in the TV or monitor. In playback, then, the reference pulses which master picture timing come from a crystal reference, usually the same one as was used for capstan speed control during record. To ensure correct tracking during replay, however, one phase control loop is essential: the control track loop. In V8-format machines the 'control track' is read out as part of the video track signal itself; the ATF tone system has already been discussed. In VHS and Betamax machines the control track is a separate longitudinally-recorded series of pulses on tape, used during replay as a positioning reference for the video tracks.

VHS and Beta control track

At the time of recording the divided-by-two incoming field sync pulses trigger a flip-flop to provide a 25 Hz square wave. It is used, as already discussed in this and the last chapter, for head-drum phasing and for head identification in the colour-under circuits. It is also passed to the stationary control-track head, which is part of the audio head assembly, placed about 6 cm 'downstream' of the video head drum exit point. At each change of state of the head flip-flop waveform, i.e. at 40 ms intervals, a mark is made in the magnetic pattern of the control track. Because the head drum-to-control head spacing is standardised, each of these marks will be made on the tape in a fixed position in relation to the start points of alternate video tracks. During replay the same control-track head reads out the pulses. By establishing a fixed phase between these and the head-drum PG pulses a relationship is set up between video head positioning and the physical disposition of video tracks on tape – this is what is required for tracking control. On replay, then, a local reference crystal is used to establish correct speed for both head-drum and capstan. The error voltage coming from the phase detector comparing control track and head-PG pulses can be applied to either the head-drum motor *or* the capstan motor. In either case it will establish and maintain a constant head path with respect to the prerecorded video tape tracks; to make them concide a suitable MMV delay is inserted into the path of either the control track pulse or the head PG pulse. The time-constant of the MMV can be varied by the user tracking control over (typically) two track widths, corresponding to about 180° of head-drum rotation. This enables the user to set up correct tracking on any tape/machine combination under any circumstances – except those of a faulty machine. The click-stop setting of the tracking control corresponds to format-standard and to a specific drum-to-control-head spacing. It is used during replay of the machine's own recordings, and those recorded in other correctly set-up videorecorders.

ATF replay tracking

V8-format videorecorders have no separate control track as such. The need for tracking correction is indicated by imbalance in the two crosstalk-beat frequencies. As described in Chapter 12 and Fig. 12.7 an error voltage is produced from this, used to directly adjust capstan speed. In this way perfect and automatic tracking is assured, with no need for a tracking control.

PULSE-COUNTING (DIGITAL) SERVOS

The basic function of the electronic section of a videorecorder or disc-player servo system is to measure time (i.e. the period between arrival of reference and sample pulses) in the case of the phase control loop; and frequency (FG rate) for the speed control loop. Both these functions can be carried out with great speed and accuracy by means of digital counter/timer circuits using a crystal clock as a basic 'metronome'.

An arrangement for a digitally-based phase-control servo using an LSI chip is given in Fig. 14.5, in which the crystal clock on the left produces 1 μs-interval pulses. The input reference pulse is used to enable counter 1, which commences to count clock pulses from 0000000000 upwards. In this 10-bit counter the maximum count is 2^{10}, which corresponds to decimal 1024. At the clock rate of 1 MHz the counter will take about 1 ms to reach maximum count. Before this happens, however, a sample pulse appears and activates the latch, which effectively 'freezes' the count at that instant and transfers it to the hold register of a digital comparator. If the sample pulse comes 500 μs after the reference pulse the count will have reached about 512 (binary 1000000000). The latch operates and binary 512 is loaded into the comparator as an indication of the time lapse between the arrival of the two pulses.

Now consider the upper section of Fig. 14.5. On emergence from the ÷2 stage the clock pulses are at 500 kHz, 2 μs interval. They are fed to a second 10-bit counter (counter 2) which also counts

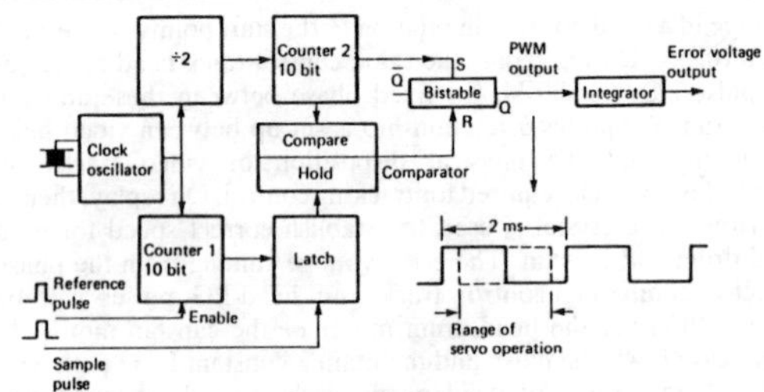

Fig. 14.5 *Basic form of digital servo for phase correction*

from zero to 1024, resetting itself each time it fills up. The count-and-reset process for counter 2 is continuous, and because it is counting 500 kHz (2 μs period) pulses it resets at 1024 × 2 μs = 2 ms intervals. At each reset a trigger pulse is applied to the *set* input of an SR bistable, whose output is thus set high. The continuous count made by counter 2 is also fed to the comparator which is designed to detect coincidence between the binary numbers in its 'hold' and 'compare' registers. After 1 ms, counter 2 will have reached 512 so that the counts in the two comparator registers match. Under these circumstances the comparator output goes high; this pulse is passed to the 'R' input of the SR bistable, resetting its output low. The bistable is being set and reset at 1 ms intervals, to give an output whose mark/space ratio is 1:1.

Suppose the motor speeds up. The sample pulse will come early, giving counter 1 little time to accumulate a count before the latch operates. A correspondingly low number, say 256, is loaded into the hold register of the comparator. Counter 2, having set the SR bistable high when it passed zero, will take only 500 μs to accumulate a count of 256 to satisfy the comparator and reset the bistable low again. It will remain low for 1500 μs (1.5 ms) before being set high once more by counter 2 passing zero. The mark/space ratio of the bistable output signal is now 1:3. The opposite applies if the motor slows down for any reason. Whereas the rising edges of the bistable output waveform always occur at 2 ms intervals (see Fig. 14.5) due to the regular resetting action of counter 2, the timing of the falling edges is determined entirely by the time lapse between reference and sample pulses.

The pulse-width-modulated (PWM) squarewave output is converted to a d.c. error voltage by passing it through an RC integrating filter. The output from this is used to modify motor speed in the same way as the error voltage in analogue servo configurations.

Digital speed correction

The arrangement of Fig. 14.5 is fundamentally a measurer of time. In order to use it in a speed-control loop some modification is required, as shown in Fig. 14.6. Waveform a is the FG tone, amplitude-limited to produce squarewave b. Its rising edge triggers a short monostable to produce pulse train c; its falling edge triggers a second monostable whose output is pulse train d. Each pulse 'c' enables counter 1 and each pulse 'd' resets the counter and operates the latch. The latch count is *inversely* proportional to FG frequency,

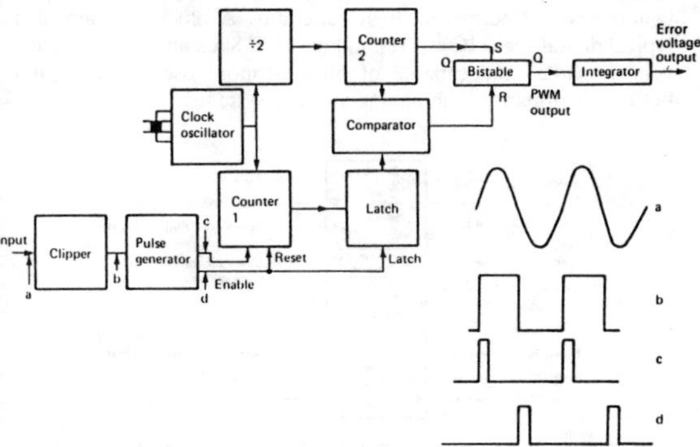

Fig. 14.6 *Digital servo arranged for speed control; compare with Fig. 14.5*

and is held in the comparator's hold register until counter 2 (whose configuration and function are the same as in Fig. 14.5) reaches the same count, whereupon the bistable is reset. The varying M/S ratio is processed as already described, and now produces an error voltage which reflects the *frequency* of the FG input signal. For this speed control application the bistable set/reset rate is required to be faster than the 1 kHz rate typical of a digital *phase* corrector, and an output rate between 4 and 17 kHz is general. In either case the bistable rate is determined by the clock rate and the number of bits (maximum possible count) of the recirculating counter – counter 2 in the present Figs 14.5 and 14.6. These are chosen to suit the sampling rate to the application loop in which it is used.

In some videorecorder designs the counter bit capacities and clock rates vary with different loop requirements in drum and capstan servos. Advanced designs also incorporate a ROM in the digital servo chip to provide different counting conditions for varying deck conditions, i.e. SP/LP operation and 'trick-speed' replay modes; the ROM is addressed by a mode select line whose origin is the user's function keyboard.

ADVANTAGES OF DIGITAL SERVO OPERATION

Although the operation of pulse-counting servo systems may appear to be more complex than that of analogue types, their operation is similar: in place of the linear ramp is the 'stair-case' of the digital counter and instead of a sampling gate a latch and comparator is used. The need for timing capacitors and pre-set controls is eliminated – even the record head-switching preset can be dispensed with in a counting circuit which counts line and field periods. More accurate timing and greater reliability and freedom from drift can be expected; the opportunity exists, too, to build-in programmable counting systems to cater for different modes of operation.

Component count is reduced in digital servos – most functions are carried out in an LSI chip, where often both capstan and head drum servo circuits are incorporated, along with pulse and timing generators and peripheral logic functions. A block diagram of a typical digital servo IC is given in Fig. 14.7. Such an arrangement is very versatile, and capable of offering more user features and better performance than analogue servo systems.

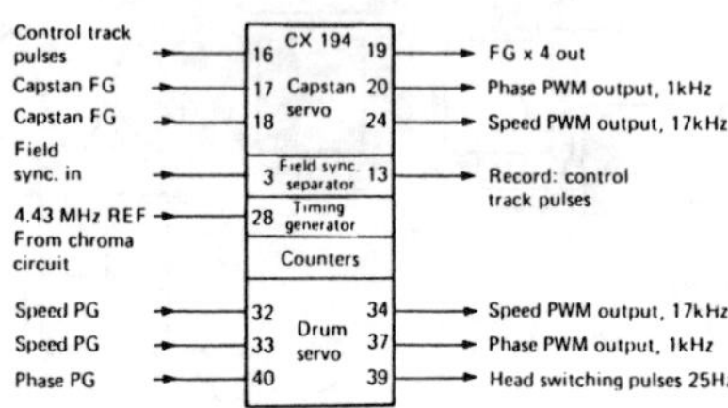

Fig. 14.7 *LSI digital servo chip, purpose-designed by Sony*

MOTORS

For reliability and versatility it is common practice to provide *direct-drive* motors for head drum and capstan, in which the motor shaft mounts the drum itself or forms the capstan respectively. These brushless motors have built-in FG generators and a multi-pole drive stator, around which rotates a multi-pole magnetised ferrite disc or cup. A typical arrangement is shown in the circuit diagram of Fig. 14.8. The motor itself is on the right, and contains three main coils split into six poles; and eight-pole rotating ring magnet; and three Hall ICs which are solid-state magnetic-field detectors. The drive circuit in IC2006 switches current into each coil in turn at 120° intervals. In this way, one coil-pair at a time will pull the ferrite disc round while a second coil-pair pushes it, the third being inactive. The sequence of coil-switching is controlled by the three rotor-position-sensing Hall ICs built into the stator assembly, and currents flow in both directions through the stator coils. To avoid flutter in motor speed due to any imbalance in coil currents or fields, the sampling resistor on pin 2 of IC2006 continually monitors motor current, passing in turn through all six coil halves. Any changes are compensated for by feedback to the torque control input at IC pin 20.

Motor control and switching is also carried out within IC2006. A speed control voltage (basically dependent on the error voltage from the servo circuit) enters on pin 15, where a falling potential will drive more current through the switching transistors and stator coils to accelerate the motor. Reverse, stop and forward commands from the system control block enter the IC on pin 11, where they are decoded in the *motor rotation detection* block.

A photograph of a direct-drive motor of this type appears in Fig. 14.9. This design is particularly flat and compact; it forms part of a camcorder by Panasonic.

SERVO OPERATION IN SEARCH AND STILL MODES

VHS–LP operation involves identical tape and capstan speeds during record and replay, and has little effect on servo operation:

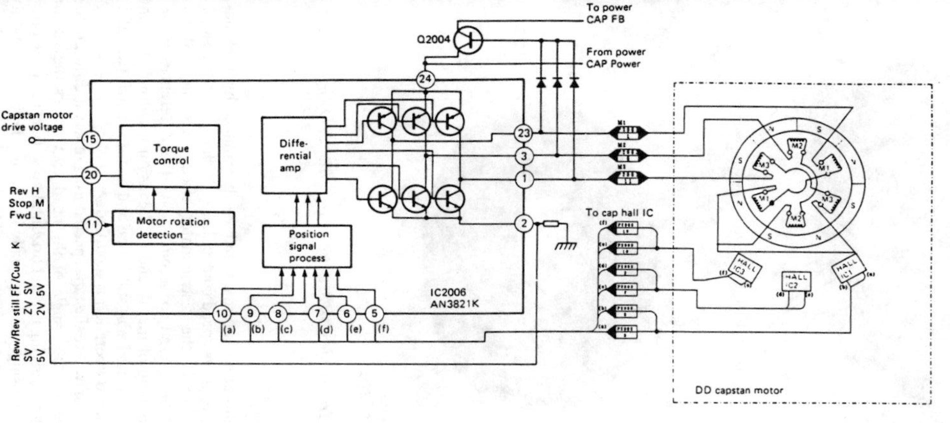

Fig. 14.8 *Electrical drive system for DD motor*

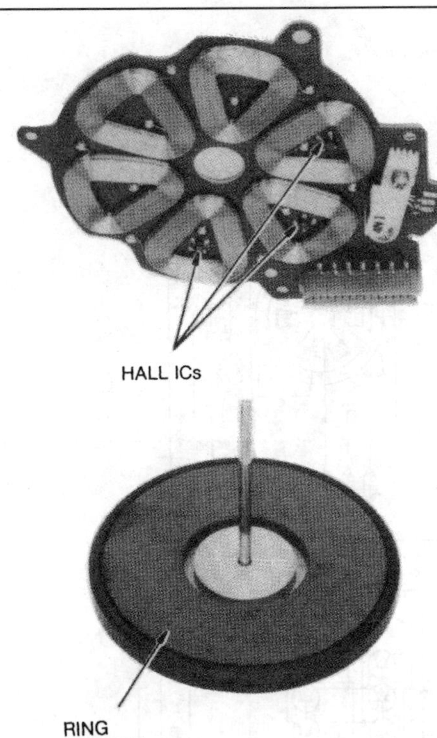

Fig. 14.9 *Internal construction of flat DD motor by Panasonic*

the capstan runs at half normal speed, easily arranged by introducing a '×2' factor in its speed control loop, or changing ramp slope or counting rate in the discriminator circuit. The head drum phasing must be altered to accommodate the difference in the physical positioning of the SP and LP heads on the drum. It is in such 'trick' replay modes as still-frame and picture search (cue and review) that servo operation is modified.

In any situation where the tape speed during replay is different to that during record, the angle of the head scan across the video tracks will change, giving rise to horizontal noise bars in the picture at each track-crossing and (especially in cue and review modes) a change in the number of lines per TV field. Non-standard line timing can cause misregistration between luma and chroma components on the TV screen, and loss of line hold if the error exceeds a few per cent. To prevent these effects speed compensation is applied to the drum motor – it is speeded up in cue mode and slowed down during review. These speed offsets are provided by switched pre-sets in simple machines, by ROM-controlled counter programming in sophisticated ones.

Trick-speed operation, then, mainly concerns the capstan servo. For cue or review the system control section sets the motor direction according to the command keyed in by the user, then capstan speed is increased by a factor of three or more. To lock the resulting track-crossing noise bars stationary on screen, capstan phase-control is referred to suitably-divided off-tape control-track pulses. Alternatively the pinch roller can be disengaged during these modes and tape speed control given over to the appropriate reel-drive motors, which in some machines (especially portables) are also direct-drive types; others have a single reel motor with swinging idler, or depend on a belt-driven clutch for reel drive. Noise-bar locking is also possible here by means of a link between reel motor and replayed control-track pulses.

For still-frame operation the capstan is stopped. In simple videorecorders this will leave a mistracking bar at some random position on the TV screen. For noise-free still frame the capstan stopping point is under close control, determined by the relative positions of the 25 Hz head flip-flop waveform and the noise bar in the replay f.m. envelope. Correct phasing of these two ensures (in conjunction with the wide-head system described in Chapter 12) that the noise occupies the field blanking interval where its effect is nullified by the synthetic field sync pulse generated and inserted into the video waveform at this time, as already described. In some machines the capstan stop-and-shunt motor drive waveforms are generated and timed by a purpose-designed chip, or a microprocessor with suitable built-in ROM. Frame-advance facility is also provided in these cases, for which the capstan motor is stepped-on by one track-width for each touch of the advance button, while the position of the noise-bar is monitored and corrected each time. Slow-motion is a development of this technique, whereby the capstan motor steps forward very rapidly at short intervals under the control of off-tape control track pulses. New and correctly-aligned video tracks are thus presented in the path of the video head sweeps, each remaining in position for many revolutions of the drum before the tape is smartly advanced to display the next field.

SERVO AND MOTOR FAULT SYMPTOMS

A fundamental point to remember in servicing servo and motor circuits is that capstan-speed faults will upset sound reproduction to give wrong pitch, wow or flutter – picture *tracking* will also be affected. Head-drum speed fault symptoms are confined to the picture; wow and flutter here gives rise to a lateral wobble of the picture, which will break into horizontal lines if drum speed deviates far from the norm. Loss of the reference signal (i.e. PAL or local crystal oscillator stopped) will usually greatly increase motor speed, and in many designs loss of feedback signal – faulty FG or PG generator, for instance – will do the same. In the case of a fast-running head drum, it can be slowed by friction from a finger to check for correct line frequency at normal speed; at the same time the effect on feedback signals (and their influence) can be monitored. If continuity is present, they should be acting to drive the motor faster, and the diagnosis then consists of finding out why the motor is not responding to the 'turn-down' signals being developed at excessive motor speeds.

A head or capstan motor running at the correct speed, but whose phase control loop has failed, will drift in phase to give the following symptoms: Head servo out of control on record – head switching point disturbance drifts up or down screen – check for 25 Hz head PG and field sync pulses. Head or capstan servo out of control on playback – cyclical tracking errors in which part or all of the screen is affected by noise – check PG pulses, tracking delay MMV and particularly the control track pulses from the stationary head. A worn, dirty or misaligned control head will pick up insufficient pulse amplitude to operate the servo. This malfunction is often masked by the action of a *muting* circuit, which only unblanks video signals when the servo is locked up: the idea is to prevent unstable pictures being displayed.

In general the electrical components of a servo system are much more reliable than the mechanical components. First checks, then, should be for the presence of reference and feedback signals, which depend on crystals, plugs, sockets and transducers – in magnetic and optical form – and on transfer of control pulses on and off tape. Motors, belts and bearings are also high on the suspect list, though brushless direct-drive motors have a lower failure rate than their earlier permanent-magnet brush-and-commutator counterparts, still sometimes encountered and still widely used for the more mundane deck functions such as tape- and cassette-loading and reel drive.

Once the mechanical components have been exonerated, the fact that both speed and phase correction sections are closed loops is a considerable aid to fault diagnosis. A fault condition implies that the loop is broken, and at the 'severed end', as it were, a strong corrective signal will appear in an attempt to restore normality; it is upon tracing this that the diagnosis should be concentrated.

Setting-up procedures for servos (especially in trick playback modes) vary widely with machine type, age and manufacturer. Except in simple machines with few presets and obvious functions no attempt should be made to adjust the servo circuits without the manufacturer's service manual and all necessary instruments. More on test equipment and diagnosis procedures will be found in Chapter 20.

15

Videorecorder deck control

Modern videorecorders require a comprehensive deck control system to act as a 'clearing house' for user instructions and feedback information from deck status sensors, and to ensure correct sequencing of deck functions. It must protect the tape and deck mechanism from damage, prevent the user invoking conflicting or damaging commands, and present (in most machines) a front panel display of the function in progress, the presence of the tape cassette and a warning of any malfunction or danger situation. An overall block diagram of the *syscon* (systems control) section of a videorecorder is given in Fig. 15.1. As can be seen there is a multiplicity of inputs and outputs, now to be dealt with in turn:

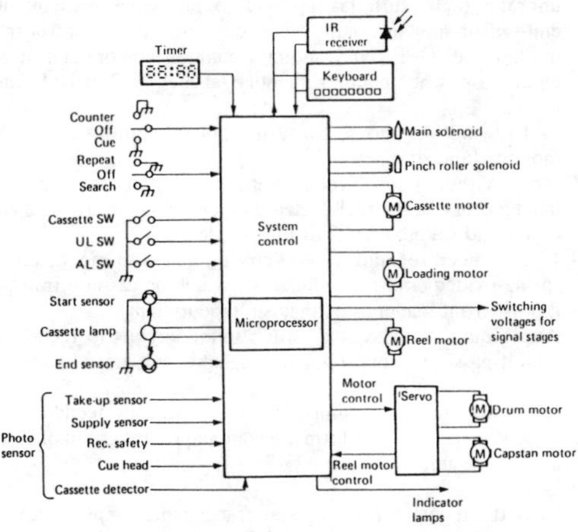

Fig. 15.1 *Overview of system control functions*

SYSCON INPUTS

The primary input lines to system control come from the user's keyboard, be it on the front panel or on a remote handset. The main key functions, and the resulting actions of the syscon are as follows:

1 Play: Check cassette lamp and end sensor; unbrake reels, lock cassette cradle, start capstan and head motors, initiate threading procedure; stop threading motor at threading end, unblank video and audio replay channels when servos locked; monitor deck functions thereafter

2 Record: As above, but first check for presence of cassette record-safety tab; switch on erase oscillator, switch sound and vision signal circuits to record; route head flip-flop squarewave

to control-track head; switch servos to record mode; lock channel selector

3 Pause: Stop tape motion by braking capstan motor or withdrawing pinch roller; override deck rotation-sensor outputs to prevent stop mode being entered; start pause-time clock to prevent tape damage by entering 'stop' after 3–15 minute period. In play-pause: shunt tape to correct point for noise-bar elimination and invoke artificial field sync pulse generator; in record-pause, some machines: rewind tape 20–25 frames and prime edit-start circuit (see later)
4 Cue: Speed forward motion of tape via capstan or reel drive motor; speed up head drum to maintain correct *f*h; switch to 'trick' video heads where applicable; disable vision and sound blanking circuits
5 Review: Reverse and increase speed of capstan and/or reel drive motors; slow down head drum to maintain correct *f*h; switch to 'trick' video heads where applicable; disable blanking circuits; switch servos as necessary
6 Fast forward: Stop, unthread tape (except some late types), unbrake reels, turn takeup reel to fast clockwise, monitor end-sensor and any auto-cue system based on control-track markers i.e. QPF, APS; monitor counter-memory sensor and enter 'stop' when counter memory reaches 0000 or end-sensor fired
7 Fast rewind: As above, but turn supply reel anticlockwise and monitor tape start-sensor
8 Stop: Withdraw pinch roller, unthread, switch off capstan and head motors, brake reels, release lock on cassette cradle, switch vision and sound circuits to E–E mode
9 Eject: Check for and if necessary initiate stop mode; release spring-loaded cradle (top loaders); switch on cassette transport motor (front loaders); extinguish 'tape-in' lamp
10 Audio dub: As 'play' but switch sound circuits to record and inhibit passage of bias oscillator signal to full-erase head

In addition to these command inputs, various feedback and guard sensors on the deck form a second important group of syscon inputs. These are:

1 Cassette-in detector: An optical or mechanical sensor activated by the plastic cassette shell. With no cassette present all deck functions are inhibited
2 Record tab sensor: A 'feeler' to detect the presence or absence of the removable erase-prevention tab on the cassette shell. With no tab, record mode is inhibited
3 Drum rotation sensor: Head PG or flip-flop waveform is monitored to assure continued rotation of the head; its absence will invoke stop mode
4 Spool rotation sensors: As above, but derived from Hall-Effect magnet or optocoupler on spool turntable. To prevent tape damage, syscon enters stop when alternating sensor signal ceases
5 Tape start- and end-sensors: At each front corner of the cassette is mounted a sensor which detects the presence of the leader tape at the extreme ends of the ribbon. For VHS and V8 a lamp shining through the clear leader tape is used; for Beta, a metallic strip which inductively loads a sensor coil. When tape start is detected, any rewinding function is disabled; at tape end, only rewind commands will be accepted. Many machines have

an auto-rewind feature, in which stop then rewind modes are consecutively entered by the syscon on receipt of 'tape-end' signal
6 Cassette lamp: In machines other than Beta, failure of the lamp used for end sensing would prevent tape start- and end-detection. Lamp current (filament bulb in old models, infra-red LED in later types) is monitored – if it ceases, stop is entered
7 Slack sensor: If at any point the tape becomes slack, the machine has malfunctioned and the tape could get damaged. Tape slack is detected by a spring-loaded feeler arm or a wide opto-coupled light pair placed where a slack tape bulge would interrupt the light path. A slack tape signal causes the syscon to enter stop mode
8 Dew detector: A resistive humidity detector fitted to the head drum assembly inhibits all deck functions via the syscon if moisture has gathered. This prevents tape, drum and motor damage from the ribbon sticking to the drum surface. Very often a dew warning is provided on the front panel of the machine, and in some designs a head-heating element is switched on to dry the drum
9 Loading start/end sensors: All videocassette recorders have electrically driven tape loading/threading mechanisms. Until load-end is reached the loading motor must remain on, and many other mechanical functions inhibited; similarly, the tape must be fully unthreaded before head, capstan and loading motors can be switched off and the cassette released from the machine
10 Loading motor lock: If the loading motor stalls during load or unload the machine switches off altogether; this is particularly relevant to battery-operated portable videorecorders and camcorders.

In most videorecorders and in portable types, some of these deck status signals are given by a *mode switch*, a multi-contact slider or rotary type mechanically linked to the mechanics of the reel drive and tape-loading mechanism.

A further set of commands come to the syscon from areas other than the keyboard and deck sensors, as follows:

1 Timer command: At times pre-set and programmed by the user the deck is given 'record' and 'stop' signals from the timer section, which itself will select the programme-channel chosen by the absentee user. Some types of videorecorder use a single microprocessor, custom-designed and internally programmed for syscon, timer clock and display-drive functions
2 Power interrupt: If a power failure occurs during record or playback all motion ceases instantly; on restoration of power the machine will unload and stop. Some designs permit resumption of *timed* (pre-programmed) recording after a power cut. If the power switch is turned off during any 'moving' function the machine will unload and enter stop before turning off
3 Low battery: In portable equipment the battery voltage is monitored and at about 88% of normal voltage the unit enters stop and turns off completely to prevent over-discharge damage. The approach of this situation is often warned of by a flashing light on the control panel or in the viewfinder
4 Counter memory: A stop command passes into the syscon when the tape counter passes 0000 with the memory button depressed. In more sophisticated designs a 'counter go-to' number can be

programmed into the keyboard, whereupon the syscon will drive the tape in either direction to the required count point

5 Remote control: A full remote control system duplicates the control panel functions, and will be dealt with below and in Chapter 19. Particularly relevant to portable equipment is the camera trigger which operates the record-pause function described early in this chapter.

SYSCON OUTPUTS

The syscon has access to all the mechanical movers on the deck, and switches command lines to various electronic sections. Not all of the below-listed outputs will necessarily be provided, depending on the vintage, price and degree of sophistication of the machine.

1 Motor controls: start, stop and up to three speed conditions for the *drum* motor; for the capstan motor, stop, run and where applicable run forwards and backwards at various speeds – half speed for LP operation; run, stop, reverse for the loading motor; run, stop, reverse for any cassette loading motor; run, stop, reverse and speed control for reel motor(s)
2 Solenoid controls: since all mechanical operations of the deck must be carried out electro-mechanically, solenoids may be provided for the following purposes: pressure-roller application; fast-forward/rewind lever; play lever; loading-drive engagement where no dedicated loading motor is employed; and reel brake application
3 Indication lamps: front-panel or viewfinder indications of machine function and status, they can range from simple LED point-emitters to dot-matrix pattern displays in fluorescent or LED display panel matrices, or electronically-generated symbols or characters on the viewfinder screen
4 Signal switching: output lines are provided to switch on and off sections of the machine as appropriate to the mode in use. These may typically be REC + 9V, PLAY + 9V, AUDIO DUB + 9V, REC/PLAY + 9V, MUTE HIGH, CH LOCK. The latter inhibits channel change during record so that servo instability is prevented; CH LOCK signal disappears during rec. pause mode.

CENTRAL PROCESSOR

The heart of the syscon is invariably a microprocessor. A four-bit type is most usual, with on-board ROM containing an instruction set appropriate to the videorecorder design and deck members. Very often this ROM is permanently programmed by or at the request of the *equipment* manufacturer to suit his design, the rest of the micro being of a standardised type; this ROM programme is defined by the *suffix* of the type number, very important when the device is replaced in a repair situation. Increasingly, microprocessors are being custom-designed for specific videorecorder or camcorder applications, particularly where the equipment manufacturer is also in the business of designing and producing ICs. This approach greatly simplifies the interfacing circuits between the syscon and its peripheral devices such as keyboards, remote control systems, motors and solenoids. It also permits the use of a single micro for *all* 'intelligent' operations within a budget-priced machine, in which timer, clock, display drive and tape counter operations may be dealt with inside the same package as the syscon process itself, reducing cost, complexity, interconnection links and component count.

A small RAM capacity is also provided on board the μP chip to store user instructions and deck status data pending decisions or execution. Unlike conventional computing systems where memories, interfaces and codecs are separate from the CPU, the one-chip microcomputer used here contains parallel processing CPU, ROM, RAM, I/O ports, programmable timer, control circuit and clock oscillator, see Fig. 15.2. Typical ROM and RAM capacities in a syscon micro chip are 3000 × 8 bits and 96 × 8 bits respectively. No great speed in operation is required, especially as the micro spends virtually all its time waiting instructions – a clock oscillator rate of 400 kHz is typical, with an instruction cycle of 10 μs.

A typical syscon's functional diagram is shown in Fig. 15.3. Here two microprocessors are used, μP1 as the main operator and μP2 as a slave/expander device. All inputs are applied to μP1, which judges the conditions and outputs mechanism drive instructions according to its ROM data. Many of the inputs discussed earlier can be seen entering μP1 at left, along with a *reset* pulse at pin 15 – this essential 'start from' pulse is applied at power on, and resets all the RAM circuits within the micro to 'stop' condition; μP2 gets its reset pulse on pin 10 via μP1. μP2 is subservient to μP1 and outputs instructions according to the latter's commands. Data transfer between the two devices takes place via the four data lines linking pins 36–39 of μP1 to pins 15–18 of μP2. The fifth transfer line (DO) contains clocking pulses and framing code data to synchronise the transfer of information. This parallel data transfer system is most common in inter-micro links in video and disc recorder control systems, though serial data is used in some designs in conjunction with codecs – see later; and is necessarily used on long inter-equipment links and in infra-red remote control systems. In the

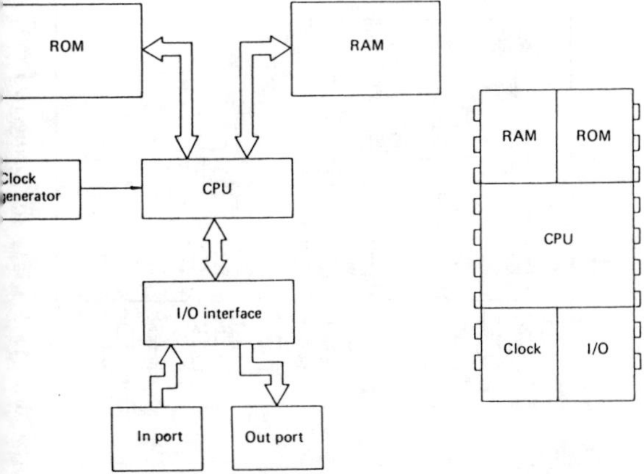

Fig. 15.2 *Internal architecture of typical mask-programmed 4-bit microcomputer as used for video-recorder syscon applications*

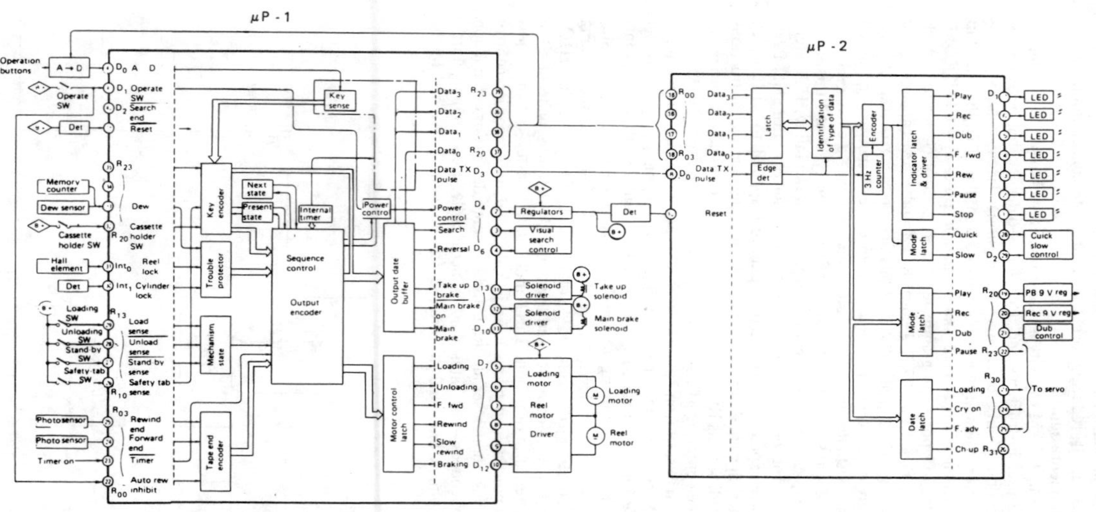

Fig. 15.3 *A syscon using two microprocessors – μP1 is dominant (Hitachi)*

diagram of Fig. 15.3, parallel-bus lines (which may be up to 8-bit) within the micros are shown as broad paths.

Closing the 'operate' switch puts a 'high' on pin 41 of μP1 whose pin 2 goes low as a result, turning on the power supply regulators from which the 'operate' LED and μP2 are powered. At this point, too, μP2 is reset by the detector block on its pin 10. Operation commands from the keyboard enter μP1 on pin 40, and as an example of a syscon programme the *play* sequence will be followed: A check is made on the cassette holder switch, then loading starts. The single reel motor is pulsed via μP1 pin 7 to set its idler in 'neutral' position, and via pins 12 and 13 the main brake is released to free both reel discs. The loading motor starts running to pull a loop of tape from the cassette and lock in place the cassette holder; simultaneously a soft brake is applied to the supply reel disc to provide back-tension during loading; and a hard brake to the takeup reel disc to prevent tape spillage. Shortly into the loading cycle the drum and capstan motors are switched on via μP2, and run quickly up to speed.

At completion of tape loading the loading-end switch closes, putting a 'high' into μP1 pin 29. The loading motor is switched off and the hard brake on the take-up reel disc released. The pinch wheel moves into engagement with the capstan, and the reel motor idler moves in the direction of the take-up reel disc to drive it clockwise via a slipping clutch. During the loading phase the signal system was muted to prevent spurious noise and instability effects; the mute is now disabled. The 'play' LED is illuminated from μP2 pin 7 and PB9V generated at μP2 pin 19.

SYSCON INPUT MATRICES

The large number of operating keys associated with modern videorecorders and camcorders necessitates some form of matrixing system to reduce the number of input pins required on the microprocessor. Two approaches are possible, key-scan and A–D conversion. The key-scan method is illustrated in Fig. 15.4, which is taken from a Panasonic camcorder. Here IC6003 pulses its key scan ports P00, P01, P02, P03 and P21 at 11 ms intervals, each port having a different pulse timing. When an operation key is pressed one of these scan pulses is fed back into one of the input ports P10–P13 of the same microprocessor IC6003. The micro's programme now compares output and input pulse timing to detect which button was pressed, and implements its ROM-based operation accordingly. Note the date manipulation keys at left of Fig. 15.4: these commands are routed to an electronic character generator. Five pulse phases and four input ports give a possible total of twenty key combinations, of which fifteen are used here, with only nine lines in the keyboard link. Even greater is the economy of link lines in the A–D converter system:

An outline of the principle of a control system using A–D conversion is given in Fig. 15.5. The operation depends on a 4-bit data bus D0–D3 which presents a μP-generated running count of 0–15 in binary terms as shown by the lower waveforms of Fig. 15.5(b). This is applied to a *D–A* converter consisting of an R/2R network (top of Fig. 15.5(a)) to generate the staircase waveform shown at the top of Fig. 15.5(b): it has sixteen levels ranging from near-zero to near-supply voltage, which might typically be 10 V. This continuous staircase is applied to one input of an op-amp comparator as 'V + '. Now consider the bottom section of Fig.

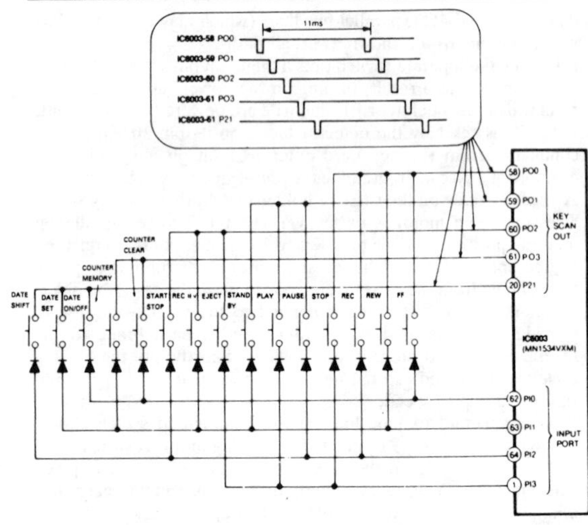

Fig. 15.4 *Key-scanning system with specially-programmed microcomputer (Panasonic)*

15.5(a). Here is a ladder network of resistors with each operation key arranged to ground a section of it. The result is a high voltage at the right-hand side of R7 with no key pressed; and some lower (but closely-specified) voltage for each key – 'play' may give rise to a voltage of 8.63 V, 'stop' 4.87 V and so on, according to the nature of the precision resistor chain R7–R20. This specific 'function voltage' is presented to the inverting input of the op-amp comparator.

When any function key is pressed the inverting input of the op-amp moves negatively; output (V_D) will rise as soon as the staircase waveform at its + input permits. This signals to the micro that a command has been keyed in. Acting on this, the micro now resets the data lines D0–D3 to 0000 (V_D reverts to low) then increments from 0001 upwards to raise the staircase signal, applied as V +, one step at a time. At some point in the sixteen-step count the V + input to the op-amp will exceed that of the V – input, whereupon V_D will go high once more. The running count is now frozen and examined within the micro. For example, the count may be 1001 which ROM will say corresponds to 'rewind'. This will then be implemented by the microprocessor, subject to the constraints of deck status sensors. By means of this A–D conversion process, up to fifteen keys can be accommodated by five microprocessor ports, D0–D3 plus switch-data input. The actual keyboard depends on only two connections (V – and ground) provided it incorporates the ladder resistor; this paved the way to providing a *full-function* corded remote control system using only one pair of conductors in the link-wire – the ladder resistor and keyboard of Fig. 15.5 is merely duplicated in the remote handset and linked to the op-amp's V – input by a panel-mounted jack socket.

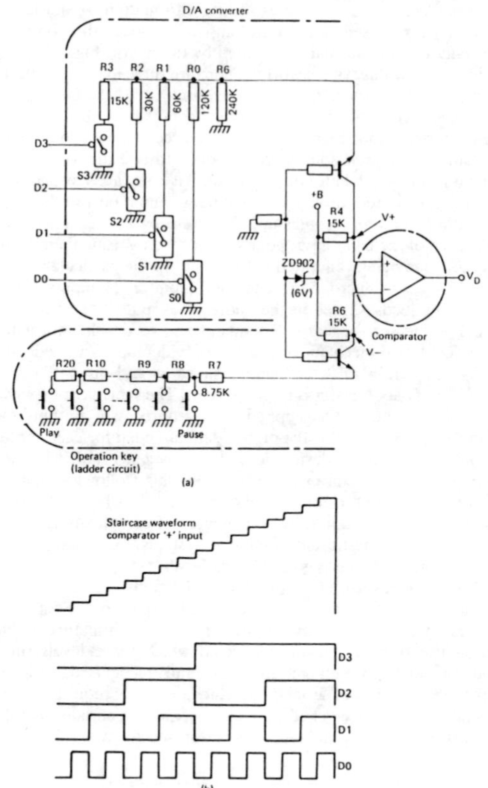

Fig. 15.5 *A–D conversion system for operating-key identification: only two conductors link the key-pad to the rest of the circuit. (a) basic circuit; (b) waveforms on data line and internal D–A conversion*

MICRO PORT EXPANSION

The two methods of input-key matrixing described above represent one form of port expansion, and the 'help-micro' μP2 in Fig. 15.3 another. In many cases the computing power required (small in relation to that of home computers and calculators) can easily be provided within the compass of one IC package. Difficulties arise, however, with the sheer number of pins required on the package, and particularly with the physical arrangement of printed conductors on the chip's mounting panel. Sixty pins is normal for a micro, through 80 and 100-pin types are now much used in VCR syscon applications.

Expander systems are used to route information to and from a micro on a time-sequential (strobing) basis under the control of *expander-address* bus data generated by the micro. Fig. 15.6 gives an idea of how this system works. There are three expander address inputs to a *port expander* chip: E0, E1 and E2. Three binary input lines give eight possible combinations from 000 to 111, and these eight addresses in the expander chip are accessed on a continually-rotating basis. Each address corresponds to one input (usually a 'latched' port which holds one signal until it is replaced by another). The input is routed through a switch to one input port of the micro each time its address comes up. The pre-programmed micro thus polls each of the eight input points in turn, recognising them by the address-code being generated at that time. In the particular case of Fig. 15.6 three micro ports can thus monitor 24 inputs via six connecting leads – three in the address bus and three in the data bus. For the sort of status, command and feedback information used in electro-mechanical control of videotape and videodisc decks and peripherals, the relative slowness and discontinuity of this form of data transfer is not important. The same port-expander principle can be and is applied to microprocessor outputs too, whereby the micro holds the output data intended for each specific output point until its destination address is generated, when it is released onto the data bus. It is also possible (following standard computer practice) to utilise a bi-directional data bus system with programmable I/O ports, but this degree of complexity is seldom necessary in domestic entertainment systems. An example of a bi-directional data bus is given in Chapter 19.

Other artifices to reduce the interconnection- and IC pin-count are used as alternatives to strobe port-expansion. Some processors – typically custom-designed types for miniature equipment – use ternary (tri-state) logic in which three levels (high, medium, low) of voltage are used and recognised. Another approach is the use of serial data, which generally requires the use of shift-registers as clocked parallel-to-serial and serial-to-parallel converters at sending and receiving ends respectively.

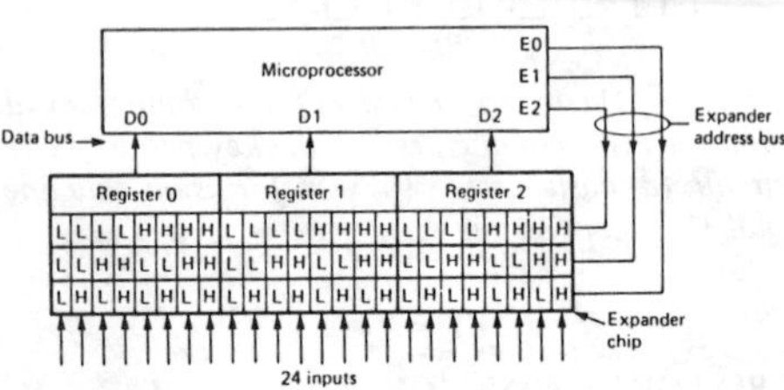

Fig. 15.6 *Port expansion using special port-expander IC under microprocessor control*

CLEAN-EDIT FUNCTIONS

In a basic videorecorder, invoking the pause function will merely stop the tape transport. When the pause key is released once more it is not possible for the tape to instantaneously attain normal speed, so that in effect, video tracks and (where applicable) control tracks on the tape become 'bunched up' at the pause point. The result is particularly noticeable on record pause because during subsequent replay severe picture and sound disturbance results from the mistracking and momentary servo instability at the point where the tracks are disordered. At best, a second or so of programme is lost while the blanking system waits for a new servo lock.

To prevent these effects the more elaborate home-base videorecorders – and all portable types, whether or not in camcorder form – have a syscon equipped for clean *assemble-edit*. This normally takes the form of a 'back-space' system, as illustrated in Fig. 15.7. The upper shaded section of the diagram represents the tape travelling towards the right in record mode. At point (A) the pause key (start/stop key on camera) is pressed, whereupon the tape rewinds for about 1–1.6 seconds then comes to rest in the *record-pause* state (B). It is still laced up. When the next recording segment is ready (scene changed for camera, commercial break finished, or alternative video source selected from tuner or auxiliary video player) the pause key is once again pressed, (C). Tape transport restarts immediately but the syscon does not yet switch the electronics to record. A 'play' period (D) of up to one second is permitted, during which time the capstan runs up to normal speed and its servo attains lock. At this time the capstan servo is directed by the syscon to lock incoming vertical syncs to existing replayed control track pulses in readiness for the changeover from old to new programme material.

A few frames (tracks) before the end of the old recording a changeover to record mode (E) is made in signal circuits, servos and control-track pulse routing, and this is arranged to take place during a field blanking period. The result is a completely smooth changeover from old to new material, with regard to both video tracks and control pulses. The presence of old and new tracks simultaneously on tape momentarily can give rise to crosstalk, especially where the old scene is highly coloured or contrasted and the new one lower-key. For the short period of over-recording the luminance writing current is increased by about 2 dB in order to provide a more effective erasing action – the full-width erase head is too far removed from the drum to take any part during this period. The resulting edit is very effective, though under some circumstances a burst of spurious colour appears momentarily at the edit point – at low colour-under frequencies the recording-erase process is less effective. Some domestic machines incorporate separate *flying* erase heads on the drum itself for use during in-camera assemble edits.

Although the backspace record-pause cycle takes less than two seconds in total, the number and speed of output manipulations by

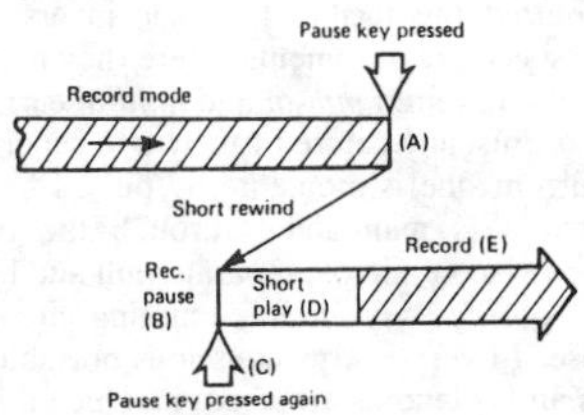

Fig. 15.7 *The stages in the automatic back-space edit process*

the syscon at this time are many and high. In a typical machine the following parts are accessed and instructed at least once: loading motor, pause LED, camera beacon, play solenoid, reel brakes, capstan motor, pressure roller solenoid, reel idler solenoid, servo circuits, recording f.m. amplifier, video signal routing, and (where applicable) flying-erase head switching.

Insert edit

The process just described will give continuity of replay servo synchronisation in circumstances of *assemble* edit, where each new sequence follows on from the previously-recorded material, i.e. when the camera stop/start trigger is used to select each 'live' sequence in turn; or in a post-production situation where a master tape is being assembled from one or more 1st-generation tapes.

Where it is required to modify an existing recording by inserting new material, the method is not effective at the end of the inserted section because video and control tracks will be disordered at the point of reversion to the original material. The insert-edit system is designed to overcome this problem. Here only the video and audio tracks are erased during the insert recording, leaving the original control track to 'master' the head drum phase and capstan speed. The continuity of the control track ensures a disturbance-free transition at each end of the inserted section.

In formats using tracking tones within the vision tracks, other methods are found to achieve edit control.

SYSCON MICRO INTERFACING

The syscon microprocessor is a wholly digital device and deals with all inputs and outputs in binary form. Since most commands and feedback indications appear as on-off signals there is no difficulty in matching them to the requirements of the chip – beyond the need for the port expansion, strobe or codec systems already described. Most syscon outputs, too, are easy to apply to their recipients; motor commands merely toggle electronic switches in motor drive amplifiers (MDAs) and signal-routing is also carried out by 'local' electronic switches. The current-sourcing capability of a microprocessor port is not sufficient to drive any 'end-user' beyond a fluorescent display panel, however, so for indication-LEDs, relays and solenoids, buffer stages incorporating further ICs and/or transistors are used; they have the additional advantage of protecting the micro from electrical damage; providing 'fan-out' capability; and if required the facility for logic inversion. Relays and solenoids have special requirements where they may be held in for long periods – the required *pull-in* and *hold-in* currents are greatly different, and are usually catered for by two separate windings: a heavy, high-current one is momentarily pulsed to pull-in, then a low 'hold' current is maintained through the other. In some custom-designed syscon micros, separate pull and hold output pins are provided. Alternatively an RC charging circuit provides the initial pull pulse. In very energy-conscious portable video systems *latching* relays and solenoids are used, in which a magnetic armature holds the selected position after a single 'pull' pulse in the right direction through the coil.

KEY PRIORITIES

Another vital function of the syscon is to assign priorities and prevent conflicting functions being keyed. Timer systems are pre-programmed to reject impossible requests like 'record for twelve hours', 'record two programmes at once' or 'stop recording before start time'; attempts to pre-programme a recording on a tabless cassette will result in eject function. Similarly, such mechanically-destructive orders as 'pause' during rewind mode, and pointless commands like 'search' during record mode are rejected. In most machines, pressing two keys simultaneously will have no effect on the function (if any) in progress; obvious exceptions are record + play, audio dub + play and play + still. A typical mode shift table for a mains machine is given in Table 15.1.

SYSCON TROUBLE-SHOOTING

Microprocessors are inherently very reliable devices, as are their attendant expansion, bus-buffer and slave chips. Their internal workings are neither obvious nor important from the point of view of servicing work. The physical problems involved in removing and replacing a 60- or 80-pin chip are considerable, especially where double-sided PC boards and miniature high-density construction methods are used. Before condemning any syscon-associated chip it is important to establish that the peripheral devices are correctly coupled and fault-free.

Mechanical and physical problems are most often at the root of what may appear to be an obscure system-control fault. Mechanically-operated switches are perhaps the most unreliable devices in the ensemble, and typically cause wrong indications in the feedback system: a machine which refuses to accept a cassette but whose motors are running will probably have a faulty unload-end (mode) switch; one which makes no response to its deck-function keyboard should be checked for a faulty cassette-down switch or cassette-lamp; one which unloads within seconds of loading completion may well have a load-end switch problem or a slipping loading belt. Wherever wear- and corrosion-prone links in the chain are suspect, they should be checked first – belts, switches, lamps, relays and solenoids are high on the list. Opto-couplers and to a lesser extent Hall-effect rotation sensors are suspect where a persistent 'shut-down' situation arises; oscilloscope and meter checks of deck sensors' outputs should quickly ascertain the cause. Do not forget the head-rotation sensor, based on its PG pulse generator.

Much can be eliminated by a close study of the symptoms and a knowledge of the syscon's ground rules. A machine which continually goes into auto-rewind may have some leakage problem in its tape-end sensor; a situation where control keys operate wrong functions via an A–D converter circuit should lead to a check of the keys and keyboard for electrical leakage and then the A–D converter circuit and ladder resistor; one *group* of keys inoperative in a key-scanned machine suggests the loss of one strobe pulse; a refusal to accept a 'record' command can often be quickly traced to a faulty recorder-tab detector switch or the failure of its 'OK' message to reach the syscon centre; and so on. In all situations suspect the ICs last, and make the diagnostic process one of checking that all control and feedback information is correctly arriving at the input

Table 15.1 *Key priorities and mode shifting for a videorecorder*

Mode *Key*	*Stop*	*Play*	*Still*	*Search*	*FF*	*Rew.*	*Rec.*	*Rec. pause*	*A dub play*	*A dub pause*	*Insert play*	*Insert pause*	*Instant rec.*	*Timer rec.*
Stop		○	○	○	○	○	○	○	○	○	○	○	○	×
Play	○		○	○	○	○	○ (rec. play)			○ (A dub play)		○ (Ins play)	×	×
Still	×	○	○ (Fadv)	○	×	×	○ (Rec. pause)		○ (A dub pause)	○ (Fadv)	○ Ins pause)		×	×
Search	×	○	○	○	×	×	×	×	×	×	×	×	×	×
FF	○	○ (S. ff)	○ (S. ff)	○ (S. ff)		○	×	×	×	×	×	×	×	×
Rew.	○	○ (S.rew.)	○ (S.rew.)	○ (S.rew.)	○		×	×	×	×	×	×	×	×

Rec. 'still'	○	○	○	○	○	○	○		○	○	○	○	×	×
A dub play	○	○	○	○	○	○	×	×		○	×	×	×	×
A dub 'still'	○	○	○	○	○	○	×	×	○		×	×	×	×
Eject	○	○	○	○	○	○	×	×	×	×	×	×	×	×
Instant rec.	○	○	○	○	○	○	○	○	○	○	○	○	○ (*1)	×
Ch. up down	○	×	×	×	○	○	×	○	×	×	○	○	×	×

Key:
○: Enabled (mode changes)
×: Inhibited (mode does not change)
*1: Rec. time advance

ports of the micro, and that all commands from its output ports are getting to their destinations, and there being correctly acted upon.

Complete lack of action and response in the micro will usually be due to failure of its VDD line (+5V or +12V) or cessation of the clock oscillator – which generally depends on an external ceramic filter or RC network tuned to around 400–600 kHz. Random functions at switch-on, 'disobedience' or no response may be due to a lack of reset pulse. Occasionally, interference spikes on the mains supply (or static charges around a portable) can 'unhinge' a micro, leading to random and bizarre functions; de-powering for a period to invoke a reset pulse usually clears the trouble. A similarly-obscure set of symptoms can arise from one line in a data-, address- or control-bus becoming 'stuck' high or low – physical faults as well as faulty chips can cause this, and an oscilloscope and multimeter can be used to trace it. A logic probe is useful here; a logic analyser (see Chapter 20) is only required when it is necessary to check the timing and nature of the data on the bus, and that is quite rare.

16

Audio record and playback

Except for the Video 8 system, the video formats were originally designed for use with longitudinal sound tracks written-onto and read-off the tape by a stationary head assembly fitted between the head-drum and the pressure roller. The techniques used are identical to those employed in audio tape recording, except that the tracks are much narrower (1 mm for mono, 0.35 mm for stereo) and the linear speed of the tape is low, varying from 2.4 cm/s to 1.17 cm/s in various formats and modes. The narrow audio tracks are not capable of better S/N ratio than about 43 dB, or 50 dB with sophisticated noise-reduction systems. The low linear tape speed sets an upper frequency limit of about 10 kHz in normal modes and 5 kHz in LP modes. Wow and flutter is typically 0.25% w.r.m.s.

While this standard of performance is adequate for time-shifting of serial programmes and for use with TV sets having small loudspeakers, its shortcomings become obvious when the video-recorder is used with high-quality input signals and good reproduction equipment. Linear-track stereo videorecorders are often linked-in to the high-quality audio system in the same room; this tends to emphasise that the 0.35 mm tracks give poorer S/N ratio than the 1 mm mono tracks. In programmes where sound is an important feature (mainly concerts and feature films) the longitudinal sound system early became a considerable drawback to the well-established formats.

The consumer's awareness and appreciation of high-fidelity sound has been brought about by the long availability of good quality sound timers, amplifiers and loudspeakers, and by compact audio disc systems and the provision of hi-fi amplifiers and stereo loudspeakers in TV receivers and 'unit' systems.

A solution to the problems of longitudinal sound recording cannot be found in further development of the basic system; the limitations are in the nature of the tape's magnetic layer, and in the physical wavelengths of the frequencies involved: they are immovable within the constraints of available video-tape track-width and speed. A more promising approach is to record sound in the helical tracks used for video, where it has the benefits of high writing speed and (provided signal-conditioning and a modulation system is used) a high S/N ratio and wide dynamic range. Three different methods of achieving this have been evolved for use in consumer video-recorders: Depth-Multiplex, Frequency Multiplex and PCM, which stands for Pulse Code Modulation. These will be described in turn.

DEPTH MULTIPLEX

The principle of depth multiplex recording is illustrated in Fig. 16.1, and depends on the use of separate heads for the audio and video f.m. carriers. In Fig. 16.1(a) the drum-mounted audio and video heads are moving towards the right in record mode. Generally there is an optimum relationship between the wavelength of the signal recorded on the tape and the depth (d) of its penetration into the tape's surface, expressed as $d = \lambda/4$. For the audio Hi-Fi head the gap is cut wide (0.7 or 1 micron) and a relatively low

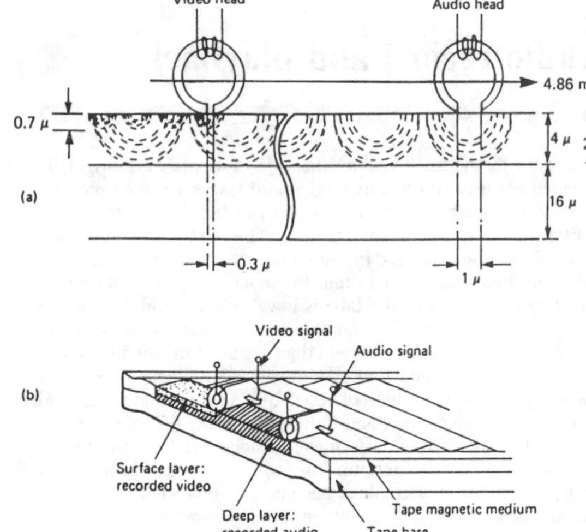

Fig. 16.1 *Depth-Multiplex recording: (a) pattern-penetration into the magnetic layer of the tape; (b) related to helical scanning*

frequency around 1.6 MHz is used for recording. The result is that the audio signals penetrate deep (about 4 microns) into the tape's magnetic coating. Following closely behind the audio head comes the video head, writing higher-frequency signals with a smaller head-gap. In this case pattern depth d is about 0.7 micron, and so a shallow pattern is recorded – the down-converted chroma signals (and track-following tones where applicable) have too low a recording current to achieve greater depth during record. The *top* layer of the depth-audio magnetic pattern is thus erased by the recording action of the video head, to be replaced by a shallow 'pool' of video pattern. During replay the presence of the over-recorded video track attenuates the replayed audio signal by 12 dB or so, but the use during record of an f.m. modulation system and high writing current for the audio carrier overcomes this.

The two audio signals are modulated onto separate carriers for passage through the head/tape interface – for VHS the carrier frequencies are 1.4 MHz (stereo left) and 1.8 MHz (stereo right) each with a maximum deviation of ±150 kHz; for Beta they are 1.44 and 2.10 MHz respectively, maximum deviation ±200 kHz. Significant sidebands extend the total audio f.m. bandwidths to over 500 kHz each, as shown for VHS and Beta respectively in Fig. 16.2(a) and (b). Plainly there is potential here for mutual crosstalk between f.m. sound and f.m. video carriers during playback. To prevent it the audio Hi-Fi head-gaps are given large offset azimuth angles of ±30° in both VHS and Beta systems. Except in VHS-LP mode it is also arranged that the audio and video heads which share one track are given opposite azimuth angles so that the track-pattern disparities become 36° for VHS (vision heads at ±6°) and 37° for Beta (vision heads at ±7°). In fact this is not wholly true of

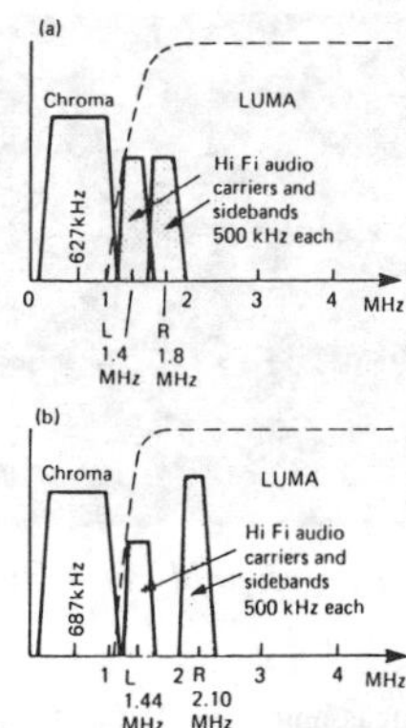

Fig. 16.2 *Hi-Fi recording frequency spectra for (a) VHS, and (b) Betamax*

Beta for reasons which will be explained shortly: in all cases the crosstalk levels are sufficiently low to give immunity from interference effects, however.

The Hi-Fi sound heads are mounted at a large angle to the video heads around the spinning drum. The angle varies between different makes and designs and matters only from the points of view of (a) correct 'height' mounting of audio heads to ensure that the relative placement of video and audio tracks is correct; and (b) correct timing of the audio-head changeover point during playback with reference to the head tacho-pulse. Synchronisation between vision and sound is not relevant where the passage of half the drum circumference only occupies 20 ms. For VHS the width of each f.m. audio track is 26 microns, about half of that of the corresponding video track. The 'buried' audio track lies centrally beneath the video track as shown in Fig. 16.3(a). In Beta format the f.m. audio tracks are comparable in width with the vision tracks, so they are offset by one-half of a track-width, see Fig. 16.3(b). This is easily arranged by suitable setting of their mounting height on the head drum (taking into account their 'lead' angle with respect to the video heads) during manufacture, and ensures that during replay the wide video heads (wide for trick-replay purposes) do not embrace *three* audio tracks simultaneously. The photo (Fig. 16.4)

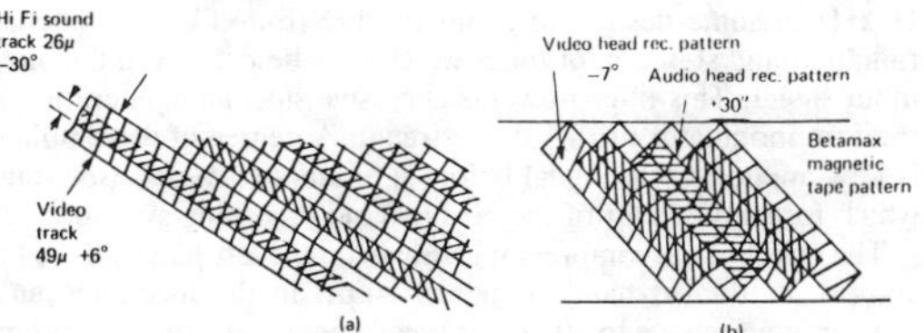

Fig. 16.3 *Relative positioning of Hi-Fi audio and video tape tracks in (a) VHS tape and (b) Betamax tape*

Fig. 16.4 *Head drum assembly in a Hi-Fi videorecorder by JVC*

shows a Hi-Fi drum assembly by JVC – the chip visible at 'six o'clock' on the drum periphery is the audio head; that at 'seven o'clock' is the corresponding video head. Their opposite numbers are on the far side of the drum. The audio Hi-Fi heads have a separate rotary transformer to themselves; in Fig. 16.4 this is under the drum with the video transformer assembly. In other designs, and particularly where multiple heads are used for video trick-play, the audio transformer is mounted on top of the upper drum. In all cases it has separate sections for each audio head. *Both* f.m. carriers are fed to each head during record, even though only one head at a time is actually scanning the tape and writing L *and* R f.m. carriers onto the tape. During replay, head switching at 20 ms intervals is used to maintain continuity of output signal, as per standard video head practice. The two f.m. carriers are separated by bandpass filters during the replay process, then individually dealt with.

Hi-Fi audio recording

As with the video signal, a large amount of conditioning is required by the audio signal in its preparation for f.m. recording, and in its restoration during playback. Fig. 16.5 is a simplified block diagram of the processing of the left-hand audio signal during record – the right-hand channel is identical, and their two f.m. signals are added in the '+' block at the bottom centre of the diagram. First comes an input select matrix to route the required audio input from line, AV or TV tuner sources. A choice of manual or automatic level control is provided, the former by a front panel slider control and the latter by an a.g.c. circuit. The level-corrected signal now enters a bandpass filter wherein its upper range is restricted to 20 kHz, or 15 kHz in some designs to avoid trouble from TV line timebase radiation and stereo pilot tones which may be present in the audio input signal. This filter prevents excessive sideband-generation by the f.m. modulator further downstream. A degree of pre-emphasis is now applied to the signal before it enters the *compressor* stage, which forms the heart of the Hi-Fi sound recording system.

The effect of the compressor is shown on the left-hand side of Fig. 16.6(a). A total dynamic range of 80 dB in the incoming audio signal is compressed to 40 dB for recording on tape in a logarithmic amplifier/attenuator whose gain or loss is determined by the amplitude of the audio signal itself. The latter is closely monitored in a true-r.m.s. detector, whose output is applied as a control

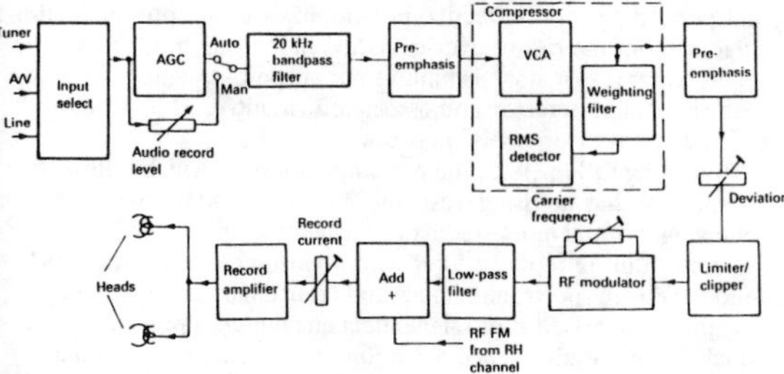

Fig. 16.5 *Audio record signal processing for one channel*

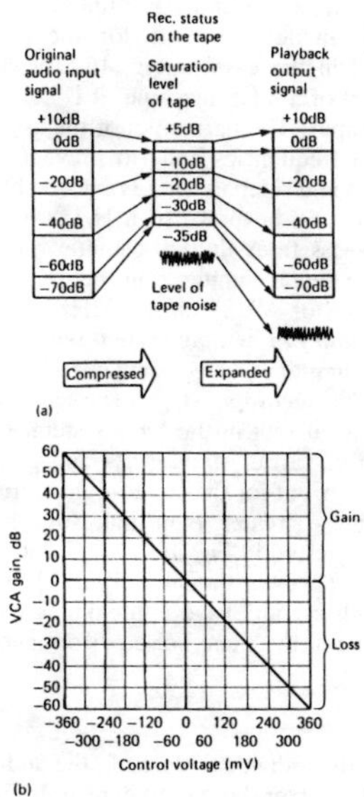

Fig. 16.6 *Companding as an effective noise-reduction system. The graph in (b) shows the r.m.s. detector/VCA characteristic*

potential to the voltage-controlled amplifier/attenuator (VCA). The logarithmic law by which it operates is shown on the graph of Fig. 16.6(b): at standard (0 dB) level the signal is unaffected. For every 60 mV increase of 'raw' signal 10 dB of attenuation is applied, and for every 60 mV decrease of raw signal (from 0 dB) 10 dB of gain is applied – the derivation of Fig. 16.6(a) is now clear. What neither diagram of Fig. 16.6 shows is the frequency selective nature of the compressor, introduced by incorporating a *weighting filter* in the path to the r.m.s. detector. The filter has a rising characteristic above 1 kHz, which has the effect of further compressing high-frequency components in the final output signal, and permitting more effective pre-emphasis in the pre-modulator stage without the risk of over-deviation in the f.m. modulator. The record compressor stage is built into a purpose-designed IC, along with the r.m.s. detector and associated circuitry, while filtering is catered for in external RC networks.

Returning to Fig. 16.5, the pre-emphasis stage which follows the compressor has a rising response between 2 kHz and 20 kHz, following normal noise-reduction technique in f.m. modulation systems – during replay a filter with opposite characteristic will be used to restore spectrum-balance and reduce tape noise in so doing. The pre-emphasised audio signal next encounters a pre-set pot with which its amplitude (hence deviation of the audio f.m. modulator) is set. Accidental over-deviation is prevented by a double-diode clipper stage.

F.m. signal is generated by an IC-based voltage-controlled oscillator (VCO). As with the vision modulator stage it is basically an astable circuit depending for basic timing on an RC network, part of which is made adjustable for the purpose of carrier frequency-setting; in the case of Fig. 16.5, which illustrates the stereo-left channel of a VHS machine, it is adjusted for 1.4 MHz with zero audio input. The harmonics of the astable output signal reach up to high frequencies and (to prevent interference with luminance carriers and sidebands) are removed by an LC bandstop filter with sharp cut-off beyond 1.65 MHz.

After the low-pass filter the left-channel f.m. carrier signal is joined by a similar signal coming from the stereo-right modulating circuit and based (for VHS) on 1.8 MHz. Together they pass through a pot (*audio f.m. writing current set*) en route to a class B push-pull power amplifier stage similar to that used for head-driving in the video recording stage. The two audio f.m. carriers have equal writing current in the VHS system. For Beta, with its wider separation of carrier frequencies and greater deviation of each, the writing current for the stereo-right carrier $f2$ (2.10 MHz) is made four times greater than that for $f1$, (stereo-left) at 1.44 MHz – as suggested in Fig. 16.2(b). $f2$ is thus made to act as recording bias for $f1$, even though both are in f.m. carrier form; during replay both carriers have approximately the same carrier/noise (C/N) ratio and the same noise performance.

Hi-Fi audio replay

The functions of the individual blocks in the audio replay chain of Fig. 16.7 generally mirror those used in record. First come a pair of sensitive head preamplifiers fed from the two audio rotating transformers. Their outputs are sequentially selected by an electronic head switch operating in accordance with a delayed head PG flip-flop signal; the delay is necessary to synchronise switching with actual audio head tape-sweeps, whose timing is offset with regard to those of the vision heads – due to their different position on the drum periphery. The delay time must be very precise and stable to prevent excessive drop-out at switching points, and is determined by a precision MMV in some designs, and by a precision clock pulse counting process (i.e. from $f$sc at 4.43 MHz) in others.

An a.g.c. stage follows the audio head-switch; its level-controlled output passes next into a pair of bandpass filters in which the left-channel and right-channel carriers are separated. Fig. 16.7 follows the left-channel processing from the (VHS) 1.4 MHz filter output. A conventional limiter/clipper precedes the demodulator, which uses the same VCO as was used during record. It now

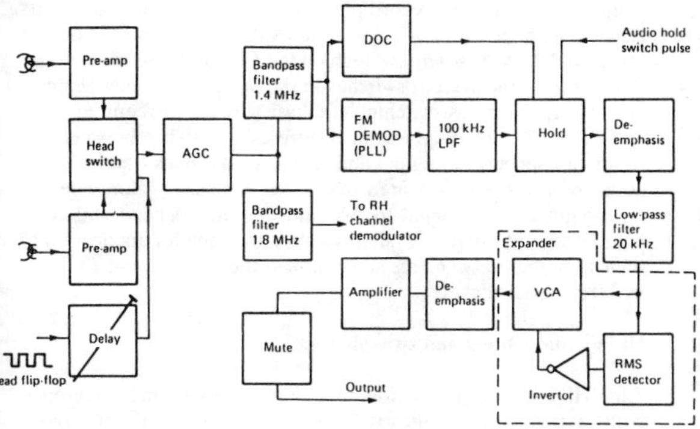

Fig. 16.7 *Audio replay signal processing for one channel*

becomes the 'steered' element of a PLL, whose error voltage forms the demodulated output signal – this type of f.m. detector was described in Chapter 4 and Fig. 4.14. A second path for the f.m. signal is provided to a dropout compensator (DOC) whose operation is quite different to that of the vision channel covered in Chapter 13. Here a dropout is made to produce a pulse which operates a post-demodulator 'hold' circuit by which the instantaneous level of the output signal is held constant for the duration of the dropout. A head-switch pulse is also fed to the hold circuit, and there used to instigate a 'bridging' pulse to mask the inevitable head-switching noise pulse at the moment of changeover. Some circuit designs (i.e. Sony Beta) have separate f.m. demodulators for each of the two audio heads in each (l. and r.) channel, permitting head switching after demodulation – this gives lower switching noise. In either case the demodulated signal now enters the first de-emphasis network where much of the tape noise is lost in its falling h.f. response.

To restore normal dynamic range to the reproduced audio signal according to the right-hand side of Fig. 16.6(a), an *expander* must be used, whose operating law is the exact inverse of that used during record. Again a 0 dB level in the replay signal is allowed to pass unmodified, but now a +5 dB replay-level signal is boosted to +10 dB, whereas *each* progressive 10 dB reduction in off-tape demodulated signal undergoes a 10 dB attentuation in the expander. An illustration of the effect of the expander on replayed tape hiss is given at the bottom of Fig. 16.6(a). It normally comes off tape (in any tape-recording system) at about −55 dB, and here emerges from the expander stage at a point more than 80 dB below the reference level: it is here that the secret of the superb S/N ratio of Hi-Fi 'video'-sound resides, and it is to preserve this level of performance that so much trouble is taken with dropout compensation.

The replay expander consists of the same components as were used for compression during record, the dual-purpose device in fact being called a *compander*. For replay use the r.m.s. level detector's output is *inverted* before application to the VCA so as to reverse its law of operation, effectively reversing about its centre the vertical scale of Fig. 16.6(b), where the upper half now becomes an attenuation scale, and the lower half an amplification scale. The compander chip has record/playback switching pins to set its function: a high on the REC pin routes the r.m.s. detector output direct to the VCA, whereas a high on the PB pin (these voltages are derived from the syscon) switches-in the inverter between detector and VCA, as well as switching emphasis circuits as required.

After further de-emphasis to restore exact balance between the frequency spectra of original and reproduced signals, the left-hand audio replay signal is routed out of the machine – alongside the right-hand channel signal to AV and line-out sockets; and combined with audio-right signal into a monaural one for application to the r.f. modulator when the signal-link to the mono-sound TV is via its UHF aerial socket.

Hi-Fi audio muting and switching

All VHS and Beta Hi-Fi videorecorders are additionally equipped with stationary audio heads, either stereo or mono, to confer compatibility with all other machines and tapes. During record both Hi-Fi and longitudinal tracks are recorded on tape; during replay the Hi-Fi tracks are always used if they are present. An automatic monitoring circuit examines the output of the f.m. audio heads for the continued presence of a carrier signal and switches the replay channels into the audio output section accordingly. Where the duplicate-longitudinal tracks are in stereo their left and right channels will be substituted for those of the Hi-Fi system to maintain stereo separation. During replay the f.m. audio signal may disappear as a result of severe dropout, mistracking or other problems. In this case the muting and switching circuits act quickly to source output signals from the conventional sound replay circuit for as long as necessary.

FREQUENCY MULTIPLEX

An alternative approach to the provision of high-quality sound with video is the frequency-multiplex system, used in NTSC-based Beta videorecorders and in the V8 format. V8, as part of its specification, makes use of metal-powder and metal-evaporated (MP and ME) tapes, whose magnetic coating thicknesses are only 3 and 0.15 micron respectively, and therefore unsuitable for depth-multiplex techniques. The V8 sound system caters for a monaural sound track conveyed by a single f.m. carrier at 1.5 MHz with maximum deviation of ±100 kHz, see Fig. 13.3(c). Separate audio heads are not used here: the 1.5 MHz f.m. sound carrier is added to the luminance f.m. and colour-under signals for passage via the recording amplifier to the *video* recording heads.

To avoid mutual interference the audio carrier writing current is held to 12 dB below nominal chroma writing current, which itself is some 6 dB below luminance writing current. Further, the relatively high video f.m. carrier frequency (4.2–5.4 MHz) ensures that little luminance sideband energy is present in the 300 kHz-wide spectrum-slot reserved for the f.m. audio carrier and its sidebands. In V8 the colour-under frequency is based on 732 kHz with sideband spreads of about 500 kHz, so that the upper chroma energy limit on the tape-frequency spectrum is about 1.25 MHz, again avoiding interference from the sound carrier.

The electronic processing circuit for V8 f.m. audio is just the same as that described above, using 2:1 logarithmic compression and expansion (Fig. 16.8) carried out by the same form of r.m.s.

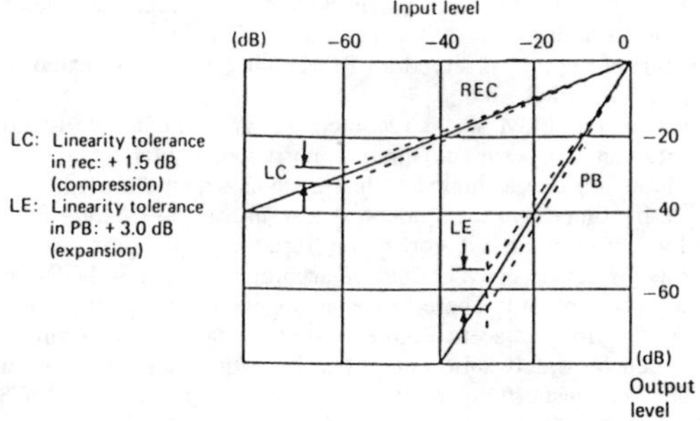

Fig. 16.8 *Compander characteristic for Video 8 format*

detector and VCA. A similar VCO and PLL f.m. modem system is also used. For camcorder application an audio-recording high pass filter is used to cut off frequencies below 200 Hz in order to suppress wind, len-motor and handling noises. An upper frequency limit of 15 kHz is also set in the baseband signal chain to permit correct operation of the noise-reduction circuit. During replay the off-tape f.m. audio signal is picked out by a sharp cut-off bandpass filter centred on 1.5 MHz, then applied to a 2-field dropout compensation circuit. For this simpler 1-channel system a single miniature 48-pin chip caters for all audio-f.m. and noise-reduction processes during both record and playback, for which internal electronic switches are provided; such external components as are required are limited to RC and LC networks for filtering and response shaping.

PCM RECORDING

Pulse-code recording is a relatively new technique in the consumer field. It is based on a quantisation process in which the analogue signal (here the audio waveform) is regularly sampled at a rate at least twice as high as its likely maximum frequency. The level obtained at each sampling point is applied to an A–D converter, which for audio applications needs to have at least 10-bit resolution to give 1024-level sampling. For V8 format, where it is a high-quality alternative to the mono-f.m. system described above, the 10-bit digital signal is brought down to 8 bits by a sophisticated bit-reduction technique. Even so, eight bits within 32 μs (corresponding to $2fh$, 31.25 kHz sampling rate) equates to a bit-rate of around 250,000 per second, requiring a bandwidth too great to accommodate in any form of track-multiplexing system so far described in this chapter.

For videotape recording the digitised audio signal is read into a memory continuously, and read out at about seven times speed. This 'compresses' the signal up to a bit-rate of about 2 Mbit/sec, but leaves a long waiting period between read-out periods – the process is similar to that used in the MAC TV transmission system described in Chapter 4. To accommodate the PCM-stereo track on the V8 tape the effective head wrap is increased from 180° to 220° (Fig. 16.9(a)) to increase the length of the video head sweep, the first 30° or so of which are used for PCM audio recording, with the recording (and subsequent playback) *video* amplifiers switched to the digital audio-memory for this brief period. Fig. 16.9(b) shows the part of the tape reserved for PCM audio; it forms an extension of the video track area.

The digital PCM signal recorded on tape contains correction (parity) bits to permit repair of a corrupted digital signal, as is common practice in digital coding systems – mention of this was made in connection with videotext transmission in Chapter 8. To further ensure against corruption resulting from tape dropout effects the digital signal is *scattered* according to a precisely defined code during record. The effect is analogous to that of shuffling a pack of cards: adjacent segments of the digital pulse train are recorded at widely different physical positions on tape. During replay an 'unshuffling' process takes place, in which the PCM segments are once more rearranged in correct order, but now with any damage due to dropouts etc. distributed throughout the data pulse train, and nowhere so bad that the inbuilt correction/parity check bits cannot adequately restore the output signal. The process is identical in principle to that used in the Nicam transmissions described in Chapter 9.

Further details of the V8 PCM sound signal are as follows: the baseband audio signal is compressed to 1:2 before quantisation and expanded 2:1 after D–A conversion in a logarithmic compander like those already described in connection with Hi-Fi f.m. sound systems. This raises the 48 dB dynamic range ordinarily available from an 8-bit quantisation system to the equivalent of 13 bits, comparable to the 14-bit system used in EIAJ PCM format and the 16-bit Compact Disc system, which latter is wholly dedicated to sound and represents the highest quality (<90 dB dynamic range) programme reproduction system available in domestic entertainment equipment. Error correction in V8-format PCM is carried out by two interleaving error correction codes on each data block every eight-bit word; this is called a Cross-Interleave Code (CIC). The audio sampling rate is twice line frequency: 31.25 kHz for PAL/625, 31.5 kHz for NTSC/525. Data words are recorded for each field as $625/2 \times (2 \times 2) = 1250$ for PAL, and $525/2 \times (2 \times 2) = 1050$ for NTSC. The compressed digital audio signal is f.m.-modulated for recording via the video heads, and similarly demodulated during replay.

AUDIO-ONLY RECORDING ON VIDEOTAPE

Whatever the type and format of a videorecorder, its automatic programme-timer facility and long running time (compared to audio Compact Cassettes) give it useful potential as an audio-only recorder, offering progressively higher levels of reproduction quality in Hi-Fi and PCM versions. There are several possibilities for using a videorecorder wholly for audio signals. With a conventional longitudinal-sound machine, an add-on 'box' is required to generate TV sync signals in order to keep the machine's servos operating correctly to enable the recording of audio signals. Although this arrangement is very wasteful of tape area, and renders lower quality sound than an audio-cassette machine, it can sometimes be useful.

Commercial Hi-Fi/f.m.-sound equipped videorecorders all have an audio-only facility invoked by a concealed front- or rear-panel mounted switch. In this mode an internal timing generator provides TV-sync-like pulses to maintain servo lock during record, and to establish a control track for the same purpose during replay. With no video signal to present a mutual interference threat, the possibility of increasing audio-f.m. writing current (to reduce the effects of possible dropout and increase replay limiter margin) is there. Up to eight hours (VHS–LP mode, E240 tape) of high-quality sound recording and playback is thus possible.

PCM audio-only recording offers a high standard domestic *record-and-playback* sound system. For use with conventional (i.e. Beta and VHS) videorecorders, a PCM processor can be used. In effect it is a codec, digitising audio signals and presenting them to the videorecorder in a form that it can recognise as a video signal. On replay the same processor decodes the video-like digital replay signal to render a very good quality audio output.

The Video 8 format, already designed to cater for a *with-vision* PCM sound system, has also the capability for high quality audio-only use. The digital-compression system already described shows that only 30° of head sweep is required for one stereo sound programme. If the entire video signal area is used for PCM recording as shown in Fig. 16.9(c), a total of six segments, each occupying about 30° of head rotation, is possible. If these segments are used exclusively for audio, either six simultaneous tracks can be recorded and replayed (i.e. for sound-studio use and subsequent mixing); or the six segments can be used sequentially for a total (with a P5–90 tape in LP mode) *eighteen* hours of very high quality sound. The arrangement of the six three-hour segments is shown in Fig. 16.9(d). Identification of the individual segments is made by a fifth ATF-like tone laid down during record.

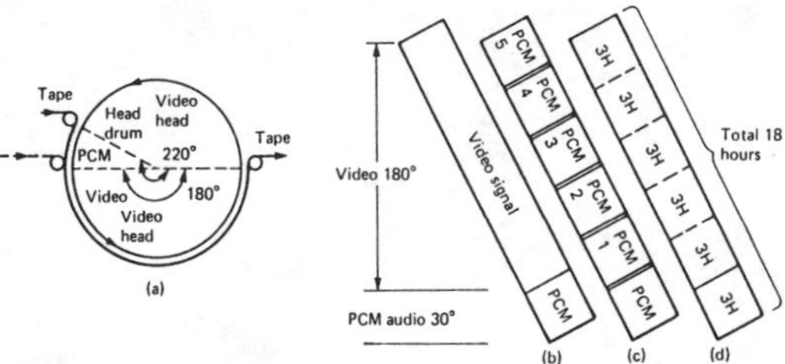

Fig. 16.9 *PCM audio in Video 8 format: (a) extended drum wrap; (b) resulting track formation; (c) six PCM segments can be accommodated in an audio-only configuration; (d) in LP audio-only mode the six segments of (c) each offer three hours record/play time*

FAULT DIAGNOSIS IN AUDIO SYSTEMS

Longitudinal sound systems are not difficult to service; the electronics are simple, and identical to those of audio cassette recorders. Hi-Fi audio stages are very similar indeed to those used for the luminance signal, with the same sorts of pre/de-emphasis, modulator/demodulator, switching and clipping circuits, and similar recording amplifier and head pre-amp designs. The servicing techniques for both are similar, then, and the oscilloscope is the most valuable diagnostic tool here; test-cassettes are available from videorecorder manufacturers with Hi-Fi audio test signals recorded to factory-model specifications.

For PCM audio systems much diagnostic work can be done by examining key test-points for the presence or absence of waveforms and operating voltages. *Analysis* of the signals present in the digital sections, however, calls for very sophisticated test equipment which will rarely be found in an ordinary service workshop (see Chapter 20).

17

Tape deck mechanics and servicing

The video tape deck is a high-precision ensemble of mechanical components, containing essentially the video head drum, a capstan, a reel drive system and a means of loading (threading) the tape around the head drum.

THREADING THE TAPE

All current formats use co-planar cassettes in which the tape spools lie side by side. The feed spool is on the left when the cassette is correctly inserted into the machine; both spools are lifted just clear of the floor of the cassette shell as it is lowered onto the deck, which action also lifts its front plastic flap to permit the tape ribbon to be drawn out and loaded. There are two basic methods of loading tape: The *travelling-guide* system, used in VHS and Video 8 machines in an M-wrap configuration, and the *loading-ring* system, used in all three (VHS, Beta, V8) formats in the so-called U-wrap configuration. The choice of loading system is a question of mechanical convenience rather than any inherent requirement of the format in use; provided the tape achieves the necessary wrap of the head drum (180° for standard VHS, Beta and some V8 types, more for 'small head' formats like VHS–C, Betamovie and V8 where the PCM facility is used) any type of loading system can be used.

Fig. 17.1 shows three stages in the tape-loading process of a typical M-wrap VHS machine. A pair of loading poles enter behind the tape loop at the front of the cassette as it is lowered onto the deck. When the loading phase begins the motor-driven arms move away from the cassette, drawing with them a loop of tape; the half-way point in the loading process is depicted in dotted outline. At loading completion the poles (adjustable tape guides in fact) locate in precision-machined V-grooves on cast pillars on each side of the head and are locked in position by a pair of latches. At this *loading-end* point the loading motor stops as instructed by the

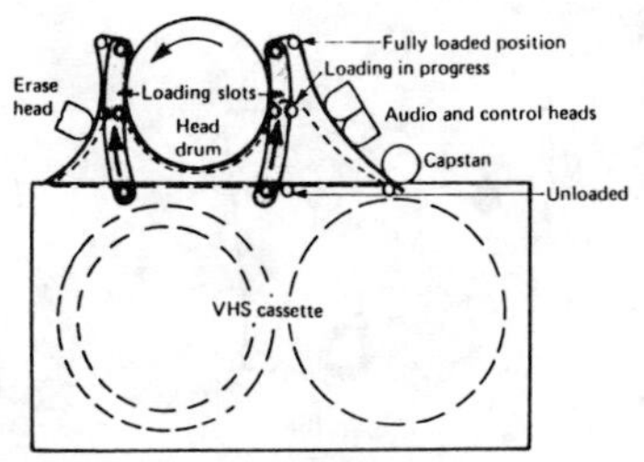

Fig. 17.1 *Three stages in the M-loading process for standard VHS machines*

loading-end switch via the syscon. The location of the moving guides in the V-grooves is very critical, since these guides define the path of the tape over the head drum; absolute accuracy and repeatability is essential for consistent tracking, a subject to which this chapter will return later. The advantage of a moving-guide M-wrap system is a relatively small and simple mechanism and short loading time.

The alternative loading method involves a *loading ring* which surrounds the rotating head-drum, and usually carries the pressure roller along with several tape-route defining pins or rollers. As an example, Fig. 17.2(a) indicates the initial (unloaded) position of the ring in a Betamax machine. The front moulding of the cassette is deeply indented, and as its plastic shell is lowered onto the deck a ring-mounted loading pole (and the pressure roller) penetrate the space between the tape and the shell. In most machines, tape-loading takes place as soon as the cassette is presented, so the cassette-down switch now signals the syscon to power the loading ring, usually via a dedicated loading motor driving through a worm-and-pinion system. In the case of Fig. 17.2 the ring rotates anticlockwise (intermediate point shown in (b)) taking the tape-loop with it; in some designs an articulated arm is provided on the ring to carry a tape-guide-pin which is intercepted by a deck-mounted slot-guide assembly. By this means the outer tape loop is held clear of the head drum itself. At completion of loading the ring has turned about 270° (Fig. 17.2(c)) and the tape is wrapped 186° around the head drum; the ring-mounted pressure roller is now opposite the deck-mounted capstan shaft. In some designs the two latter members are actually brought together over the tape by a roller moving into a cam on the periphery of the loading ring. Ring-loading in these forms has the advantage that the crucial head-entry and -exit guides are *fixed* and stable.

An alternative loading-ring configuration is used on later, more compact Beta decks, see Fig. 17.3. Here the loading ring is smaller and closely surrounds the head drum itself. It rotates in a clockwise direction, so that the tape emerging from the feed (left-hand) spool takes a long curved path around the tape-guide pins on the loading roller before entering the head-wrap. With this design there is no room for the fixed tape-guide posts which are a feature of the larger loading rings; instead the posts are hinged at their loading-ring mountings and spring-loaded to keep them erect. When the loading ring is fully retracted (*unloaded* position) both guides are lying flat on the ring in what amounts to a curved tunnel under the audio head assembly. As the ring advances to load the tape the guides

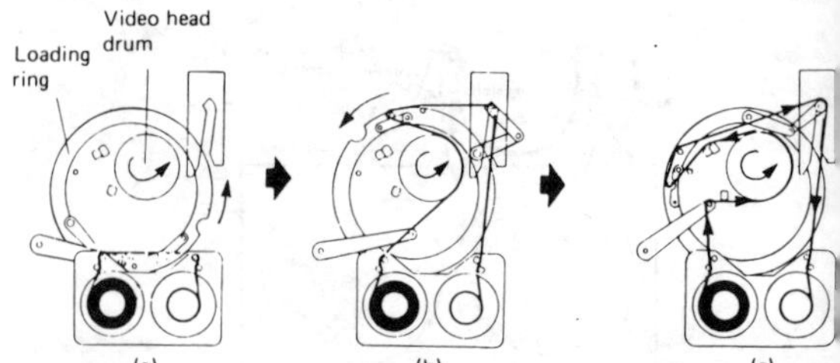

Fig. 17.2 *U-loading with a ring: (a) at rest; (b) halfway point of loading; (c) loading complete. The pinch roller is mounted on the loading ring*

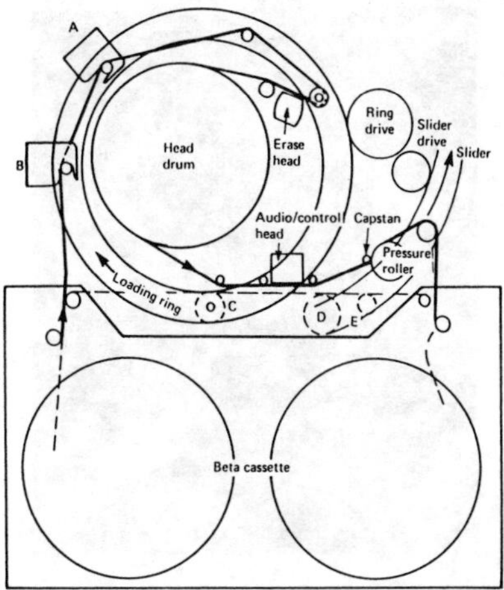

Fig. 17.3 *Alternative U-loading threading ring layout used in later Beta videorecorders. Catching slots A and B position and brace retractable tape guides fixed to the loading ring. The initial (unloaded) positions of the far tape guide, the pressure roller and the final tape guide are shown in dotted outline at points C, D and E respectively*

emerge from the tunnel and spring upright (within the tape loop) as they are released. Further progression of the ring carries the top ends of these guide posts into stationary support-slots A, B fitted at intervals around the ring-path: graded guide-post and slot heights ensure that each tape guide correctly locates in its appointed place. During unloading the guide-pins are retracted and folded down by the 'tunnel mouth' as they are drawn into it. A slider (on the right of Fig. 17.3) moves, during tape loading, in the opposite direction to that of the main ring. It carries the pressure roller and a tape guide, and pulls the tape loop away and to the right of the cassette front, positioning it across the audio/erase head and the capstan shaft.

Tape loading around small heads

The VHS–C cassette is designed for use with loading pole/guides as described earlier for standard VHS practice. Here the M-wrap is extended into what amounts to an inverted omega (ʊ) wrap to embrace 270° of the head circumference as shown in Fig. 12.9(b). In small-drum VHS videorecorders, regardless of the size of cassette package used, the 'steering slots' for the two loading pole/guides extend round towards the back of the head drum where they locate in the V-grooves of a catcher block for precise positioning as shown in Fig. 17.4. Here the moving guides are transported by contra-rotating loading rings *beneath* the deck-plate; for use with small (C-type) cassettes a further (*middle*) pole, pivoted on the deck surface, springs up at a late stage in the loading process to prevent the *outer* threading loop contacting the right-hand side of the drum; the same function at the left is performed by the tension pole, to be described later.

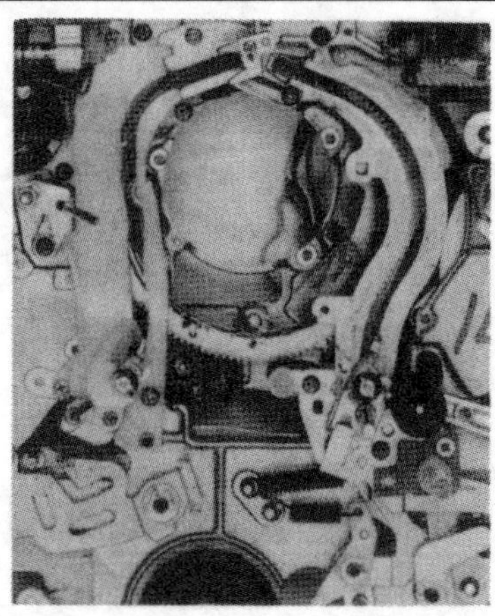

Fig. 17.4 *Compact VHS deck in a Panasonic camcorder. Note the long curved guide paths embracing the small head-drum, and compare with Fig. 12.9(b)*

For the Betamovie configuration (Fig. 12.9(a)) the required tape wrap is 313°, set up by a pair of loading pole/guides which initially penetrate the cassette behind its front tape loop, then move away on circular paths in opposite directions, conveyed by a pair of contra-rotating loading rings. When the rings stop, the guides are almost touching at the far (12 o'clock) side of the head-drum.

Many Video-8 format machines use a combination of travelling-arm and loading-ring techniques. A method used by Sony is illustrated in three progressive stages in Fig. 17.5. At (a) the cassette has just been inserted with the machine in standby mode. The first part of the loading process involves a pair of arm-mounted poles AA moving from their initial position behind the cassette's front tape loop to resting-places on each side of the head-drum, and drawing out a loop of tape. When this phase is complete (Fig. 17.5(b)) the loading ring itself begins to rotate anticlockwise; mounted on it is pole B which picks up the tape loop and carries it around the drum. Loading is complete when the tape embraces 220° of the drum periphery as shown in Fig. 17.5(c). The ring-mounted tape-spacing rollers CC prevent the tape falling back on the drum, aided by arm-poles AA. The tape is now ready for record or play mode, impelled by capstan D pressing the tape against ring-mounted pressure roller E. The pole F is the back-tension regulator, shortly to be described.

Unusually the V8 cassette package has no internal tape guides – Table 17.1 gives further information on videotape cassette packages.

TAPE PATH

Apart from V8 format which (where a *flying erase* head is used) has no need for any stationary heads at all, the progress of the tape through the deck is fairly standardised between formats. On emerging from the cassette feed (left side) spool, the tape is

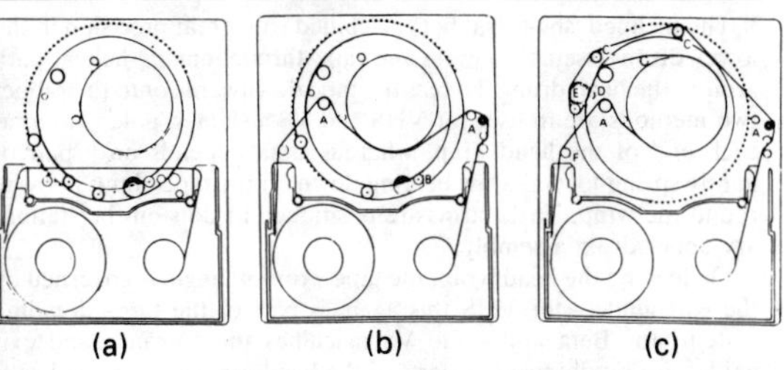

Fig. 17.5 *Three stages in loading Video 8 tape: (a) at rest, (b) first (M-configuration) stage complete, and (c) threading ring fully turned*

Table 17.1 *Characteristics of cassette packages and videotape*

Cassette	*VHS*	*Beta*	*VHS-C*	*Video 8*
Size, mm	188 × 104 × 25	156 × 96 × 25	92 × 59 × 23	95 × 62.5 × 15
Volume, cc	489	374	125	89
SP max. time, hrs	4	4	0.5	1.5
SP recording density, hrs/m^2	0.93	1.16	0.93	1.67
Tape thickness, mm	21	21	21	10*

*MP (Metal Powder) and ME (Metal Evaporated) tape

leaned-on by a spring-loaded feeler (*back-tension pole*) which governs the friction applied to the feed spool, either by a very simple felt-lined tension band around the turntable (a purely mechanical negative feedback system) or by an electrical feedback system which governs the (reverse) current in the direct-drive feed spool motor. In the latter case the tension-arm position sensor is generally some form of opto-coupler. By means of the feeler the *back-tension* of the tape is regulated to a constant value regardless of the weight of tape on each spool.

Next the tape passes over the *full-erase* head which during record mode generates a strong a.c. field at about 60 kHz to remove all previously-recorded magnetic tracks from the tape. In VHS machines the erase-head's gap is sufficiently long to accommodate any vertical movement of the tape ribbon, whereas Beta tape is at this point about to enter the head-wrap, so the erase head assembly incorporates a long tape guide whose adjustment governs the critical head run-in angle. For VHS an *impedance-roller* is sometimes provided downstream of the erase head to remove any tension fluctuations in the tape, now approaching the head-wrap and its entry guide, the latter being part of the moving tape-loading system already described.

The inclined 'shelf' (rabbet) machined with great precision in the lower drum assembly guides the tape throughout its helical path around the head drum. To bias the tape downwards onto the rabbet two methods are in use: for VHS and V8 a slanted pole is used at each end of the head-wrap, whereas Beta depends on a pair of lightly spring-loaded arms bearing down on the tape about halfway round the wrap. These arms are positioned in slots on the stationary upper drum assembly.

On leaving the head wrap, the tape's run-off angle is governed by the exit guide – for VHS this again is part of the tape-threading system; for Beta and some V8 machines the entrance and exit guides are rigidly fixed as parts of the head-casting assembly itself. Next is encountered the fixed head assembly used for audio and control-pulse transfer. The audio head is at the top of the assembly and the control-track head at the bottom; in some VHS designs another impedance roller is present between video and audio/control head assemblies, where it prevents sound flutter by smoothing the progress of the tape ribbon.

Finally the tape reaches the capstan which (aided by the heavily-sprung pressure roller) has pulled the ribbon through the entire path so far described. The capstan itself is a precision-machined shaft about 3 mm in diameter, on which, in the very common *direct-drive* system, is mounted the actual rotor of the drive motor below. The pressure roller is made of rubber and is typically 12 mm in diameter; its mounting is often designed to permit a degree of axis-tilt in order to make it self-aligning against the capstan shaft, whereby the pressure is even over the full width of the tape ribbon.

The slack paid out by the capstan is taken up by the take-up reel on the right-hand side of the cassette. Although the 'feed-in' rate is constant, the required take-up spool speed varies tremendously, depending on the amount of tape (hence diameter) on the spool. What is required is a constant *torque* in a clockwise direction, and it is achieved by a slipping clutch or by a suitably-regulated current through the reel motor, which in some videorecorders is a direct-drive type.

VIDEO HEAD DRUM

The heart of a videorecorder is its head drum assembly. The lower (stationary) section contains one half of the rotary transformer in most designs; and consists of a monobloc cast-and-machined assembly whose most critical features are its peripheral surface finish and the angle and finish of the guide rabbet. For all formats except Betamax the whole upper section of the drum rotates, carrying the heads and the second half of the rotary transformer. The heads themselves consist of tiny chips of ferrite in 'ring' form, around which is wound a dozen or so turns of very fine enamelled wire. The protruding section of each head chip is precision-ground to the required dimensions, after which the gap is cut across the face – at an angle dictated by the azimuth requirements. The effective 'width' of the head and the magnetic track it writes is determined by the length of the magnetic gap in fact, and by grinding indentations in the chip at each end of the gap, 'head-width' is precisely defined as shown in Fig. 17.6(a); some heads have double gaps (with separate windings for each), often with opposing azimuth angles and different widths, all achieved by micro-grinding of the gap and head face. An idea of the construction of such a head is given in Fig. 17.6(b). The heads are fixed to brass mounting tabs which in turn are screwed to the lip of the head drum. The positioning of the

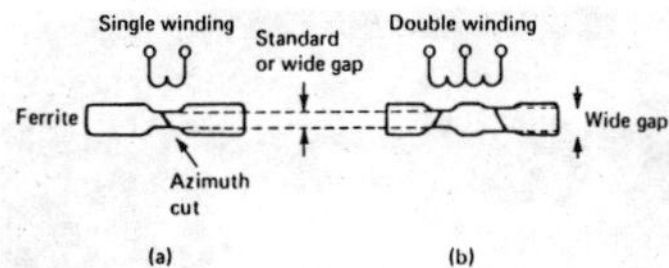

Fig. 17.6 *Head-chip configurations*

heads is very critical indeed; it is set up in the factory using precision optical equipment whose resolution is better than one micron. In Betamax machines the heads are mounted on a thin disc which forms the rotating centre part of a 'sandwich' whose other components are the stationary upper and lower drum assemblies.

There are two alternative methods of managing the gradient on which the tape must pass the head-sweep path in order to record the required slanting tracks. In M-loading machines (i.e. VHS) the drum assembly itself is tilted with respect to the deck plane, permitting the tape to travel parallel to the deck and tape spools throughout its path. Where ring-loading is used (Beta and V8) it becomes possible to mount the head drum parallel to the deck. Either the entry-level or the exit-level of the head wrap is aligned with the cassette reels; the necessary change in tape level around the head wrap is compensated for by an inclination of the tape path around the threading ring, most simply arranged by tilting the threading ring itself.

All head drums spin anticlockwise in domestic formats, and the tape passes anticlockwise around the drum, except in review-replay (backward search) mode. In all cases the head enters onto the tape at its lower edge to read or write its slant track, leaving the tape at its top edge, as shown in the diagrams in Chapter 12.

Head service

The most expensive and vulnerable component on the deck is the video head drum assembly. As a general rule it is also the one most vulnerable to wear – 2000 operating hours is an oft-quoted life expectation. As the head-tips wear, their penetration ability decreases to the point where replayed pictures from known-good tapes are intolerably marred by dropouts and snow, as depicted in the photo of Fig. 17.7(a). A common effect of head wear is the streaking and transient-distortion pictured in Fig. 17.7(b). The effects shown can easily be caused by defects in the replay amplifiers, so after head cleaning (see later) the heads themselves should not be condemned before the replay circuits have been checked with regard to: (a) correct setting of DOC; (b) condition and operating point of preamplifiers, demodulator and limiter circuit. Very often the noise, streaking or other effect will have a heavy flicker component at 25 Hz rate, a sure indication that the trouble stems from *one* of the two head channels. Examination of the replay video f.m. envelope at a point after the head-switch but before the limiting stage (a suitable test point is given in the manufacturer's service manual) will reveal a large difference in output levels between the heads as shown in the oscillogram of Fig. 17.7(c) which is taken from an oscilloscope whose timebase is triggered from the head PG or flip-flop waveform. The performance of the suspect head in record mode (replay its tape in a known-good machine to check) is a useful clue as to whether it is faulty.

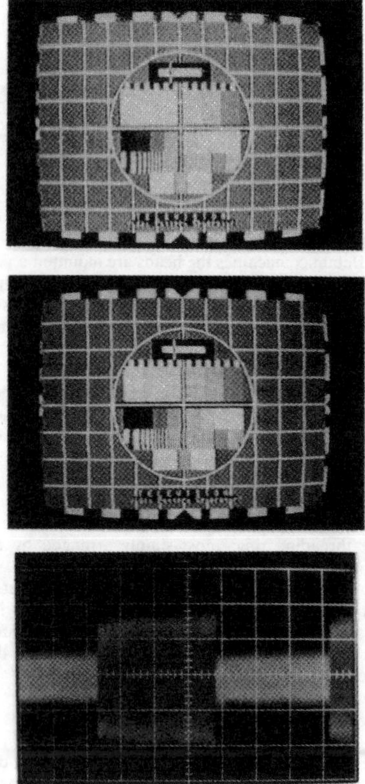

Fig. 17.7 *Head problems: (a) snow and dropout; (b) transient distortion and streaking from verticals; (c) oscilloscope envelope pattern – one head worn*

Sometimes the first indication of the onset of head wear is excessive dropout during replay of 'self-made' recordings – the double passage of the video f.m. signal through the sub-standard head(s) emphasises the problem, which at this stage may not be apparent during replay of well-recorded (i.e. library or alignment) tapes. With experience the state of wear of the video head tips can be judged by their 'feel' to a fingertip through a thin layer of cleaning material; a close examination of the ferrite tips (even with a powerful magnifying glass) is unlikely to reveal the state of wear that may be present, but *will* reveal any physical damage, e.g. chipped or cracked face.

The symptoms shown in Fig. 17.7 will often be due to a build-up of tape oxide and other debris on the head tips, forming a barrier between head and tape; in severe cases no picture at all can be recorded or replayed. Cleaning of the heads is best done by hand rather than a cleaning tape. Various solvents can be used, including the specially-prepared types offered for sale by videorecorder manufacturers and component distributors; surgical spirit is an adequate alternative. Using a lint-free cloth (or, better, a fine chamois or buckskin surface) well-moistened with solvent, rub each video head *sideways*, that is in the direction of tape travel. Gentle-to-moderate pressure should be used, and great care taken not to move the head-chip vertically, which will break the adhesive by which the head is held in place on its brass mounting tab. Fig. 17.8 shows how the head is held steady with one hand while being cleaned with the other – here a special cleaning stick is being used.

In Beta machines it is not always easy to manipulate the rotating disc section, and for these (and other-format heads where expedient) it is possible to clean the head chips by holding the cleaner still on the peripheral surface of the drum then rotating the latter by direct or indirect means. Whenever this is done, however, it is essential that the head is turned *anticlockwise* or the ferrite chips may be damaged. Sometimes a head will continue to display wear/'blocked' symptoms after a thorough 'wet' clean; before condemning it (and since at this point there is nothing to lose) it is worth trying the effect of bearing moderately hard on the front surface of the head with a stiff card (like a business- or visiting-card) while rotating the drum anticlockwise by hand. Sometimes this will restore normal operation. Cases where heads 'block' and need cleaning at regular intervals may occasionally be due to faulty (rough-surfaced) head chips, but are more often attributable to the use of one or more tapes which are shedding oxide excessively, perhaps as a result of a roughened or torn surface sustained in an earlier 'tape-chewing' incident in a faulty deck.

When head cleaning fails to cure the symptom, and electrical tests exonerate the drive and pre-amp circuits, the head-disc must be replaced. It is important to ensure that the new head is fitted and wired correctly according to the colour-code of individual head leads, since a head fitted 180° 'out of phase' will cause puzzling symptoms like no colour. Provided that no dirt particles enter under the head during replacement, and that the securing screws are equally tight, correct running level of the heads is assured by the factory-sealed settings. For some machines the exact centring of the head disc on its mounting platform must be checked and corrected by a *dial-gauge* with which eccentricity can be reduced to less than 2 microns; any greater error may cause fluctuating tape tension and flutter on sound. Whether or not a dial-gauge is used, great care is necessary to avoid damage to the delicate head tips during handling and installation.

At the time of head replacement, the entire tape path should be cleaned (description follows) and the following setting points checked and adjusted as necessary: control-track head positioning; record writing current; pre-amplifier alignment; and record and replay head-switching points. Sometimes guide alignment may be necessary, and this, too, will be described later in this chapter. Never use an alignment tape in a newly-repaired deck in case it gets damaged: check first with a less valuable tape.

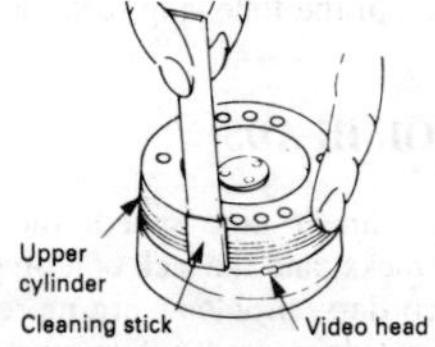

Fig. 17.8 *Video head cleaning by hand*

TAPE PATH CLEANING

After many hundreds of hours' use a video deck will be in need of cleaning and servicing. Every component that the tape contacts along its entire path is cleaned with alcohol, applied with a soft cloth or cotton bud as necessary. The inside angles of tape guides require special attention, since grease, oxide and other debris can build up there to upset tracking. The drum surfaces often develop patches of black dirt, most easily removed by scrubbing with a solvent-moistened cotton bud; this same agent can be used to clean-out and polish the guide rabbet on the lower drum. The front surface of the audio/control head is treated in the same way, then polished off with a soft cloth. In some Betamax videorecorders the audio/control head face is not easily accessible or visible. Here the use of a bent cotton-bud stick is recommended for scrubbing, and an angled dental-type mirror for inspection.

The capstan shaft will often be found to have built-up rings of encrusted dirt at points corresponding with the upper and lower edges of the tape ribbon; these can be difficult to remove, and are best tackled by soaking them with solvent initially, leaving it to soak in and soften the deposits while other cleaning is progressing; hard vertical rubbing with a cloth held between thumb and fore-finger will then prevail. The use of a fibre pencil (available from component distributors) makes the task of capstan cleaning very easy. The pressure-roller requires similar surface treatment, though the process is easier. Do not apply any abrasive agent to the surfaces of capstan or pressure roller.

Where a general service of the deck mechanics is required, various other components need to be checked. Specific details of these depend very much on the type and age of the videorecorder, and are fully covered in the maker's service manual. In general it will be necessary to check and replace as necessary drive belts and idlers which are showing signs of (or are prone to) slipping. In the case of idlers used for tape-loading or reel drive, removal, degreasing and a roughening of their drive surfaces with fine glasspaper is good precautionary practice. For sliding- and bearing-surfaces a drop of light machine oil is required, but several cautions must be observed: most drive motors must not be oiled – follow maker's instructions; nylon and plastic bearing surfaces may need no lubrication, or a special type; and beware of contaminating friction surfaces (belts, idlers, pulleys) and particularly tape-contact surfaces (guides, heads, rollers) with lubricant. Where old grease, which may well have hardened, is being replaced, a light graphited grease is recommended.

Other aspects of routine deck maintenance or fault diagnosis are checks of reel-brake operation; confirmation of correct winding and take-up torques; checking and adjustment of back-tension; alignment of tape guides; adjustment of audio/control heads; and the position-setting of such things as spool turntables, loading-rings/gears, and sensor- and mode-switches. The more important of these will be covered in the following sections.

AUDIO/CONTROL HEADS

Because of the low linear tape speed, the narrowness of the longitudinal audio tracks, and the lack of a pressure-pad as used in audio-only tape recorders, problems are more prevalent with the audio head area of a videorecorder. Symptoms of a worn or dirty audio head are low, muffled sound lacking in treble response; and of a worn control-track head erratic servo lock on playback – especially of its own recordings, since the head will have been used twice. In machines where a signal-mute circuit is used on playback there will be no output signal with the servo unlocked, though trick-mode pictures will be displayed.

For checking and setting up A/C heads an *alignment* tape is required. This has a standard audio track with which adjustment of height, level and azimuth can be made. Height setting is only required when the head assembly has been replaced, and is made by adjustment of a single nut or three screws (VHS) or two nuts (Beta) for maximum volume on the test tape. A lack of treble response from 'foreign' (i.e. recorded elsewhere) tapes indicates an azimuth error; it is corrected by a spring-loaded screw or nut at one side of the head-mounting platform. Adjust for maximum level of high-frequency (typically 6 kHz) sound from the appropriate section of the test-tape; if a large adjustment is necessary, re-check height before finally setting and sealing the azimuth-adjusting screw.

Whereas the azimuth adjustment rocks the A/C head assembly sideways, a further tilt adjustment screw is provided to rock the head fore-and-aft. This is called *tilt* or *zenith* adjustment, and ensures that the top edge of the tape (audio track) bears correctly against the head for consistent sound. Where sound level fluctuates (especially with three-hour and longer tapes) the back-tension should be checked before the azimuth adjustment screw is adjusted to slightly tilt out the upper face of the head: too much tilt will result in intermittent transfer of the bottom (control) track.

The final aspect of A/C head adjustment is its positioning *along* the tape path, which governs the relative placement on tape of control- and video-tracks. Its main importance is in establishing compatibility, whereby a correctly-recorded 'foreign' tape will not require any offset of the tracking control during playback. It is set by lateral adjustment of the A/C head for perfect tracking of an alignment tape, with the tracking control in its normal (click-stop) position.

ALIGNMENT TAPE

For each format a reference cassette, called an *alignment* or *interchange* tape, is available from videorecorder manufacturers. It is recorded on a specially produced and aligned 'model' machine at the factory, and all its characteristics are centre-tolerance. It contains colour-bars, monochrome step-wedge, and test-card images for checks on all aspects of the replay machine. An important feature is an *r.f. sweep* signal in which the entire tape-frequency spectrum is covered in one 20 ms field period. An oscilloscope connected to the f.m. replay signal and triggered from the head flip-flop waveform will thus display a graph of overall replay frequency response; suitably-positioned markets fascilitate the accurate setting of the replay preamplifier response – the peaking and damping trimmers referred to in Chapter 13. An oscilloscope-type display of the r.f. sweep pattern is reproduced in Fig. 13.12.

Audio aspects of the alignment tape include an l.f. tone for audio level checking and adjustment, at an accurately-specified frequency for replay capstan speed checks. An h.f. tone checks A/C head azimuth setting. Test tapes are also available with Hi-Fi sound tracks; and recorded to LP specifications for VHS and V8 formats.

Alignment tapes are expensive, and the test sections on them very short. To avoid wear, and particularly to eliminate the risk of damage, they should never be used where their particular qualities are not essential, and should *never* be placed in a machine which has not been *proved* mechanically safe. Much work which requires the use of an alignment tape can be carried out with a locally-recorded substitute: Take a high-grade tape and record colour-bars, grey-scale step-wedge and test-card, with tones from an audio generator or the broadcast signal. Use a new, well set-up machine on which the real alignment tape plays perfectly at tracking-control centre. For all applications (except sweep-adjustment of video f.m. preamps) use this tape, followed by one pass of the alignment tape as a final check. In the text that follows the term 'test-tape' refers to the alignment tape or the above-described substitute.

TORQUE AND TENSION CHECKS

Torque is a turning force, and is applicable, in videorecorder service, to the tape spool turntables. It is measured in gram/centimetres (g-cm) the second term referring to the radius of the tape reel. The most important such reading is that of *take-up torque*, the 'twisting power' of the right-hand reel during record and playback modes. It must be sufficient to reliably pull in the tape issuing from the capstan, but not so great that the tape is stretched – a typical figure is 120 g-cm. To measure it a special torque-gauge is available. It fits over the take-up turntable and has a spring-loaded dial/pointer scale on top, directly calibrated in g-cm; in use it is gently held at the rim, permitting the upper section to *slowly* rotate while the reading is being taken. An out-of-spec torque normally calls for cleaning, adjustment or replacement of the slipping-clutch in the take-up drive – generally a worn clutch will increase torque.

In fast-forward and rewind modes the torque will typically be more than 400 g-cm, and the absence of any form of driver clutch means that any shortcoming is likely to be due to slipping belts or idlers, or a defect in the reel motor or its electrical drive circuit. The type of torque-gauge mentioned above can also be used for this check – an alternative in either case is a special cassette containing spring-loaded spools with dials and pointers instead of tape spools.

The most important tape-tension check is that of *running back-tension*, the degree of braking on the left-hand (supply) tape spool during record and playback. On this depends the video-head tip penetration into the tape; the chroma-luma image registration (via the 'stretch-factor' imparted to the tape); the skew-error (sideways tilt from head switch-point) in the picture; the intimacy of tape contact with the sound and control-track heads; correct interchange with other tapes and machines; and the risk of permanently damaging the tape. The correct figure varies between manufacturers and formats, depending on the number and type of guides between feed spool and video head: typical figures are 30 g-cm for VHS, 45 g-cm for Beta types.

There are several ways of measuring back tension. The simplest is the use of a spring-loaded straight- or sector-type tension gauge, which is in effect a weighing-machine calibrated in grams. It is attached to the end of the tape of a full reel recovered from a discarded cassette, then (with the videorecorder in 'play' mode) the tape is passed over the back-tension pole and pulled to the right at approximately the correct (format) speed. The reading is taken from the scale as the gauge is moved. This is not easy or accurate, and a simpler (but much more expensive) method is to use a directly-calibrated tension gauge (e.g. *Tentelometer*) which has two fixed arms and one central 'deflect-able' one; the tape is threaded between these to give a direct readout of tension. In some machines, however, it is difficult to find room to fit this instrument's probes into the tape path, and like the reel-and-pull system just described, account must be taken of the diameter of the tape reel on the feed-spool in use. For these reasons, a third method is favourite: a specially produced cassette containing two spools linked by a few minutes-worth of ordinary tape, which is played in the normal way while a calibrated dial on the feed side indicates back-tension directly in g-cms. They are available from video-recorder manufacturers.

TAPE GUIDES AND THEIR ALIGNMENT

The most demanding and critical adjustment procedures on the tape deck have to do with the tape guides. The number of guides on the deck varies with formats and threading arrangements, and is least with moving-arm M-wrap systems and most with loading-ring systems. All guides define the *shape* of the tape path; the more important ones determine the angle and running-level of the tape across the heads.

Guide adjustment is normally only required when the guides themselves have been replaced or disturbed by necessary replacement of associated parts. In all other cases of mistracking or tape-running error, every other possibility should be explored before breaking the factory paint-seals and attempting to reset guides. Their adjustment is carried out with reference to (a) an oscilloscope trace of the envelope pattern of the output signal of the heads during replay; and (b) careful observation of the 'lie' of the tape ribbon on the guide and head surfaces it passes over.

Fig. 17.9(a) shows the sequence of components on a typical VHS deck. The two crucial guides are the entry and exit guide rollers at each end of the tape's head wrap. Their height is initially set up by use of a jig which rests on the deck's surface. Using an alignment tape in replay the height of the entry guide is now set for a flat shape at the beginning (LHS) of the envelope waveform, avoiding the 'bottleneck' effects shown in the waveforms of Fig. 17.10(a). When it is correct there should be no wrinkling or curling of the tape at the guide; if there is, trouble upstream (typically a bent tension pole, or incorrect supply-reel height) is indicated. The exit guide height is now trimmed for a flat waveform at the end of the head sweep. Correct setting is when the bottleneck effects at RHS of waveform (Fig. 17.10(b)) are eliminated.

The more complex Betamax tape path is depicted in Fig. 17.9(b). Here guides 0, 1 and 2 all influence the entrance waveform, and nos. 3, 4 and 5 the exit waveform. Only the bottom edge of guide 0 contacts the tape. With guides 1 and 2 screwed up, and out of contact with the tape, no. 0 is adjusted (tracking control offset to the right) so that the tape entrance envelope *rises*, when the tape ribbon is fractionally above the head's rabbet at the lead-in point. Guide nos. 1 and 2 have a common upper flange-plate, and are now adjusted downwards to achieve a flat entrance waveform. At this point there should be no curl on the tape, and it should be in contact with the lower edge of guide no. 0, and the common upper flange of guides 1 and 2. If not, check reel height and perpendicularity of the tension pole and the full-erase head.

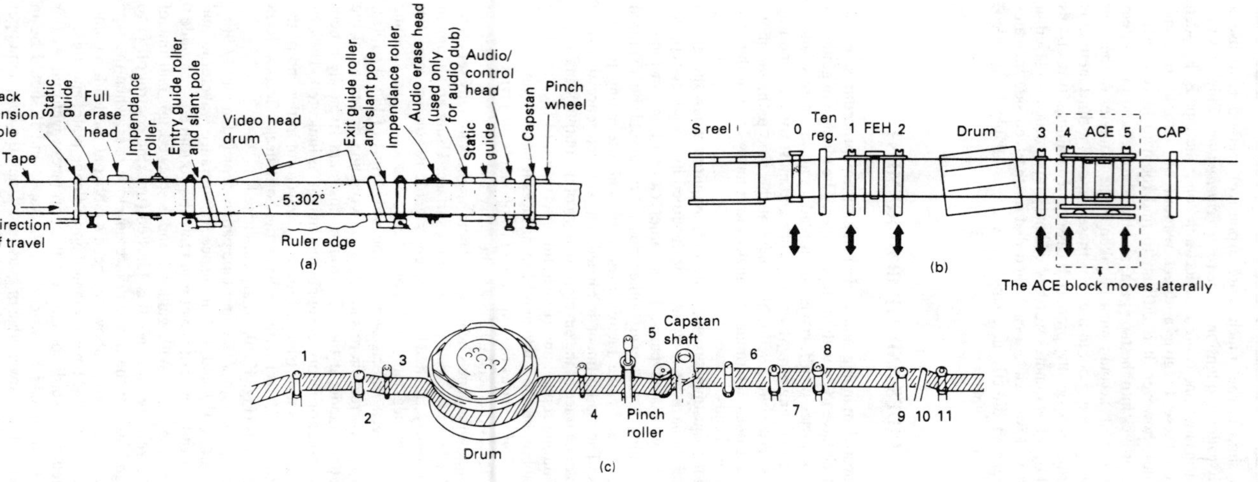

Fig. 17.9 *Tape running diagrams: VHS at (a), Beta at (b), Video 8 at (c)*

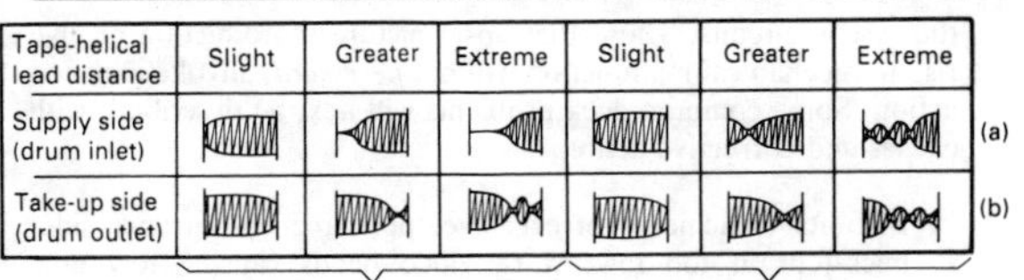

Fig. 17.10 *FM envelope patterns with maladjusted guides. Row (a) is concerned with the entry guide, and row (b) with the exit guide*

On the exit side, the tape contacts only the upper flanges of guides 3, 4 and 5; the audio head sits between the latter two. With the same offset adjustment of the tracking control as before to reduce envelope height, all three guides are raised until they are clear of the tape. Guides 4 and 5 are now adjusted for a *rise* at the exit point in the envelope waveform, then guide 3 for a flat exit-shape. At this point alignment is complete; using an alignment tape on replay, rotating the tracking control should increase and decrease the envelope amplitude without significantly altering its shape, demonstrating that tape paths and head sweeps are truly parallel, the indication of perfect tracking. This, of course, applies equally to Beta, VHS and the V8 system to be described shortly. In general a maximum variation of 30% in envelope amplitude is permissible over the sweep period of each head. This tolerance is taken up by the clipping action of the amplitude limiter in the replay path of the luminance f.m. signal.

A representation of the tape path of a V8-format videorecorder is given in Fig. 17.9(c). The first guide, no. 1, moves vertically and sets the running angle of the tape at the entrance side. It is set to poise the tape marginally above the guide rabbet at the entry side. Guide no. 2's flanges do not contact the tape at all, and it has two adjustment points: height and tilt, the latter biasing the tape downwards onto the head-rabbet, as per VHS practice. It is set for a flat entrance waveform. Guide 3 has little effect on tracking or tape running – it absorbs tape tension fluctuation, like the impedance roller described earlier for VHS.

At the exit side, guide 4 comes first, and has the same function as no. 3: it absorbs fluctuations in tape running. Guide 5 is the main exit governor, and like no. 2 is adjustable in respects of height and tilt. It is set for a flat exit waveform from the test tape. Alignment of guide no. 6, beyond the capstan, is concerned with tape running during reverse mode. Succeeding guides 7 and 8 are non-adjustable, being merely *tape-steering* rollers on the threading ring; guides 9 and 11 are deck-mounted pillars which define the tape's routing on its way into the take-up spool; they work in conjunction with guide no. 10, which in fact is a pull-out pole used for initial tape threading. Its action was illustrated in Fig. 17.5, where it forms one pole A.

DECK FAULT SYMPTOMS

Some possible deck faults were covered in Chapter 15, where malfunctions of deck members, especially the feedback sensors, were described in terms of the effect they have on the operation of the syscon circuits. Those that upset picture reproduction or give rise to mechanical malfunction will not *necessarily* invoke a syscon action. Some common deck problems will next be described, with causes and corrective action:

1. Inability to achieve correct envelope shape on entrance side: back-tension too low; worn video heads causing low tape penetration; faulty or maladjusted entrance guide(s); dirt on lead-in section of head rabbet
2. Tape path across guides wrong when envelope waveform correct: tape-path biased by incorrectly-aligned members beyond the guides, i.e. tilted stationary heads, bent tension pole, faulty pressure roller, incorrect reel height etc.
3. Tape creased during play or record: dirt or hairs on capstan or pressure roller; faulty or misaligned tape guides; foreign body or swarf along tape path
4. Tape damaged or chewed during threading or unthreading: incorrect braking action on spools; insufficient reel torque for take-up of slack
5. Slow or laboured fast-transport functions: slipping reel-drive idler or belt; faulty reel motor; in Beta machines where the tape remains loaded in these modes, excessive tape friction due to a worn upper drum surface
6. Wow and flutter on sound: where the capstan servo circuit is proved innocent, the capstan drive mechanics are implicated: faulty motor, bearings or drive belt should be suspected. Further possible causes are insufficient pinch-roller pressure (should be about 1.6 kg), faulty or 'tight' pinch-roller, bent capstan shaft and eccentric mounting of the head-disc or drum. Many of these faults will give rise to picture problems, primarily:
7. Lateral wobble of picture: the visible equivalent of wow on sound. Where capstan or head-drum servo faults are not responsible, tightness of entry- and exit-guide rollers (VHS) on their shafts may be at the root of the problem. In such cases a squeak will often emanate from the offending guide. A faulty capstan or drum motor can give rise to the same symptom
8. Mechanical squeaking, especially in fast transport modes: In Beta videorecorders a common cause is lack of lubrication on the shafts of rotating guide-rollers on the threading ring. In VHS types 'dry' bearings are also the usual cause; careful listening will pinpoint the problem area, typically the bottom bearing of the capstan shaft or the counter-belt pulley
9. Replay picture rolling: symptomatic of a poor 'entry' r.f. envelope pattern, see (1) above
10. Excessive tape and head wear, misregistration of colour on tapes recorded elsewhere: back tension too high, check and adjust as described earlier in this chapter
11. Inability to match A/B output levels of new head assembly, and tracking control has differential effect on f.m. output levels of the two heads: this suggests that the heads are not operating in the same vertical plane, and may be due to the head disc/drum being tilted on its mounting platform during installation. Check for true running in the vertical plane
12. 'Stop' mode entered during threading or (front-loaders) cassette transportation: jammed mechanics or mode switch. Dismantle and investigate.

18

Video disc technology

Compared with videorecorders using tape-cassette systems the video disc concept is a relative latecomer to the domestic market. Like the more recently developed videotape formats, however, it has benefited from the higher technology available at the time of finalising the format details and specifications – once this is done (in any consumer equipment sphere where large and long-lived markets are envisaged) development is effectively frozen. Compatibility, and in the case of home-playback systems, software availability, dictate that the basic parameters cannot be changed.

The main limitation of the video disc concept is that its current technology does not permit recording at home, so its usage is confined to playback of bought-in or hired software; the corollary to this is that player sales are dependent on the easy availability of a wide range of software, whose price would have to be at least comparable to the well-entrenched VHS cassette. Software availability is beyond the control of the disc-player manufacturers to a large degree (at least at the very local level required by potential customers), leading to a chicken-and-egg situation which hampers the development of disc-player sales. However, provided that the picture quality is high (i.e. Laservision) this alone may swing the consumer in favour of discs for vision, as it has in the audio world – the growth in usage of the Compact Audio Disc is phenomenal.

Of the video disc systems currently available to the home user, the most popular is Laservision, originally developed by Philips in Europe. It has the best performance, but is the most expensive and complex system. This chapter will concentrate on the Laservision system exclusively.

LASERVISION

Laservision is the only home-playback system to offer virtually full-bandwidth video reproduction, and the only one capable of handling the broadcast colour signal *en-suite* as it were; other disc systems, and all videocassette formats are limited to about 3 MHz vision bandwidth, and require the chroma subcarrier to be frequency-shifted in a colour-under system. The vision and sound information is encoded on the disc in the form of a series of tiny pits in its surface, which is then aluminised and sealed with a coat of plastic. Ordinary video discs are 30 cm (12 inches) in diameter, and double-sided. The signal-bearing pits are arranged in a continuous spiral, starting near the disc centre and finishing at the outside edge. They are very closely spaced at around 600 lines per mm, giving a total track length of about 34 km, 21 miles.

The read-out system is optical, and the pick-up sensor does not touch the disc at all – it depends on reflections from the pitted surface. Thus there is no wear or deterioration of the disc, even in still-frame. Since the optical system focuses on the sub-surface pits, dust, fingerprints and (within reason) superficial damage to the disc surface have no effect on reproduction quality. The specifications and characteristics of the Laservision system are given in Table 18.1.

Table 18.1 *Specifications for Laservision system*

Disc material	Aluminised plastic
Disc diameter	200–300 mm
Disc thickness	2.7 mm
Centre hole diameter	35 mm
Rotational rate	1500–570 r.p.m.
Fields per rev.	2–6
Recorded band	107–290 mm
Sides	2
Duration per side	30–60 min
Reading light	1 mW laser
Tracking system	Optical servo
Recorded signal	6.76–7.9 MHz
Luminance bandwidth	5 MHz (−6 dB)
Chrominance bandwidth	500 kHz
Video S/N ratio	37 dB
Audio S/N ratio	60 dB
Audio channels	2
Audio carriers	684 kHz and 1066 kHz
Audio carrier deviation	±50 kHz
Audio bandwidth	40 Hz–20 kHz
Channel separation	55 dB

FIELDS, TRACKS AND MODULATION

There are two ways of arranging the television fields on the surface of the disc, both illustrated in Fig. 18.1. At (a) is depicted the 'active' disc in which each TV field occupies one half of the disc's rotation, with all the field sync pulses lined up across a diameter of the disc. These play at a constant speed of 1500 r.p.m. and have the advantage of excellent trick-speed replay: the pick-up is 'skipped' sideways during the field blanking interval for still-frame or special-speed playback. This disc is a CAV (Constant Angular Velocity) type, and since the track-length for 1 field of 312½ lines varies greatly from the middle to the outside of the disc the pit-density is great at the beginning of play, but sparse at the end. CAV discs have 36 minutes playing time per side.

The alternative arrangement is the CLV (Constant Linear Velocity) disc shown at Fig. 18.1(b). Here the pit-density along the tracks is constant so that each TV field has the same track length. At replay start (disc centre) 2 fields are read out per rev at 1500 r.p.m. As playback continues the disc slows down to maintain constant track-scanning speed until at the outer edge the pick-up is reading six fields per rev at about 550 r.p.m. This disc is capable of 54 minutes playing time per side, but no trick-replay is possible.

The pit-track pattern is shown in Fig. 18.1(c). The track pitch is 1.7 micron, the pit width is 0.4 micron and pit depth 0.1 micron. The surface of the disc is scanned by a very fine (0.9 micron) spot of light from a laser, and the information is read out by a photodiode which discriminates between the reflected light level during the presence or absence of a pit. In the absence of a pit most of the light is reflected onto the pick-up diode which passes high current; when

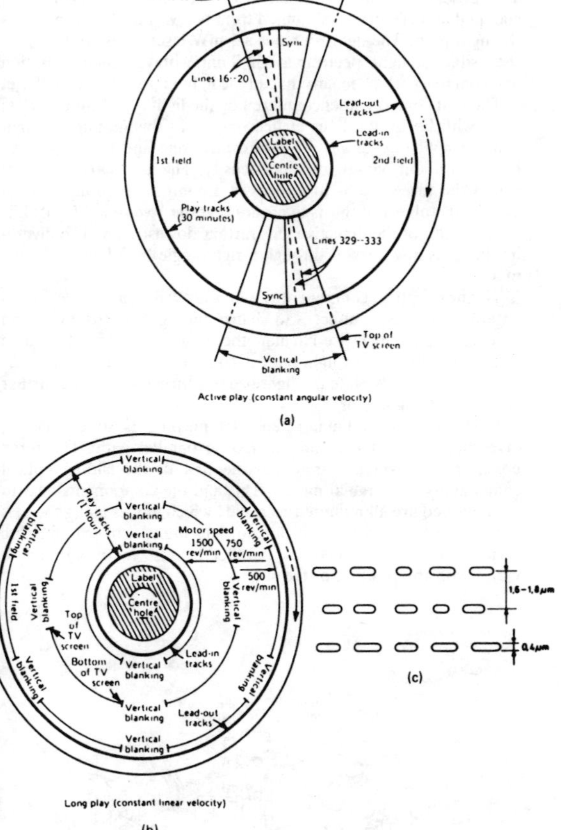

Fig. 18.1 *Laservision disc-track layouts: (a) CAV type; (b) CLV type; (c) pit width and spacing*

a pit is present most of the light is scattered and little returns to the photodiode, whose current is now low as a result. The diode output contains all the video, colour and sound information.

LIGHT PATH

The Laservision disc does not have a turntable as such – it is clamped at its centre and scanned from below. Fig. 18.2 represents the light path. The light source is a 1 mW laser whose output is in the visible red light spectrum at 632.8 nm, with vertical polarisation and *coherence* which means that all the light emissions are in phase.

The first component encountered by the light is a grating, a glass plate with horizontal lines etched into it. In this grating the light beam is split into three: a bright central one and two secondary beams at about one-quarter its intensity. The associated spot-lens brings the three beams to a focus at a point in space about 1 cm away – the object of this is to ensure that the *beam-bundle* just fills the aperture of the objective lens further downstream. The diverging beam is now turned through a right-angle by a beam-splitting prism.

The next optical component is a quarter-wavelength (λ/4) retardation plate, whose effect is to change the light polarisation from vertical to anti-clockwise circular; the reason for this will become clear when the return light-path is considered shortly. On emergence from the λ/4 plate the light beam is turned through a further 90° by a folding mirror.

Next comes a collimator lens. Its purpose is to collect the diverging beam-bundle and set it on a parallel path. The three beams now travel in parallel to the first of the sliding optical components – the radial mirror. This and the components next to be described are all mounted on a slide which moves along the axis of the light beam from the collimator lens in order to scan the disc surface – hence the need for parallel beams: their path-length varies with the position of the slide.

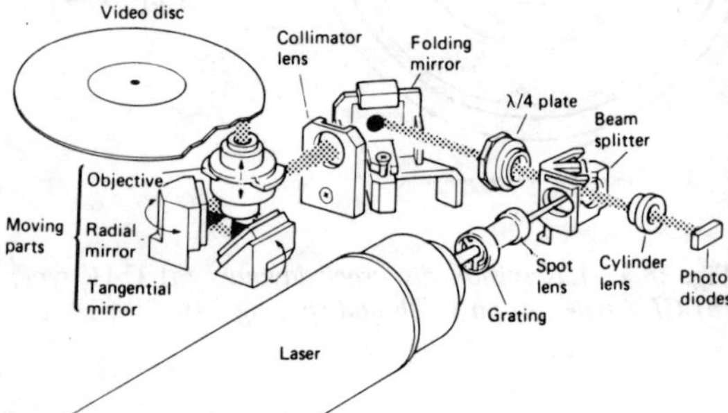

Fig. 18.2 *Light path and optical components in a Philips LV player*

The radial mirror pivots on a vertical axis under servo control, reflecting the beams to the surface of an adjacent tangential mirror pivoting on a horizontal axis, and also closely governed by a servo system. The alignment of these two 'steered' mirrors determines the exact position of the light spot on the disc surface. Reflected light from the tangential mirror surface passes up through the objective lens which focuses the three light beams to sharp pin-points of light on the video disc. The diameter of the focused central spot is less than 1 micron, which is comparable with the wavelength (0.63 micron) of the light waves themselves. The outer light spots are used for tracking purposes, and the central one to read out the information on the disc surface.

After reflection at the disc the (now modulated) light follows the same path in the opposite direction, passing through the objective lens and via the tangential and radial mirrors, collimator lens and folding mirror back to the $\lambda/4$ plate. The outgoing and returning light beams have a phase-difference of 180° because the depth of the pits on the disc is one-quarter of the light wavelength. The difference in path-length between disc-surface and pit-bottom for a 'bounced' light signal is thus $2 \times \lambda/4$, corresponding to half a cycle, 180°. The $\lambda/4$ plate turns this 'antiphase' anticlockwise-polarised beam into a linearly-polarised one, but now the light is *horizontally* polarised.

In this form the modulated returning light beam passes into the beam-splitting prism, whose surfaces are polarised such that for horizontally-polarised light no deflection takes place. As a result the return beam passes directly through to a cylindrical lens, and finally onto a bank of photodiodes, whose outputs provide not only the video and audio output signals, but tracking control signals to maintain correct focusing of the objective lens. The operation of the beam focusing servo will now be examined.

BEAM FOCUS SERVO

The objective lens has a very small depth of focus, typically less than 2 microns. In order to maintain correct focus on the pit-surface in the face of tolerances in disc manufacture and mounting (and slide height) a servo system is required to drive the lens vertically. The lens assembly itself is mounted on a moving coil which moves in the annular gap of a permanent magnet, the assembly being very similar to the centre section of a moving-coil loudspeaker. Lens position is proportional to the current in the moving coil. The coil forms one element of a closed-loop servo system.

The combination of objective lens and cylindrical lens forms (for the return path only) an *astigmatic* lens, whose characteristic is that a perfectly-focused circular light spot will render a circular image, whereas elliptical images will result from out-of-focus circular light spots. The angle of the major axis of the ellipse produced depends on the direction of defocusing, as shown in Fig. 18.3. A group of four photo-diodes ABCD is arranged in quad formation and placed at a distance from the cylindrical lens such that with the disc in perfect focus all four diodes receive equal light, and pass equal current. If the focal point should fall short of the disc the circular spot closes down to an ellipse whose light falls mainly on diodes C and D; their current increases while that in diodes A and B decreases. The resulting imbalance is detected, amplified and turned into a current for passage through the objective lens coil in the correct sense to reduce the focus error. If, alternatively, the

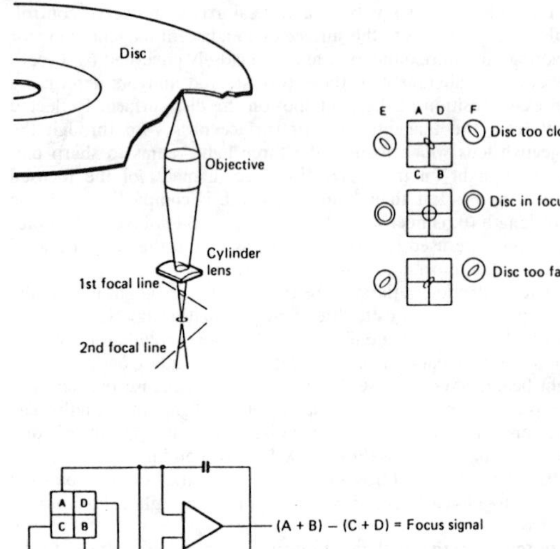

Fig. 18.3 *Focus tracking of the objective lens*

focal point falls beyond the disc surface, the narrow ellipse-image falls across diodes A and B whose current increases at the expense of that in C and D, whereupon the objective lens is driven by the servo amplifier to restore correct focus, signalled by exact balance in the quadrant photodiode matrix.

Although the maximum vertical movement of the objective lens is limited to about 150 microns, its response time is fast enough to cope with the changes in effective disc height which vary mainly at disc-rotation rate of between 25 Hz and 9 Hz.

TRACKING SERVO

The two side-beams generated by the grating in Fig. 18.2 are used for guiding the objective lens along the pit-spiral. To achieve this the entire slide (carrying the objective lens and radial and tangential mirrors) must be slowly moved from near the centre of the disc to the edge. The slide is motor driven, but its inertia (and that of the motor and drive system) is too great to enable it to follow the possible sideways 'track-wobble' which may typically be 100 microns – the light spot must remain centred on the disc-track to within 0.1 micron. The resolution of the tracking servo, then, must be better than 1 part in 1000.

To obtain this degree of accuracy the radial mirror in Fig. 18.2 is used to steer the light beam on the disc surface. It is fitted with permanent magnets and a coil in which the strength and direction of the current determine the mirror's angle. The coil is part of a closed-loop servo whose feedback signals are derived as follows:

The two side-beams (tracking beams) generated at the grating early in the outgoing light path are displaced on either side of the main (scanning) beam by half the track width at the disc surface, so that they straddle the edges of the pit-row. Their reflections from the disc surface are conveyed to separate pick-up photodiodes (E and F, Fig. 18.3) sitting at either side of the main diode quadrant already described. The amount of reflected light received by each of these diodes depends on the tracking beams' view of the pit-row. If the triple-beam should wander to the left, the left-hand beam will see flat disc-surface and a great deal of light will be reflected back into the 'left-hand' photodiode as a result; simultaneously the right-hand tracking beam will be continuously viewing pits whose reflectance is lower, causing the 'right-hand' photodiode surface to go dark. The converse is also true. By amplifying and inverting the diode currents for passage through the radial-mirror coil a feedback loop is set up whereby the main beam is kept centred on the pit track by continual maintenance of a balance in the light falling on the tracking photodiodes, hence a balance in the pit/disc views taken by the equi-spaced tracking light spots. The concept has much in common with the ATF track-following systems described for videotape in Chapters 12 and 14.

The radial mirror assembly is very small and light, enabling it to respond quickly to tracking errors. Its range of movement is limited, however, and it needs to be kept in the centre of its operational range as the slide assembly gradually tracks outwards from the disc centre. The current in the radial mirror coil is monitored in a long time-constant circuit which only produces an output when a *sustained* deflection is taking place. This output controls the tracking motor which drives the slide assembly, and the overall action is to keep the *average* voltage across the mirror coil at zero.

SPEED-CORRECTION SERVOS

For CAV discs the required motor speed is exactly 1500 r.p.m., as with a video head drum. For CLV discs the speed is variable, falling from an initial 1500 r.p.m. to around one-third that speed at programme end. In both cases the speed of the disc-drive motor must be closely and accurately controlled. Unlike a videocassette recorder the disc system is a replay-only one, so speed control need consist only of ensuring that off-disc line sync pulses come at intervals of 64 μs precisely. This is easily arranged in a servo identical in principle to those used for control of a videorecorder's head drum during replay mode, employing speed and phase loops. Here the reference signal will be a stable crystal whose divided-to-*f* h output is phase-compared to off-disc line syncs to produce an error output drive to the disc motor.

Such a motor-servo system will ensure correct replay timing in the long-term, but is unable to handle timing errors having a frequency higher than the 25 Hz disc rotation rate. For the correction of short-term speed errors the tangential mirror of Fig. 18.2 is used. If it deflects the beam in the same direction as the disc is travelling it effectively *slows* the readout rate, reducing the frequency of off-disc signals; and if it deflects the beam *against* the disc rotation direction the effective scanning rate is *increased*, increasing the frequency of off-disc signals. By this means the timing of off-tape signals can be, in effect, bunched-up or stretched-out, an essential requirement for maintenance of correct phase (hence hue) in a colour TV system, where acceptable colour is only possible if the timing error is held below 8 ns.

For a sufficiently accurate readout of off-disc frequency a special burst signal is recorded on the disc during cutting. It consists of a 3.75 MHz (240 × fh) sinewave, placed in the period of the line sync pulse. During replay it is gated out of the video signal and compared with a crystal-generated 3.75 MHz signal in a phase detector, whose error output drives the tangential mirror to compensate. The result is that off-disc subcarrier and burst become locked to a multiple of the local reference frequency with sufficient stability to ensure complete freedom from line jitter and hence perfect colour rendering.

A block diagram of the servo systems of a Laserdisc player is given in Fig. 18.4.

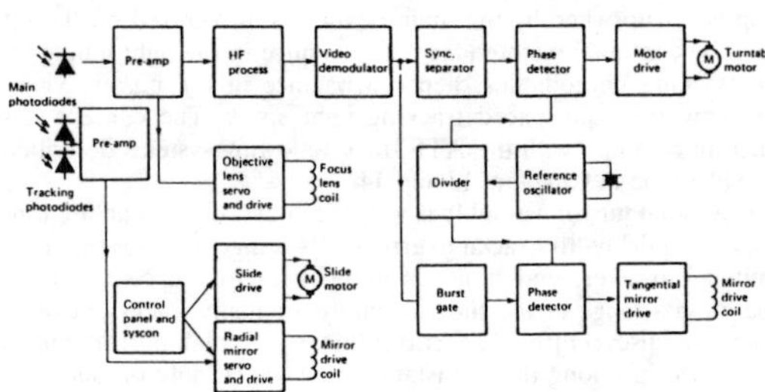

Fig. 18.4 *Block diagram of servo systems for a Laservision player*

SYSCON, FIELD- AND CHAPTER-INDEXING

Laservision players, like videorecorders, have a comprehensive syscon section governed by a microprocessor containing RAM and ROM. As in tape machines it governs motor running, interpretation of user commands, safety functions, go-to, search and other trick modes. There are, however, several differences between videorecorder and Laserdisc syscons; the most fundamental being that the disc-syscon receives commands and feedback from the disc programme itself. These are in the form of digital codes, very similar to Teletext signals, inserted in some of the TV lines during the field blanking interval. The lines used are 17, 18, 280 and 281, and their signals (extracted from the replay signal circuits and decoded) have the following functions:

1 Lead in: the first 1000 or so tracks contain code 88FFFF to send the slide at 9 × speed to the programme start point
2 Lead-out: the last 600 or more tracks contain code 80EEEE to return the slide to the beginning at 75 × speed; during this time the signal circuits are muted.

   The codes used during the programme itself depend on disc type. For CAV discs:

3 Picture code: a unique number for each individual picture in a programme, running from 1 upwards; about 45 000 individually-addressable pictures is the capacity of a CAV disc. The picture number can be displayed in one corner of the TV screen if required, and memorised for subsequent quick access
4 Chapter code: a chapter number which identifies each segment of a programme; used for chapter search functions. Again the

chapter number can be displayed on the TV screen at will. For CLV discs the range of functions is more limited, and the control data here is:

3 Code 87FFFF, corresponding to 'normal play' in which the special operation modes described above are disabled; and
4 Time code: a running count similar to the tape counter in a videorecorder. It provides a readout of elapsed disc time in minutes and seconds and can be displayed on the screen at will; and used with a go-to function, whereby the required time point is programmed by the user into RAM in the control microprocessor for automatic finding.

LASERDISC SIGNAL PROCESSING

The CVBS signal, in standard PAL form, is frequency modulated onto a carrier signal (see Fig. 18.5(a)), such that peak white corresponds to 7.9 MHz, black level to 7.1 MHz and sync tip to 6.76 MHz. Very little bandwidth-limiting is applied to the signal, so that its lower sideband extends down to below 2 MHz, and a replay response approaching 5 MHz is possible; the major area in the sideband for chroma signals is centred on about 2.5 MHz. Audio left and right signals are f.m.-modulated onto carriers at 683 kHz and 1066 kHz respectively, each with a maximum deviation of ±100 kHz. The amplitude of the sound carriers is about 25 dB down on that of the vision carrier.

In the record system the signals may be represented as in Fig. 18.5(b), where waveform 1 corresponds to the frequency-modulated vision carrier based on 7.1 MHz, and waveform 2 the sound carrier. Adding the two renders waveform 3, which is now clipped or amplitude limited at fixed points equidistant from the zero line. The result is a PWM (Pulse Width Modulated) signal whose positive period determines the spacing between disc-pits, and whose negative period determines the length of each pit. This and the pit configuration is depicted in line 4 of Fig. 18.5(b).

During replay, the PWM signal from the disc surface appears as intensity-modulation of the spot of reflected light on the quad-formation pick-up photodiode array of Fig. 18.3. The outputs of all four diodes are summed to form the h.f. signal output, which is processed to recover CVBS vision and separate L and R sound signals.

The complexity and high precision of the servo circuits and optical components, and the great bandwidth of the system considerably simplify the signal circuits compared to those of a videorecorder; in fact the only complication in the disc player is a need for phase-correction of the chroma signal in track-hopping modes with CAV discs. At each outward-hop (cue mode) the phase of the subcarrier jumps forward by 90° per track, and at each inward-hop the phase of the subcarrier jumps backward by 90°. To maintain correct burst phase sequence (Bruch blanking) in the field blanking period, and to thus avoid upsetting the subcarrier regenerator in the monitor TV, these phase errors are corrected by a phase-shifter in the chroma processing section of the player.

A much-simplified block diagram of the signal-handling stages is given in Fig. 18.6. The carrier signal is preamplified and a.g.c.-controlled, then split off in several directions. One path feeds the servo circuits (see Fig. 18.4) and a second the sound circuits. Each sound carrier frequency is selected by a bandpass filter 100 kHz

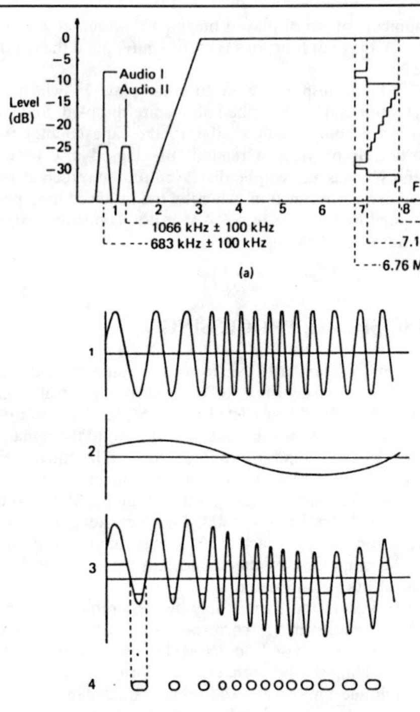

Fig. 18.5 *Laservision signal transfer. The frequency spectrum at (a), and the pit-coding method at (b). Derivation of the waveforms at (b) are explained in the text*

wide then amplified, limited and f.m.-demodulated to baseband after which de-emphasis takes place.

The vision signal process starts with an h.f. compensation stage, which is mainly concerned with equalising the h.f. signal throughout the playing time of a CAV disc, whose inner tracks are more densely packed with pits than the outer ones, leading to an initial shortfall in replay h.f. response. The 'lift' given to high frequencies is governed by the mean level of colour burst gated out of the demodulated CVBS signal. This process is called Motional Transfer Function (MTF).

Next comes a limiter to prepare the f.m. signal for demodulation. In fact there are two demodulators; the secondary one is fed by a 64 μs delay line so that it is working on a '1-line old' signal. Incoming f.m. carrier level is monitored by a drop-out detector which, when dropout is detected, throws the switch to select a good signal from the previous TV line, in just the same way as was described for videorecorders in Chapter 13. Because a conventional glass delay line does not have sufficient bandwidth to handle the full spectrum of f.m. signal there is a risk of spurious colour effects during the patch-job, and since no-colour is more acceptable than

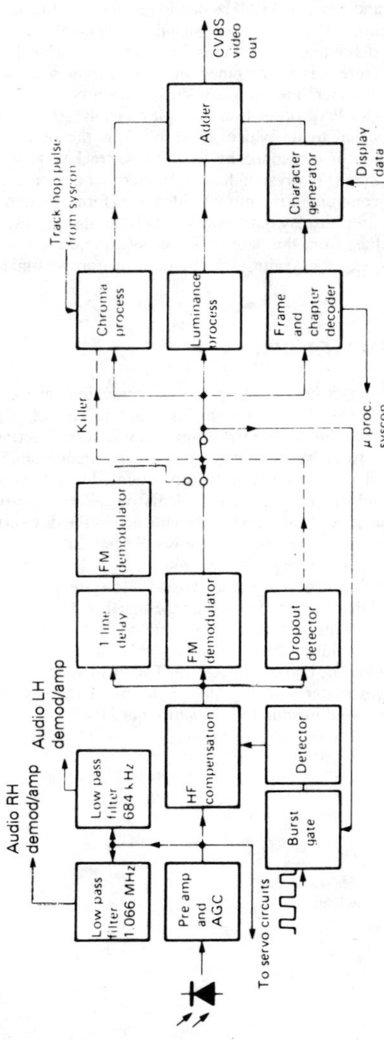

Fig. 18.6 *Outline of Laservision signal processing*

wrong-colour, a fast-acting colour killer is switched into the chroma channel for the duration of the dropout.

At the demodulator output the video signal splits three ways: to the luminance amplifier/process block; to the frame/chapter code detector (a simplified version of the text decoder described in Chapter 8); and via a 4.43 MHz bandpass filter to the chroma processing stage. The luminance signal is edge-enhanced and passed via a delay line (for chroma registration purposes) to an adder block. Here it is re-combined with the chrominance signal, which has now undergone the phase-correction process necessary to restore proper PAL order to trick-replay signals.

The third signal to the video adder block is the output of a character generator controlled by the off-disc track-code signals; this inserts the digits (corresponding to the picture number, chapter code or time-counter) in the output video waveform. Its output is enabled by a user 'display data' command. Data also passes, via a parallel data bus, from the decoder to the syscon microprocessor, conveying the essential control information for transport management.

AUDIO COMPACT DISC

The audio Compact Disc (CD) system has much in common with the Laservision system outlined in this chapter. The CD disc is 12 cm in diameter, and uses a similar pit-track system. It is tracked centre-to-edge from below, but for CD a very small aluminium-gallium-arsenide (AlGaAs) laser is used, mounted with the objective lens and all other optical components on a servo-controlled arm; the whole is gradually tracked radially across the disc surface. A simpler method of tracking control is used here, depending on the *angle* of the single return beam.

The main difference between laser-read disc systems for sound and vision is in the method of encoding the signal. Audio CD uses a truly *digital* encoding system with an equal-to-16 bit quantisation system. The techniques involved in this type of signal encoding were described at the end of Chapter 16. The PCM system used for audio CD gives better sound quality than any of the f.m. audio carrier systems used in sound-with-picture machines.

19

Control systems

The increasing sophistication of TV and video equipment (reflected in earlier chapters of this book) and its interactive nature has necessitated the development of control systems which are largely automatic in operation. They devolve into three broad groups: user-control of equipment function; equipment-internal management of data and commands; and inter-equipment links, in which the operation of associated units is co-ordinated by 'command' links between them.

The most tangible and familiar of these is the cordless remote control handset by which much modern consumer entertainment equipment is 'driven'. The serial data link takes the form of an infra-red (IR) transmission, in which the carrier is a beam of light whose wavelength is about 950 nm (frequency 316,000 GHz), which lies just below the visible spectrum. This very high carrier frequency permits the use of advanced modulation systems: the data is invariably transmitted in serial PCM form with the IR carrier turned fully on or off in a closely-defined time sequence. As with all PCM systems, it is the pulse timing and nothing else which defines the command, and the use of check-codes and filters – electrical and optical – gives great immunity to interference and misinterpretation of commands.

Internal data management has already been touched upon in the syscon arrangements described in Chapter 15. Various serial and parallel data bus formats are used within single equipments, their complexity depending on the features offered. Internal data systems are required to interface with RC receiver/decoders, and generally require access to ROM and manipulation of RAM; this is particularly relevant to FS tuning systems (Chapter 3), teletext and viewdata (Chapter 8) and deck control for both videorecorders (Chapter 15) and disc players. For the latter some very sophisticated control systems are used in conjunction with a computer in *interactive video* applications.

Systems are also available to control signal-routing and operating conditions in separate, but inter-linked equipments, and can be implemented by remote handset or even over the telephone. One such system will be described towards the end of this chapter.

IR REMOTE SENDER

As can be seen from the circuit diagram of Fig. 19.1(a) the component count of a modern handset is very low, consisting here of twelve electrical components plus the battery and keyboard. The single IC is designed for minimal current consumption ($<2\ \mu A$) in standby to conserve battery energy. The clock oscillator has no need of high precision or stability, and the cheap ceramic resonator connected between chip pins 11 and 12 provides an adequate frequency reference around 450 kHz. When no button is depressed the oscillator is off. Pin 1 of the chip is low, transistor TB01 off and the transmitting LEDs DB01 and DB02 off.

When a key is pressed a current is detected within the IC and the oscillator starts. To prevent false operation due to key-bounce a

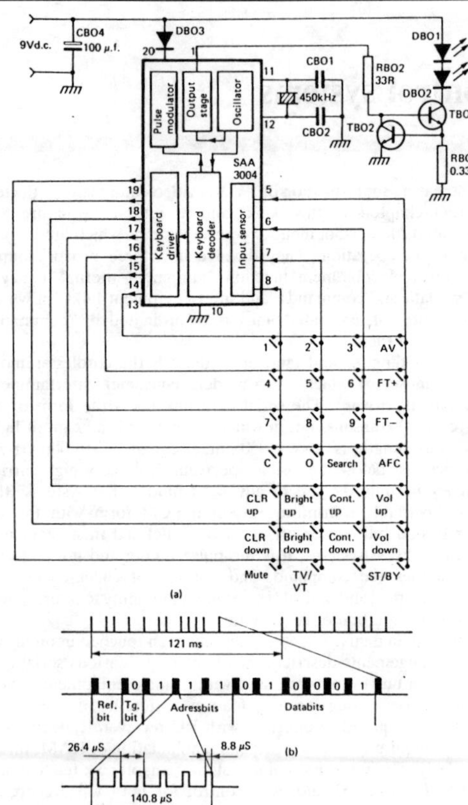

Fig. 19.1 *Infra-red multifunction remote control: transmitter diagram and pulse train analysis*

20 ms period is allowed before the key-detect process starts, when IC output pins 13–19 are strobed via a key-scan system (refer to Fig. 15.4 and associated text). A return pulse enters the chip on one of pins 5–8 and is decoded to identify the function requested. Even if the key is released at this point, the entire command word is generated and transmitted before the circuit returns to standby; if two or more keys are pressed simultaneously the commands are rejected.

Each key retrieves a specific command code from chip-internal ROM, and the required bit-sequence is made up by a processing section within the chip, driven by the clock. Remote control commands are pulse-position coded, each pulse consisting of a burst of 38 kHz carrier – this permits the use of a sharply-tuned filter at the receiver for immunity from noise and interference. The spacing between pulses determines whether the pulse represents 0 or 1: a 7.59 ms period indicates a 1 and a 5.06 ms period a 0. A complete command consists of eleven bits: a reference bit, a toggle bit, three address bits and six bits for the actual command, as shown in Fig. 19.1(b).

The first bit is always 1, and is for use as a time reference in the decoder – its duration is measured, stored and used as a time base for the serial-to-parallel decoding process of the pulse-train which follows. The second (toggle) bit changes state each time a key is pressed, so that the decoder can discriminate between 'new command' and 'end of interruption in transmission' e.g. someone passes between handset and receiver. The need for the toggle bit arises because the data transmission is continuous while any key remains pressed, in order to operate analogue functions like brightness and volume. On the other hand such functions as teletext page selection need sequential number keying, for which the toggle bit resets the decoder.

The next three bits are address bits which identify the sender and receiver/decoder, and act as a turnkey for the decoding of subsequent bits. In simple RC systems like this one a single address is used; here it is address 0, whose code (Fig. 19.1(b)) is 111. Finally comes the command itself in the form of a six-bit code. Six bits offer 64 combinations, not all of which are used. The code 010001 is shown in the diagram, corresponding to 'channel 6' in this system; 001100 is brightness-up; 011110 will switch the set into standby, and so on. If any key is held down continuously, its command is repeated every 121 ms.

The pulse-coded output appears at pin 1 of the IC, and via RB02 switches output transistor TB01 between heavy conduction and cut-off. The sampling resistor RB01 and feedback transistor TB02 maintains peak LED current at around 1.3 A. The internal resistance of the small battery used is too great to supply this order of current, so large reservoir capacitor CB04 is essential. Because of the low duty-cycle of the pulse signal, however, the average battery current is only 14 mA during command transmission. Even at the rate of 1000 commands per day the battery life is many months. DB03 protects the IC from the effects of reversed connection of the battery. The circuit will operate at battery voltage levels between 11 V and 5 V, though imminent exhaustion is signalled by insensitivity.

MULLARD-PHILIPS RC5 SYSTEM

In the description above, mention was made of the address code, which forms the third section of the RC command word. By changing the address codes and programming receiving decoders accordingly, the three bits offer eight possible addresses, which means that eight different pieces of equipment can be operated by the same handset. A more sophisticated application of the same technology is embodied in the SAA3027 encoder/transmitter IC, which can handle up to 2048 separate commands, placed in 32 addressable groups of 64 commands each. The transmitter has a similar start/debounce cycle to that already described. Here the code is transmitted in bi-phase form, whereby a digital 1 is signalled by a rise in potential during one bit period, and a digital 0 by a fall in potential during one bit period. See Fig. 19.2. Each bit period is 1.78 ms, and as long as a key is depressed the data word is transmitted at intervals of 64 bit periods, 114 ms.

The bit structure for the SAA3027 is shown in Fig. 19.2. The first two bit periods are occupied with debounce and key scanning. The transmission begins with two start bits to set the operating point in

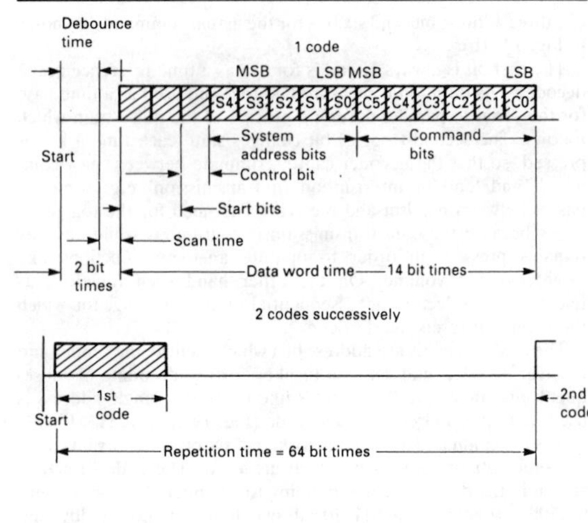

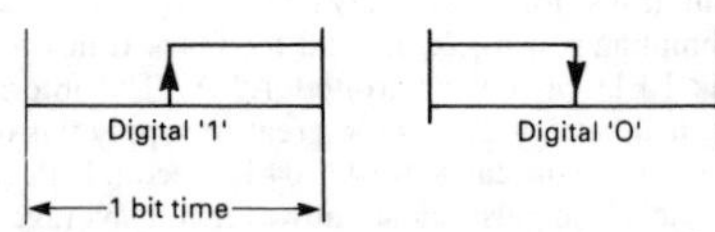

Fig. 19.2 *Data format for the Mullard/Philips RC5 remote control system*

the receiver's a.g.c. circuit, followed by a control bit (similar to the previously-described toggle bit) to indicate a new transmission. There follow five system address bits S0–S4 which can be set by a selector switch on the handset or (for 'dedicated commander' applications) hard-wired in one of the 32 possible configurations. The command is conveyed by the next five bits C0–C5.

Because of the large number of possible slaves for the RC5 system, and to ensure standardisation between different manufacturers' equipment using it, the address codes have been standardised by the IC maker as shown in Table 19.1. The command codes have also been standardised so that the same (symbol marked) buttons on the handset are relevant to all equipment addressed. Thus 'play' command code 110101 will be recognised by video-recorder, disc player, audio cassette player etc. once correctly addressed, as will 'volume up' (010000) 'go to standby' 001100 etc., the latter two commands also being relevant to a TV set.

IR RECEIVER AND DECODER

The infra-red RC signals are detected by a photodiode whose standing current is modulated by the incoming light pulses. A sharply-tuned LC filter immediately follows the diode to reject

Table 19.1 *System addresses and address codes for domestic electronic equipment – RC5 concept. The spare addresses (1, 6, etc.) are either reserved for future standardisation or free for experimental/OEM use*

	System address	System code S4	S3	S2	S1	S0
TV receiver	0	0	0	0	0	0
Teletext	2	0	0	0	1	0
Viewdata	3	0	0	0	1	1
Video disc	4	0	0	1	0	0
Video recorder	5	0	0	1	0	1
Video camera	9	0	1	0	0	1
Audio pre-amp	16	1	0	0	0	0
Radio tuner	17	1	0	0	0	1
Audio recorder	18	1	0	0	1	0
Audio compact disc	20	1	0	1	0	0
Electric lighting	29	1	1	1	0	1

noise and out-of-band (38 kHz) components. Next comes a preamplifier whose main characteristic is its very wide a.g.c. range of about 140 dB, required to cope with the large variation of IR signal level which may be encountered.

In simple receivers the coded message is simply converted into parallel data and decoded to give a series of output lines, each of which change state when the corresponding button of the remote handset is pressed. Such outputs are used for channel selection via latching ICs which switch in pre-set tuning potentiometers; for off- or standby-switching via a solenoid on the mains switch or a 'pull-down' line to the PSU; and for control of such analogue functions as brightness, colour and volume, where the appropriate control line feeds an interface IC whose PWM output is varied in respect of duty-cycle for as long as the command is received, and held constant thereafter. Integration of this PWM pulse train in an

RC circuit renders a d.c. control voltage for application to the voltage-controlled attenuators (VCAs) within the signal-processing chips described in earlier chapters, e.g. colour decoder TDA3562A (Chapter 7).

MICROPROCESSOR CONTROL

While the simple decode-and-command system outlined above is adequate for videorecorders, disc players, audio equipment and *basic* TV sets, it offers little versatility or flexibility. Particularly for full-function TV sets where a sophisticated data-decoder (text/Prestel) is fitted, and where self-seek tuning, signal routing, function switching (i.e. PAL/SECAM/NTSC and CCIR system B, G, I etc.) and perhaps control of peripherals are required, a much more advanced control system is needed. By using a microprocessor in conjunction with a memory system a most comprehensive control system can be built up, represented by the block diagram of Fig. 19.3. The central processor is a microcomputer containing 4 K of ROM and 128 bytes of RAM. It has an output port 0, a bi-directional port 1 (eight wires each), a four-wire port 2, an interrupt input, a clock output and a power-monitoring input. Its main functions are (a) decoding of the remote control commands; (b) scanning the local keypad and decoding any requested function; (c) generating data for the 2 × 7-segment numeral display and status-indication LEDs; (d) communicating and controlling the FS tuning; (e) communicating via a serial bus with other devices, i.e. text decoder, tuning memory, signal-routing switches etc. The RC signal is applied to the interrupt (INT) input.

The system memory is a LOCMOS chip with 1024 bit (128 × 8) RAM capacity, and is used to store essential data. This memory has only eight pins, and since its address (several such memories can be used with the microprocessor) is hard-wired to 0, has only four essential connections – ground, operating voltage VDD (1.2 V),

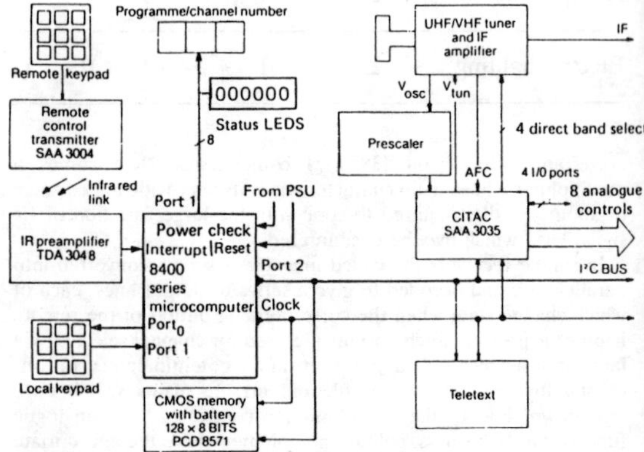

Fig. 19.3 *Computer controlled television using Mullard/Philips LSI devices*

lock input, and serial data in/out. The following information can be stored in the memory:

Programme channel numbers	29 × 8 bit = 232 bit
Frequency offset for each channel	29 × 8 bit = 232 bit
Favourite Teletext pages (progs 1–9)	9 × 24 bit = 216 bit
TV standard/mode (2 bit)	29 × 2 bit = 58 bit
Personal settings for 7 analogue functions	7 × 8 bit = 56 bit
Flywheel sync time constant (1 bit)	29 × 1 bit = 29 bit
Satellite switch (1 bit)	29 × 1 bit = 29 bit
AFC switch (1 bit)	29 × 1 bit = 29 bit
AV switch (1 bit)	29 × 1 bit = 29 bit
NTSC switch (1 bit)	29 × 1 bit = 29 bit
Spare bit (1 bit)	29 × 1 bit = 29 bit

This totals 968 bits, leaving 56 bits of the available 1024 free.

The fact that the microcomputer is programmed in software permits the setmaker to use the I/O ports as he wishes. An interesting application of this is the operation of ports 0 and 1. They provide strobed drive signals to individual segments of an '88' channel indicator readout, but also provide, at 9 ms intervals, a key-scan pulse with which the local keyboard is interrogated. Bidirectional port 1 is by turns a segment drive output and a key-scan input, its role being defined by two outputs from port 0.

CITAC

The CITAC chip (Computer Interface for Tuning and Analogue Control) is interposed between the microcomputer and the controlled sections of the TV set. Tuning, colour processing, video/audio switching, sound control and satellite receiver switching are handled by the CITAC, which has basically just two connections with the microcomputer – the same clock and serial data lines as the memory already described. The CITAC is individually addressed; the data word containing its address consists of 8 bits plus an acknowledgement bit. Next comes an eight-bit word containing a CITAC-internal address to determine which output register is to be loaded, followed by the data for that register. As an example the volume control register is 00100001, and it would be loaded with 00111111 for maximum volume, 00000000 for minimum (zero) volume, and typically 00010100 as a 'reset' level at switch on. The six-bit data for analogue functions gives 64 voltage levels on each, in the range of 0.5 V to 10.5 V: the data for each D–A output is latched in an on-chip register. This avoids the need for RC integrating networks in the analogue control lines.

FSS tuning is carried out by reference to the channel number stored in the C-MOS RAM, and is based on the principles described in Chapter 3. Again the setmaker can programme the system in software. Tuning steps of 50 kHz (dividing an 8 MHz-wide TV channel into 160 segments) are possible, with or without a.f.c. Any user-required offset which may be stored in memory is applied to the appropriate channel. From software it is also possible to adjust the length of the measuring window to suit the prescaler in use; the tuning characteristic to suit the type of varicap tuner in use; the speed of self-seek tuning; and the a.f.c. characteristics.

THE I²C BUS

The simplicity of interfacing between the computer, memory and CITAC chips described above is due to the use of a Philips-designed internal data-exchange system called *Inter-IC (I²C) bus*. Its other significant destination (see Fig. 19.3) is the teletext decoder, which again is individually addressed and instructed by the microcomputer when text (or Prestel) mode is selected. Unlike a true computer-system, the control lines in a TV set are quiet for most of the time, so that an eight-wire parallel bus system would hardly be justified in terms of speed; it would also add greatly to the number of pins required on each IC (command and peripheral). The board area required for connections and chips, and the wire/plug/socket count would all increase, as would the cost, complexity and the risk of failure.

The I²C bus is a simple two-wire system, on which the data is sent in serial form. One line (data) is called *SDA*, and the other, carrying clock pulses for synchronisation, is called *SCL*. When the bus is not carrying information both lines are held at logic 1 by pull-up resistors to the +ve supply line. All devices connected to the I²C bus must have an open-drain or open-collector to be able to use the wired-and function.

Although the TV control system described above has only one master in the control microcomputer, the I²C bus is arranged to be bi-directional and to permit the use of more than one master. The pulse generator is called the master, the sending unit is called the transmitter and the receiving unit the slave. The addressing procedure on the I²C bus is such that the first byte of data sent determines which slave has been selected by the master. The most significant seven bits of this byte hold the slave address, and the least significant bit indicates whether the data will be written to or read from the slave. If two masters attempt to use the bus simultaneously, an arbitration process is initiated, in which the master addressing the slave with lower address will predominate; when that transaction is complete, the second master is permitted use of the bus.

For each clock pulse on SCL there is a corresponding data pulse on SDA. The level must be stable on SDA when there is '1' logic level on SCL, so that data on SDA may only be changed while SCL is at 0. The most significant bit is always sent first, and if SDA changes when SCL is at 1, either a start or stop condition is indicated, see Fig. 19.4(a). An example of I²C bus addressing and data from the microcomputer is given in Figs 19.4(b), (c) and (d). In Fig. 19.4(b) message start is signified by a drop to zero of SDA during an SCL 'high'. Now comes the seven-bit CITAC address code 1100000 followed by a 0 to indicate that 'write into CITAC' is required. This is now acknowledged by the CITAC, inviting further data. It comes in the form of a register address 00100010 which is the store for brightness information, Fig. 19.4(c), and its successful receipt is acknowledged on the next clock pulse after the 8-bit word. Finally the required brightness information (set by the user) is loaded into the selected register, overwriting the information already held. Here (Fig. 19.4(d)) the command is 'full brightness' corresponding to 00111111. It is loaded on the eight clock pulses of the word and acknowledged on the ninth. The stop (end of message) indication is given by SDA rising during SCL 'high'. The new information in the brightness control data register raises the d.c. control voltage to the luminance clamp section of the colour decoder chip.

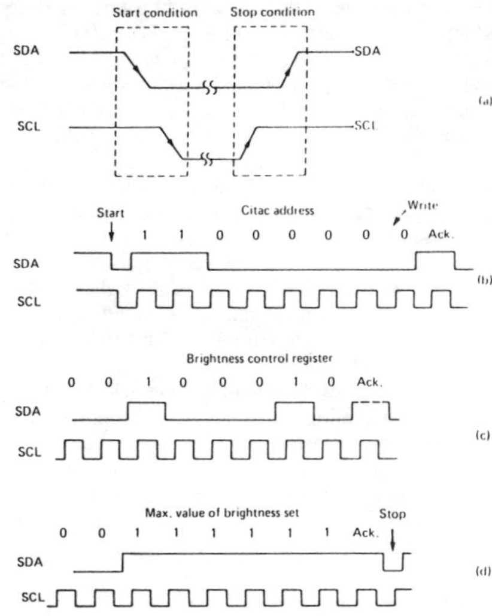

Fig. 19.4 *I²C bus data format, addressing and command*

The 'acknowledge' procedure does not involve the direct transmission of a pulse from slave to master; the ninth bit is passed out onto the bus by the master as a high (1) but held low (0) by the slave during the appropriate clock pulse if the preceding bits have been received. If the acknowledge bit is allowed to remain high, the master is thus informed that the data has not been accepted . . . or that no slave occupies the address given. All 'TV-internal' peripherals for use with the I²C bus have this acknowledge facility; in a Teletext/Prestel decoder it is provided by an interface chip whose other (decoded) outputs are distributed to the LSI chips for VIP, TROM and TAC – see Chapter 8.

SCART SYSTEM AND D²B BUS

Details of the SCART plug/socket connector system are given in Chapter 21. There are two controls systems associated with it; the simplest consists of a source switching line at pin 8. By raising a high (+12 V) on this line a source-peripheral (tape- or disc-player, satellite converter, computer etc.) can automatically switch the vision and sound circuits of the TV receiver/monitor to baseband operation in order to transfer signals at CVBS or RGB (plus sound) via the appropriate SCART signal-pins. The second control system – on SCART pins 10 and 12 – is more comprehensive, and has much in common with the I²C bus already described, though the serial data flow is slower, and includes a security system to overcome the effects of possible data corruption. This control system is called D²B (Domestic Data Bus), and can be interfaced with I²C (and associated cordless remote control systems) by special transcoding chips.

The two D^2B data lines take the form of a floating differential pair, in which logic 1 corresponds to a level above 100 mV and logic 0 to a level below 50 mV. The information is transferred at one of three standard speeds, 110, 2400 amd 8300 characters per second, based on clock frequencies of 0.554, 2.217 and 4.436 MHz. The signalling is bi-directional and self-synchronising, with an arbitration system similar to that of I^2C. To satisfy the auto-synchronising requirements each bit is more complex than that for a separate-clock pulse system, and consists of an initial period at logic 1; a following period at logic 0 for synchronisation; a period defining the bit value, i.e. 0 or 1; and a final stop period at logic 1.

The formation of a complete D^2B message is given in Fig. 19.5. First is a start period at logic 0, then a *mode* indication to define which of the three speeds is to be used. A 12-bit code to identify the master is now sent, followed by a parity bit for truth checking. The next 12-bit word addresses the intended slave, which will be a piece of AV equipment, a lighting circuit or perhaps even an oven. Parity and acknowledge bits follow, then a 4-bit control signal to define direction of transfer and type of message. Finally comes the control data itself, an eight-bit word to convey a possible 256 different commands, followed by a 'sign-off' set of continuity, parity and acknowledge bits.

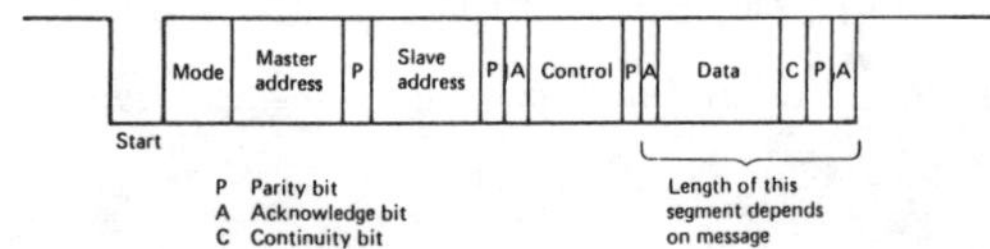

Fig. 19.5 *D^2B (Domestic Data Bus) bit format*

INTERACTIVE VIDEO USING LASERVISION

The use of a separate code to identify each individual chapter and picture on a Laservision disc (Chapter 18) opens the way to a whole new system of controlling replay picture sequencing by an external computer, which can generate picture and chapter addresses for the disc player's syscon. The computer program determines the order and rate-of-change of the images, and is itself under a degree of control by the viewer – hence the term *interactive*. In an interactive learning programme at any level from primary school to university, the student's progress will depend on his own abilities, as reflected by his answer (or multiple-answer choice) to the questions presented to him. In a simulation exercise for car drivers, aircraft pilots or railway signalmen the results of their actions are graphically displayed in a situation representing, if necessary, the actual working environment involved. For computer shopping the disc's picture code number can be passed over a Prestel link to identify and order goods from a Laservision disc 'catalogue'.

The master computer links up with the disc player's syscon via a multi-pin socket on the player, typically to standard RS232 interface specification. The presence of some 'local intelligence' in the disc player's syscon microprocessor is fully used, with feedback passing to the control micro. Extensions of the technique include the possibility of superimposing computer- and disc-sourced pictures, alphanumerics and graphics for advanced learning programmes, computer-aided-design (CAD) and very advanced TV games with detailed and realistic settings.

VIDEORECORDER EDIT CONTROLLERS

In post-production editing of videotaped material the operator has two roles – an aesthetic and a 'mechanical' one. To help with the latter, professional editing studios have long had available automatic editing systems, in which the master copy is assembled in a recorder whose record-pause function is automatically controlled by a microcomputer-based auto-editor. It works from a software program in which the edit-in and edit-out points of the visual and sound material from one or more 'source' playback machines are stored. The reference points for these come from cue codes or true frame codes recorded on longitudinal (sometimes helical) video tape tracks.

These techniques are now available in domestic hardware for 'home-movie' enthusiasts. These less sophisticated (but still microcomputer-controlled) auto-editors require access to the pause control of the assembly recorder (which must have backspace editing) and the pause input jacks of the source machine(s). They operate by counting field pulses from some chosen 'start' reference point in each source tape. A photo of a domestic video-edit controller appears in Fig. 19.6.

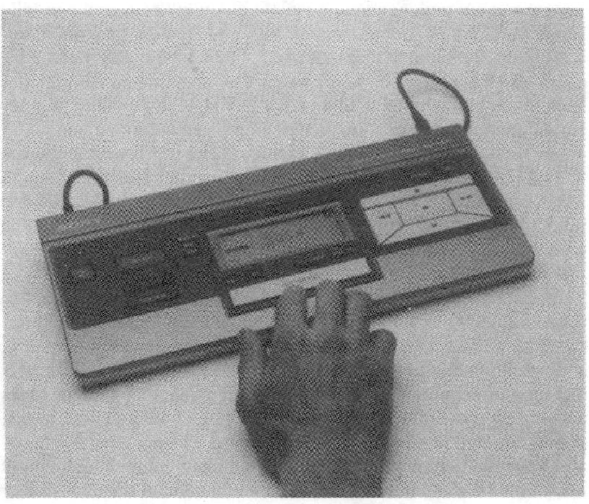

Fig. 19.6 *A domestic edit controller by Sony. It automatically runs a pre-programmed editing sequence*

20

Test equipment and fault diagnosis

Several of the previous chapters in this book contain servicing and setting-up hints relating to the equipment dealt with there. It is the purpose of this chapter to concentrate on servicing and diagnostic matters entirely, since many readers are likely to be concerned with maintenance and repair to a greater or lesser degree.

SAFETY

For all equipment which operates from domestic mains supplies the first concern in servicing should be safety, particularly from electric shock hazard. While a risk of shock from internally-generated voltage is present all the time the covers are removed, the most dangerous shock hazard is that of completing a circuit from mains live to earth. Since TV aerial systems can be expected to be earthed, and many other surfaces and equipment which surround the engineer may be earthed, it is essential that the mains supply to the equipment under service is isolated. A double-wound and fully insulated isolating transformer is required, and to provide a suitably 'stiff' (low impedance) supply a 500 W type is recommended, especially where TV sets using thyristor-controlled power supplies may be serviced. Suitable fuses are a 5 A HRC type in the primary circuit, and a 2.5 A anti-surge type in the secondary circuit.

For field engineers the shock hazard on site is greater than in the workshop. Possible solutions are a large rubber mat on which to work, or the use of a portable isolating transformer: provided service is confined to reasonably modern TV sets a 250 W type suffices for diagnosis work. Test equipment for TV field work *should not be earthed*.

A second aspect of safety is the need for consumer equipment to maintain BS415 and BEAB safety standards, as it did when it left the factory. These standards are mainly concerned with user-safety, and are implemented by the OEM (Original Equipment Manufacturer); the requirement of the service engineer is that he does nothing to compromise the equipment safety. In practical terms, shock, fire and implosion risks are avoided by using OEM-sourced and approved components wherever a safety component (clearly marked by the symbol ⚠ or shading on the circuit diagram and/or parts list) is replaced, and by mounting it in the same way as the original. Particular care is necessary in the event of repairs to – or replacement of – back covers, cabinets, picture tubes and user-controls.

TEST EQUIPMENT

In effect his test equipment forms the eyes and ears of the engineer, and he depends on its accuracy and reliability to interpret what is happening in the circuits he is dealing with; but it is important to understand the limitations of the test-gear and the effect of its use on circuit operation. Brief descriptions of the main classes of test instrument follow:

Multimeter

The traditional analogue multimeter is based on a sensitive large-scale moving-coil meter whose dial is calibrated in ohms, volts and milliamps, the latter two usually on a 3- and 10-full-scale deflection (f.s.d.) basis. Except for resistance readings it is a passive device, drawing energy from the circuit under test, the amount depending on the sensitivity of the moving coil. A basic 50 μA fsd movement offers a sensitivity of 20 kΩ per volt on d.c. ranges, and the best known high quality multimeter (AVO models 8, 9 and derivatives) have this specification, though more sensitive types, up to 100 kΩ/V, are available. The ranges of these types of meter are typically d.c. voltage from 3 V to 3 kV f.s.d.; a.c. voltage ditto, but at lower sensitivity; d.c. current from 50 μA to 10 A f.s.d.; a.c. current from 10 mA to 10 A f.s.d.; and three resistance ranges with which measurement between 1 Ω and 20 MΩ can practically be made. Lesser meters do not offer such wide ranges, especially of current measurement, but in all cases the ranges offered are quite adequate for servicing all types of consumer equipment. Since most general-purpose multimeters are subjected to accidental overload from time to time, a reliable cut-out/protection system is important. The AVO types score particularly here, with their electro-mechanical safety cut-out.

The passive multimeter is the most used general-purpose instrument in service work, but it has some limitations. Its accuracy is generally between ±1% and ±7% of f.s.d. depending on type and circumstances. Its loading effect on the circuit under test depends entirely on the impedance of that circuit. In high-impedance circuits an *active* meter must be used to prevent loading and thus achieve an accurate reading. It contains an amplifier to drive the meter movement, and typically has an input impedance of 10 MΩ on all ranges. This increase in sensitivity permits provision of much wider measurement ranges, which may now extend down to 10 mV a.c. and d.c., and up to 200 MΩ for resistance tests. On low a.c. voltage ranges it is important to bear in mind the effect of mains-hum and time-base-radiation pickup, however, especially when working on high-impedance circuits.

Digital meter

While the active multirange analogue meter overcomes the loading effect of ordinary multimeters, its *intrinsic* accuracy of reading is little better. A digital multimeter has much greater accuracy and higher resolution. It consists basically of a high-impedance precision voltage divider for range selection, an A–D converter and a digital readout system using a neon, LED, liquid-crystal or fluorescent display similar to those on videorecorder front panels. A typical instrument for general service work has a 3½ digit display whose maximum reading is 1.999 and decades thereof.

Digital multimeters (DMMs) come in various sizes and specifications; in all cases their greatest virtue is accuracy, which ranges from ±1% in inexpensive types to ±0.02% (two parts in 10^4) in precision 4½ digit bench instruments. Portable types are pocket size and offer typically 500 hours operation between battery changes due to a low-consumption LCD display. At the other end of the scale, mains-powered instruments have bright light-emitting displays and wide ranges – 29 or 30 ranges may be offered, though resistance ranges seldom go beyond 20 MΩ. Some sophisticated types have auto-ranging, in which it is only necessary to set the function (i.e. voltage, current, resistance) whereupon the level is automatically sensed, and units (mV, V; μA, mA, A; Ω, kΩ, MΩ) are displayed alongside the readout digits, together with an indication of polarity on d.c. ranges. DMMs are not easily damaged by the sorts of overload which would ruin analogue meter movements, but *are* vulnerable to accidentally-applied pulse and e.h.t. voltage.

The main drawback with digital meters is the confusing display (known as *fruit machine effect*) where the measured quantity is not constant, i.e. a voltage line with superimposed mains hum-ripple. The instrument samples the input condition several times per second, and if each 'update' is different, readings are difficult to take. Analogue meters make no such confusion, settling at the mean level of the varying quantity being checked.

Oscilloscope

While the multirange meter is the most used test instrument, the oscilloscope is perhaps the most useful. Basically it provides a continuous plot of voltage against time, so that period, amplitude and waveshape of the applied input can be read off against a calibrated graticule over the screen. A typical bench osilloscope for general service work is pictured in Fig. 20.1.

The most important section of the oscilloscope is its Y amplifier, to which the signal is applied – two are incorporated in dual-trace types, which are essential to modern service practice. For general TV and video work, a bandwidth of 10 MHz is the minimum

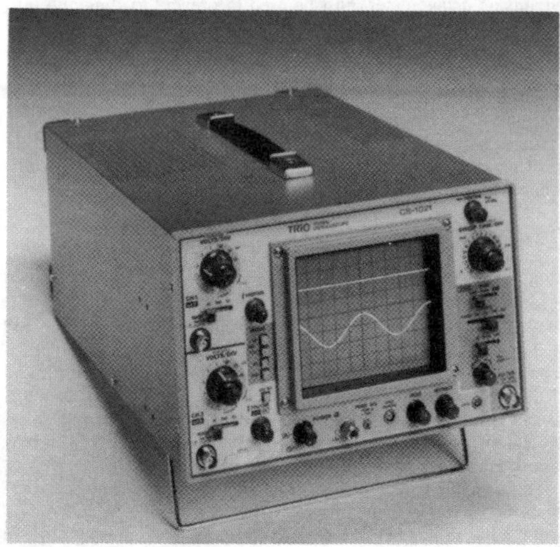

Fig. 20.1 *TV/Video servicing oscilloscope by Trio of Japan. Photograph courtesy House of Instruments, Harlow*

requirement; 20 MHz is better if it can be afforded. The second important factor is Y-sensitivity, invariably measured in millivolts per screen division: the screen is typically divided into 1 cm squares. A minimum sensitivity of 10 mV/div is the requirement, though 5 mV/div is better, and 2 or 1 mV/div better still. In all 'scopes a calibrated step-attenuator is used to set Y-gain, and at its maximum setting (greatest attenuation) a figure of 10 V/div is typical. Normally the Y amplifier is a.c.-coupled via a large internal capacitor at the input socket to keep the trace centred on the screen, but maintain response down to about 10 Hz. For use as an accurate and *fast-acting* d.c. voltmeter this capacitor can be by-passed by setting the input-select switch to 'd.c. coupling'.

A typical Y amplifier has relatively high input capacitance, and to reduce its loading effect on the circuit under test, a 10:1 attenuating test-probe is generally used. This gives an effective load of 10 MΩ and 12 pf, but reduces the oscilloscope's Y-sensitivity by a factor of ten. The test probe's compensation trimmer must be set up on a squarewave input (often available at the 'scope's front panel) for 'square corners' – only then will readings at high frequencies be accurate.

The timebase section of the oscilloscope sweeps the light-spot over the tube face from left to right at constant speed, in identical fashion to that of a TV line timebase. Its sweep-speed control is calibrated in terms of time per division, and typically has a range (in conjunction with a vernier control) from 1 s/div to 200 ns/div, often multiplied by a factor of five if required by an 'X-expand' switch. For examination of TV field rate waveforms a typical setting would be 5 ms/div, and for line-rate waveforms 20 μs/div. The output from the sweep generator is passed to the tube's horizontal (electrostatic) deflection system via an X-amplifier. Most oscilloscopes have facilities for application of an external signal to it, for use in *X–Y* applications.

The sweep generator must be triggered by some Y-signal-associated pulse to display a locked waveform, and trigger circuits are built into all servicing oscilloscopes. They can be driven via a separate front panel socket (EXT TRIG) or from either Y-amplifier. Switches permit selection of positive- or negative-flank triggering; trigger level; and a built-in sync separator to permit locking at line or field rate from a composite video waveform. For TV and video work external triggering is recommended wherever it is possible. Some trigger circuits incorporate a variable delay (monostable type) in their path, useful for analysis of complex or transient waveforms.

The cathode ray tube is the heart of the oscilloscope, and the larger its screen the better. For best legibility a PDA (Post Deflection Acceleration) type operating at high EHT voltage (up to 15 kV) should be chosen; it gives improved performance in 'strobe' (short beam duty-cycle) applications.

Dual-trace 'scopes have only one electron beam. At high X-scanning speeds the two Y amplifiers are gated to alternate sweeps, and at low X-scanning speeds a *beam-chopper* circuit switches between the two Y amplifiers to give the effect of two separate traces; in both cases traces 'Y1' and 'Y2' can be independently positioned on the screen by separate shift controls.

Other 'scope terminals may be: sweep output; probe-calibration output; and Z (intensity modulation) input.

Frequency counter

The frequency counter is a digital instrument like the DMM, but is distinguished by its large readout length, typically 7½ or 8 digits. A precision internal reference crystal is used to time the open period of a signal gate – downstream of the gate is a pulse counter, whose accumulated count over (say) 1 second is read-out on the display. With long gate periods considerable accuracy can be achieved, depending only on the accuracy of the internal crystal which may well be 2 ppm (2 in 10^6). The instrument can be easily checked and recalibrated if necessary by using a standard TV locked to a broadcast transmission: three widely different and highly accurate standards are available – field rate 50 Hz, line rate 15.625 kHz, and subcarrier frequency 4.43361875 MHz.

The main use for a frequency counter is in setting up colour-under circuits in video equipment, checking and setting SSG systems in colour cameras, and testing the operation of divider circuits. It is important to bear in mind that the digital frequency meter operates by counting zero-crossings of the waveform under test, so that where spurious components, or more than one frequency is present, erroneous or confusing readings will be obtained. A service-type counter commonly has a frequency range of 10 Hz to 200 MHz, and prescalers are available to extend this range upwards. Sensitivity is of the order of 10 mV r.m.s.

Test-pattern generator

The advance of IC technology has made possible the production of a wide-range of relatively inexpensive pattern generators, ranging from battery-operated pocket types to full-facility bench models. All generate colour bars, grey-scale step wedge and a crosshatch pattern of white on black for check and adjustment of picture-tube convergence. The more elaborate types can generate coloured rasters in red, green and blue for purity checks; circles and edge-castellations for tests of scanning geometry and picture centring; 'multiburst' in monochrome for frequency response and focus evaluation; special patterns for adjustment of colour decoders, etc. There are now available complete composite pattern generators which provide a test-card similar to those used by the broadcasters – one such is featured in some of the off-screen photographs later in this chapter.

Simple generators have an output at a spot frequency in the UHF band – usually around Ch.36. Bench-type instruments will generally have r.f.-modulated outputs over the UHF broadcast bands, and often at VHF and i.f. as well. Also incorporated will be a sound facility in the form of a 1 kHz tone, a baseband (1 V p–p) CVBS video signal, and possibly line and field sync pulse outputs. The composite-test-pattern generators are particularly useful in the service workshop, where their r.f. output can be 'spliced' into the UHF signal distribution system for use simultaneously at all benches.

For colour bars, most generators provide 100% modulation, 100% saturation signals as used by the BBC. Other configurations are possible, however, and their effect on decoder and RGB waveforms should be borne in mind in decoder-RGB service and alignment. They are detailed in Fig. 20.2.

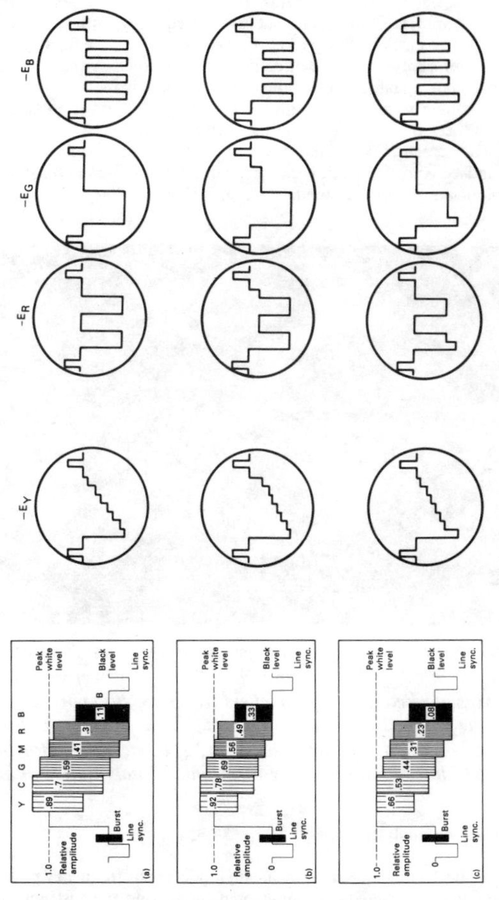

Fig. 20.2 *Three forms of standard colour bar waveforms. (a) Basic signal 100% amplitude, 100% saturation, as rendered by most workshop and portable pattern generators; (b) BBC colour bar signal, 100% amplitude, 95% saturated; (c) EBU/IBA colour bar signal, 75% amplitude, 100% saturated*

Vectorscope

The vectorscope finds its main use in the setting-up and alignment of colour-picture sources, particularly those using analogue devices, i.e. colour TV cameras. The circular screen represents one complete cycle of the colour subcarrier frequency, with the U axis at 'three o'clock' and V axis at '12 o'clock'. At rest the light spot is at screen centre; its angle of deflection is governed by the phase of the colour signal, and its strength of deflection by the amplitude of the colour signal. These instruments have two basic inputs, a reference subcarrier feed and the chroma signal itself.

The screen is calibrated in terms of the vector positions of the standard colour bars. A vectorscope display showing the burst and colour-bar axes for a standard signal is shown in Fig. 20.3.

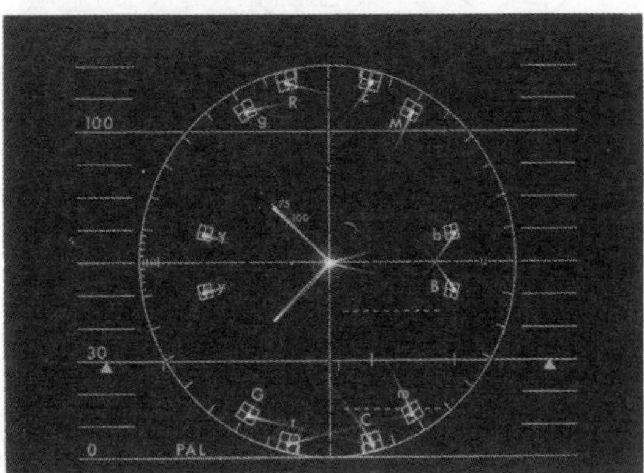

Fig. 20.3 *Off-screen photograph of vectorscope display. The input signal is a standard colour-bar waveform. The boxes marked with capital letters (R, G, B, etc.) correspond to the colour bar vectors on the 'standard' TV line, and the boxes marked with small letters (r, g, b, etc.) those for the 'PAL' line. Photo courtesy Electronic Visuals Ltd, Woking*

Spectrum analyser

The spectrum analyser gives an amplitude versus frequency plot of the signal applied to its input, and by varying the instrument's scanning width, the user can examine energy distribution of a modulated signal, its sidebands and harmonics. Markers are provided to identify frequency and verify bandwidth. Spectrum analysers are useful and revealing instruments for checking filter response, videorecorder f.m. modulator characteristics, camera front-end electronics, and for identifying spurious signals, but in wide-coverage form are expensive and not sufficiently often used to justify economically except in large and specialist workshops. A very useful (and less expensive) version for service and aerial/distribution work is the UHF *panoramic monitor*, which uses a varicap tuner to scan the entire broadcast band, displaying the response on the screen. Adjustment of 'shift' and 'zoom' controls permits close and useful examination of individual broadcast carrier characteristics, as well as identification of spurious and interfering signals.

Logic probe

The logic probe is a relative newcomer to the TV/video service scene. It generally takes the form of a hand-held probe with an internal battery, a clip-lead for the ground connection, and a pointed prod for connection to the circuit under test. The logic indication is given as high or low, generally indicated by red and green LEDs respectively. Some types of probe have an audio output with separate tones for H and L indication. Where the probe is connected to a point carrying a pulse train the relative brightnesses of the H and L LEDs is proportional to the duty-cycle or pulse frequency at the point in question. Some probes have a third (e.g. orange-coloured) LED to indicate the presence of pulse activity – also signalled, where audio output is provided, by a warbling tone.

The logic probe is an inexpensive and convenient way of checking out operation in digital systems, especially in videorecorder syscons where parallel and single-line data is often used. Even for serial data lines and on parallel bus systems it can quickly indicate the presence or absence of pulse activity, and any 'stuck'-high or -low lines. A great deal of diagnosis work in home-computers, allied systems and peripherals can also be carried out with a logic probe.

In choosing a logic probe the important requirements are adequate overload protection; wide operating range, i.e. 5 V–15 V; wide frequency response to at least 10 MHz and ability to detect pulse trains with 'mark' widths down to 50 ns; compatibility with TTL, CMOS and MOS technology in microcomputers, microprocessors and the various forms of memory chip; an input impedance of 100 kΩ or more; and light but robust construction.

Logic analyser

While the logic probe is capable of indicating the status and the presence of information on a data line, it is unable to give an exact picture of the pulse train regarding pulse width, pulse spacing, and timing with respect to other data lines and to the clock signal. A dual-beam oscilloscope can indicate some of these things, but a stationary readable display is impossible with continually-changing data on a serial-transmission line, and is time-consuming even on a 4- or 8-wire bus carrying 'static' data. The need to analyse digital data fully arises surprisingly seldom except during in-depth diagnosis of computer malfunctions; in most domestic entertainment equipment an analogue meter, 'scope and logic probe are adequate for diagnosis to component level, and for diagnosis of the faults in peripheral and 'mechanical' components which are so often at the root of problems.

For full investigation of the operation of digital circuitry a *logic analyser* is required. Logic analysers can operate on serial or parallel data, and consist in essence of a series of latched registers, one for each line of the data bus, and where applicable the memory and/or control buses. At the required point in the program the data is 'frozen' by the latch system, then the register contents are continually read-out into the Y-channel of an oscilloscope for analysis. The many parallel traces are generated by a beam-switching circuit operating synchronously with the 'scope's sweep generator. The data words are displayed in time-coincidence. Only one input to the oscilloscope is required – all other functions are handled by the logic analyser. A photo of an LA time-domain display is given in Fig. 20.4.

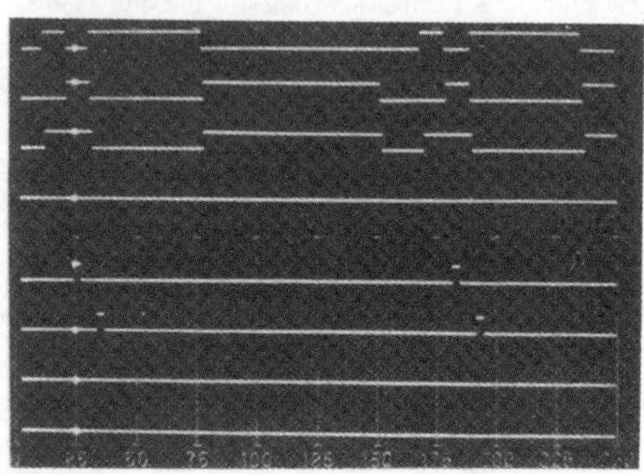

Fig. 20.4 *Logic analyser 'scope display of eight data lines, here applied to a videorecorder syscon*

Picture tube tester/reactivator

The picture tube is the most expensive part of a TV or monitor, and since it depends on thermionic emission, it is subject to wear. An indication of its condition is given by an emission tester, which plugs onto the tube base socket (*discharge e.h.t. first*) and sets up heater and gun electrode supplies to monitor beam current. In the best instruments three separate meters are used to simultaneously show the goodness of R, G and B guns for comparison. Such defects as inter-electrode short-circuits, slow warm-up and loss of vacuum are also indicated at this stage.

If low emission is indicated a reactivation process is possible. It is carried out by overrunning the tube heater for some seconds, then applying a *positive* voltage to the control grid. The resulting very heavy K–G current strips the oxide deposits off the cathode coating to expose a new emissive surface. This treatment is very effective, and can give a new lease of months or years to the tube's life. A second 'repair' facility is provided to clear inter-electrode leaks due to conductive flakes lodging in the gun: a large capacitor is discharged across the afflicted electrodes, destroying or dispersing the conductive particle.

Signal strength meter

A useful indication of the strength of the received broadcast signal is given by an r.f. signal strength meter, which contains a standard UHF (and/or VHF) tuner, an i.f. amplifier and a meter, which generally monitors the a.g.c. control voltage required to maintain some specific level of detected video signal. Such an instrument cannot discriminate between signal and noise, and gives no indication of reflections unless it incorporates a miniature TV monitor; in the absence of this a sound detector and amplifier is usually incorporated to assist with identification of the broadcast being received. For a noise-free picture a signal level of 1 mV at the TV aerial socket is generally required, though modern TV sets give acceptable results down to below 500 μV provided the signal is reasonably free of noise.

Miscellaneous test gear

Apart from the main items so far described, the video-service jigs, tools and test cassettes covered in Chapter 17, and the variac and external power sources discussed in Chapter 11, there is a range of 'secondary' test equipment which is needed less often, or which is not fundamental to the servicing process.

Having to do with picture tubes are *degauss coils*, with which the set, tube and magnetic shield, as well as external objects, can be demagnetised for correct purity; *a microscope* for checking of beam-landing accuracy in purity evaluation; and a *reference light source*, generally a fluorescent tube with the correct phosphor and ND filters incorporated to give a source of illuminant D at several levels for grey-scale matching. An e.h.t. meter or probe is also useful – an f.s.d. of 30 kV and impedance of >300 MΩ are typical of a practical instrument.

An *insulation tester* is necessary for safety checks to BEAB and BS415 requirements. Be it self-powered or hand-cranked, a high applied voltage (see OEM specifications) and high resistance-reading capability are required.

A *signal injector* is useful for first-line and field checks on signal-dead equipment. It consists of a transistor- or IC-multivibrator whose basic output is in the a.f. range, but whose harmonics extend to very high frequencies. It will often help locate the point of loss of a signal – audio, video, chroma or even pre-detector, but misleading effects can result from breakthrough or radiation.

A component *test-bridge* can check passive components out-of-circuit with great accuracy, but seems to find little use in the average workshop.

PRACTICAL SERVICING

In general the servicing process consists of three distinct steps: (a) diagnosis of fault; (b) repair or replacement of faulty component or assembly; and (c) setting-up, alignment and test. All three apply equally to mechanical, electronic and optical aspects of TV and video equipment. It is important to separate these three aspects of service work as far as possible. While diagnosis by substitution may be necessary where information, expertise, test equipment or (in some circumstances) time is lacking, it is far better to carry out a careful analysis of the symptom and a logical process of reasoning – aided by progressive test readings – to identify the faulty component.

There are several exceptions to the rule, especially where (as is usually the case) the labour time in diagnosis must be held to the absolute minimum. Where the fault is an intermittent one, cross-substitution (e.g. of picture-tube cathode feeds, or of L and R channels in audio systems) is invaluable, especially where – as in the examples given – the fault can be made to give a *positive* indication of its origin when it appears. For complex faults the problem area can be considerably narrowed down by substituting complete sections or PC boards where possible. In cases where components (ICs, tuners, modules etc.) are pluggable and a substitute available, it is expeditious to test in this way. On the other hand, haphazard trial-and-error methods of faultfinding are likely to damage printed circuits and delicate components, multi-legged ICs and wound components, especially where tightly-packed PC boards (many double-sided) are used in miniature and portable equipment. The time spent in this pursuit can often be more profitably used in analysing TV-screen images, voltages and waveforms.

It is good practice to spend the first few minutes (or more) of service attention in a careful and close visual examination of all sections of the equipment – a high proportion of failures are due to 'physical' causes like corrosion; damaged, split or cracked circuit boards; burnt, broken or misplaced components; intermittent joints or contacts; faulty plug/socket connections; and spark- or corona-discharge of one type or another. If no obvious problems can be seen, the next logical step is a check of supply voltages to appropriate sections of the equipment – not only in respect of correct voltage, but (particularly in the case of digital circuits) the degree of ripple and spurious noise riding on them. The presence of input signals, and correct operation and connection of peripheral components should next be checked for. Failure to do this could result, for instance, in a long diagnosis session in a videorecorder servo only to find that the control track head is dirty; the replacement of a TV tuner because the aerial has been blown down; or a prolonged foray into the colour circuits of a TV camera for a no-colour fault when the problem is entirely due to defocusing of the pick-up tubes' scanning spot. Only when it is proved that there are no physical problems, power lines are present and correct, input signals present and output or load devices connected need fault-diagnosis begin in the signal-, power- or data-handling stages themselves, in the sequence: signal in, operating conditions, signal out. Reference to the OEM's service literature is essential at this stage, not only to establish the layout and operating mode of the circuit and components, but to refer to the d.c. voltages and waveforms quoted for normal operation.

ICs are always direct-coupled internally, so that an incorrect pin voltage should lead to a check of the externally-derived voltages on associated pins (refer to the IC block diagram) before condemnation of the chip itself. Where a clamping or gating action takes place inside an IC, incorrect 'static' voltage levels may well be due to a missing or badly-shaped keying, trigger or gating pulse. In digital and especially counting chips, *all* relevant inputs should be checked in the event of an incorrect or missing output, bearing in mind that apparent loss of an input signal can be due to a stuck-low input gate within the chip itself.

Many circuits, analogue and digital, have feedback loops. While his may appear to complicate the task of fault-finding, it can often ielp, in that under fault conditions the two 'loose ends' of the loop nove (electrically) in opposite directions in an attempt to restore iormality. Thus the loss of an FG feedback signal will usually vastly icrease a videorecorder's capstan speed to aid diagnosis; a low ain UHF tuner in a TV will result in a 'go-to-full-gain' a.g.c.-line iessage to the tuner even with high applied r.f. input level; the iopper transitor in a switch-mode PSU will have a high duty-cycle aveform applied to its base in the event of no output due to its illector lead opening, and so on. Again, analysis of all symptoms, d rational thought, should lead to a speedy diagnosis.

Experience, both of diagnosis and fault patterns in general, and especially of the particular equipment under service, counts for a great deal. Many a problem has been very quickly solved on the basis of 'hunches' and a knowledge of the habits of various classes of components. Large electrolytic capacitors tend to dry-up and reduce capacitance, especially when mounted in hot places; some sorts of transistors are prone to go b–e open-circuit in certain circuit configurations; heavily-loaded drive belts in video decks will slip under heavy loading conditions – the list is very long. An experienced engineer is aware of all these things, and thus often able to short-cut much of the diagnostic procedure.

Some quick checks are easy to understand and follow. A 10 kΩ wire-wound resistor with 200 V across it is intact if it is very hot, and open-circuit if it is cold to the touch. A multirange meter's prods form a handy and instant shorting link with the meter switched to its 10 A range. An analogue test meter, provided its sensitivity is known (e.g. 20 kΩ/V d.c., 1 kΩ/V a.c.), is a useful switchable substitute resistor provided the applied voltage will not overload the movement. The test-voltage on an ohms range will switch on a transistor junction. These are but a tiny selection of time- and trouble-saving techniques.

In support of the approach to fault-diagnosis suggested above, the off-screen photos on the following pages have been chosen not as simple cause-and-cure cases (diagnosis by 'stock-fault' lists is seldom relevant to modern equipment) but as illustrations of logical testing and analysis, and of how much information can be gained by careful study of picture symptoms. The same principles apply to situations (i.e. deck malfunctions, digital logic faults etc.) where the convenience of a 'screen' fault display is not present, necessitating close observation or the use of test instruments at the outset.

SYMPTOM ANALYSES

Fig. 20.5 shows a snow-and-noise bar across the extreme bottom of a videorecorder playback picture from a known-good tape. The effect is due to mistracking, and because it is confined to one section of the picture it is unlikely to be due to a servo fault, or maladjustment of the tracking control. The bottom of the picture corresponds to the top half of the tape ribbon, and is read-out by the head as the tape *leaves* the head wrap. The implication is that

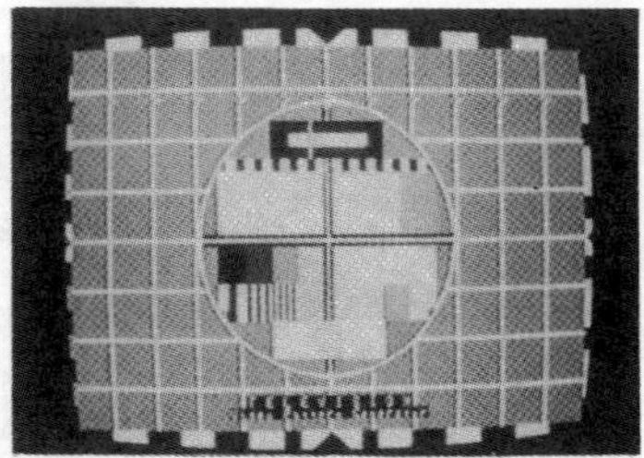

Fig. 20.5 *Mistracking at picture bottom in videorecorder replay*

the tape exit angle from the drum is wrong, and it is likely that the trouble is confined to the *exit guide* or the adjacent section of head rabbet. The need for cleaning and position checking is more likely than a need for height adjustment unless the guide is loose or has been disturbed.

In Fig. 20.6 appears another videorecorder fault, this time in the form of a glass-like bar of picture disturbance on replay of a tape recorded in a faulty machine. In fact the bar is the visible effect of a wrongly-timed *head-switch point* during record. Normally it is hidden at the bottom of the picture by the action of the head-drum servo which should ensure that the changeover point takes place at a point in time just before the field sync pulses. If the offending bar is stationary the first check should be on the setting of the record switch-point preset and the monostable it controls. If the bar drifts up or down, an *unlocked* head servo is indicated; the correct action then is to check for correct *playback* servo lock on a known good recording. If good lock is achieved the likelihood is that off-air field syncs are not reaching the head servo during record. If not, the head servo itself is suspect, and a first check would be for correct output pulses from the drum tachogenerator.

The display of Fig. 20.7 is symptomatic of *white crushing*, and could arise in a camera, TV set, monitor or videorecorder. It can normally only take place in a video signal-amplifier, and the trouble-source is easily traced with an oscilloscope, progressively checking the video waveform until the non-linearity becomes evident. At this point the bias, supply voltage, input level and feedback arrangements should be checked.

It is possible for the symptom to arise from an incorrectly-biased or light-overloaded camera tube; or (where it is present at the output of a demodulator) from overdeviation of an f.m. modulator or signal distortion ('bottom crushing') in an a.m. i.f. amplifier – check bias and a.g.c. voltages.

Another video-stage fault is pictured in Fig. 20.8. The picture is heavily shaded from left to right and badly smeared. An immediate conclusion is that the luminance signal(s) is deeply modulated at line rate, and that it stems from a large ripple on some l.o.p.t.-derived power supply line. The most heavily loaded and worked is that for the 180 V or 200 V h.t. supply for the RGB output stages.

Most sets use flyback-rectification to derive this supply, and since the picture is dark (high supply voltage) at left, which immediately follows flyback, and brightens (low supply voltage) as line scan progresses, the obvious conclusion is that the 180/200 V-line reservoir is low-capacitance due to leakage or drying up.

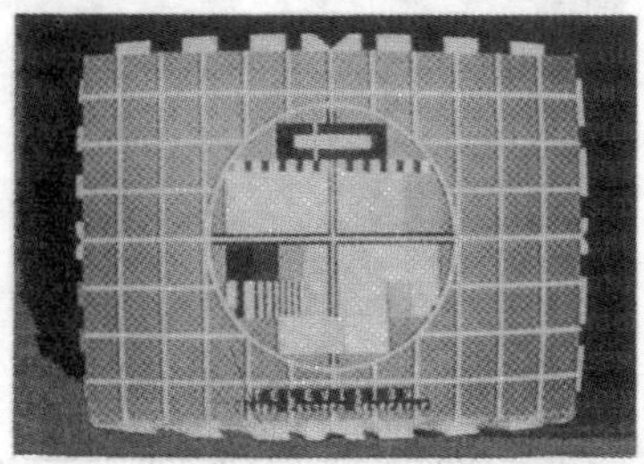

Fig. 20.6 *The horizontal tearing near the top of the circle is due to an incorrect record head-switch point*

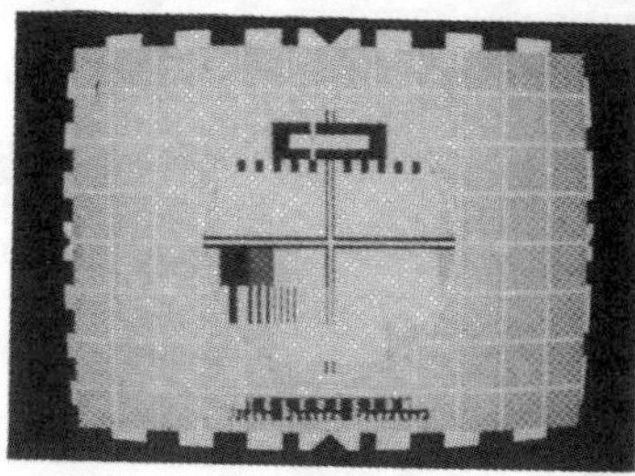

Fig. 20.7 *Severe white crushing, generally due to non-linearity in a video amplifier or demodulator*

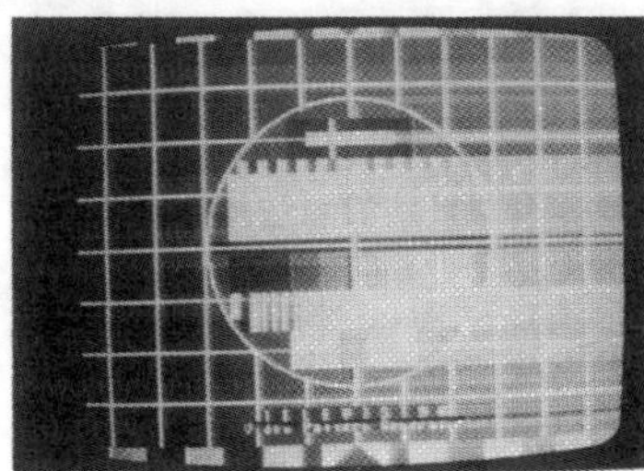

Fig. 20.8 *Smearing and shading, due here to a lack of decoupling on the h.t. supply rail to the video output amplifiers*

The display of Fig. 20.9 is a familiar one, and is due to a poor S/N ratio in the vision signal. First check (preferably with another TV) that aerial signal strength is adequate, and that the r.f. connections to the tuner are correct. If so, the next check should be of the applied a.g.c. voltage to the tuner, sometimes easiest done by applying a known correct (typically +2.5 V d.c.) voltage to the a.g.c. input pin. The persistence of the symptom with correct gain-control voltage incriminates the tuner, whereas restoration of a good picture shows that the r.f. a.g.c. circuit (or its control pot) is in need of attention. Any 'low gain' fault which gives this degree of noise must invariably be in an early stage of the signal-handling circuits; low gain in the final i.f. amplifier stage or in post-demodulator circuits gives a flat 'milky' picture rather than a snowy one.

The multiple images of Fig. 20.10 illustrate a case where the TV screen is a better diagnostic instrument than any piece of test equipment. The problem here is due to signal reflections, and the strength and position of the ghost image with respect to the main one indicates the amplitude and delay of the reflected signal, the latter easily calculated on the basis of 1 μs equals $\frac{1}{52}$ picture width, which can then be expressed if required in terms of signal path length.

While ghost images can arise from reflection of the UHF signal from hills, tall buildings etc., they can be generated *within* the equipment: This photo was taken with the ground connection of the

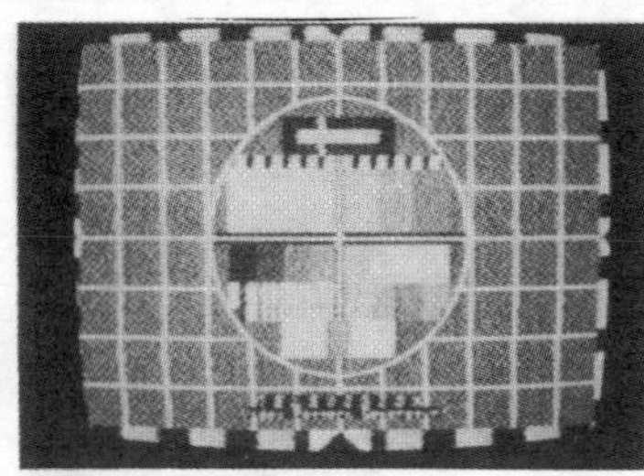

Fig. 20.9 *Severe noise on picture, most often due to inadequate signal level*

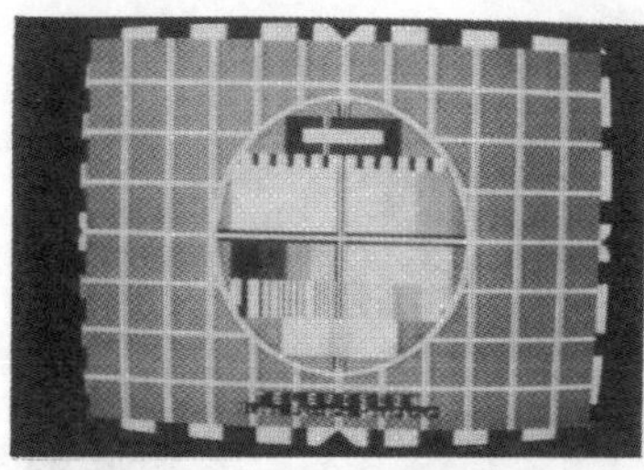

Fig. 20.10 *Ringing. Double- or multiple images are the result of reflections in the signal path – to the aerial, in the downlead or within the set itself*

luminance delay line open to give multiple reflections along the line.

A likely effect of much shorter-term signal reflections appears in Fig. 20.11. Here a page of text shows corruption, in which the incorrect and missing characters result from misinterpretation of data. It can be caused by a faulty text decoder, but this is unlikely where its power line, grounding and video input signal level are correct. Apart from an *eyeheight* check with a 'scope on the data lines, see Chapter 8, little can be done with ordinary test instruments. If the r.f. tuning and vision demodulator 'tank' coil tuning are correct, here is a justifiable case for testing by substitution – starting, perhaps, with a complete text-equipped TV set, because the aerial, distribution system, and downlead or feeder are prime suspects in these cases.

Moving onto the timebase sections of a TV or monitor, a picture display like that of Fig. 20.12 again rewards careful analysis with an almost certain diagnosis. Here the screen is grossly overscanned in the vertical direction, with evidence of bad non-linearity. This indicates a large increase in the power applied to the field scanning coils. Of several possible causes, those of an increase in the intrinsic gain of the field amplifier, or a large rise in the supply rail voltage to the field timebase are very unlikely; in the latter case, other symptoms would probably be present.

Fig. 20.11 *Severe corruption of a teletext page due to a badly damaged data pulse train*

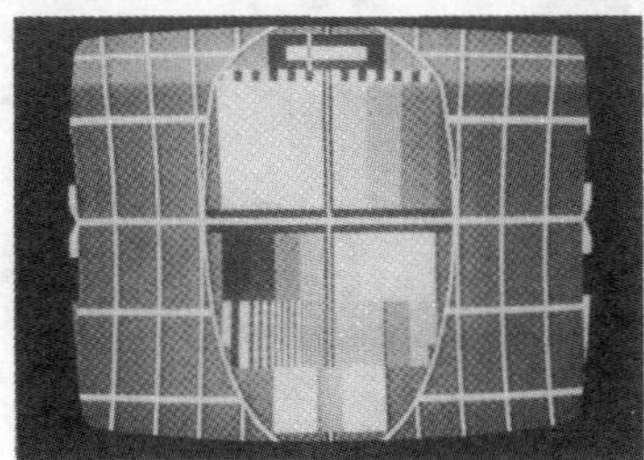

Fig. 20.12 *Vertical overscan and distortion arising from an open feedback loop in the field-scan amplifier*

An increase in generated ramp-height is again unlikely, and could be quickly checked with an oscilloscope. The first check, though, should be made at the main output negative feedback loop which here is open-circuit.

The opposite effect, field collapse, is the subject of Fig. 20.13. Careful study of the resulting single scanning line, however, reveals a slight undulation of the line at the extreme left, and this is the effect of a ringing pulse induced into the field scan coils from the line-scan pair at flyback. This arises from a lack of damping in the field coil circuit, and is indicative of an open *yoke* circuit. The field scan coils themselves are rarely responsible, and investigation is generally confined to the coupling components between coils and output stage.

A single *vertical* white line, where scan and e.h.t. are derived from the same flyback transformer, is likewise indicative of a break in the immediate circuit of the scan coil, typically due to a defective or dry-jointed S-correction capacitor or scan-balance coil.

A line timebase fault is depicted in Fig. 20.14. The basic problem here is a gross timing error between line scan and video signal,

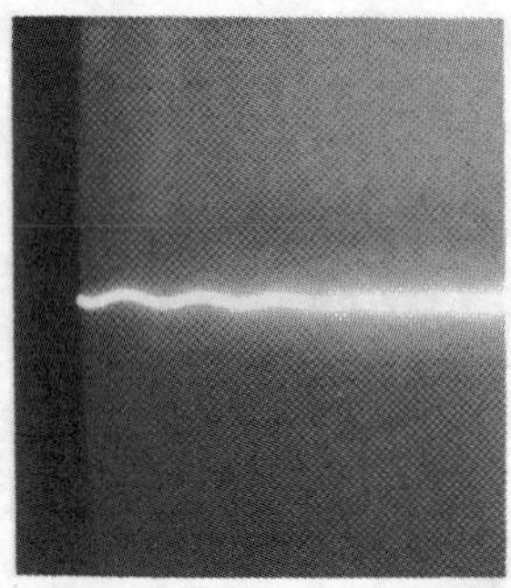

Fig. 20.13 *Close-up of left hand side of screen showing line-flyback excitation of vertical scan yoke*

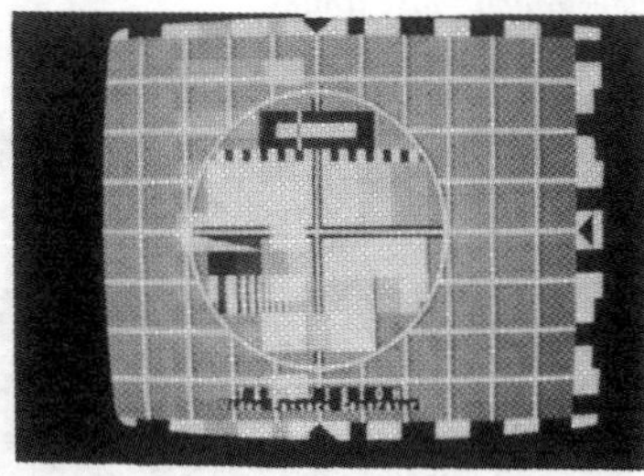

Fig. 20.14 *False line lock effect and resulting lack of flyback blanking*

causing the line blanking period to appear on the screen. Its likely causes are perhaps less obvious without some thought. It is seldom possible for this error to arise in the line sync phase detector itself in a flywheel system; much more probable is that either its reference (incoming line sync) or feedback (line flyback) pulses are suffering an abnormal time delay. A check with a double-beam 'scope will probably eliminate the former, and identify a problem in the pulse-feedback circuit between l.o.p.t. and line sync chip. A change in resistor value or leakage in a capacitor is often responsible.

Faults in PSU systems are common, and while many of them result in complete loss of picture and sound, others give a display symptom which immediately identifies the fault area, and sometimes the actual component. Fig. 20.15 shows one such. The picture has two 'wasp-waists' which shows that the main power line bears a strong 100 Hz ripple. This can only come from a full-wave mains rectifier system, and is almost certainly due to failure of the primary reservoir capacitor in the PSU. The bulging effect will generally move slowly up or down the screen because mains a.c. is not synchronous with TV transmissions.

A *single* wasp-waist, except in very old equipment using half-wave mains rectification (where the reservoir capacitor would again be suspect) is an almost certain indication that *one* of the four

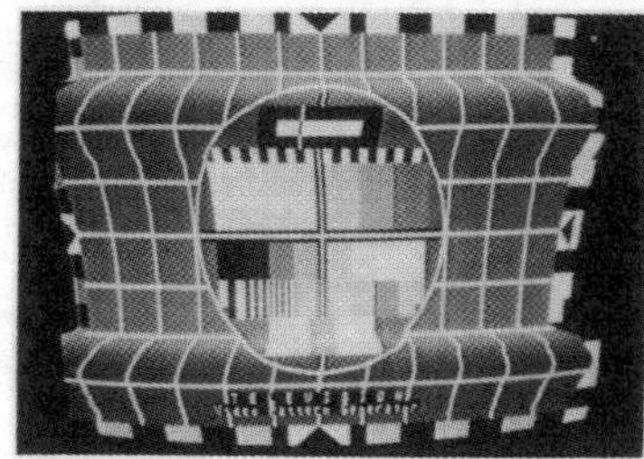

Fig. 20.15 *100 Hz ripple modulation of horizontal scan, indicating a fault in the mains section of the power supply*

diodes in the rectifier bridge is open, resulting in half-wave rectification.

The screen image shown in Fig. 20.16 is an intriguing one, in which the height is normal but a large degree of horizontal overscan is apparently present. In a TV or monitor this symptom would be most unlikely unless some rare l.o.p.t. tuning fault were present: The increase in h.t. supply line voltage otherwise necessary would have involved overload protection or damaged the line output stage before the picture reached these proportions.

In fact the monitor from which the photo was taken was operating normally, but was fed from a faulty TV camera in which the vidicon target is *underscanned* in the horizontal direction. This enigma is simply explained: Only the *centre* portion of the camera faceplate image is scanned in the 52 μs period during which the display screen is *fully* scanned; the centre of the image is thus effectively 'magnified' in a horizontal direction. Complete line scan collapse in the camera would give an 'infinitely wide' image on the monitor screen, with vague horizontal bars across the screen. In both cases the vidicon base-connector should be unplugged during fault investigation to prevent damage to the target of the tube. Symptoms like these are not applicable to CCD pickup devices.

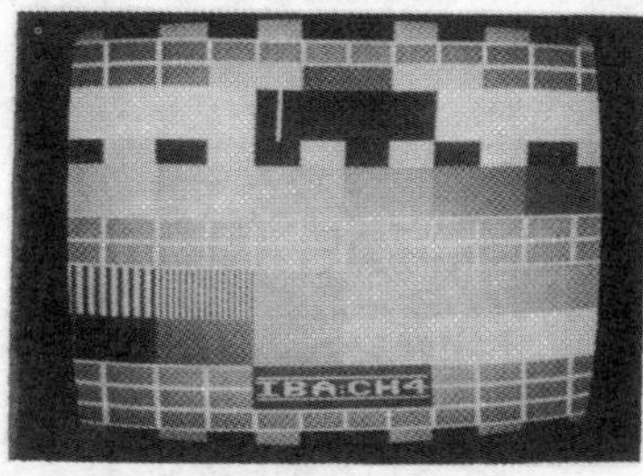

Fig. 20.16 *The effect of gross horizontal overscan, in this case the result of underscanning in a faulty camera viewing the printed card from which the next figure was reproduced*

TEST CARD FEATURES

The final screen-picture, Fig. 20.17, depicts a broadcast test-card. Between them, this and the locally-generated pattern of Figs 20.5, 20.6 etc. (both being electronically generated) represent most classes of general-purpose test chart. The main features of the card shown here are as follows:

1 Crosshatch pattern: checks convergence, best judged without colour in the picture. Colour fringing should be zero at screen centre, minimal at the edges and corners
2 EBU colour bars: This block, one-third of the way down the pattern, contains colours in the order yellow, cyan, green, magenta, red, blue, at 75% amplitude, 100% saturation, as per Fig. 20.2(c).
3 Grey scale steps: 0/20/40/60/80/100% amplitude of luminance signal. The difference in brightness between adjacent rectangles should be approximately constant
4 Multiburst: The frequency gratings correspond (from left to right) to 1.5, 2.5, 3.5, 4.0, 4.5, 5.25 MHz. All six will only be displayed on a high-quality monochrome set. On colour sets the final three will contain cross-colour patterns
5 150 kHz square wave train: These blocks immediately above the colour bars check transient and i.f. video response. There should be no ringing, overshoot, pre-shoot or 'smudging' on them
6 Black/white rectangles: These, above the squarewave train, offer an l.f. response check; poor l.f. response shows as streaking to the right of white-black and black-white transitions. The white needle pulse within the black rectangle is designed to emphasise any ghost images which may appear on the black ground to its right
7 Colour-fit pattern: At top centre of the card appear yellow-red-yellow rectangles as a check of chroma/luminance registration. The redness of the central rectangle should fit snugly between the yellows
8 Border castellations: These define the edges of the pattern, and should be at least half-visible on all four sides. The colours,

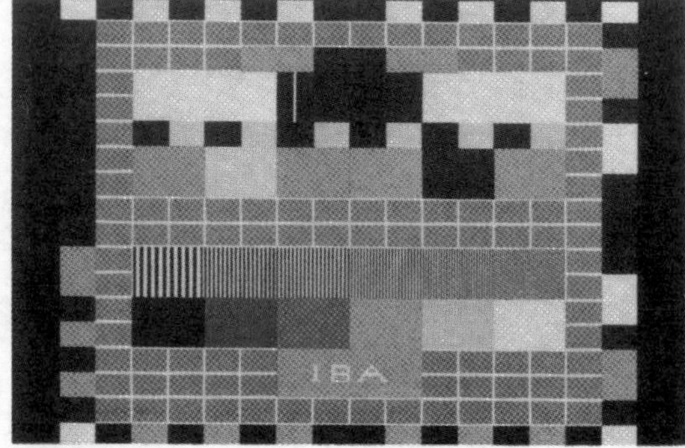

Fig. 20.17 *Broadcast test pattern. It is electronically generated*

positioning and brightnesses of the border castellations are designed to check (a) the sync-separator performance – shortcomings cause picture pulling or cogging along castellation lines; and (b) burst-gate timing, which if incorrect will cause hue errors in horizontal bands aligned with the red or blue (LHS) or yellow (RHS) castellation blocks.

TRACING INTERMITTENT FAULTS

Of all equipment malfunctions, intermittent faults are the most difficult and frustrating to trace and diagnose. Provided that operating conditions are not 'borderline' i.e. weak tacho pulses, low supply-line voltage, PSU starting resistor gone high-resistance etc., they usually have their origins in mechanical or 'thermal' effects. Bad jointing on PCBs or within components, as well as hairline board cracks etc., can usually be traced by flexing, probing and tapping of PC boards – once the fault has been made to appear, use test equipment to *prove* its origin for a definite diagnosis.

Intermittent faults which are temperature-dependent can often be traced to a single component (very often a semiconductor) by the alternate use of gentle heat from a hairdrier and an aerosol freezing spray. The most vulnerable and suspect components for thermal faults are diodes, transistors, ICs and to a lesser extent polystyrene and electrolytic capacitors. 'Mechanical' intermittent problems are most often due to dry-joints (sometimes concealed under an apparently-good solder blob), potentiometers, switches, plug/socket interfaces and board-print faults. The most vulnerable joints are those which carry heavy (e.g. scanning and primary power) currents, and those which support heavy or iron-tagged components like transformers and large electrolytic capacitors.

The main aim in diagnosis of intermittent faults should be to get *positive* indications of the identity of the faulty component or section. Thus a solder-up of suspect board joints or replacement of suspect components followed by a fault-free test period is not as satisfactory as a cross-substitution test of stages, panels or individual components, in which the fault can be reproduced *in isolation*. Whether this takes the form of transferring an intermittent blue picture to an intermittent green one by interchanging B- and G-output transistors, or an indisputable meter reading at some crucial point in the circuit during the presence of the fault, it gives complete confidence in the diagnosis and the repair.

It is important to glean every clue from the equipment user in cases of alleged intermittent faults. Analysis of these can considerably narrow down the field of search. In difficult cases, it is necessary to leave the equipment with diagnostic instruments (ideally redundant and aged test-gear saved for the purpose) hooked semi-permanently on key test-points.

PCB PRACTICALITIES

The second aspect of service after fault diagnosis is repair and component replacement. Ease of repair and access ranges enormously between different make, type and vintage of equipment. Unsoldering of PCB-mounted components, especially multi-legged types, is most easily done with a small hot soldering iron and commercially prepared desoldering wick, which consists of resin-impregnated copper braid to absorb old solder as it is melted. A useful alternative, especially for use with double-sided and plated-through-hole boards is the solder-pump, a spring-loaded vacuum device; the most effective is the type in which it is combined with a mains desoldering iron whose bit is made in the form of a hollow nozzle.

The very tightly-packed double sided PCBs used in cameras, camcorders and portable videorecorders are the most difficult to deal with – see Fig. 6.14. Many of their components are SMD (Surface-Mounting-Device) types, which are soldered direct to the print panel on both sides of the board. These pinhead-size transistors, resistors, links and capacitors are glued to the board surface in manufacture, then soldered to the print in a bath-wave operation. To remove them, one or more small hot soldering irons are required to simultaneously release all connections. For multi-legged SMDs like miniature ICs it is often necessary to either use a hot-air gun for simultaneous release of all pins, or to cut the pins through for subsequent individual removal. It is important to be sure of the diagnosis before changing components on these high-density assemblies, and to closely consult the manufacturer's service information in all cases.

STATIC PRECAUTIONS

Increasingly, C-MOS and similar IC technology is being incorporated in consumer equipment, and careful handling of these devices is required to prevent damage from static electricity charges. The necessary precautions are to ground the soldering iron and (by means of an earthed wristband) the operator; to keep the replacement device in its conductive packing until the moment it is to be fitted; to temporarily ground the circuit into which it is being fitted; and if possible to keep its leadouts strapped together until the fitting/soldering operation is complete.

SERVICE MANUALS AND DOCUMENTATION

Unless one is very familiar with the equipment under service it is foolhardy to attempt diagnosis on any but the simplest equipment without a service manual, preferably that produced by the OEM. Most manufacturers and some specialist and trade magazines produce fault-finding guides and algorithms, lists of common faults, modifications and spares ordering information. All this information should be carefully filed, along with personal notes and findings, by make and model. A list of names and addresses of major manufacturers and importers is given in the next chapter.

21
Reference data

Much reference data has been given in the diagrams, tables, charts and text of preceding chapters. That given here is confined to information which is common to more than one section of the book.

RESISTORS

The colour coding system for resistors includes information on value, tolerance and grade. These characteristics are indicated by three or more coloured rings or dots which are read from the end of the resistor body towards its centre – Fig. 21.1. The first colour indicates the first digit of the value (refer to Table 12.1); the second colour gives the second digit of the value; and the third colour gives the number by which the first two figures should be multiplied to obtain the value of the resistor in ohms. The fourth colour, if present, indicates the manufacturing tolerance: typical tolerance figures encountered are ±1%, ±2%, ±5%, ±10% and ±20%. Where no tolerance is indicated it may be assumed that the tolerance is ±20%.

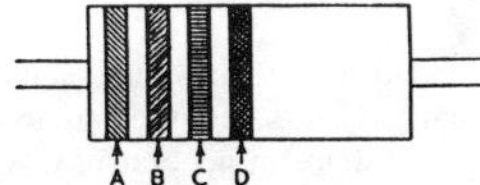

Fig. 21.1 *Ring colour code for resistors*

Table 21.1 *Resistor colour code*

Colour	*1st Figure (A)*	*2nd Figure (B)*	*Multiplier (C)*	*Tolerance (D)*
Black	—	0	1	—
Brown	1	1	10	±1%
Red	2	2	100	±2%
Orange	3	3	1000	—
Yellow	4	4	10 000	—
Green	5	5	100 000	—
Blue	6	6	1 000 000	—
Violet	7	7	10 000 000	—
Grey	8	8	100 000 000	—
White	9	9	1 000 000 000	—
Gold	—	—	0.1	±5%
Silver	—	—	0.01	±10%
No colour	—	—	—	±20%

Grade 1 high-stability resistors are distinguished by a fifth band of salmon pink, or a body of that colour.

Example

A resistor with four colour bands, the end one of yellow, the next violet, followed by orange and gold, would have a value of 47 kΩ with a tolerance of ±5%. Here the body colour would have no significance unless it were salmon pink to indicate a high stability type.

For surface-mounting colour codes, see under 'capacitors' below.

CAPACITORS

Capacitors are most often printed directly with their value and working voltage. Colour coding systems are used, and differ according to the type and shape of the device and the extent of information to be conveyed, though in all cases they use the same basic colour coding (Table 21.1) as for resistors, except for the 0.1 and 0.01 multipliers. Information typically given by colour coding includes value, temperature coefficient, tolerance and voltage rating. Since at least eight different coding systems have existed, and in many cases inspection does not reveal which of them is in use, it is impractical to give guidance here – the manufacturer's service manual for the equipment must be consulted for details of the actual component in use, or the colour-code key.

SMD R and C codes

Not all SMDs are coded with their value, making it essential to keep them in their marked packs until they are used. Those that are coded use one of two systems in general use, which give resistor values in ohms and capacitor values in picofarads. The simplest is the three-symbol code, in which the first two digits give the base figure and the third the multiplier: thus 222 is 2.2 k Ω or 2200 pF; 153 is 15 k Ω or 15,000 pF; and 7R5 is 7.5 Ω. The alternative coding method consists of a letter and multiplier number, see Table 21.2. Here B2 indicates 110 Ω/110 pF, H4 20 kΩ/20 kpF, etc.

Table 21.2

A = 1	M = 3	Y = 8.2	0 = × 1
B = 1.1	N = 3.3	Z = 9.1	1 = × 10
C = 1.2	P = 3.6	a = 2.5	2 = × 100
D = 1.3	Q = 3.9	b = 3.5	3 = × 10^3
E = 1.5	R = 4.3	d = 4	4 = × 10^4
F = 1.6	S = 4.7	e = 4.5	5 = × 10^5
G = 1.8	T = 5.1	f = 5	6 = × 10^6
H = 2	U = 5.6	m = 6	7 = × 10^7
J = 2.2	V = 6.2	n = 7	8 = × 10^8
K = 2.4	W = 6.8	t = 8	9 = ÷ 10
L = 2.7	X = 7.5	y = 9	

FORMULAE

Ohm's law:

Current flow: $I = \frac{E}{R} = \frac{P}{E} = \sqrt{\frac{P}{R}}$

Volt drop: $E = IR = \frac{P}{I} = \sqrt{(PR)}$

Power dissipation: $P = EI = I^2R = \frac{E^2}{R}$

Resistance: $R = \frac{E}{I} = \frac{P}{I^2} = \frac{E^2}{P}$

Where I = current, amps, A; E = voltage, volts, V; P = power, watts, W; R = resistance, ohms, Ω.

Reactance:

Capacitive: $Xc = \frac{1}{2\pi fC}$ ohms

Inductive: $XL = 2\pi fL$ ohms

where C = capacitance, farads, F; L = inductance, henrys, H; R = resistance, ohms, Ω. f = frequency, hertz, Hz.

Series and parallel combinations:

For resistors in series Rtot = R1 + R2 + R3 etc.

For resistors in parallel $Rtot = \cfrac{1}{\frac{1}{R1} + \frac{1}{R2} + \frac{1}{R3} \ldots \text{etc.}}$

For resistors in series $Ctot = \cfrac{1}{\frac{1}{C1} + \frac{1}{C2} + \frac{1}{C3} \ldots \text{etc.}}$

For capacitors in parallel Ctot = C1 + C2 + C3 . . . etc.

Frequency and wavelength:

The velocity c of an electromagnetic wave through a given medium is constant, and in space is equal to that of light:

$c = 3 \times 10^8$ m/s.

$f = \frac{c}{\lambda}$ or: $f(\text{Hz}) = 3 \times 10^8/\lambda$;

$f(\text{kHz}) = 3 \times 10^5/\lambda$;

$f(\text{MHz}) = 300/\lambda$

where f is frequency and λ is wavelength in metres. Table 21.3 gives reference points for frequencies between 1 MHz and 3 GHz.

Table 21.3 *Frequency/wavelength conversion for propagation in air and space*

f(MHz)	1	3	10	30	100	300	1000	3000
λ (m)	300	100	30	10	3	1	0.3	0.1

DECIBEL CONVERSION

Field signal strengths for r.f. transmissions are often given in microvolts per metre (μV/m) of free space. The boundary of the service area of a UHF transmitter is taken to be the 60 dBμV/m contour, corresponding to 1 mV/metre. Table 21.4 converts dBμV/m to voltage.

Table 21.4 *Basic open-circuit field strength conversion*

dB μV/m	*Voltage*	*dB μV/m*	*Voltage*
20	10 μV	70	3.2 mV
30	32 μV	74	5 mV
40	100 μV	80	10 mV
48	250 μV	88	25 mV
54	500 μV	90	32 mV
60	1 mV	94	50 mV
68	2.5 mV	100	100 mV

Because the voltage given is an open-circuit one at an untuned 1 metre rod, several factors must be taken into account in calculating a figure for signal strength at the aerial socket, as follows. Field strength is related to signal strength by the factor λ/π where λ is the wavelength. Average figures are 0.2 (−14 dB) in band IV; 0.15 (−16 dB) at the lower end of Band *V*; and 0.12 (−18 dB) at the top of Band *V*. Next must be added the gain of the aerial, typically 6 dB for a 4-element Yagi type, 10 dB for an 8-element Yagi and 13 dB for an 18-element Yagi. Account must also be taken of the loss in the downlead – 10 metres of 'low-loss' coaxial cable introduces a loss of about 3 dB. Finally, allowance must be made for the fact that a practical feeder is terminated in 75 Ω, rather than open-circuit, and so a further loss of 6 dB is incurred. Table 21.5 gives two examples of widely different situations, in each case calculating the signal strength at the receiver aerial socket.

Table 21.6 gives an accurate dB conversion chart applicable to r.f. levels as well as video and audio baseband signals. Standard levels for signal interchange between equipment are composite

Table 21.5 *Typical calculations for signal strength at a TV receiver. At (a) a strong local signal low in Band IV renders 1 mV from a small simple aerial; at (b) a weak distant signal high in Band V requires a large expensive aerial to secure a barely-adequate 250 μV at the set's aerial socket*

Strong signal, primary service area:		*Weak signal, distant transmitter:*	
Channel	27	Channel	62
Field strength, μV/m	+72 dB	Field strength, μV/m	+57 dB
(Equivalent voltage)	(4 mV)	(Equivalent voltage)	(700 μV)
Aerial gain (8 element Yagi)	+11 dB	Aerial gain – 'fringe' type	+18 dB
Feeder loss	−3 dB	Feeder loss	−3 dB
Conversion loss, Ch. 27	−14 dB	Conversion loss, Ch. 62	−18 dB
Set termination loss	−6 dB	Set termination loss	−6 dB
Signal strength at aerial socket	60 dB	Signal strength at aerial socket	48 dB
Equivalent voltage	1 mV	Equivalent voltage	250 μV
(a)		(b)	

video 1 V p-p in 75 Ω; CVBS 1.235 V p-p in 75 Ω; audio 0 dB = 0.775 V in 600 Ω.

CONNECTOR PINNING

All contemporary videorecorders and many TV sets have baseband video and audio input and output sockets. The standard pin configuration for several types of plug/socket are given in Fig. 21.2 (overleaf). Details of camera plug/socket types were given in Fig. 4.14 and of the SCART D^2B bus in Fig. 19.5.

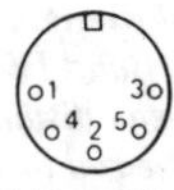

(a) 5 pin DIN

1,4 Audio in
2 Chassis
3,5 Audio out or stereo
1 L audio in
2 Chassis
3 L audio out
4 R audio in
5 R audio out

(b) 6-pin DIN

1 AV select. For VCR high = all outputs, low = all inputs. Opposite for TV set
2 Video in/out
3 Chassis
4 L audio in/out
5 12V
6 R audio in/out

(c) 7-pin DIN

1 L audio in
2 Chassis
3 L audio out
4 R audio in
5 R audio out
6 Remote control data
7 Chassis

(d) 8-pin DIN

1 L audio in
2 Remote control data
3 R audio in
4 Chassis (audio)
5 Chassis (remote control)
6 Chassis (video)
7 Chassis (audio)
8 Video in

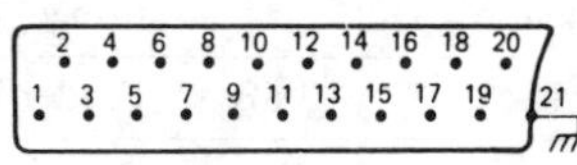

(e) SCART

1 R audio out
2 R audio in
3 L audio out
4 Chassis (audio)
5 Chassis (B video)
6 L audio in
7 B video in
8 Source switching
9 Chassis (G video)
10 Data bus
11 G video in
12 Data bus
13 Chassis (R video)
14 Chassis (data bus)
15 R video in
16 Fast video blanking
17 Chassis (composite video)
18 Chassis (fast video blanking)
19 Composite video out
20 Composite video in

Viewed from front:
1 Y ground
2 C ground
3 Y signal
4 C signal

(f)

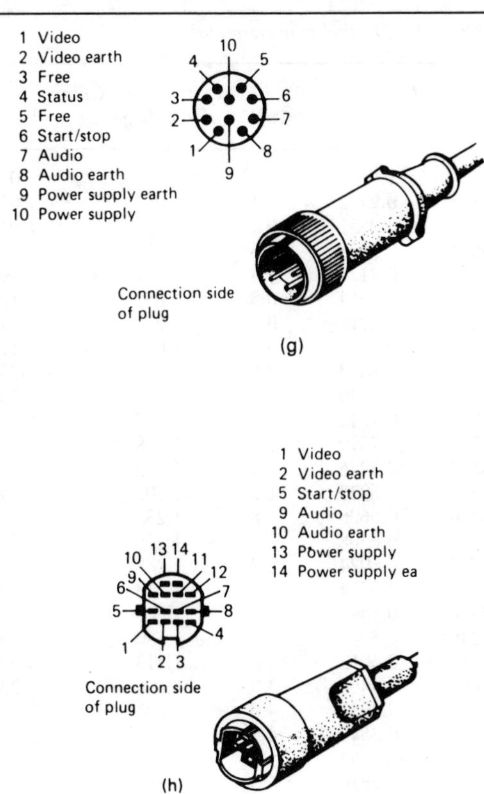

Fig. 21.2 *Pin connections of commonly-used AV connectors. At (a), the 5-pin DIN plug for audio, as fitted to audio equipment and videorecorders, and generally compatible with type (c). At (b), 6-pin DIN fitted to TV and videorecorder: signal flow direction is determined by the switching voltage on pin 1. The 7-pin DIN socket (c) is an alternative to type (a), fitted to some videorecorders incorporating remote control facilities. For videorecorder audio channels, L = Ch. 1, R = Ch.2. (d) depicts the 8-pin DIN input type provided on some TV sets. The SCART connector (e) (also called* Peritelevision *or* Euroconnector*) may be fitted to all types of TV and video equipment, though not all its facilities will necessarily be used Then: At (f) is shown the S-connector, used with high-band domestic videorecorders for Y/C signals, and at (g) and (h) the early types of camera plug connections*

Table 21.6 *Decibel conversion table*

Loss			*Gain*	
Voltage	*Power*	*dB*	*Voltage*	*Power*
1.0	1.0	0	1.0	1.0
0.9883	0.9772	0.1	1.012	1.022
0.9777	0.9551	0.2	1.023	1.047
0.9661	0.9328	0.3	1.032	1.072
0.9551	0.9120	0.4	1.047	1.097
0.9442	0.8914	0.5	1.059	1.122
0.9328	0.8711	0.6	1.072	1.148
0.9223	0.8509	0.7	1.084	1.175
0.9120	0.8320	0.8	1.097	1.202
0.9023	0.8130	0.9	1.109	1.230
0.8914	0.7942	1.0	1.122	1.259
0.8711	0.7590	1.2	1.148	1.318
0.8505	0.7246	1.4	1.175	1.380
0.8320	0.6920	1.6	1.202	1.445
0.8130	0.6606	1.8	1.230	1.514
0.7942	0.6308	2.0	1.259	1.585
0.7762	0.6024	2.2	1.288	1.660
0.7590	0.5754	2.4	1.318	1.733
0.7414	0.5494	2.6	1.349	1.820
0.7246	0.5247	2.8	1.380	1.905
0.7078	0.5012	3.0	1.413	1.995
0.6682	0.4466	3.5	1.496	2.239
0.6308	0.3981	4.0	1.585	2.512
0.5955	0.3549	4.5	1.679	2.818
0.5624	0.3162	5.0	1.778	3.162
0.5307	0.2819	5.5	1.884	3.548
0.5012	0.2512	6.0	1.995	3.981
0.4467	0.1995	7.0	2.239	5.012
0.3981	0.1585	8.0	2.512	6.310
0.3548	0.1259	9.0	2.818	7.943
0.3162	0.1000	10	3.162	10.000
0.2818	0.07943	11	3.549	12.59
0.2512	0.06310	12	3.981	15.85
0.2239	0.05012	13	4.467	19.95
0.1995	0.03981	14	5.012	25.12
0.1778	0.03162	15	5.623	31.62
0.1585	0.02512	16	6.310	39.81
0.1413	0.01995	17	7.079	50.12
0.1259	0.01585	18	7.943	63.10
0.1122	0.01259	19	8.913	79.43
0.1000	0.01000	20	10.000	100.00
0.056	0.00316	25	17.78	316.2
0.03162	0.0001	30	31.62	1000
0.01778	0.000316	35	56.23	3162
0.010	0.001	40	100.0	10 000
0.0056	0.0000316	45	177.8	31 620

0.003162	0.00001	50	316.2	100 000
0.001778	0.00000316	55	562.3	316 200
0.0010	0.0000001	60	1000	1 000 000
0.00056		65	1778	
0.0003162		70	3162	
0.0001778		75	5623	
0.00010		80	10 000	
0.000056		85	17 780	
0.0000316		90	31 620	

EQUIPMENT MARKING CODES

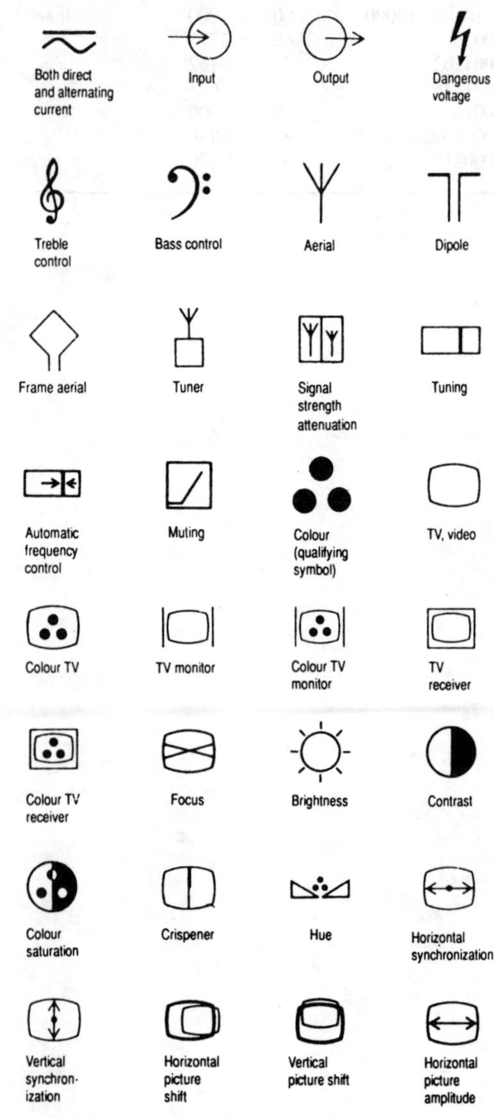

Fig. 21.3 *Commonly-used codes and symbols in service data, and on the control keys of consumer electronic equipment.*

Fig. 21.3 *(cont.)*

Vertical picture amplitude

Picture size adjustment

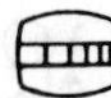
Horizontal linearity

Vertical linearity

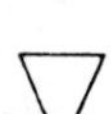

Monophonic

Stereophonic

Balance

Omni-directional microphone

Bidirectional microphone

Unidirectional microphone

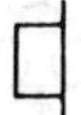
Earphone

Headphones

Stereo headphones

Headset

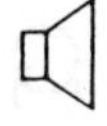
Loudspeaker

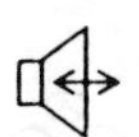
Loudspeaker microphone

Microphone

Stereophonic microphone

Amplifier

Music

Pick-up for disc records

Stereophonic pick-up for disc records

Piezo-electric pick-up, crystal or ceramic

Dynamic pick-up

Telephone adapter

High-pass filter

Low-pass filter

Tape recorder

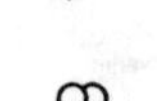
Magnetic tape stereo sound recorder

Recording on tape

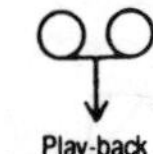
Play-back or reading from tape

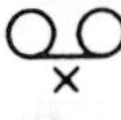
Erasing from tape

Fig. 21.3 *(cont.)*

Monitoring at the input

Monitoring from tape after recording on tape

Monitoring during play-back

Recording lock on tape recorders

Signal lamp

TV camera

Colour TV camera

Video tape recorder

Colour video tape recorders

Video recording

Colour video recording

Video play back

Colour video play back

Transformer

Band-pass filter

Band-pass filter with variable centre frequency

Band-pass filter with variable pass-band

Band stop filter

Fast start

Fast stop

Test voltage

Variability in steps

Sound

Clock

Rejection filter

Rectifier

Frame adjustment

d.c./a.c. converter

Variable band-stop filter

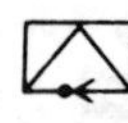

Demodulator

Modulator

Modem

Fig. 21.3 *(cont.)*

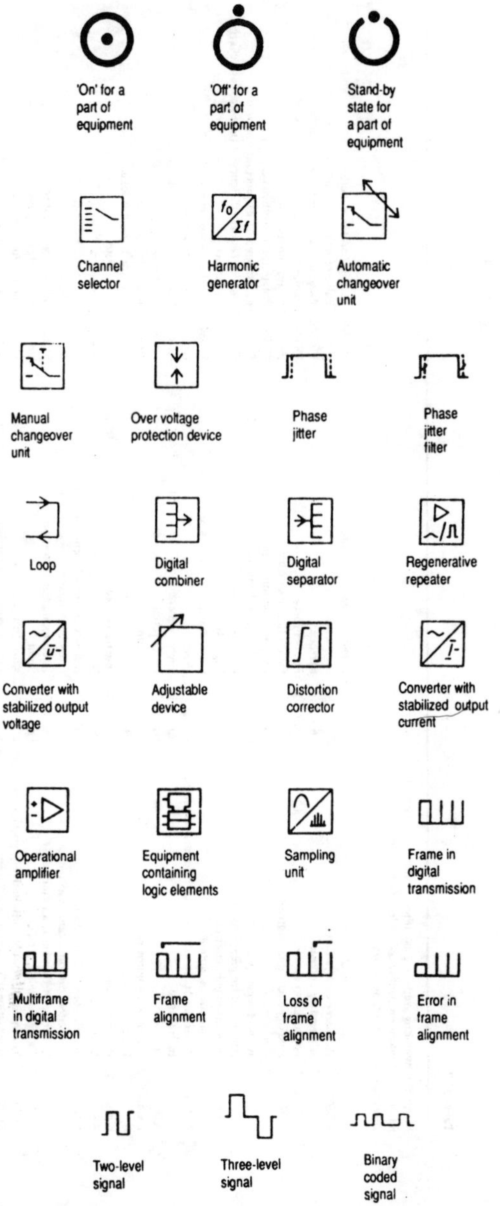

'On' for a part of equipment

'Off' for a part of equipment

Stand-by state for a part of equipment

Channel selector

Harmonic generator

Automatic changeover unit

Manual changeover unit

Over voltage protection device

Phase jitter

Phase jitter filter

Loop

Digital combiner

Digital separator

Regenerative repeater

Converter with stabilized output voltage

Adjustable device

Distortion corrector

Converter with stabilized output current

Operational amplifier

Equipment containing logic elements

Sampling unit

Frame in digital transmission

Multiframe in digital transmission

Frame alignment

Loss of frame alignment

Error in frame alignment

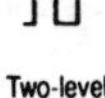

Two-level signal

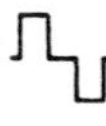

Three-level signal

Binary coded signal

Table 21.7

Many abbreviations are found as either capital *or* lower case letters, depending on publishers' styles. Symbols should generally be standard, as shown.

Abbreviation	Meaning
A	Ampere or anode
ABR	Auxiliary bass radiator
a.c.	Alternating current
A/D	Analogue to digital
ADC	Analogue to digital converter
Ae	Aerial
a.f.	Audio frequency
a.f.c.	Automatic frequency control
a.g.c.	Automatic gain control
a.m.	Amplitude modulation
ASCII	American Standard Code for Information Interchange
AUX	Auxiliary
a.v.c.	Automatic volume control
b	Base of transistor
b.p.s.	Bits per second
BR	Bass reflex
BSI	British Standards Institution
C	Capacitor, cathode, centigrade, coulomb
c	Collector of transistor, speed of light
CCD	Charge coupled device
CCIR	International Radio Consultative Committee
CCITT	International Telegraph and Telephone Consultative Committee
F	Farad, fahrenheit or force
f	Frequency
Fe	Ferrous
FeCr	Ferri-chrome
f.e.t.	Field effect transistor
f.m.	Frequency modulation
f.s.d.	Full-scale deflection
f.s.k.	Frequency shift keying
G	Giga (10^9)
g	Grid, gravitational constant
H	Henry
h.f.	High frequency
Hz	Hertz (cycles per second)
I	Current
IB	Infinite baffle
IC	Integrated circuit
IF	Intermediate frequency
IHF	Institute of High Fidelity (U.S.)
I^2L (IIL)	Integrated injection logic
i.m.d.	Intermodulation distortion
i/p	Input
k	Kilo (10^3) or cathode
K	Kilo, in computing terms ($=2^{10} = 1024$), or degrees Kelvin
P.P.M.	Peak programme meter
p.r.f.	Pulse repetition frequency
PROM	Programmable read only memory
PSTN	Public Switched Telephone Network
PSU	Power supply unit
PTFE	Polytetrafluoroethylene
PUJT	Programmable unijunction transistor
Q	Quality factor; efficiency of tuned circuit, charge
R	Resistance
RAM	Random access memory
r.f.	Radio frequency
r.f.c.	Radio frequency choke (coil)
r.m.s.	Root mean square
ROM	Read only memory
RTL	Resistor transistor logic
R/W	Read/write
RX	Receiver
s	Source of an f.e.t.
s/c	Short circuit
SCR	Silicon-controlled rectifier
s.h.f.	Super high frequency
SI	International system of units
S/N	Signal-to-noise
SPL	Sound pressure level

CTD	Charge transfer device	LIN	Linear	s.w.	Short wave (approx. 10–60 m)
CLK	Clock signal	LOG	Logarithmic	s.w.g.	Standard wire gauge
CrO_2	Chromium dioxide	LOPT	Line output transformer	s.w.r.	Standing wave ratio
CMOS	Complementary metal oxide semiconductor	LS	Loudspeaker	T	Tesla
c.w.	Continuous wave	LSI	Large scale integration	TDM	Time devision multiplex
D	Diode	l.w.	Long wave (approx. 1100–2000 m)	t.h.d.	Total harmonic distortion
d	Drain of an f.e.t.	M	Mega (10^6)	t.i.d.	Transient intermodulation distortion
D/A	Digital to analogue	m	Milli (10^{-3}) or metres	TR	Transformer
DAC	Digital to analogue converter	MHz	Megahertz	t.r.f.	Tuned radio frequency
dB	Decibel	m.c.	Moving coil	TTL	Transistor transistor logic
d.c.	Direct current	mic	Microphone	TVI	Television interface; television interference
DCE	Data circuit-terminating equipment	MOS	Metal oxide semiconductor	TX	Transmitter
DIL	Dual-in-line	MPU	Microprocessor unit	UART	Universal asynchronous receiver transmitter
DIN	German standards institute	MPX	Multiplex	u.h.f.	Ultra high frequency (approx. 470–854 MHz)
DMA	Direct memory access	m.w.	Medium wave (approx. 185–560 m)	u.j.t.	Unijunction transistor
DPDT	Double pole, double throw	n	Nano (10^{-9})	ULA	Uncommitted logic array
DPST	Double pole, single throw	NAB	National Association of Broadcasters	V	Volts
DTE	Data terminal equipment	Ni-Cad	Nickel-cadmium	VA	Volt-amps
DTL	Diode-transistor logic	n/c	Not connected; normally closed	v.c.a.	Voltage controlled amplifier
DQPSK	Differentially encoded quadrature phase shift	n/o	Normally open	v.c.o.	Voltage controlled oscillator
	keying	NMOS	Negative channel metal oxide semiconductor	VCT	Voltage to current transactor
DX	Long distance reception	NTSC	National Television Standards Committee	v.h.f.	Very high frequency (approx. 88–216 MHz)
e	Emitter of transistor	o/c	Open channel; open circuit	v.l.f.	Very low frequency
EAROM	Electrically alterable read only memory	o/p	Output	VU	Volume unit
ECL	Emitter coupled logic	op-amp	Operational amplifier	W	Watts
e.h.t.	Extremely high tension (voltage)	p	Pico (10^{-12})	Wb	Weber
e.m.f.	Electromotive force	PAL	Phase alternation, line	W/F	Wow and flutter
en	Enamelled	p.a.m.	Pulse amplitude modulation	w.p.m.	Words per minute
EIRP	Effective isotropic radiated power	PCB	Printed circuit board	X	Reactance
EPROM	Erasable programmable read only memory	PCM	Pulse code modulation	Xtal	Crystal
EQ	Equalisation	PLA	Programmable logic array	Z	Impedance
ERP	Effective radiated power	PLL	Phase locked loop	ZD	Zener diode
EROM	Erasable read only memory	PMOS	Positive channel metal oxide semiconductor		

ABBREVIATIONS

Table 21.7 lists abbreviations used in service data and specifications.

ELECTRICAL RELATIONSHIPS

Table 21.8 shows relationships between electrical units.

Table 21.8

Amperes × ohms = **volts**
Volts ÷ amperes = **ohms**
Volts ÷ ohms = **amperes**
Amperes × volts = **watts**
$(\text{Amperes})^2$ × ohms = **watts**
$(\text{Volts})^2$ ÷ ohms = **watts**
Joules per second = **watts**
Coulombs per second = **amperes**
Amperes × seconds = **coulombs**
Farads × volts = **coulombs**
Coulombs ÷ volts = **farads**
Coulombs ÷ farads = **volts**
Volts × coulombs = **joules**
Farads × $(\text{volts})^2$ = **joules**

LOGIC SYMBOLS

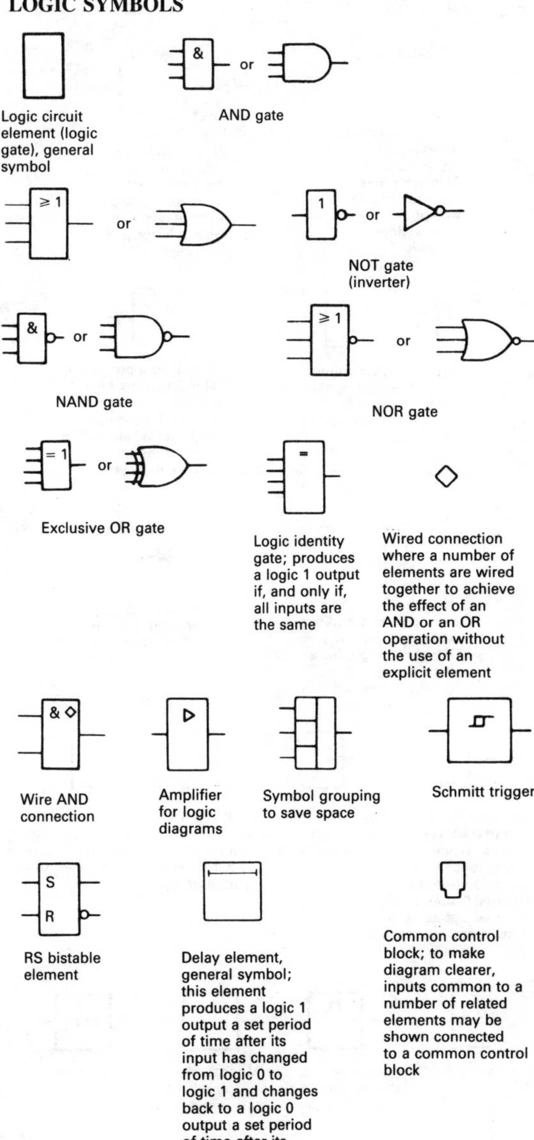

Fig. 21.4 *The form used by most manufacturers in service data*

Fig. 21.4 *(cont.)*

Direction of data flow should normally be from top to bottom. This symbol is used to indicate exceptions to the normal flow direction

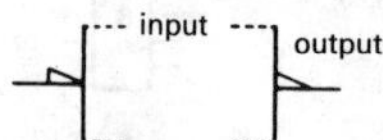

Input/output polarity indicator indicating that the logic 1 state is the less positive level, ie negative logic is in force at this point

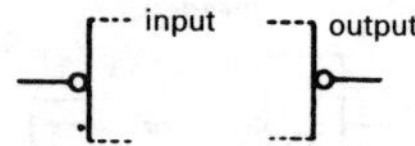

Logic negator input/ output, indicating the state of the logic variable is reversed at the input

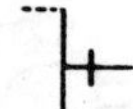

Inhibiting input; when standing at its logic 1 output (or a logic 0 output if the output is negated) whatever the state of the other input variables

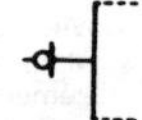

Negated inhibiting input; when standing at logic 0, prevents a logic 1 output (or a logic 0 output if the output is negated

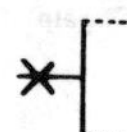

Input or output not carrying logic information

Dynamic input
The (transitory) internal 1-state corresponds with the transition from the external 0-state to the external 1-state. At all other times, the internal logic state is 0

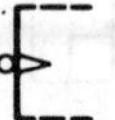

Dynamic input with logic negation

Bi-threshold input
Input with hysteresis e.g. Schmitt trigger

Open-circuit output (e.g. open-collector, open-emitter, open-drain, open-source)

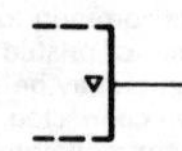

3-state output

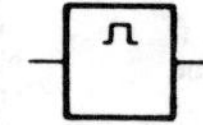

Monostable, retriggerable (during the output pulse)

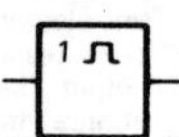

Monostable, non triggerable (during the output pulse)

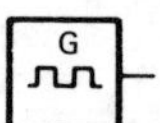

Astable

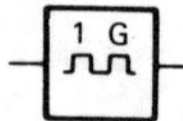

Synchronously starting

PROCESS SYMBOLS

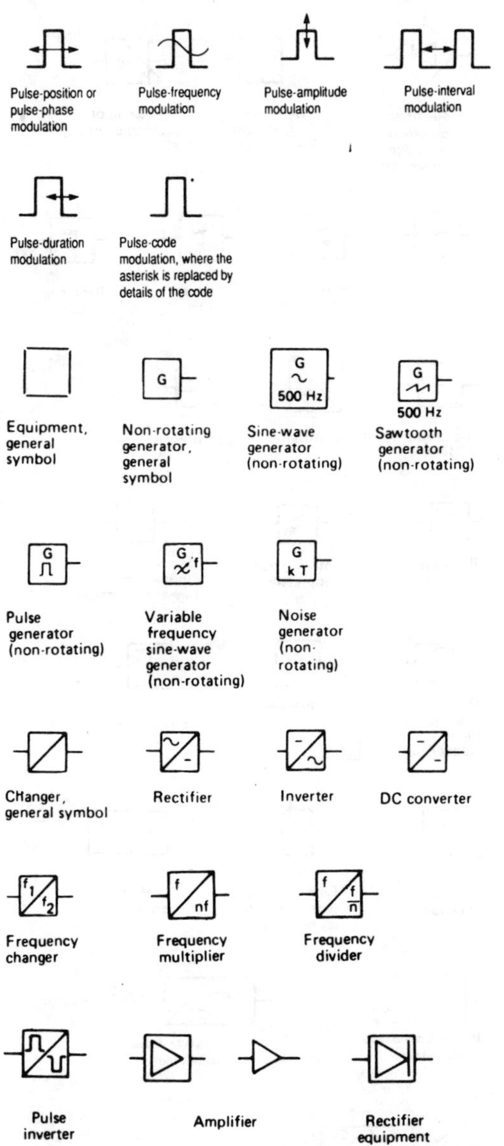

Fig. 21.5 *Symbols used (mainly by European manufacturers) in block diagrams*

Fig. 21.5 *(cont.)*

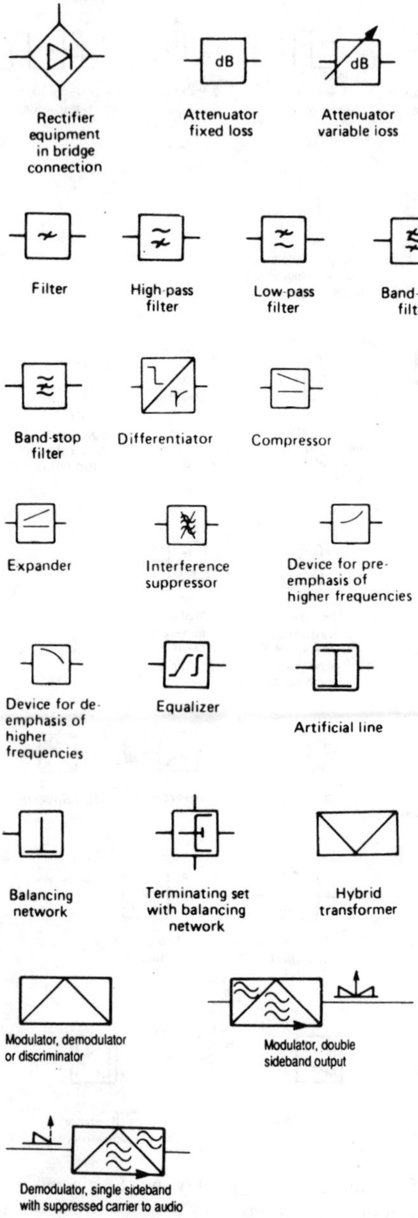

Rectifier equipment in bridge connection

Attenuator fixed loss

Attenuator variable loss

Filter

High-pass filter

Low-pass filter

Band-pass filter

Band-stop filter

Differentiator

Compressor

Expander

Interference suppressor

Device for pre-emphasis of higher frequencies

Device for de-emphasis of higher frequencies

Equalizer

Artificial line

Balancing network

Terminating set with balancing network

Hybrid transformer

Modulator, demodulator or discriminator

Modulator, double sideband output

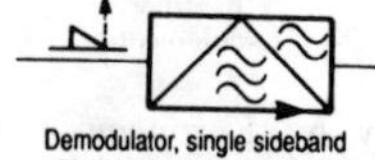

Demodulator, single sideband with suppressed carrier to audio

FREQUENCY SPECTRUM

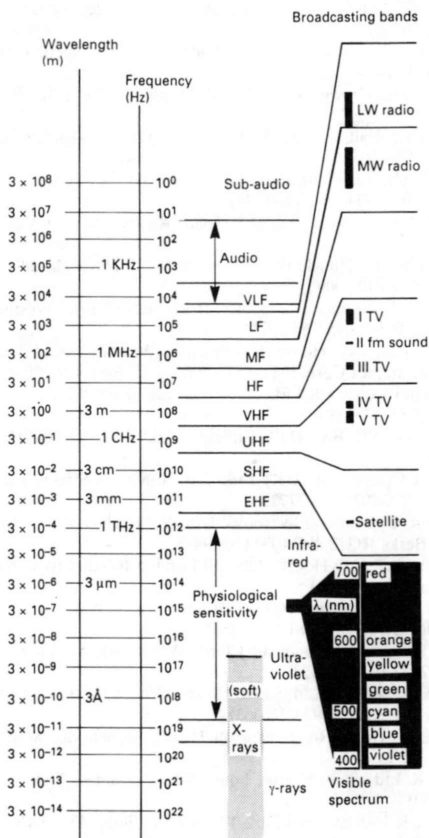

Fig. 21.6 *The electromagnetic spectrum*

NAMES AND UK ADDRESSES OF MANUFACTURERS AND IMPORTERS

Akai UK Ltd, Haslemere Heathrow Estate, 12 Silver Jubilee Way, Parkway, Hounslow, Middlx (081 897 6388)

Amstrad Consumer Electronics, Brentwood House, 169 Kings Road, Brentwood, Essex (0277 228888)

Bang & Olufsen UK Ltd, Eastbrook Road, Gloucester GL4 7DE (0452 307377)

Canon UK Ltd, Unit 4, Brent Trading Centre, North Circular Road, London NW10 (081 459 1266)

Ferguson Ltd, Crown Road, Enfield, Middlesex EN1 1DZ (081 344 4444)

Finlux UK, Valley Farm Way, Leeds, Yorks LS10 1SE (0532 714521)

GoldStar UK Sales Ltd, Goldstar House, 264 Bath Road, Slough, Berks SL1 4DT (0753 691888)

Grundig International Ltd, Mill Road, Rugby, Warks CV21 1PR (0788 77155)

Hitachi UK Ltd, Hitachi House, Station Road, Hayes, Middlx UB3 4DR (081 849 2000)

ITT Nokia Consumer Electronics, Bridgemead Close, Westmead, Swindon, Wilts SN5 7YG (0793 644223)

JVC UK Ltd, JVC House, 6–8 Priestley Way, Edonwall Trading Estate, Staples Corner, London NW2 7AF (081 450 3282)

Mitsubishi Electric UK Ltd, Travellers Lane, Hatfield, Herts AL10 8XB (07072 76100)

Nordmende, PO Box 1140, Enfield, Middlx EN1 1NB (081 366 4442)

Olympus Optical Co (UK) Ltd, 2–8 Honduras Street, London EC17 0TX (071 253 2772)

Panasonic Consumer Electronics UK, Willoughby Road, Bracknell, Berks RG12 4FP (0344 853943)

Philips Video, City House, 420–430 London Road, Croydon CR9 3QR (081 689 4444)

Pioneer High Fidelity (GB) Ltd, 1–6 Field Way, Greenford, Middlx UB6 8UN (081 575 5757)

Salora UK Ltd, Bridgemead Close, Westmead, Swindon, Wilts SN5 7YG (0793 644223)

Sanyo Marubeni UK Ltd, Sanyo House, Otterspool Way, Watford, Herts WD2 8JF (0923 246363)

Sharp UK, Thorp Road, Newton Heath, Manchester M10 9BE (061 205 2333)

Sony UK Ltd, Sony House, South Street, Staines, Middx (0784 467000)

Tatung UK Ltd, Stafford Park 10, Telford, Salop TF3 3AB (0952 290111)

Toshiba UK Ltd, Units 6/7, Admiralty Way, Camberley, Surrey GU15 3DT (0276 62222)

BROADCASTERS' ADDRESSES

British Broadcasting Corporation, Engineering Information Dept, 201 Wood Lane, London W12 7TS (081 752 5040)

British Sky Broadcasting, 6 Centaurs Business Park, Grant Way, Isleworth, Middlx TW7 5QD

EBU (European Broadcasting Union), Av. Albert Lancaster, 32 B–1180 Bruxelles, Belgium

ITV: for transmitter breakdowns etc: contact local programme company at regional studios. Policy, planning, coverage: ITC Engineering Information Dept, 0962 848647

Radio Telefis Eirean, Donnybrook, Dublin 4 (Dublin 693111)

SES (Société Européene des Satellites), Chateau de Betzdorf, L6832 Betzdorf, Luxembourg (operates Astra Group)

Index